BLACK PRESENCE

IN

WORLD HISTORY

BLACK PRESENCE IN WORLD HISTORY

By

ROBERT EWELL GREENE

R.E. Greene Publisher
Fort Washington, Maryland, 1997

COPYRIGHT   1997 by Robert Ewell Greene
ALL RIGHTS RESERVED
Published in 1997 by R.E. Greene Publisher
Fort Washington, Maryland

Library of Congress Catalog Card Number 97-092912

ISBN 0-94-573315-1

ILLUSTRATION CREDITS

I am always indebted to my sister, artist Ruth Greene Richardson, for her outstanding creative cover paintings. I thank you again, my loving sister, Ruth.

To David and the memory of Robert II who were taught that the color makes no difference because they should always be proud of their multi-racial genetic heritage of African, Causasian, Jewish, and Indian.

TABLE OF CONTENTS

AUTHOR'S PREFACE . . . .

ACKNOWLEDGEMENTS . . . .

ORIGIN OF MAN 1

MESOPOTAMIA 8

EARLY EGYPTIANS AND HUMAN GENETIC DIVERSITY 10

DRAVIDIANS OF INDIA 25

MINOANS 30

CARTHAGE AND HANNIBAL 30

AFRICAN PRESENCE IN THE GRAECO ROMAN EXPERIENCE 31

CATHOLIC SAINTS AND CARDINALS 34

BYZANTINE EMPIRE 36

ITALIAN RENAISSANCE 36

JAPAN 38

ISLAM AND MOHAMMAND 40

AFRICAN KINGDOMS AND SOCIETIES 50

ETHIOPIA 72

EARLY EXPLORERS 92

SLAVE TRADE AND AMERICAN SLAVERY 102

ENLIGHTMENT AND ABSOLUTISM 133

TABLE OF CONTENTS

AMERICAN REVOLUTION	137
FRENCH REVOLUTION	152
ROMANTICISM	159
SECOND EMPIRE, AND NAPOLEON III'S INTEREST IN WEST AFRICA	163
PARTITION AND DOMINATION OF AFRICA	164
TREATIES BETWEEN GREAT BRITAIN AND OTHER COUNTRIES	166
LATIN AMERICA	167
SIGNIFICANT HIGHLIGHTS OF BRAZILIANS OF COLOR	173
WAR OF 1812, 1812-1815	180
MEXICAN WAR	183
UNITED STATES CIVIL WAR	186
SPANISH AMERICAN WAR, 1898	202
PHILIPPINE INSURRECTION 1900-1901	206
CHINESE BOXER REBELLION	208
HAITI	209
LIBERIA	216
PUNITIVE EXPEDITION TO MEXICO	255
WORLD WAR I	264
LEAGUE OF NATIONS AND MANDATE	276

TABLE OF CONTENTS

WORLD WAR II	282
KOREAN WAR	307
AFRICAN NATIONALISM AND INDEPENDENCE	311
VIETNAM WAR	322
PERSIAN GULF WAR	325
UNITED NATIONS PEACE MAKER, RALPH BUNCHE	332
WEST INDIES	335
EARLY AFRICAN PRESENCE IN MEXICO	338
WORLDS's MUSICIANS AND ARTISTS OF COLOR	344
SOUTH AFRICA	349
SOUTH PACIFIC ISLANDS	351
EMPLOYMENT OF BLACK CANNON FODDER	359
ROBERT AMBROSE THORNTON AND THE EINSTEIN YEARS	361
A CANADIAN PHYSICIAN OF COLOR	381
DIPLOMATIC HISTORIAN OF COLOR, MERZE TATE	384
COLOR OBSESSION	386
DIVERSITY OF AFRICAN AMERICANS	392
BIBLIOGRAPHY	401
INDEX	408

PREFACE

I was motivated to write this book because after twenty-eight years of teaching secondary and college levels, I wanted to document and share with others, especially my future students the experiences of meticulous and extensive research over the years using rare documents, papers of individuals, oral interviews, unpublished papers, visits to county and state archives, hours of research in the National Archives and Library of Colleges and my travels abroad to Asia and Europe. All of these experiences and years of scholarly study were fortunate to culminate into the writing of 23 books which four of them were published by other sources and some by me in order to make my research available to the public. I was privileged to have a very distinguished publisher, John H. Johnson of Jet and Ebony, the Johnson publications to print and market my first book, *Black Defenders of America 1775-1973* which was one of his best sellers. My book, *Black Courage, 1775-1783 Documentation of Black Participation In The American Revolution* was published by the National Society of The Daughters of the American Revolution (DAR). There is a copy of this book in each DAR Chapter's library. I am also pleased, that 15 of my publications have been accepted into the Library of Congress's permanent collection. My extensive research over the years has been an attempt to balance out the omissions by design or otherwise that have prevented the accurate portrayal of the black presence in world history, in study after study and volume after volume. I seriously believe that historiography must recognize the black presence in world history past and present. In this book, I have broadened the foundation for the thesis that much of the success in the Western world was due to the capacity of the Europeans to conquer, and mobilize the creative talents of people of color through the centuries. I have presented the facts, both glorious and inglorious.

I have been able to blend my professional careers as a biologist, chemist, staff officer, and the director of the first United States Army Race Relations School, Germany and a historian, in writing this book. This book includes researched papers that I have prepared and used in my college teaching of African, World and American histories. I have used some of the articles as summary of teaching points and student handouts to supplement the respective courses that in most instances do not address thoroughly and sometimes accurately the black presence in history.

Black Presence in World History is a book that can be used as a college and secondary textbook in World History courses. This book is also a valuable reference for the librarian, social science teachers, and above all the student. I believe that this book can help to educate and reeducate blacks, whites, Asians and Hispanics about the black presence in the world.

I believe that the fertile seeds of Mother Africa have been spreaded across the continents of the world and created a genetic admixture of her children. The significant result is that her offsprings have survived through the years of oppression, slavery and colonial empires' domination with a legacy of courage and faith.

**Robert Ewell Greene
January 6, 1997**

ACKNOWLEDGEMENTS

I wish to express my sincere gratitude and appreication to a most caring, understanding and patient lady, Janice Wood Hunter for her exemplary administrative assistance in the preparation of this book. Please remember Janice, your assistance beyond any doubt has made my twenty-fourth book possible. I thank you again Janice.

I most sincerely thank Viola F. Smith for her outstanding scholarly expertise in the grammatical editing and proof reading of this book.

I also wish to express my sincere gratitude to the following people for their contributions to this book.

Larry C. Mucha
Bill Grant
David A. F. Greene
Janice Wood Hunter
Kimberly Cherie Hunter
Viola Smith

My appreciation is also hereby expressed to the wonderful persons who have assisted me and their names may have been inadvertently omitted.

Black Presence

ORIGIN OF MAN

In 1871, the noted naturalist, Charles Darwin published his book on the *Descent of Man*, a study believed that the species of animals and humans originated from lower forms by evolution. He also believed that the volutionary descent started in Africa. An analysis of DNA and serum (blood) protein in recent years show a close relationship of humans, chimpanzees and gorillas. It is believed that the evolution of human beings originated in Africa many many years ago and over thousands of years modern human being ancestors of years ago migrated through the world to Europe, Asia, Australia and the arctic. The human behavior of man came about 3-4 million years ago by walking upright, using tools, controlling of fire, burying their dead and using art. Language is possibly 50,000 years old. Some 15,000 years ago, man learned to build shelters and huts. These hypothesis and theories and some facts have been made possible in recent years due to scientific research and new methods and techniques such as the examination , identification, and dating of fossil remains, bones and teeth. The scientists have dated the past by using absolute and relative methods, potassium argon dating and radio carbon dating. There is a regional continuity theory that Homo sapiens originated in the area of Africa. Some scientists say that all living human beings descended from a common first mother in South Africa who lived about 200,000 years ago and call this the "Eve Theory". In 1988, a professor offered some credence to this theory when DNA of 14 humans from around the world and he was able to determine 13 branching points and concluded that Africa was the ultimate homeland. Mitochondrial or mitochondrion DNA is explained by realizing that the cell part mitochondria is a specialized structure of the cell that provides cells with energy or as I call it the power house of the cell. The DNA molecules located in the cell's nucleus contains our genes. The mitochondria or mitochondrion provides cells with energy and also carry some genes for their own manufacture on a ring of DNA. When a sperm and an egg unite, they contribute equally to the DNA in the nucleus of the resulting cell. The mitochondria and DNA comes from the egg. Therefore, the mitochondrial DNA can reveal an individual's maternal ancestry. Understanding this chemical genetical and molecular biology research, the professor concluded from his protocol that there is a possible common ancestor who was an African woman whose mitochondrial DNA all humans have descended.

There have been various theories and inferences over the years in relationship to the physical description changes that occurred if man and woman did originate from Africa. It is believed by some researchers that the physical changes possibly occurred due to anatomical structure and physiological (function) that could have occurred during the glacial or Ice Age. Some scientists state that the early Cro-Magnon people were confronted with a harsh climate in Europe and through adaptation and mutant changes, little by little their skin color became lighter to facilitate the absorption of vitamin D from the weak sunshine of the north. They needed different requirements for survival. Gradual mutation (a change occured in body form, possibly skin color, lack of melanin). The northern areas of northern Germany, England and Ireland were covered with ice sheets. Other views of the adaptation theory are associated with ecological factors. Some scientists state that there was a physical descriptive transition in skin color and hair texture mainly. (When we refer to hair texture differences, I always pose the question to my students, how many have observed newborn babies in a hospital nursery just after birth? Because regardless of their skin color or ethnicity, if the baby has hair on its head, is it straight? The majority of the babies regardless of race have straight hair). It is also believed by some scientists that the first Europeans who were immigrants from Africa, left by the way of Gibraltar Isthmus or Western Asia. Their phenotype or descriptive characteristics could have been "pepper corn hair, brown to black skin color, small stature and their jaws were similar to the Hottentots of South Africa today. There have been theories on the Mongolian race, possibly a cross between African and Causasian type with yellow brown skin. I realize that many readers, scholars and laypersons will offer their pros and cons to these theories or hypotheses that I have discussed. However, it is my intent to present other views than what is normally presented by the multi media and other communiation means. I want the students to analyze the information and possibly become motivated to search further for their own understanding and acceptance of what is possibly true or could be false. In 1997, students in some colleges and universities do use textbooks that allocate a few lines to discuss the origin of man.

Scientists have offered theories about evironmental adaptations. They state that the long nose of north Africans and Europeans reveal they evolved in a dry or cold climate, because the nose moistens air before the air reaches the lungs. Some say that the tall, thin bodies of the Masai of Kenya helps them to dissipate heat and the Eskimos short bodies assist them in retaining heat.

There have been some logical and thought provoking views on man's descent and birth place in Africa by distinguished historians of color. The late Dr. Charles Wesley wrote years ago that the conclusions of some archeologists and anthropologists who have studied the material remains in the Nile Valley and territories in Africa believed the origin of man was in Africa. Wesley said the earliest known traces had been found in Tanganyika (Tanzania) and a report on the subject was made to the Pan African Congress of Pre History at Leopoldville, Belgium Congo in August, 1959, *The Ghana Times* reported the following in their edition, November 14, 1959. *"For some 30 years now, the continent has yielded discovery after discovery which has revolutionalized early concepts of the remote origins of humanity and which indicate that it may be well that the white race had its parentage in Africa, that all the Europeans, Americans, Asians as well as the present population of the continet are the descendants of an African race"*. This theory stated in 1959 was asserting that there is a possibility that Spain and North African were joined by land and there were different Nomadic tribes who settled in Europe, wrote Dr. Wesley. He also said it is possible that the paleolithic men and women were of African origin and migrated to Europe and Asia. One should also consider that the early racial groups in Africa, the Bushmanoid, Caucasoid, Mongoloid, Negroid and Pygmoid has no valid scientific bases for racial definition. Because over many years these populations have been miscegenation or mixed, especially the non Negro ancestry with people belonging to the Caucasian group. The African type used by some anthropologists over the years can be challenged when they use the typical skin color, black, wide features and wooly hair. Because the Bantus have shown Caucasian like features, the Pygmies skin as brown, red and light to yellow. The Fellatahs complexion varies in skin color.

The dark melanin of the so-called Negro strain of Africans is present in the Berbers of the North Bantu tribes of the south and tropics, the Bushmen and Hottentots of the Southwest, the Fulani and the Hausa of West Africa, East African peoples, Kaffirs, or Basutos, Bechuanas and Zulus of South Africa. Therefore, what is the meaning of a Negro, the major groups of dark Africans or really anyone who calls himself a Negro in considering the ancestral gentic diversity in the motherland of creation.

There have been studies by molecular biologists that indicate that blood groups show close relationship of non African races to Africans and adds some support to the belief that all humans orginated from the early type and gives some credibility to monogenetic evolution that says all people in the world are possibly descendants of populations which left Africa years ago.

A medical doctor and Africanist (a specialist in African history and culture) has said that there is considerable scientific evidence that support the belief that there is a detectable African element present in populations of countries in other parts of the world. This African element is the sickle cell hemoglobin gene. I have presented some of my research ten years ago on the subject of sickle cell disease and its variants that are also associated with abnormal hemoglobins (red proteins of red blood cells that transfer oxygen from the lungs to the body's tissues).

When I attended a seminar and a conference in 1987 on sickle cell disease, I realized that I had been misinformed about the prevalence of the disease. I learned that it was more prevalent among African American in the United States, however, a variant of sickle cell disease called thalassemia is present in the population in other countries beside America and Africa. I will dicuss briefly what sickle cell disease is and also the variant that is found mostly in other countries.

The illness called Sickle Cell Disease (SCD) includes variants of hemgolobin SCD, and sickle cell thalassemia. The sickle cell trait is an inherited condition which affects the red blood cells and the cells normally are round in shape, but in SCD, they beome distorted in shape or sickled. The disease is described when both parents carry the trait. Because if only one parent has red blood cells which sickle, then the children will have either sickle cell trait or normal red blood cells.

The sickle Beta Thalassemia affects mostly people of Mediterranean, African and Asia descent. There is also a relation between malaria and thalassemia, where the gene could provide some protection against malaria. The term thalessima is derive from the Greek (sea) to show the occurrence of the disease in the Mediterranean areas. In the variants the sickle thalassemia cells are called alpha and beta. There is a greater tendency for the cells to sickle because of two abnormal genes that reduce the amount of normal hemoglobin present, which in turn can reduce the oxygen intake.

Considering the presence of the sickle cell disease gene in the population of other countries outside of Africa, it is quite possible over thousands of years ago the original human beings could have migrated out of Africa and some did remain. The knowledge of the SCD gene present today in other populations can raise some questions how did this occur, especially when one consider the geographical distribution.

Geographical Distribution Sickle Thalassemia

Thalassemia B and abnormal hemoglobins S, C, D, and E have affected peoples in the countries of Italy, Greece, Sicily, Thailand, Cyprus, Turkey, Spain, China, Puerto Rico, Brazil, Surinam, Central Africa, Saudi Arabia, India, China, Vietnam, Philippines, Pacific Islands, Iran, Egypt, Sri Lanka (Ceylon), Marlaysia, Cambodia, Laos, Burna, Indonesia, Pakistan, Afganistan, South Africa, Kurdish Jew, Taiwan, Japan Melanesia, Jamaica, England, France, Mexico, Guyana, Kuwait, and Africa. These countries that I have mentioned were cited as having some forms or variants of thalassemia from research articles that I had obtained when I was conducting research on sickle cell disease in 1987. Therefore, I was able to learn that there were reported incidences of cases in the above list of countries and the affected person had been identified with some variant of thalassemia, mainly sickle B thalassemia.

I have discussed the scientific research, hypothesis and theories that support the belief that the human being originated from the continent of Africa. A distinguished family of archaelogists and paleontologists, anthropologist have made outstanding contributions to the hypothesis that man originated in Africa. On December 9, 1986, the matriarch of the Leakey family died. Mary Leakey died at the age of 83 years in Nairoba, Kenya where she had worked with her late husband Louis S.B. Leakey for many years. During her lifetime, she was able to confirm the theory of Charles Darwin that at least some of mankind's earliest ancestors could be traced to the continent of Africa. In 1978, she discovered a 3.6 million years old homind's footprint in hardened volcanic arch at Laetow on the Serengeti Plain in northern Tanzania. When she found the skull fragments of an early homind that was 1.75 million years ago in the Olduvai Gorge in Tanzania in 1959, Leakey worked for 18 months to put together 400 fragments of the skull known as australopithecus. In 1947, she located a skull of Proconsul Africanus on an island in Africa's Lake Victoria, it was an apelike ancestor of apes and humans about 25 million years ago. This discovery focused wide attention on her and her husband's work in East Africa, because it was alluding to evidence that East Africa could be the cradle of mankind. Her studies were supporting the theories that man and woman's early evolutionary descent could have started with Homo habilis to Homo erectus to Homo sapiens.

The following discussion will address some archaeological findings in recent years of this decade, the 1990's. A skull was found in Java, Indonesia and it was stated that it was the oldest fossil found outside of Africa, representing the first pre-historic people who could have migrated out. They were bones of Homo erectus (immediate ancestor of Homo Sapiens). The species Home erectus was first collected in 1936 and called Pithecanthropus erectus and also Java Man. The oldest species of Homo erectuss was found in 1976 in Kenya 1.95 million years old. Java individuals were thought to have left Africa earlier. Scientists raised some questions, why did the East Asians not have a stone tool culture developed like the Africans? Some responded by saying, it is possible that the Asian population departed African before the hand ax was invented, and it did not go as far as Indonesia. In a cavern near China's

Black Presence 7

Yangtze River, a scientist identified fossils remains and primitive stories of possile first known human ancestor who left Africa and migrated to subtropical Asia 1.9 million years ago, 100,000 years earlier than presumed. The researchers found an upper jaw and incisors of the tooth. Some scientists have postulated that it is possible that human evolution in China is another argument for the theory that man could have originated from some place other than Africa. However, this species found in China resembles two species Homo habilis and Homo ergaster which were found earlier in East Africa with a date of 2 million years ago.

There has been considerable debate in recent years about the different views of the origin of early man. Some scientist are saying that the molecular structure of modern apes and human evolving lines did diverge about 4-6 million years ago. But there is some doubt about how the human being came about. There is disagreement about when man began to migrate out of Africa, 2 million years ago or 1.5 million years ago?

A jaw bone was found in the former Soviet Union Republic of Georgia and it indicated that our ancestors could have left Africa at least 1.6 million to 1.8 million years ago. There is another species that was found and dates some 2.5 million years ago. It is Homo rudolfensis and was found in the Rift Valley of East Africa. Some paleontologists believe that this Homind that was found in China could have evolved in Asia and spread back to Europe and Africa. They call this the *"Back Migration Theory"*. They also state that Homo erectus and the early Homind found in China were sisters species and spread out of Africa in successive migrations or evolved in erectus, which is referring to early Java man, Peking man and fossils found before the ones recently excavated in Africa. One migration theory states that Homo erectus could have evolved in Africa 800,000 to 1.8 million years ago. However, a continuous transition among regional population occurred from Homo erectus to Homo sapiens. Scientists call this a parallel evolution and that among the dispersed populations to other geographical areas outside of Africa, a gene flow was created between populations. This scientific controversy centers around a hypothesis that says could all non Africans descend from an anatomically modern Homo sapien or ain the simple meaning, could people that are not "pure black Africans" descend from original man or woman if they were pure black in Africa?

Now in view of all the information that I have presented about the origin of man in Africa to consider the continuing controversy whether it could have occurred else where, the latest finding reported in 1996 is that an African jaw bone was found and the dated fossil is approximately 2.3 million years old. This jawbone was found in fossils sendiments in the Hadar highlands of Northern Ethiopia. This finding gives more evidence to support the theory that there is a link between the chopping tools, and the species. The link is that the first tooll maker were members of the African Homo groups. The jawbone was first discovered in 1994 and it took two years for a more positive analysis. The controversy will continue and scientist will continue to conduct their resarch to support their thesis. However, I believe that current findings support the hypothesis greatly that man and woman did evolve out of the continent we call Africa and possibly if it difficult for some people to reach a sincere state of mind and agree that it is a possibility that those in the past for whatever reason they believe when they said the Motherland, that others in the multiracial world need to reclaim their ancestors homeland the genesis of human civilization's native land, Mother Africa.

MESOPOTAMIA

Early Mesopotamia civilizations were located near the Euphrates and Tigres River. A early racial group was known as Sumerians. They had cities along the rivers. They had their Gods, stone temples, Ziggurat, 2,000 B.C. The political power was the king or a local class system with a governor, free citizens, commons and slaves. The slaves included foreigners and prisoners of war. The Sumerians gave the basic, social, economic and intellectual pattern of Mesopotamia. Around 233 B.C., the people were conquered by the Semites.

The Sumerians had cities located in the valley and they were called city-states consisting of 10-50,000 inhabitants. The cities had roadways, waterways, boats and barges. They built defensive barriers. They had a Goddess of fertility, earth and vegetation. The Sumerians introduced early writings.

Black Presence

A group of people called Semitic Amorites lived in an empire building state. Their ruler was Shargon I. The people organized the cities of Sumer and Akkad into an empire called Babylon. The people were called Babylonians. The Babylonians improved the Sumerian math, science and astronomy. Their deity or God was Mareluk. The people had 280 body laws or codes called Hammurabi. The laws addressed the subjects of business, contracts, debts, adultery, divorce, incest, treatment of slaves and class societies.

A people of Indo European origin and a language related to Greek, Persian and Latin were called Hittites. They possibly migrated from central Europe or central Asia around 2700 B.C. (present day area of Turkey). The people used horses and wheeled carts. They attacked the Syrians, Babylonians, and threatened the Egyptians. They had an agricultural society producing grain, olive oil and cultivated wine. The Hittities discovered some techniques of iron smelting. Their legal codes were used to organize the society. They had a patriarchal society. The father gave their daughters away involving a financial contract. The Hittite people were eventually overcome by some Indo-European invaders. They had fought the Egyptians under the rule of Ramses II around 1200 B.C.

When one considers the numerous migration theories, it is possible that black Africans over the centuries migrated from east to west across the continent and other areas of the world. Some historians and anthropologists have stated that the first Babylonians could have been of a Negroid race prior to the presence of the Semite and could have migrated from Africa to Chaldia through East Africa by way of Arabia to the Indus or Euphrates Valley. Later the Aryans or Indo Europeans would arrive in the valley and over thousands of years the physical difference would occur reducing the black African's dominant genes.

Many distinguished scholars of all races over the years have written and documented their research about the possible migration of dark skin Africans to the geographical areas of India, Malay Peninsula, eastern Archiapelago, Italy, France, Ireland, Spain, Wales and southern Ireland and the Persian Empire

W.E.B. DuBois stated in one of his books that the Hammurabi code had a line that said *"Go forth like the sun of the black race"* Malcolm X wrote in his book, <u>Afro American History, 1967</u>, that *"at least 5,000 years ago they had a black civilization in the middle east called Sumerians."*

Whether or not there is any validity to the above statements we must realize that over the years people have been writing and discussing about the possibility that black Africans were present in early civilization. One cannot ignore the biological reality that Mother Africa's fertile egg cells have been transplanted throughout the world.

The above information is nutritional reasoning or food for thought.

EARLY EGYPTIANS AND HUMAN GENETIC DIVERSITY

The Egyptian civilization 3100-1200 B.C. consisted of an isolated country in the Nubian deserts, cataracts of the Nile. They had some Mesopotamia influences when they were ruled by foreign invaders, the Hyksos. They believed in a God 3100 B.C. known as Menes. There was an Egyptian God, Osiris and his wife Isis. Horus was the son. The Egyptians had the old and New Kingdoms, pyramids, and unusual method of embalming and believed in spirits. The New Kingdom 1570-1200 B.C. had Pharaohs, Ahmose who overcame the Hyksos. Pharaoh Thutmose I overcame Nubia, and Syria. The Hebrews came to Egypt during this period. The kings of the 18th dynasty created the first Egyptian Empire, region of Nubia.

There exists today in the scholarly anthropological and historical schools of thought a controversy as to the true racial identity of ancient Egyptians. Were they considered black or white? Some historians have considered the research of the late Cheikh Antar Diop by referring to the African influences on early Egyptian culture and social similarities. However, they avoid discussing the current beliefs by many past and present historians that Egypt is actually Ethiopia's oldest daughter. How can one support this statement, first we must examine known facts, theses, inferences and simple logic.

Black Presence 11

As a biologist and historian, I must consider the facts that over thousand of years, Egypt has been visited by many foreign nations to include Persians, Macedonians, Romans, Arabs, Turks, French, and English. One can not deny that there was cross miscegenation or race mixing among the Egyptians over the years. Egypt's conquerors have changed the physical descriptions of Egyptians, somehow the African genetic structure still remains today.

Historians have discussed the pros and cons about the following: the Egyptians called their country, Kemit which means black, possibly referring to the soil. The first inhabitants were people of the black Anu race. After the conquest of Egypt by Alexander under the Ptolemies race mixing occurred between white Greeks and blacks. Some credible researchers have said that the Egyptians were of Negroid origin and that Egypt's civilization began in the lower Nile Valley and later moved northward. The civilization of the Nile Valley began in the southern part of Ethiopia and passed as the Nile flows northward to Egypt. The Ethiopians and Egyptians were closely together in the early prehistoric periods. The coins, implements remains and records of trade support the relations of Egypt and Ethiopia. The early historian Herodotus believed Egyptians were of black skin color.

In February 1978, there was tour throughout many American cities that included artifacts and relics from the pyramid of King Tutankhamen or King Tut of Egypt. Scholars representing Egyptologists, biologists, archaeologists, anthropologists and historians were debating and writing about the ethnic origins of King Tut. I received a paper from my second cousin in California on an article about King Tut and the 18th Egyptian dynasty. The article discussed some selected royal members of the dynasty. They were Queen Ahmose Nefertari, Ahmose I, Amenhotep II, Thutmose III and his mother Tio, Amenhotep III, Thutmose I, Hatshepsut, Queen Tye, mother of Tutankhamun, Akhenaton, and brother of King Tut. The article stated that if King Tut's nearest relative were of black ancestry then obviously this was the case for King Tut. I received this article from my cousin in 1989. My cousin Eric MacCalla has made contributions to previous articles on King Tut for a Los Angeles newspaper. When I met my young cousins Eric and Johnetta Maccalla in 1989, I was pleased to learn that they had continued their pursuit of excellence in education, besides having an admirable interest in ancient Egyptian royalty of black ancestry. They had completed their academic studies and were both the recipients of the doctor of philosophy degrees in electrical engineering.

In 1992, I wrote two articles on Egyptians racial identity. These articles will provide the reader some serious nutritional reasoning or food for thought.

Egyptians are of a black origin genetically.

During the past 180 years many scholars in the disciplines of anthropology, archaeology, egyptology, ethnology, genetics, history, linguistics, and sociology have debated written papers and books on the racial identification of the original Egyptians.

There also exists even today an academic division of thought on the race of Egyptians. While teaching European history at a predominantly white college, I mentioned during a lecture that the ancient Egyptians were black Africans and have possibly descended from the Ethiopians. A caucasian colleague well-versed in European history and a respected scholar told me directly, that Egyptians were caucasians and that I should not be teaching a non-accepted school of thought. At this time, I was not privileged to know the following facts that have been related to me by my loving cousin and only remaining senior citizen of my maternal ancestral genetic line. My cousin, Harriet Johnson Allen clearly, logically, and seriously related to me three years ago, that I, like many African Americans have a very distinctive diverse genetic background. She said not only through the oral tradition but a pictorial analysis of family photographs that your mother's father, your grandfather, and my mother's father, my grandfather's father was an English Jew and my mother's mother and your grandfather's mother was a brown skin Egyptian who was brought to Biloxi, Mississippi by her husband, Ewell Conway, the English Jewish man. During the past three years, I have tried very diligently to ask my cousin Harriet, was she sure that this

Black Presence

information is valid or true and could my great grandmother be of Ethiopian origin. She has convinced me with her consistent knowledge and other information that her grandmother was an Egyptian woman and that my great grandmother was an Egyptian woman. Ironically, as we now reflect about family memories we can see the biological similarities of our Egyptian and Jewish genetic origins in our family.

I have related this story for one specific reason and that is women and men scholars of all ethnic and social groups continue to agree, disagree or give no attention to it at all, the original Egyptians were black. My reason is that if we logically look at the biological and historical aspect of the white Americans renaming of African peoples in Africa and often they were genetically mixed in North America. Of course, the school of thought that Egyptians were caucasians will prevail in the minds of many scholars and lay persons. My cousin, Harriet's mother lived to be 100 years and she knew that she was of Egyptian African origin and was proud of it. I sincerely believe that she did not let the mulatto and white looking appearance confuse her racially and politically, because she was black in spirit and in genes.

During the past three years, I have read and researched more on the subject of the racial origin of Egyptians. However, my greatest source toward the veracity of the fact that Egyptians are and/or were black is the oral tradition of the Ewell Conway family presented by a perceptive cousin, Harriet Allen. It is with this information that I pursued my interest to increase my knowledge of the Egyptian racial identity knowing that if my family background is one example, I ask those experts, how many more are there out there? How many more stories of the truth were buried with the deceased descendants of Egyptian origin in America? Therefore, I state emphatically and would tell my former colleague if I knew her whereabouts that yes, Egyptians of yesteryears were black Africans and just as my great grandmother's offspring or children were hybrids. I believe that mother Ethiopian's millions of Egyptian daughter's children were tinted with the genetic male sex cells of many foreigners over the centuries. Those foreigners were the Greeks, Romans, Turks, Arabs, Syrians, Iranians, English, and many others. Somehow in the mystic of genetics, that powerful, durable and dominant gene of black Mother Africa did not disappear. This dominant gene of blackness still glows in the diverse rainbow colors of its descendants in the diaspora of African children worldwide. It is with these facts and complexities for some scholars that they strive so hard to designate people by color, language, custom, tradition, and geography instead of looking at the simplistic realistic fact that we cannot undue God's most complex creativity and that is of the genetic biological structure of people.

The following researched statements are representative of scholarly views, opinions, and supported research on the subject Egyptians are of Black African racial origin.

"Herodotus wrote that these people are black skinned, have wooly hair, practice circumcision like the Ethiopians."

"Realizing that circumcision is of Egyptian and Ethiopian origin and the Egyptians and Ethiopians were none other than Negroes occupying different regions."

"The thinking about kinship between Black Africans and Egyptians are similar."

"Present day Egyptians' ancestors descended from the countries of Nuba, land of the Aman, territory of Kush, South of Egypt."

"Herodotus wrote that of the 300 Egyptian Pharaohs, from Menes to the seventeenth dynasty, 18 were of Sudanese origin."

"Pyramids found in Nubia were similar to those in Egypt."

"The Gods Amen and Osiris were black and Isis and Horus were black goddesses."

"The Negro Anu race were the first inhabitants of Egypt."

"Upper and lower Egypt were unified for the first time by the first Pharaoh of Egypt, Narmer."

Black Presence 15

"The builder of the great pyramids were Cheops, 4th dynasty pharaoh."

"The Pharaoh who founded the Crooked Dynasty was the son of a Sudanese woman. He was Pharaoh Tuthmosis III." Ironically, one of Egypt's greatest presidents of the twentieth century was the late Anwar Sadat. He was the son of a Sudanese mother and an Arabic father and he was called by the Egyptian people an Egyptian and accepted by the world as an Egyptian. At the time of his death, a literature search of available newspapers and a magazines revealed that Time Magazine was the only known American magazine owned by the majority population that identified Sadat's true biological ethnicity, which, of course, is an African Egyptian. I use the term African Egyptian just as our forefathers of democracy called Africans of a hybrid structure "Negroes, colored, and they echo the words African Americans.

"The Dynasty II Pharaoh was of color, Pharaoh Ba-en-netes."

"The Black Queen Mother of the eighteenth dynasty was the Queen Mother Ahmose-Nefertari. Her son was Amenhotep I."

"Egyptians were people of the Anu group. Their melanin deposits were evident with their black skin."

"Cheops or Khufu was the builder of the Great Pyramid."

"Khofre (Chephren) was the builder of the second Great Pyramid located at Gizeh."

The 1894 edition of Adolph Erman's Life in Ancient Egypt discussed the question of the race origin of the Egyptians. Erman stated that ethnologists believed that nothing exists in the physical structure of the Egyptian to distinguish him from the native African and that from the Egyptians to the Negro population of tropical Africa. The inhabitants of Libya, Egypt, and Ethiopia have probably belong to the same race since prehistoric time. Erman said in response to an Asian origin that Egyptians were "natives of their own country, children of their own soil."

In 1992 a perusal of books, almanacs, and other references indicate the "so-called" accepted or popular description of the ethnicity of the Egyptians.

A World Almanac and Book of Facts, 1990: "Ethnic groups Eastern Hamitic stock 90%, Bedoun, Nubian."

A book on peoples and cultures of Africa contains an article on "Human Biological Diversity" shows Egyptians as "Eastern Hamites ancient and mixed. However, the writer concedes that they are now mixed semitic speaking elements, Nubians, Beja, Galla, Somali, Danakil, and most Ethiopians.

A book on Tutankhamen written in 1923 by E.A. Wallis Budge stated that:

"Although the Pharaohs of the 12th dynasty were Thebans, it is possible that they and many of their finest warriors had Sudani blood in their veins." An illustration in the book depicts some native people presenting gifts to Pharaoh Tutankhamen. The native people and the Pharaoh's face and skin are painted jet black."

There have been many discussions, writings, pros and cons on the racial identify of Pharaoh Tutankhamen. A book written by a journalist and writer with an interest in archaeology includes a picture of the gold and enamel death mask of the mummified face of Pharaoh Tutankhamen. Now if one would apply the visible perception rules that many Europeans used to identify black people, then this illustrated mask of the Pharaoh includes the physical index of large lips.

The author of a book, Ancient Egypt Its Culture and History, published in 1952 display stereotype writing style when he distinguishes the 25th Dynasty as the Ethiopian dynasty and writes, "it appears strange that the former colony of Nubia could exert its will over Egypt. The royal son, Kush, introduced into savage Nubia a replica of the manners and mode of government of the royal court of Thebes. The viceroy (18th dynasty), comforted himself as a miniature Pharaoh, and in consequence the Negroes became acquainted with the ways of civilization.

The author believed that the "Nubians or Negroes" departed upper Egypt and went back to Nubia because the Negro felt ill at ease among the fair skinned Egyptians, perhaps due to their splendors of the land which had been a legend to the Nubians. These statements help readers today to develop their own individual impression that are based on writings similar to this author. The most unfortunate situation is that in America we still have separate schools of learning depending on the geographical location and economic status of individuals and their God-given right and choice to select where they want to live if they have the finances and to select the school. We must also realize that regardless where the school is located, the great majority or 98% of the selected textbooks for the curriculum have been written by caucasians and sometimes they invite a minority or African American guest author, or advisor to say it is integrated. Therefore, the African American, Caucasians, Asian, Hispanic, and other students matriculate at their different secondary and collegiate institutions of learning and in most cases are still misinformed and miseducated on the true facts of the black experiences in Africa and the United States. In simple lay terms, this is what African centered curriculum means to some people. If they did not tell me, the white majority authors and educators, then who will tell us all. It is not essential for anyone to have as a priority to know which Pharaoh was black or white. They should have a priority to learn that there was a rich talented civilization in ancient Egypt thousands of years ago that happened to possess the biological genetic structure of African chromosomes, genes, and DNA. These genes have survived through the centuries and those melanin deposits or melanocytes have created a visible multi-color skin texture of peoples of color throughout the world.

A department of the army DA Pamphlet, "Area Handbook for the United Arab Republic" (Egypt) stated that origin of the people - food gatherers and hunters from North Africa were drawn to the Nile Valley. The northern Sinai provided a route for incoming peoples from Asia. In upper Egypt, predynatic peoples from farther south were of African Nubian stock." Upper Egypt was essentially Nubian-African in character, whereas northern kingdom of lower Egypt showed a stronger influence of neighboring peoples to the west in North Africa and to the east in Asia Minor.

"The Pharaoh of the twenty-fifth dynasty were Nubians and Ethiopians."

"The people of modern Egypt are an amalgam of several dominant strains. Of these, the earliest known were of African Hamitic stock. The Hamites were Caucasians, who constituted the chief native population of North Africa. Those original Egyptians later mixed with African Negroes."

These views, opinions, and researched statements of scholars over the years in support of their thesis that Egyptians are of a hybrid have been challenged by those who contend and possibly will always in their dominant command of the current literature and its distribution to their collegiate world. A perusal of many different sources of literature relevant to the subject still indicate that the ancient Egyptians were not of the African race but Caucasians. These authors have used as previously stated in this manuscript anthropology, anatomy, linguistic,, ethnology, egyptoloqy, and history to support their conclusive findings. They continue to use terms such as Eastern Hamitic and the physical descriptions and the race or ethnic group. I talked to several veterans of Desert Shield-Desert Storm, Persian Gulf War, when I was collecting material for my recent book on blacks in Desert Storm and many of the veterans told me that they were amazed to see so many people of Arabic descent who would be called Negroes or blacks in these United States. To state it clearly and to the point, television has portrayed to the world the "so called physical characteristics of blacks, curly or wooly hair, thick lips, a range of skin colors from light, brown, dark, to black and various nose sizes. The physical characteristics depicted are also characteristics of foreigners of the Persian Gulf allied armies', civilian ambassadors and so distinctively a prince from the major country in question during the conflict. This only says further that there is an obsession of color by American people. But when they ignore the fact that people in areas of the world other than the United States realize that race is a myth, the terms of ethnic, hamitic, true Negro, linguistic categories and even some anatomical indexes can all be challenged. People of color throughout the continents are varied hybrids because they have been genetically mixed

Black Presence 19

continents are varied hybrids because they have been genetically mixed over thousands of years with possibly the first Adam and Eve's sperm and egg out of Africa; and, of course, color blind sex calls in whatever mutation or change came over the centuries somehow show dominant genes for blackness never disappeared.

Confronting The Smithsonian Institution

An African American, Jacques Hall of Washington, D.C. had visited Egypt in 1988. He was able to observe the descriptive physical characteristic of the Egyptians and was convinced not only by their appearance but from other knowledge about Egypt that Egyptians were black people.

One day in 1989, Jacques Hall happened to he visiting the Smithsonian National Museum of Natural History when he noticed an exhibit on Egypt, The Human Origin and variation section of the exhibit read mainly Caucasoid (Egyptian) African, realizing that he had observed Egyptian as having skin color ranging from jet black to brown, he questioned the Smithsonian's rationale. Hall wrote a letter on July 15, 1989 and asked the Director of the National Museum of Natural History what was their rationale.

On August 9, 1989, A Public information Specialist from the Department of Anthropology answered Jacques Hall's letter by stating:

"Egyptians as well as other people who inhabit the mediterranean coast of North Africa are characterized by dark brunt skin color, with good tanning capacity, that does not differ much from the skin color in Southern Europe. The range in skin color among the people of Egypt reflects; the mobility of population over time. For instance, migration from south of the Sahara and the Prosperity to intermarry his created a mingling of characteristic that overlap between adjoining and even distant population. This may help explain why it is difficult today to assign individuals to one and only one race. Such designation more often reflect cultural or ethnic identity rather than physical characteristics. The exhibit information as therefore correct in stating that Egyptians as Africans are mainly Caucasoid."

Jacques Hall did not accept this reply as the answer to his initial question. Therefore he wrote another letter to the Director of the National Museum of Natural History on February 27, 1990. Hall wrote, In order to inject an element of perspective, we note that pure blooded Caucasoid (Europeans) have a skin color that's generally considered to be white. Pure blooded Negroids have both black and brown skin. Below the sahara (in Africa) there are many brown people, as well as black people. Are they mainly Caucasoid, of course not. Right here in the U.S.A., there are many black and brown people. Are they mainly Caucasoid? Of course not, and yet we claim that the black and brown people od Egypt are mainly Caucasoid."

"I seem to recall that when I was a youngster, before World War II, that there was a branch of the Caucasoids called the Mediterranean Race. It contained Middle Easterners and extended all the way into India. All of these people were supposed to be white, even the black Ethiopians. And of course the black and brown Egyptians as well. But what happened to the good old Mediterranean Race? Well, it seems to have just sort of faded away. Probably because now we realize that we can no longer obscure the unpleasant truth that most of these folks are simply a mixture of black and white. Thus, some of these people are mostly black and some are mostly white. Some of them that are truly 'mainly Caucasoid' are the Greeks, the Italians and Spanish."

"Now for what purpose do we display this 'mainly Caucasoid' sign? Is it to inform the public as to the peoples of the globe that are 'mainly Caucasoid'. If this is so, then such is a worthwhile objective. But then, why are the Egyptians signled out? Where are the signs that proclaim that the Greeks, Italians and Spanish are mostly caucasoids? (Not recommended).

The big barrier between white Europe and black Africa is not the Mediterranean sea but the Sahara desert. Nature provides an excellent highway via the Nile River from black Africa to Egypt. It is undoubtedly

Black Presence 21

because of this link that other North Americans tend to be more white than the Egyptians. Such being the case, why don't we have signs proclaiming that the Moroccans, the Algerians, and the Tunisians are mostly Caucsoids. Could it be because they have no outstanding civilization? And again, why are the Egyptians singled out? And where, Oh, where is the sign that say that the black Ethiopians are mainly caucasoids?

European civilization has been dominant and has led the world for the past several centuries. Thus, it is little more than human nature that many would develop the feeling that the Europeans are simply special people. But then it develops that the ancient Egyptians have a most magnificent civilization millennia before the awakening of the Europeans. And that a great deal of this early Egyptian culture and civilization was absorbed into the beginnings of the European civilization. This throws a monkey wrench into things as it tends to cast doubt upon the idea that Europeans are special. Is this why we, in decades gone by, have declared the Egyptians to be white? Could it be that we still today suffer from this hangover of the past but that now since it is obvious that the Egyptians are not white have fallen back to the position that they are mainly Caucasoid simply because of their past magnifient civilizations? Is this simply a case where wishful thinking causes us to continue to try to horn on the credit for their marvelous ancient culture? Are we simply creating "facts" and rationalizations to support our predetermined conclusions? Or are there indeed valid reasons why the Egyptians are deemed to be mainly Caucasoid? Reasons of which I am as of yet unaware.

They say that it looks like a duck, walks like a duck, and goes quack, quack, quack, then it's a duck. If the Egyptians are black and brown, and they most certainly are, then the thought strikes me that this at least opens up the possibility that they just could be mainly Negroid. It seems to me that if in this case you are mistaken it would tend to indicate an error, to white kids that perhaps they are indeed special. To black kids it would rob them of a mist glorious segment of their heritage and history.

I am sure that the Smithsonian is as interested as am I in the unvarnished truth here as we are all concerned that its worldwide reputation for integrity and credibility be maintained. So therefore, I again respectfully ask "what is the Smithsonians's rationale for the idea that the Egyptians are 'mainly Caucasoid'? Your response would be greatly appreciated."

Three months later, June 1990, Hall had not received a reply from the Smithsonian to his letter. He then decided to contact the Black Caucus realizing that three black congressmen were on the House Appropriations Committee. He was also aware that the Smithsonian Institution is partialy funded by the U.S. government. Hall discussed the matter with the black caucus staff. They in turn contacted the Smithsonian by phone in July. Hall received a call from the black caucus and they told him that the Smithsonian was going to effect necessary changes. Realizing that he had nothing in writing, Hall sent a telegram to the Director of the National Museum of Natural History. The telegram read, "sent you a letter dated February 27, no answer, very surprised and disappointed."

The Director of the National Museum of natural History wrote Hall a letter, dated July 12, 1990. It read,

[The Public Information Specialist] regrets the typographical error, and the confusion it caused, in her letter to you regarding the racial characteristics of the Egyptian people. She intended to say that the exhibit label was incorrect in describing Egyptians as 'mainly Caucasoid'". This was confirmed with the accompanying material she sent you. Our Human Origin and Variation Hall was installed in 1952 and reflects the biases, attitudes, and state of knowledge at that time. We are aware that the exhibit contains some material that is outdated or, by today's standards, occasionally inappropriate or insensitive. We have begun making changes to the hall to bring it more in line with current thinking. In fact, the hall is scheduled to be dismantled and replaced with a new hall on human origins. However, given the time required to design and raise funds for the project of this scale, we do not anticipate a new exhibit before 1995 at least. Early works on race identified European sub-races (Nordic, Mediterranean, and Alpine) generally by stature, head and nose shape, and hair color. When these categories did not surface, other sub races were constructed. Alice M.

Black Presence

Brues does an excellent job in discussing this and other issues your letter mentioned in her book, *People and Faces*.

Jacques Hall was very appreciative of the response that he had received from the museum director. He wrote the Director a letter on July 24, 1990 to address some issues that he believed were significant. Hall wrote,

There are many things obviously wrong with your exhibit entitled, 'The Negroid Racial Stock Arose In Africa'. So much so that it is my view that this exhibit in total does considerable violence to the Smithsonian's high standards of integrity and creditability. I do not think that I go too far in saying that this exhibit is an insult to the Negroid people of the world. It blatantly attempts to surreptitiously deny Negroid credit for ancient's Egypt magnificent civilization by claiming that the Ancient Egyptians were, and that the present day Egyptians are predominantly white. The exhibit contains two photos of full figured Africans. Both are of horribly grotesque looking women. Regardless of intent, the impressions that is given is that these two photos represent typical examples of Negroid peoples.

It is very disturbing to realize that this offensive exhibit has existed since 1952, a period of 38 years. Thirty-eight years of distorted information. Distortions that 38 years have been negatively inaccurate and thus harmful to blacks.

I am delighted to read that you realize the need of change and that you do plan to thusly proceed. But in 1995? Five years from now? This exhibit for 38 long years has short changed some 30 million of our black citizens. Everyday that this biased exhibit stands represents still another day of injustice to these 30 million black American taxpayers. Somehow to me, there seems to be something wrong here. In your letter to me, you spoke favorably of Alice Brues' People and Races. I happen to be familiar with this book. On page 285, Ms. Brues states that the ancient Egyptians were archetypal (same type, model or origin) Cauasoids. I fail to understand the apparent contradictions here. In your letter you indicate that the Egyptians are not mainly Caucasoid while at the same time you suggest her book that states just the opposite. This seem somewhat confusing; however, I would suggest that the Black African, Dr. Cheikh Anta Diop, in his book *The African Origin of Civilization* dispels decaded and decades of this type of confusion. He says how can the black and brown Egyptians be white, and that they are simply members of the Negroid race as are the rest of the black and brown peoples of Africa. Dr. Diop, a former Dean at the University of Paris, and of impeccable credentials, devotes nearly half of his book to an analysis of this strange phenomenon whereby Caucasoids continually dream up creative reasons to explain why the black and brown Egyptians are white. The motive of course, is obvious - attempts to back off with the credit for the Ancient Egyptian civilization. Dr. Diop, himself a historian and an Egyptologist, sets the records straight as he debunks one after another of these sometimes very clever rationalization. Nevertheless, this myth has been with us for so long that still many, many sincere well meaning people continue to believe it. It is my view that Mrs. Brues' statement here represents an excellent example of the type of wishful thinking anthropology that Diop so successfully exposes.

Could it be without being confrontational or perhaps even a trouble maker, that I respectfully make several suggestions as follows:

1. Please dismantle and remove this offensive exhibit as soon as possible.

2. From your vast annual funding, please fund the relatively small amount necessary to complete and install (within perhaps a year) an honest replacement exhibit.

3. In preparing the new exhibit, please seek, and accept counsel from qualified blacks. Howard University as a source is suggested.

4. And last of all, I would respectively request that you please be kind enought to answer this letter."

Hall sent copies of this letter to the Executive Director, Congressional Black Caucus; Secretary of the Smithsonian; President, Charles Wesley Branch Association for Study of Afro American Life and History; Assistant Secretaries of Public Service and Institutional Initiatives, Smithsonian Institution.

As a result of Jacques Hall's letter of July 24, 1990, the Smithsonian Institution invited Hall to come in for consultation. He had an opportunity to express his honest views and specifically told them that the entire exhibit was biased including several rooms and that the exhibit should be immediately removed. Hall simply said no information is better than wrong information. The Smithsonian Institution listened and heard the message Hall brought to them in person. The whole entire exhibit was almost immediately dismantled.

The thought that still remains is where were our African American anthropoloists, Egyptologists, historians, and museum curators, with and without doctorates. Where were they while Hall whose orientation is business had to step forth and correct a serious and offensive error that had been in place for 38 years.

I personally applaud Jacques Hall for his initiatie and successful actions in challenging the Smithsonian Institute to correct an inaccuracy in historical and biological true facts. I challenge African American and European, Asian and Hispanic scholars in this subject elated disciplines to use Jacque Hall's approach to correct many inaccuracies in the history of African Americans and Africans. One specific area for them to start is to reeducate young black, European, Asian and Hispanic youngsters about the truth by including African American History in their school curriculum.

DRAVIDIANS OF INDIA

The year was 1965 and I had arrived in Germany for a miliary tour of three years. One evening, I was visiting Frankfurt and the main train station to purchase some newspapers and magazines as I was walking through the large train station, I observed walking a few feet ahead of me, three Catholic sisters that were very short but from a side perpective as I was passing them, I could see their very Negroid features, mainly black skin, quite dark and nasal features also. I was just about to stop them and ask, how long have you been in Germany? Suddenly, I could see their black straight Asian hair and I realized that they were not black like me, an American black. That experience was my first introduction to the people of India, known as the Dravidians or untouchables.

Over the years, I have read newspapers, magazines, books and have conversed with some Indian friends who were helpful in giving me a clear and intellectual understanding of the Dravidian people. As a biologist and historian, I believe I have a greater appreciation of the facts beyond inferences that these people do have some profound genetic relation to the black African possibly over thousands of years, originating in the Indus Valley. There are historians who believe that there was a social contact between the Aryans and early inhabitants of the Indus Valley that eventually evolved in a caste system. There are many theories, inferences and continuing debate about the origin of the Dravidians. It has been stated that they possibly lived one thousand years ago in the Indus Valley and then migrated into central and southern India. Some scientists will categorize them as being related to the Austroloids. Writers have stated that they were conquered by the Aryans and made slaves (Dasa) and were driven south into the Deccan. The Aryans probably referred to them as Dasa because of their dark skin.

During my class lectures, I explain to my students the meaning of the term caste. There are dictionaries and references that will define caste as *"to be without, split division of society based on wealth, prestige, profession, occupation, hereditary status, social barriers sanctioned by custom, law or religion."* I also tell my students that the caste system existed in other countries, because years ago the Ndebele Social Groups placed people in a class or caste system which were major divisions, Southern Baptu, Sotho and Nguni and sometimes were classified by language. In researching the caste system in India. I learned the system was passed on religion occupation. There was a distinction between Aryan from Non Aryans and people were designated by birth or descent. The name of the Indian Caste system is varna (which interestingly means color). It is believed that when the Nomadic Aryan Turks conquered the

Black Presence 27

present day areas of Pakistan, and Northern India, a caste system began: Military administrators - identified by red colors, the Kshatriyas, merchant and farmers, vaisyas, yellow color and the lowest level were the Sudras, Dalits or Dravidians, known as the outcasts or untouchables.

The term varna has some meaning to color, however throughout many of my readings did not refer to color or skin color and even today, the popular term that disguises color in my inference is "untouchables". I was able to read an article on India by the late Dr. W.E.B. DuBois, the noted historian of color. He wrote the following 50 years ago or earlier about the dark peoples of India. I provide this information for nutritional reasoning or food for thought on this subject.

"What is India? It is 1,500 thousand square miles of territory, with four hundred millions of people. They are mixed descendants of Negroes and Negroids, mongolians, Western Aisiatics and Eastern Europeans". These comments explain so simply what I mean about bio human genetic diversity, but in reality is very easy to call people in Indian black without any discussion or interest in their genetic makeup. That is probably why Americans of all colors get very upset when a young professional golfer decides to acknowledge his genetic diversity.

DuBosis also stated that three or four years before Christ, a black people established civilization in the Valley of the Ganges, they had a fine civilization that was posed on a black Dravidian foundation. He also said five centuries prior to Christ's birth, one of the greatest religious leaders, usually depicted as black, crisp-haired Gautama Buddha was preaching a religion of sacrifice and development. I am sure many scholars of note will say "lies". I do not dispute the authenticity of DuBois's views, however, I repeat again. I am only trying to present the other side of world history as it was being discussed by my predecessors years ago on the subject of the black presence in world history. I am only challenging the reader to evaluaate what is true or false in their sensible thoughts in 1997.

When we examine the lifestyles of the Dravidians years ago, we see some parallels with American slaves as far as separation and ostracism. At one time, the untouchables were required to enter the Hindu community only at night, beat a drum announcing their arrival, and attach a broom to their back to erase evidence of their presence in the area. They were also required to tie a cup around their neck to carry their spittle and some were not allowed to read or write. Their primary duties were sweeeping streets and emptying toliets. Some were required to make fuel cakes from animal dung and then dry them in the sun and store them in cool places. This was generally done by the women. The Dravidians have lived on one side of the village away from the Hindus. They could not use roads that were in the Hindu's areas.

In 1995, I read an article in a newspaper about 4,000 people demonstrating in the Indian state of Maharashtra near Bombay. The violence erupted because the government made a decision to rename a prestigious university in the honor of a former Indian social leader and hero for the Dravidian cause. He was credited with the struggles to obtain rights for the lower class or untouchables. His name is B. Ambedicar. Now I often tell my college students that when you read information in papers, books and magazines and you really do not know the meaning of the words, names, places and overall clarity of the subject, you are sometimes just reading the "tip of the subject." Because when I read the article I found myself applying a phase of a teaching technique that I learned from the late Dr. Robert Thornton, Master Teacher, Physicist and a friend fo Albert Einstein, the celebrated physicist. I tell my students at the beginning of the semester that they should use the simple method of the learning process and that is to comprehend, recall and analyze. I was able to recall what I had comprehended about Mr. Ambedicar that I had learned previously. I referred to my research note book and realized that the man the article was referring to in 1995 was this man: B.R. Ambedicar, the son of an Army officer in the Mahar Regiment. When the Indian mutiny of 1857-8, occurred the British realized that it was necessary to incorporate into their army some untouchables. This decision would, of course, cause animosity among the Hindu ruling class. Some of the Dravidians were able to receive commissions and promotions and in many instances were given better treatment by the British rulers. Many received their first education when they went into the army. Ambedkar father's was able to obtain permission to educate his sons. They were able to attend children. Ambedkar was able to overcome the oppressions and dehumanzing conditions of his early life and was able to enter politics and advanced to a high position of a minister of labor. He also was able to force the Hindus and the Congress Party to reconsider about restrictions on the political progress of Dravidians.

Since the late Jawaharlal Nehru and M. Gandi led India to the independence in 1947, the Congress Party has made some political gestures to attract religions, ethnic and social classes to their party, of course the Dravidians. In 1950, the Indian constitution banned discrimination based on caste, but one must realize that prejudices that originated some 3,000 years ago, will not disappear in 1997. Because America the Beautiful is learning that today, because racial prejudice in America that is only 222 years old cannot be eradicated in 35 years as some honorable politicians and innocent supporters believe. There are many Dravidians today who have been successful in developing their own identity and self concept by improving their income status, education and competing in the capitalist economic system. Yes, many of them have come to America and can be found in the work force representing many occupation and probably living in middle class communities with those priviledged life styles. However, it must be known that in this decade of the 20th century there are millions of people who are classified as Dalits, untouchables, low caste, and Dravidians are still living in India and still being subjected to the veils of the caste system which is still visible. In 1995, an incident occurred when a Dravidian lady was assulted by a gang of the upper class because her son had stopped n upper caste boy for stealing peas from his garden. She was paraded through the streets after her clothes had been ripped off and she was prodded with a bamboo cane or stick.

There are some concerned Dravidians in India who are informing the world through the pen and press that there is racism in India today. V.T. Tajshekar is the editor and publisher of a limited distribution of the *Dalit Voice*, or magazine. He denounces what he calls *"Brahmanism, the father of racism which originated in India"*, a calls for *"the overthrow of the upper class social order"*. He also quotes the writings of B.R. Ambedclar who he calls the author of India's constitution and a former revered leader of the untouchables. When I see a Dravidian in America

There are some concerned Dravidians in India who are informing the world through the pen and press that there is racism in India today. V.T. Tajshekar is the editor and publisher of a limited distribution of the *Dalit Voice*, or magazine. He denounces what he calls *"Brahmanism, the father of racism which originated in India"*, a calls for *"the overthrow of the upper class social order"*. He also quotes the writings of B.R. Ambedclar who he calls the author of India's constitution and a former revered leader of the untouchables. When I see a Dravidian in America today, I am pleased to know about their heritage even though some could be acculturaled in white Ameria or as a friend would say, *he is a Dravidian also, Et tu (you too) brothers are of African descent."*

MINOANS

The middle Minoan period (1900-1700 B.C.) has been represented on fragments of plagues and panels, by individuals of Negroid types. There has been research by some scholars that indicated that there was contact between Ethiopians and the Minoans along the southern coasts of Crete in the Missara plain. A particular fresno painting shows a brown skinned Cretan or Minosan officer with Negro troops.

CARTHAGE AND HANNIBAL

Carthage was a city state located in and near the Gulf of Tunis, in the present day areas of Tunis, Tripoli, Algeria and Morocco. The geographical areas extended westward to the Pillars of Hercules (Strait of Gibraltar) and southward to include areas where they traded with African social groups.

Carthage was founded in the eight century B.C., a wealthy commercial state and intermarriage with African peoples were common practices and were encouraged at times possibly because of wealth and control over subject peoples they met. There were many soldiers of black complexion who fought in Carthage's military. They were also employed as Numidian horsemen and elephant mahouts.

Black Presence

Scipio Africanus negotiated with the Numidian Kings to assist him in the conquest of Carthage. There was a distinguish African general in Carthage who fought in Spain. He was Hamilcar. It has been stated by creditable sources that Hamilcar's son, Hannibal was also of dark skin complexion and was an outstanding General. Hannibal led the Carthagenian armies into Italy and across the Pyrennies and Alps. When he went into winter quarters at Capua, his armies were defeated by opposing forces.

When I had the unique opportunity in 1966 to travel from Turin, Italy, to Munich, Germany by car, I was able to cross the historical Italian Alps and viewed the remains of the historic paths or roads that Hannibal had traveled around 218-201 B.C. Hannibal's success in crossing the Alps was due to his black or African mahouts who guided those elephants with mounted military and subsistence equipment. Those brave Africans of color participated in the Second Punic War (218-201) B.C.

The Ethiopian Mahouts were quite familiar with elephants. They had used elephants in ceremonies and they were well trained to lead the elephants in a military situation. Because some lasting bronze coins were struck relating to Hannibal's military invasions, history has preserved the truth about the black mahouts. The bronze coins portray the head of a Negro with physical descriptive features of a broad nose, thick lips, curly or wooly hair, and an elephant appears on one side of the coin. Even though Indians from India are considered as the primary mahouts, however a picture is worth a thousand words or a picture in this situation on a preserved bronze coin of centuries ago tells the true facts that blacks were present in Hannibal's military expeditions into Italy during the Panic Wars.

THE AFRICAN PRESENCE IN THE GRAECO - ROMAN EXPERIENCE

History books have unfortunately excluded in many instances the presence of Africans especially Ethiopians in early Rome and Greece. The following documented facts illustrate the real black presence.

Black soldiers were among the Carthagenian prisoners in 480 B.C. They also participated in the revolt during the Roman occupation in North Africa. The King of Ethiopia brought his troops from Meroe to the assistance of Troy in Greece in the 13th century B.C. It is believed that Ethiopians troops fought with Constantine in the siege of Verona.

The early inhabitants of Italy were the Etruscans who migrated from Asia and the Carthaginians from Africa. Later these people were of mixed Mediterranean and African groups. One must remember that the Italian peninsula was one of the European areas for centuries to which some African migrated across the Mediterranean sea. There were Roman expeditions to Egypt and trade was promoted with Central Africa, Arabia and India. When the Romans annexed Egypt to their Empire, they also went into the Nile Valley with intentions of conquest. The Romans visited the Nubian Kingdom of Napata. Emperor Nero was interested in expansion and sent an expedition to locate the origin of the Nile river. The Romans were furnished troops and boats by the Nubians and Ethiopians at Meroe.

Some historians have stated that Aesop who was born at Ammonius in Central Asia Minor was possibly as slave at Samos, an island in the Aegean sea. His famous fables were of African origin. Some of his stories are the *Lion and the Mouse, The Belly and its member, The Lion and other Beasts, The Wolf, The Lamb, The Goat, The Wolf In Sheep's Clothing, and the Eagle In the Fox*.

Ethiopian soldiers were present in the invasion of Greece, 480 B.C. under the leadership of Xerxes. Some Ethiopian actors entertained Nero in 66 A.C. Greek writers mentioned Ethiopians in their writings. Some of the writers were Aristotle, Plutarch, Sophocles, Euripides and Homer. Ethiopians are mentioned in the Iliad and Odyssey. Ethiopians had an active role in Isiac worship. Isis was a deity. The temple of Isis was located at Meroe, Third century A.D. There was an early Ethiopian influence in Isiac worship in Greece and Italy. They called the deity, Regina Isis. It has been stated that the herald of Odysseus was black skinned and black women were present in a ceremony associated with the festivals of Isis and Serapis.

Black Presence

The citizens of Meroe honored the Gods Zeus Amasis and Dionysus (Osiris). Ethiopians were with the Egyptian ruler Amasis, (569-525 B.C.) during the occupation of Cyprus. One of Cleopatra's Ethiopian attendants was a lady named Iras.

The Blemmyes were people with black skin and wooly hair. In later years, they were known as member of the Beja tribe near the Red Sea. There was a black warrior, Garamantes, who was described as an Ethiopian.

Historians have presented evidence that reveals that there was an Ethiopian present in Greece and Rome during the Hellenistic period and earlier through sculpture and art figurines. The art treasures depict pictures and images of Ethiopians in numerous descriptive occupations. The Ethiopian's presence has been portrayed on the following:

1. Etruscan coin with the head of a black Mahout (driver) and elephant head image of Queen Ty, wife of Amenophis III

2. Black and white priests in an Isiac ceremony

3. Occupational statutes of black acrobat, bath attendant, lamp bearer, street singer, jockey and groom

4. A marble bust of a black man during the Augustan or Julius Claudian era with descriptive black features

5. A head of a black woman during the Trojan period

6. An image of black warriors appeared on a plate, 5th century B.C.

7. There were pictures of black attendants on the vases of King Busiris, 470-460 B.C

8. Terra cotta statute of a juggler at Thebes

9. Figures showing blacks as prisoners during the Flavian period and black Isiac cultists figures during the Neronian age

10. Some fresnos have depicted black at Pylos and some were wearing Minoan Kilts

Students in colleges and universities throughout the United States study in their world history courses about Athens, Rome and Greece and very few are aware of the early black presence. It is quite possible that the Ethiopians arrived in Greece around the 4th or 5th century B.C. The presence of some mulattoes on the vases and art pieces suggest that race mixing or miscegenation did occur between the Romans and Greeks in the early period or antiquity.

CATHOLIC SAINTS AND CARDINALS

Saint Martin de Porres

St. Martin de Porres was born on December 9, 1579, the son of Do John, a Spanish Cavalier and soldier of fortune and Ann Velasquez, a free black from Panama. The Castilian father of St. Martin abandoned his family. Later he returned briefly and took St. Martin to Guayaquil, Ecuador, where he placed him under the instruction of a tutor for two years. When he returned to Lima, he was apprenticed at the age of twelve to a surgeon. He learned how to make medicine from herbs and to treat sore, wounds and to set broken bones. He gave medical assistance to the poor.

St. Martin became a brother at the convent of the Holy Rosary Black Friars. Some of his duties were caring for the sick, being in charge of the wardrobe, sweeping the cloisters, and being the convent's barber. He was always available to help people with medical and social assistance. The official name of his order was the Order of Preachers of St. Dominic. It has been estimated that he fed on an average of a hundred and fifty daily. He had orchards of olive trees planted for the benefit of the poor.

St. Martin died on November 3, 1639. Thousands of friends came to the convent to pay their last respects. His black and white robes had to be replaced three or four times because people would tear off little

Black Presence 35

pieces. After his death, the friars decided to give his remains a more suitable resting place in the chapel. The disinterment occurred in the presence of the Viceroy of Peru. It has been stated that a surgeon present pierced the flesh with an instrument, and it is said that red drops of blood oozed out. It was then that St. Martin's cause was brought to the attention of Rome. In 1837, Pope Gregory XVI solemnly announced to the world that Martin de Porres was blessed in health. He was canonized in 1962 by Pope John XXII.

Saint Benedict The Moor

St. Benedict the Moor was born near Messina, Sicily in 1526. He died in Palermo in 1589. His parents were slaves. St. Benedict received his freedom from his slave master. In 1807, St. Benedict the Moor was canonized by Pope Pius VIII

African Cardinals

Name	Country
Alexandre Nascimento	Angola
Bamungwabi Nzabi Etsou	Zaire
Toffo Bernardin Cantin	Dahoney (Benin)
Ignatius Dominic Ekandem	Nigeria
Michael Maurice Otunga	Kenya
Victor Razafimahatratra	Madagascar
Laurean Rugambwa	Tanzania
Maria dos Jose Alexandre Santos	Mozanbique
Ilyaciritlie Tliiandouln	Senegal
Wighan Christian Tumi	Cameroon
Paulus Tzadua	Ethiopia
Bernard Yago	Ivory Coast or Cote d'Ivoire
Francis Arinze	Nigeria
Paul M. Zoungrana	Upper Volta
Hyacinthe	Thiandoum

BYZANTINE EMPIRE

Early African Trade with the Byzantine Empire

The Ethiopians were trading with traders from Constantinople as early as the sixth century. The items that were brought from Ethiopia were gold, ivory, ostrich feathers, spices, frankincense, myrrh and slaves. The citizens of Constantinople used tortoise shells from the Somali coast.

There were some slaves and free people in Constantinople from East Africa during the sixth and seventh centuries and eventually race mixing occurred. It is unfortunate that the contemporary history books have not recorded this information.

Some early Ethiopians were able to mine their gold, operated trading posts, built and sailed ships on the Red Sea.

ITALIAN RENAISSANCE

The Black Presence

Historians have documented some factual evidence of the black presence during the era of the Italian Renaissance. The Italian painters portrayed in their works, images of the African or Negro person.

Paolo Varonese showed a Negro in his *Repast at the Home of Simon* and the *Pharisee*. Benetto Grillandajo painted Simon the Cyrene, a black man bearing the cross, *Christ Marching to Calvary*. Paolo Caliaridil Pasto had a Negro in the painting *Wedding Feast in Cana* and Nicolas Poussin, a frenchman who painted under Italian influence displays a Negro in his *Adoration of the Magi*.

There were black present in the Italian states, some 3,000 blacks were in Venice in 1459. It has said that Othello, the black moor was taken from Giraldi Cinthio's novel which was in a collection of sixteenth century

Black Presence 37

short stories. Papini introduced to Italy the Negro poet Danko or Sancho in his volume work, *Stroicature*. Angelo Solimann learned military tactics in Germany and was a soldier in the Holy Roman Emperor's army. Anton Wilhelm Amo was an African who served as professor of philosophy at the University of Wittenberg.

A Medici of Color

The classical historians will probably dispute the facts of history concerning a mulatto or person of African genes who lived during the reign of Lorenzo the Magnificent (1449-1492) in Florence, Italy. When Lorenzo succeeded his father in 1409, he ruled with his brother Guiliano for nine years. His brother was assassinated in 1478 and one of his descendants was an illegitimate son, Guilo (1475-1534) who later became a Pope of the Roman Catholic church in 1523. The *Catholic Almanac, 1992* list a Pope named Clement VIII, Giulio de Medici, Florence, November 1523 to September 1534. A late outstanding archivist and authority on black history, Arthur Schomburg wrote that prior to Giulio de Medici's elevation to Pope, he had a love affair with an African slave servant who became the mother of their child. Her name was Anna. It has been stated Anna was quickly married to the Duke of Urbino who reigned in the city. They became the parents to a child named Raphael. People would say that he was not the son of the Duke of Urbina but probably Clement's son. The disputed son was named Alessandro and his physical description was wooly hair and Negro like appearances similar to his black mother, Anna. Emperor Charles, King and Emperor of the Holy Roman Empire met Alessandro at the Medici palace. At the age of 13 years, Alessandro challenged his rights to the line of the Medici succession. The possible father of this illegitimate man, Pope Clement was interested and concerned about Alessandro behind the scenes. In 1523, the Pope made Alessandro a joint ruler of Florence with his cousin Ippolito under the guardianship of a Cardinal Passerini. When Pope Clement made a peace alliance with Charles V and the Emperor captured Florence in 1530, an agreement was signed at Bologna. The agreement provided that Alessandro became the first hereditary of Florence. Later Charles V had his daughter Margaret of Parima, at the age of 15 years, betrothed to Alessandro de Medici. The Barcelona Treaty of the marriage provided that Alessandro, natural son of Clement VII should marry Margaret and dismiss all doubts as to the subject of Alessandro's parentage. The wedding was held at San Lorenzo. Alessandro did confront some problems and internal family disputes. He was betrayed by his cousin Lorenzino who murdered him in his sleep on January 5, 1537.

Regardless of the veracity of this story, one can not ignore these inferences and possible true facts that have been known through the centuries and have been brought forth by many historians over the years. It is very difficult for many scholars to reveal the truth when it involves the biological genetic diversity of distinguished people of history especially when one was the brother-in-law of Don Juan of Austria, and the son-in-law of the Emperor of Germany, King of Spain and King of Naples and he became the first Duke of Florence. Ironically in 1997, he would not have been a mulatto in America, but a person of color distinctive classified by the government and possibly his family as an African American, just as my miscegenated legitimate great nephew who has an Italian father directly from Italy and an African American mother. Biology determines the reality of birth and social and cultural designation determines what society believes is black or white in our America the Beautiful today.

JAPAN

Sakanouye Tamura Maro was a warrior during the rule of Japanese Emperor Kwammu (782-806 A.D.). Maro was of African descent. He was a hero in the struggle against the Ainus (Ainos) people who were classified as Neolithic inhabitants of Japan's stone age, located in the areas of Hokaido, northern island of Japan. It has been stated that these people could have mixed with people of Ryukyu Island. They were primitive tillers of the soil, hunters and worshipped the bear. They occupied the Island of Yezo as far as Sendai. The Japanese wanted the area and previous armies had failed.

When Maro was given command of the military forces to confront the Ainus people, he was successful in battle, killing some thousands of the Ainus and forced them to retreat further north. This victory possibly made it easier for Japan to erect a castle there and give protection for the frontier   Later Sakanouye Tamura Maro became a shogun or generalissimo.

SUFISM

Sufism was a religious movement that started in the Ninth and Tenth centuries in Arabia, Syria, Egypt and Iraq. The followers were called Sufis (named from the simple coarse woolen garment they wore (Suf). They were people in simplicity and the men and women had a simple life style, fasting, praying and meditating on the love of God. Some people described them as mystics who desired a personal union with God.

A woman named Rabia was a mystic who expressed renunciation and devotionalism. She did not marry but made a total commitment to God. Rabia served as a spiritual guide to her followers. The movement included people from all social classes. They would welcome out caste Hindu groups into their religion or muslim brotherhood. The Sufis included in their religious ideas from Buddhism and Hinduism. The Sufis desired a dear distinction between God and humans. Some were healers and spread Islam to the non believers.

After their demise, the tombs of the Sufi mystics became objects of veneration for Indian Muslims, Hindu and Buddhist followers. Some of their critics believed they were heretical and deviated from the orthodoxy.

It has been stated that Dhul-Nun al-Misri a native of Upper Egypt whose parents were Nubians was the chief of the Sufis and founder of the Sufi school of Islamic Mysticism. He was probably the first to introduce the characteristics of the Sufi doctrine of the ecstatic slates. Al-Misri believed in the merits of penitence, renunciation (to renounce, give up voluntarily), self discipline and sincerity. He said affliction and solitude aids spiritual growth. He was the first to use the language of passionate love in his religious poems, a major feature in Arabic, Persian, Turkish and other Islamic language.

If one considers the definition of a Nubian, "a member of a Negroid people of Nubia", then Dhul-Nun al-Misri was present in the world history of people of color centuries ago.

ISLAM AND MUHAMMED

The Black Presence

When we hear the names, the late Honorable Elijah Muhammed and Malcolm X, the American Muslim Movement, and the Nation of Islam, many people relate these names to the Muslim Movements in the United States for people of color. How many people are aware of the current African states that still embrace the religion of Islam and especially those religious leaders and laypersons who opposed the Million Man March because of religious differences? How many of those individuals who wore and still possibly wear the beautiful and creative fashions from the following countries are aware of their adherence to Islam anywhere from 25 to 100 percent of their population as of 1996?

Country	Percent	Country	Percent
Chad	44	Mali	90
Gambia	30	Mauritania	100
Republic of Guinea	85	Niger	80
Burkina Faso	25	Senegal	50
Guinea Bassau	30	Sierra Leone	30
Djbouti	94	Sudan	70
Ghana	30	Tanzania	33
Egypt	94	Nigeria	50
Ivory Coast	25		

I infer that many Americans of all colors are not aware of the black presence in yesterday and today, 1997.

The following discussion will reveal some research on blacks in the Islamic Society, and the black military presence in Islam, personalities of

Black Presence 41

color Mohammed Ahmed, the Madhi of Sudan, and decisive moments in Islam history in reference to Abyssinia or Ethiopia.

During my many years of teaching world history, I have not been able to find reference in the textbooks for secondary and college level to relate to the above subjects.

Black Presence in Islamic Society

Blacks came into the Islamic world from West and East Africa. Since the beginning of the Islamic period in the 7th century, blacks were imported into North Africa and Morocco as slaves and used as servants, attendants wrestlers, wood cutters, hunters, eunuchs in the harems, concubines, farm laborers, soldiers, and custodians of tombs and sacred palaces.

The African slaves traveled the routes from West Africa across the Sahara to Morocco and Tunia, on to Chad, across the desert to Libya on to East Africa down the Nile river to Egypt and across the Red Sea and Indian Ocean to Arabia and the Persian Gulf.

The Muslims did practice some acts of racism and prejudices in Islam. There was a distinction between black African slaves and the Ethiopian slave women based on physical features.

The employment of young black men and boys as palace enunchs was very popular in Islamic Society.

In 800's Caliph Al-Amin used black and white enunchs. The blacks were separated from the whites. The blacks were called locusts and ravens. The Count of Baghdad in the Tenth century had 7,000 blacks and 4,000 whites. Later the majority were blacks.

In upper Egypt at Abu Tig, some 200 African boys were castrated yearly. They were between 8-10 years old. A powerful enunch in the Ottoman palace court was Kizlar Agass, the Aga of the Girls. It has been said that the Mohammed Ali Pasha castrated many young Dafur slave boys.

Blacks appeared frequently in Islamic literature such as *The Thousand and One Nights* and *Arabian Nights*.

During the Iraq African slave rebellions, there were 10,000 East African slave laborers who worked in salt marshes. They were called the Zanj. During a rebellion in the seventh century, they were able to defeat some Arab armies. Some of the Zanj were defectors from armies of the Abbassid Caliphate of Baghdad. The Zanj constructed the capital city of Moktara (The Elect City).

A 1930 book on *Wit and Wisdom* and a 1926 book on *Ritual and Belief in Morocco* contained several Moroccan proverbs inferring negative and prejudicial impressions about blacks.

Inference about black Arabic Children. *"A fertile Negroes is better (as a wife) that a sterile white woman"*

Prejudice Against Blacks. *"For lack of a relative I call a Negro my mother's brother (said by a woman who could find no husband in her own race."*

Black Military Presence in Islam

I can not forget the reading of United States Army Military documents written in the 1920's and 1940's that referred to decisions made by the so called educated and qualified military leaders who probably believed what they wrote when they stated that blacks were not competent or had the potential to serve as combat troops and, of course fight in integrated units in future military campaigns. I repeat this many times when we talk in 1997 about minorities and their similar problems, I must tell it like it happened and that the native American and those persons who did or did not call themselves Hispanics or Latin Americans in 1941, did serve and fight in integrated military units with whites. However, if one consider

Black Presence 43

simple logical and a historical awareness that people who had black skin and were called people of Negro ancestry had been fighting even though in separate military units at times for many centuries. The following discussion of the blacks soldiers in Islam will reveal again some true facts that are not taught today in the simple to complex presentation about people of color.

The prophet Mohammed had some black slaves in his military. There was one called Wahshi, an Ethiopia who participated in the battle of Uhud.

Blacks served in the Abbasid military forces in Iraq, serving in Baghdad in the infantry corps of the Caliphs.

When Ahmed Ibn Tulan was overthrown in 905, his black infantry was killed and in 930, a black cavalry unit was massacred by a white cavalry unit.

Black troops were present for a brief period in Egypt's Muslim armies around 1000-1100. They served under the Fatimid Caliphs Cairo's black regiments.

In the 1600's, black slave troops were present in the Moroccan Sultan Mawluy Ismali's army of 250,000 soldier. They were obtained through the means of conscription, compulsory purchase of all male blacks in Morocco, levies on slaves and slave raids in Mauritania. There was also forced breeding or mating of black slave girls and women with male soldiers in order for them to produce future slave soldiers and female servants.

In the 1800's, black slaves were observed in the Egyptian armies during Napolean Bonparte I's expedition in Egypt.

It has been stated that black troops were present in Muhammad Ali Pasha and his successor's armies when Pasha dispatched an Egyptian Expeditionary Force to Mexico in 1863 in the support of the French army.

Creditable sources have stated that in the mid 1800's, blacks were reported as being soldiers in Turkish units seeking their freedom. Some blacks served as officers and were marines. They possibly were recruited from Tripoli where there were some free blacks. A British Naval reported stated that the black men were treated in similar manner as the Turks with respect to equal pay, quarters, rations and clothing to include discharge of service. A Negro mulazim (lieutenant) and some tchiaoushes (sergeants) were used to instruct new recruits. Their performances showed very little connection between their past slavery condition and present state of existence. This report was written in the 1800's and in 1944 the United States military still maintained command officers and non commissioned officer positions for whites to command and instruct black American service men. Now I can understand a little more clearly why I was introduced to a Turkish officer in the rank of major in the Sixth Turkish Brigade in Korea in 1955 when I saw only one U.S. black Army officer in the rank of major while serving in Korea 1955-1957. Yes, I often tell my students, knowledge is powerful when you learn something new each day.

The first independent ruler of Muslim Egypt had Nubian troop in the armed forces, even though they had separate living quarters in 800.

In 1164, a Caliph's chief black eunuch led 50,000 blacks against Caliph Saladins' army.

Zayd Harrith was a Moslem black general officer.

When Abid al Beihari organized an elite praetorian guard blacks were brought as slaves from West Africa. They were part of the military similar to the Turks in the Arab Islamic world.

Personalities of Color

The late president of Egypt, Anwar Sadat's mother was a black Sudanese. In America using the one drop of black blood rule, she and her son, Anwar would have lived and died as black people.

Black Presence 45

Al-Johiz was a theologian, anthropologist, naturalist, zoologist, philosophers and philogist.

Abu Dulama was a court poet and jester for an Abasid Caliph. He once made a comment about his family. He wrote, *"We are alike in color our faces are black and ugly, our names are shameful"*.

A Caliph, Umar was a grandson of an Ethiopian woman

Suhaym was a slave ho was conscious of his blackness. He wrote, *"thought I am black of color my character is white"*.

A tribal chief, Khufaf ibn Nadba was a friend of Prophet Muhammad. His father was an Arab and his mother was a black slave.

The architect of Egypt and a conquer of the country was a mulatto named Amir ibn al-as.

A black poet, Daud ibn Salm, 700 c.a. was known as David the black (al adlam) and was called ugly and black.

A famous Muslim singer was ibn Misjah. He was of black descent.

Ali the successor to the founder of the Songhay empire. Ali was known a Mohammed Ture ibn abi Bakr. He was of Soninke origin. He was able to consolidate the areas of the Niger Valley from Jerine to Gungia, the hinterland of Hombosi and Northern Yatenga. Muhammad demonstrated his support to Islam by establishing Timbuktu as a center of learning. This African ruler also made Islam the state religion when he made a pilgrimage to Mecca (1497-81). He gave a gift of gold for the building of hostel for Sudanese pilgrims.

Nedjeh, an African slave and his descendants were rulers of Arabia from 1020 to 115.

Prior to the Norman conquest of England, a group of Persians migrated to Kilwa, East Africa. The group was led by Hassan-ibn-Ali, the son of an Ethiopian slave mother.

A ruler of Egypt named, Zahir (1021-1026) was married to a black Sudanese woman. Later their son, Mustanir, ascended to the throne in 1036 and ruled until 1094. His mother influenced him during the rule of his kingdom. At one tome, Mustanir's army consisted of 50,000 African soldiers, 30,000 white slaves, 26,000 Berbers and 10,000 Turks.

When I have discussed the Mohammedans in Europe and their crossing the Pyrenees around 719 A.D., unfortunately, my required World History textbook did not include the following: *"an independent government known as the Caliphate of Cordova was in existence and the sustenance of power dependent on an army composed of African and white Christian slaves."* Later the rule of the Caliphate passed over to a mulatto or person of color, Almanzor. He maintained order with Africans and Berbers. Almanzor conducted some 50 invasions into Christian territory.

One of the distinguished poets of Damascus under the dynasty of Ommiades (661-750 A.D.) was an African called, Nosseyeb.

Malik Ambar's original name was Shambu. He was born in Harar, Ethiopia and sold into slavery. His master Husseen provided him with an education in administration and finance. His master named him Ambar when he was converted to Islam. Later Ambar was purchased by an Indian Prime Minister of African origin named, Khan. Amar was sold to the King of Byapur and received the title or name Malik, and became a military commander. Malik Ambar decided to desert in 1590. He was able to organize his own army of 1500 cavalry and infantry men who were mercenasics. Ambar confronted a Mongol Emperor named, Akbar and established a capital at Kirkee. He organized a 60,000 horse army and enlisted some naval support from the Siddis in 1616.

Some of Ambar achievements were: (1) he improved the communication systems in his kingdom and had a postal and messenger service (2) he purchased one thousand Habshu slaves, a minority group people of the Deccans (3) he encouraged them to enlist in his army and gave them a Koranic education (5) he used the Habshu slaves as his guards (6) he granted land to the Hindu residents in his kingdom and appointed the Brahmins as financial officials and tax collectors (7) he built canals,

Black Presence 47

irrigation systems, and architectural developments to include roads, public gardens, Mosques and public buildings (8) he reduced the tax rates and permitted commural and private ownership of property. Malik Ambar was a great personality in Deccan and Indian history. Islam did provide significant opportunities for Africans in India and among the Deccan people.

Bilal ibn Rabah was born a slave in Mecca. His physical description was tall, thin and dark complexion. He was freed by his master, Abu Bakr, the father-in-law of Prophet Mohammed. He was called Bilal. He had served as a personal attendant to the Prophet and was an African Iman at Medina and Mufti at Mecca. His distinguished position in Islam was his appointment as the first Muezzin or Crier to perform the Azan or call to prayer. Bilal was also the Prophet's mace bearer, steward, adjutant and personal valet. He traveled with the Prophet and carried the prayer spears Anaza before the Prophet's public prayers at the great festivals. Bilal was a member of the tribe of Djimah. He was one of the five non Arabians to be assigned grants. It has been said that the singing of the Adhan is a developed art in Islam that requires study and practice. The melody varies. There are seven declarations of faith and one is a repetition of the first, *"Alah, is most great"*. Bilal use to sing from the roof of the Caaba at Medina. It is believed that Bilal died in Damascus and is buried in Dariya.

In the 1600's, Naubat Khan Kalawant played a vina (a vina is a stringed instrument of India with four strings on a long bamboo finger board) at a court of Jahanger.

Mabed Ibn Ouhab was the son of a black and was a mulatto. He was a herder for his master. He received his freedom and was able to study music. As a young man, he would sing a lahn (a strain) called the bird song near Mecca.

Ibrahim-al Madhi was a singer and musician of Arabia. He was the son of Caliph Muhammad al-Madhi and married a black slave girl named Shika or Shaka. It has been stated that he was directly descended from Hashin, grandfather of Prophet Mohammed and a brother to Haroun al Raschid. Al-Babbas was his uncle. In 817 at 38 years, he was chosen to succeed his father as Caliph. He then received the name of Al Mubarak, the blessed. When his troops rebelled for lack of pay, he was forced to go to Baghdad. His nephew, Almamoun then became Caliph. Mabed was of the Abbassides dynasty of Caliphs of Baghdad. He helped to build a Mosque at Ar-Ru Sofa. He was an accomplished musician and played the flute.

Antarah ben Shedad el Abs was born in the sixth century around 525 and was a member of the tribe of Abs. He was the son of a slave mother from Ethiopia. Her name was Zabiba. His father was a noble Arab. Antarah was called Antar. He raised camels as a child and was interested in horsemanship. Antar developed a real interest in writing poetry. He wrote the *"Romance of Antar"*, a free expression of Arab hero worship. The admirers of Antar's poems would recite them in the cafes of Aleppo, Baghdad and Constantinople. Antar was also called Antar, the Lion. He was a great warrior and poet of Arabia.

Mohammed Ahmed, the Madhi was a person of color. I can recall seeing the movies as a youngster of the British fighting in Khartoun and the opposing soldiers had their faces covered in their respective attire. I had no knowledge what so ever that the famous British officer, Gordon was fighting a courageous black Sudanese leader who thought he was the "Messiah", the Madhi. Mohammed Ahmed was a native of Dongola, a Nuba family of non Arabic ancestry. In 1881, he proclaimed himself the Madhi, a representative of the Prophet Mohammed. He was a fearless military tactician who was victorious in several strategic battles against the British and Egyptian forces. In 1882, the Madhi defeated an Egyptian army and captured Kordofan. On November 4, 1882, he was successful in a battle against Hicks Pasha and practically overcame an army of 10,000 men. He was able to seize Omdurman. The Madhi was later killed by the British. However, his successors were Abdullah or Kalife who was a member of the Darfur Tribe and mixed with black and Arab. He was a former chief advisor to the Hadhi. He had a powerful army that attacked Ethiopia and captured the city of Gondar where Negus or King John was killed in 1888.

Black Presence 49

Osman Digna was a mulatto general who commanded the armies that drove the English out of Sudan for 16 years to include the killing of General Gordon. The British returned in 1898 and Digria was imprisoned in solitary confinement for 25 years.

I did not perceive or learn this from the skillful entertaining movie that I saw as a young boy.

Decisive Moments In Islam History

I was surprised to see the following accounts in a book on Islam history that I purchased 25 years ago, especially the black presence in events of history in the year 627.

At one time, there were some early relations with Muslims and Christians. In the sixth year of the Hijrah (627 c.e.), the Prophet sent letters and envoys to Heracluis, Emperor of the Eastern Roman Empire to Chosroes, King of Persia, to the Roman ruler to Egypt, to the Christian King of Ghassan, to the Amirs of Yemen, Uman and Bahrain and to the King of Abyssinia. The Prophet wa suggesting that the kings and princes should embrace Islam. The letter included statements such as: *"you will be saved if you become a Muslim and God will double your reward. If you refuse you will be responsible for the sins of the infidels."*

Some of the king's responses were, the prefect of Egypt sent the Prophet a letter and present, the Amir of Bahrain replied by embracing Islam, King Chosroes insulted the envoys, and the King of Abyssinia (Ethiopia) replied in a friendly manner. *There was a real Muslim Seamen and leader of Naval forces called Ghulam Zarafa or Leo of Tripolis. He had participated in numerous military invasions. In 904, he had chased the Byzantine naval fleet to the Strait of the Hellespont and returned to Thasos. He decided to attack the city and sent an advanced guard. The Muslim divided themselves into groups and roamed the city killing, plundering and taking captives. A Byzantine historian, John Camniatis and several members of his family were among the captives. They fell into the hands of a number of Abyssinians or Ethiopians with whom they pleaded for mercy and told them there was a place where the family's treasures were hidden. One of the Abyssinians knew Greek and the chief of the Ethiopian group led Caminiates to Admiral Leo of Tripolis who accepted the treasures as ransom for the life of the historian and his family. They were taken to Tarsus to be exchanged for Muslim captives in the hands of the Byzantines.*

These above true accounts reflects how there are many stories of the early and ancient presence of blacks in world history. I often ask my college students where were we in world history other than the usual slave status that is still taught in 1997.

AFRICAN KINGDOMS AND SOCIETIES

I was very pleased to review several textbooks sent to me by college book publications and observe that after many years of neglect and possible intentional omissions they are including some information on the early African states and societies in world history textbooks. However, they concentrate mainly on the well known and popular ancient states of Songhay, Mali and Ghana. They do address leaders such as Sundiata Keita (1230-1255) King Mansa Musa (1307-1332), and Askia Mohammed I.

I have included in the following articles information on African Kingdoms and societies to include the subjects of geography, caste system, slected social groups, and African decorative dress and jewelry. These articles were researched in the early 1990's for my book *They Did Not Tell Me True Facts About The African American's African Past and American Experience.*

There were some forms of government organization and political type institutions that existed among some East African communities prior to the 1900's. The Acholi states had social groups linked to Rwot King, who appointed his village chiefs. The Royal families had their respective regalia and conducted ritual ceremonies. Prior to 1700, small Lwo groups were present as centralized states. Some ruled by Pubungu and Luo families from Northern Uganda and Bunyoro.

The Lwo had assumed kingship over the Bachwezi (Kitara). A dynasty called the Mukuma Kings was started by the Luo and succeeded for eighteen generations over four-five centuries. The Bito dynasty founders were of the Jo-Bito Lwo Kingdom called the Bunyoro. They had assumed the regalia and tradition of the Bachwezi.

The Bito families established sub-dynasties near the border of Tanzania, Western Uganda, and Buganda.

The Himia-Bito kingdoms, were modeled similar to the Sidama, Kafa, and Janjero. There was an organized hierarchy with status and power of the king, court, and state officials. The King's Mother had a position in the ruling system. There was a system of administration in the provinces of the kingdom. The selection of successors and royal burial rites were similar to the Sidama Kingdoms.

Some customs of the King's Burial rites were: "Janjero - King's body wrapped in royal gowns, a cow is killed and the body is placed in the animals hide and on the seventh day, the new king kills the maggots; Ankole - the king's body is laid in cow skin and left to decompose, milk is mixed with fluids and the king is reborn; Bunyoro - the king's body is placed in a bull's hide.

Buganda had a king as the ruler. The royal insignia consisted of drums, stools, and spears. The states were composed of different social groups united together the alligiance to the king. The Office of the Kingship Kabaka was hereditary. There was a legislative council, the Lukiko, and the provinces were represented by chief ministers. The Administration of Bunyoro included "court officials, county chiefs, county agents, county servants, pages and messengers."

The Kiganda dynasty was founded by Kintu. The Kikuyu had an age system and descent group. The age system of the Kikuyu was a system of government, control, and type of Political organization.

African Kingdoms - Past and Present

Africans had more kingdoms than just Ghana, Mali, and Songhay. African kingdoms past and present are:

West Africa

Akan
Allada
Akwamu
Asante
Basoambiri
Benin
Bono
Dahomey
Diom
Dyara
Djoloff
Ghana
Gonja
Igala
Ijebu
Jakin
Kaatra
Kanen-Bornu
Katisina

Ketu
Little Popo
Mali
Mamprussi
Merue
Mossi
Nanumba
Nembi
Oyo
Sine
Songhay
Sulimoma
Tori
Warri
Whydah
Yauri
Za
Zamfora
Zandoma
Zazzau

East Africa

Ankole
Buganda (Luapula)
Bunyoro-Kitara
Damot
Enarya (Sidamo)

South Africa

Bemba
Kazempe

Kongo
Lozi
Luba

Ethiopia
Hadya (Sidamo)
Kafa
Kitara
Sham Baa
Wanga
Wolamo (Sidmo)

Lunda
Swaziland
Zimbabwe
Zulu

Geography - True Facts About Ghana

The Republic of Ghana covers 522 miles from south to north and 355 miles from east to west, with an area of 92,100 square miles. The capital is Accra. Geographically, Ghana is bordered by three West African countries in the east, north and west. They are the Republics of Togo, Upper Volta, and Ivory Coast. The Gulf of Guinea is in the South. Ghana obtained its independence on March 6, 1957 and became a republic within the British Commonwealth on July 1, 1960. The colors of the country's flag are three horizontal bars of red, gold, and green with a black star in the middle of the gold. In 1970, the country had nine regions with their capitals as follows:

Regions	Capital
Greater Accra	Accra
Eastern	Koforidua
Volta	Ho
Ashanti	Kumasi
Brong Ahafo	Sunyani
North	Tamale
Upper	Bolgatanga
Central	Cape Coast
Western	Sekondi

The climate of Ghana is tropical, and it has two seasons. The wet season occurs between May and September, and the dry season between October and February. Main exports from Ghana are logs and timber, cocoa, gold, diamonds, bauxite, and manganese.

The country of Ghana receives its energy resources from the Volta River Hydroelectric project. In 1970, the project had an ultimate power output of 768,000 kilowatts which provide abundant cheap power for domestic and industrial use throughout the country. The project had created the largest man made lake in the world, 250 miles long and occupying an area of 3,275 square miles.

A major airport in Ghana is the Kotoka International Airport, located in Accra. Internal ports in Ghana are Kumasi, Tamale, Bolgatanga, Takorade, and Sunyani.

Ghana has major lakes and lagoons. The lakes are Lake Volta, and Lake Bosumtwi. Bosumtwi is located 21 miles southeast of Kumasi and occupies an area of about 19 square miles and a depth of between 230 and 240 feet. The lagoons are located along the country's coastline. East of Accra and West of Cape Three Points are lagoons that are the mouths of rivers ponded back and separated from the sea by low sand bars.

Ghana, A Profile

The Republic of Ghana is situated along the Gulf of Guiena. To its east lies Togo, then Benin and the Republic of Nigeria. On the west is the Ivory Coast, and on the North, the Republic of Upper Volta.

The population of Ghana is mostly Ghanians who are Sudanese Africans and some may have "Hamitic" strains in Northern Ghana. People have occupied the country during the past 700 to 1,000 years. The major ethnic groups in Ghana have moved into the country from the north. Those coming from the north included the Guan groups who came in from the Volta gorge. They are located along the coast between Winneba and Cape Coast. They were followed by the Fantis, Akans, and the Twi. Some groups came from the east. They were the Ewes. Ghana became independent on March 6, 1957. Dr. Kwame Nkrumah became the country's first Prime Minister.

Present day Ghana is very proud of the ancient kingdom of Ghana. It was a great commercial center. Ancient Ghana traded with Spain and Portugal in gold, ivory, animals skins, kola nuts, and cotton.

It has been stated that European, Egyptian, and Asiatic students studied at the Universities in Ghana. They learned philosophy, medicine, mathematics, and law. There was even exchange between the University of Sankore in Ghana and the University of Cordova in Spain during this period of ancient Ghana's prosperity.

Ancient Ghana was attacked by various nomadic races in 1240. A small empire attacked and conquered Ghana. Mali began to expand its territories and became the largest of the Sudanic kingdoms. Mali's King, Mansa reigned for 25 years. He loved his people and had a justice system. When Musa made his pilgrimages to Mecca, he displayed his wealth and was accompanied by "60,000 people, 1,200 young slaves and 1,400,000 grams of gold. He gave some gold away as gifts. Mali had a renowned University at Timbucktu. Around 1450, Mali began to decline and Songhai, a small kingdom located South of the Niger conquered Mali. In 1591, the Moorish troops of the Moroccan Prince, El Mansur, defeated the troops of Songhai on the battle field of Tondibi.

The Portuguese were the first Europeans to visit the gold areas between the Rivers Ankobra and Volta (1471). The Portuguese were amazed at the large deposits of gold and called the area "Mino (mine)" and the French called the area, "Cote de l'Or or the Gold Coast", a name the English used later to call the entire country. Later, the Portuguese built, the Castle of Sao Jorde da Mina.

The Gold Coast became an interesting economical base for other European countries to explore. The Dutch captured the Elmina Castle from the Portuguese in 1637. Then the English, French, Danes, Swedes, and Germans began to exploit the gold and slaves of the Gold Coast.

In 1874, the British established the Colony of the Gold Coast. After several Ashanti resistance movements to British exploitation, the Ashanti Empire was conquered in 1901. Since its independence in 1957, the Republic of Ghana has demonstrated considerable progress in the areas of government, economics, and the social welfare of its people. A Ministry of Cocoa Affairs was established in 1975. The ministry is tasked to formulate policies and supervise programs relative to cocoa, coffee, and industries in Ghana. A national museum opened in 1973. The museum housed archaeological, historical, and ethnographical materials. Paintings and sculptures are also present in the museum.

The Republic of Ghana has the following organizations: Ghana Academy of Arts and Sciences; Council for Scientific and Industrial Research; The Ghana Bar Association; The Ghana Medical Association;

The Institute of Chartered Accountants (Ghana); The Ghana Institution of Engineers; and the Ghana Institution of Surveyors; and Ghana National Association of Teachers.

The Christian council of Ghana was founded on October 30, 1929, a fellowship of churches in Ghana. Some of the churches are the: "Anglican Church, Presbyterian Church, Methodist Church, Evangelical Presbyterian Church, African Methodist Episcopal Church, Society of Friends, Ghana Baptist Church, Mennonite Church Christian Methodist Episcopal Church, Evangelical Lutheran Church and the Feden church."

Ghana has been very active in sports and competitive games. Ghana won the Africa cup in soccer, 1963. In 1972, Alice Anum of Ghana became the first African female sprinter to reach the 100 meters final and placed 6th in the Munich Olympic games. Ghana shared honors with kenya at the Second All-Africa Games in Lagos by winning seven gold medals.

Ghana has demonstrated successful progress in hockey. In 1975, Ghana won the Africa Continental Championship and earned a place among 12 finalists of the World Championship.

The Republic of Ghana has a strong friendship with African Americans because one of our great leaders was buried with honors in Ghana. He is the late W.E.B. DuBois.

Black Presence

An African Caste System

African societies have families with a common name, with common descent, or divine ancestors. The Ndebele society caste system involves a social stratification of individuals in a class system and groups in a caste system.

The two major divisions of the southern Bantu were the Sotho and Nguni. The Nguni people were classified in terms of language and were distinguished from the Tsonga in the northwestern border and the Sotho to the north and northwest. The area of present day Swaziland was inhabited by the Nguni as early as the sixteenth century. Around 1775, the chiefdoms developed into larger states. Three kingdoms, Mathethwa, Ndandwe, and Qwabe dominated the smaller groups in 1810. There were numerous disputes among the leaders and eventually a great warrior appeared, Shaka, who was the founder of the Zulu Empire. He established the group by defeating the leaders and had other leaders to submit.

An independent Chief, Zwangendaba moved farther north with his people and small groups of Swazi and Tsonga peoples. This newly formed group was called Ngoni (derived from Nguni). Another independent leader fled from Shaka. The chief of this group was Mzilikazi, a member of the Northern Kumalo chiefdom of the northern Nguni. His group became known as the Ndebele and called Matabele by the Europeans. In 1825, the Ndebele settled in towns at Mosega and Gabeni along the Marico River. They raided villages and with five regiments crossed cattle from the Shona people. Mzilikazi recruited Sotho youths and Nguni immigrants. The Kingdom increased to approximate 80,000 persons. Mzilikazi's kingdom was a military type. He absorbed members of other societies into the Ndebele political system and developed their loyalties. The 14 members who were of the original Nguni group obtained a high social status and called themselves the Zansi. They came from the coastlands of Zululand.

The people who came from the high veld (grass cover plains) and were of Sotho ancestry accepted the name Enhla. Those persons from Shona and Kalanga lineage who were incorporated into Ndebele society after they settled in Rhodesia were called Holi (alien people). The Holi were denied full membership in the society.

The Ndebele caste system was a three tier system. The Zansi were known as Nguni or real Matabele. The royal family and aristocrats formed this tier. The middle caste members were the Sotho or Ndebele. The third tier included the Lozwi or Holi. The clans in this caste were the Kalanga, Lowzi, Nyai, Venda, Shankwu and Nanzwa.

The Ndebele caste system possibly originated when the Nquni fled from Shaka and Mzilikazi conquered them into his kingdom. The kinships systems of the Ndebele is patrilineal. The Sothos had a form of marriage to cousins. The Tswana approved marriages between cross cousins.

The Ndebele forbidden marriage between the castes. The Zansi and Enhla wives of higher caste would refuse to eat with a Lozwi wife. There was also differences in dress. The zansi could wear headdress of ostrich feathers. The Lowzi were not allowed to wear kilts and wild cat skins. It was mandatory for young women of the three different caste to dress differently. There were caste systems in other African societies. They were present in the societies of the Marghi in Western Sudan, Rwanda Tutsi, and the Mande.

The Kikuyu of Kenya

One of Kenya's proud and industrius social groups, the Kikuya has interesting cultural traditions. Prior to the arrival of the Kikuyu into the Kiambu area of Kenya, a dense forest region was inhibated by the Pygmy people called "bumba" and the Wa-Ndorobo people. The pygmy people eventually departed the area arid the Kikuyu obtained hunting rights "Githakas" (ithaka) from the Wa-Ndorabo. The land was handed down over the years by inheritance to the descendents of the original owners. This was the genesis of a land tenure system. Later years the Kikuyu were forced to make land reserves in the highlands available for the white settlers who had immigrated to Kenya. Land tenure played a significant part in the social, political, religious and economic life of the Kikuyu. The

Kikuyu people use their land for their cattle, sheep, and goats. The soil has a spiritual meaning to them because their ancestors are buried there.

The social organizations of the Kikuyu have three major divisions. They are family group (Mbari) parents, children, grand and great grand children; clan, (Moherega) a family unity where family members have the same name and are descended from one family group; a system of age-grading (niika), where the family is united.

The Kikuyu had an annual circumcision ceremony. The ceremony is called the "Irua Ceremory."

The True Identity of The Berbers

The North African Berbers are another group of Africans who have been classified by the so-called experts, anthropologists, archaeologists, ethnologists, linguists, and historians as to their true biological race or ethnic group. The consistent name-calling of Africans with black skin, different hair texture, lips and noses created a classification system of true Negro and then people who were known to have African genes besides European genes were called "mixed" or hamitic and Caucasian people.

The experts did not and some still are not considering the variables that exist in the biological complexities of the African in Africa. The geographical dispersions, land relocation, years of small cellular groups reproducing their own kind even though ancestral wise they have some gene diversity with the addition of African genes. Even though it is of no significance, interest or matter to peoples yesterday and today, the true reality is that the people may be called anything but the fact is that the word mixed has a greater connotation than just being mixed. The reality again is that they are not of one pure racial, ethnic group and, of course, they are genetic hybrids renamed by the early so called dominant groups that visited their areas, the Greeks, Romans, Spanish, French, Italians, Portuguese, Belgium, Dutch, Germans, British and, of course, the Americans in later years.

The Berbers have been described physically, racially, and linguistically by historians and other scholars over the years as:

"Berbers are caucasians; probably white men from North Africa; original inhabitants of North Africa are Caucasoid. They are brown-skinned Berbers, but Hamitic; Berbers had some black blood mixed with Arabs and produced a race that developed in North Africa; people of North Africa were identical to early Egyptians, some had long heads, broad faces, dark skin and eyes; the Libyans or Berbers were descendants of north Africans populations and had a mixture (if Asian and Negroid; the area of Kanem had a population of mixed Negro and Berber descent; Berbers are of mixed races to include Libyans, Ethiopians, whites and black Africans; Berbers do not possess a homogeneous ethnic group, but are of mixed blood. They include the African blood of the Sahara and Morocoo."

History books will continue today and possibly many tomorrows to state without any reservations about the previous discussion on Berbers identity and state simply and definitive that Berbers are white, Caucasian, caucosoid, and hamitic. Again I repeat, in this manuscript that the continued debate over African-centered and multicultural curriculum do pose a problem when distinguished scholars on both sides continue to debate intellectually and with scholarly research as to who is the persons in question real ethnic identity. I challenge the curious with a simple statement that from the biological and historical perspective, ancient Berbers had black genes.

African Brazilians Return To Their Roots

When the late Alex Haley's best seller book, *Roots* was published there were some people of African descent in North America who were able to locate their families in Africa. They were able to visit Africa and return or become a permanent resident in Africa. Of course, it has been difficult for African Americans to search their roots to Africa, possibly due to the system of slavery that existed in America. There were many prohibitions

Black Presence 61

imposed upon the American slave. They were denied the right to use their native language and read and write.

The Brazilian system of slavery did provide opportunities for some African slaves to retain their native language and cultural traditions. An example is the African Yoruba slaves from Nigeria. When they were transported to Brazil, they were settled in the city of Bahia.

After slavery, some of the descendants of the original Yoruba slaves were able to return to their hometowns. This was made possible when some slaves were permitted prior to abolition to purchase their freedom ad return to Africa. There were some freed slaves who would return to Nigeria, Africa and marry and then return to Brazil with their children after abolition. In later years, some former African slaves in Brazil would engage in import/export business with Lagos, Nigeria. Slavery was abolished in Brazil in 1888; whereas American slavery and the Civil War was ceased in 1865.

Some examples of descendants of African slaves and former African slaves in Brazil returning to Africa are:

"An African slave in Bahia Brazil in 1879, Ainaro Marinho purchased his and his wife's freedom. He sailed with her and three children to Nigeria. His children were Andre, 19; Fortunata, 15, and Vicente, 13. He never returned to Brazil. Marinho's daughter, Fortunata, married in Lagos, to a Marcos Augusto Jose Cardosa who left Brazil in 1869 with his father. They became the parents of nine children. Marcos Cardosa was a skilled mechanic. He learned his trade from an African in Brazil. He is credited for building the first Catholic church in Nigeria in 1880. Cardosa also constructed schools and churches and built the first spiral stairway in Lagos, Nigeria.

Dorothea Manuel Reis was born in Rio de Janerio of African parents who were brought to Brazil as slaves from Aheokuta, Nigeria. Her parents purchased their freedom prior to abolition and returned to Nigeria.

Lucia Mendes and his wife were born in Nigeria and came to Bahia as slaves. He obtained his freedom and returned to Nigeria with his wife and a son, Supriana Mendes. His wife died in Nigeria and he died in 1894.

These examples of Brazilian Africans returning to their homeland Nigeria are evidence that some Africans and their descendants were able to return to their fertile soils of their original roots.

The Neur

There are a group of proud tall men called Neur, Storkmen of the Nile. They live in a swamp and plains area of southern Sudan. The Neur men generally rest upon one leg while tending their cattle.

Jomo Kenyatta

The first leader of Kenya was Jomo Kenyatta, a Kikuyu. The Kikuyu were involved in the aggressive Mau Mau Movement that eventually led to the country's independence in the 1950's.

African Kingdoms

Some kingdoms and states of Africa existed prior to 1800. They were successful and had reached a period of great accomplishments (dates indicated) Kush, 700 B.C.; Egypt, 1450 B.C.; Axum (Ethiopia/Abyssina); Ghana, 1000; Kanem, 1300; Mali, 1325; Kilwa, 1400; Hausa States, 1400; Benin, 1450; Mosi States, 1450; Zimbabwe-today) ; Monomotapa, 1475; Songhai, 1500; Kongo, 1500; Lupa, 1500; Bornu, 1600; Lunda, 1750; Oyo, 1750; Buganda, 1800; and Dahomey, 1800.

Black Presence

The Luba

The Luba descendants of people ruled the Katanga Plateau in the 15th and 16th centuries. Many of them live in present day southeastern Zaire. The Luba conduct a Roman Catholic mass called the "missa luba. The mass is sung in a vigorous, joyful style with the assistance of drums.

King of Ashanti

In July 1970, Nana Opoku Ware 11 was installed as King of the Ashanti in a ceremony using the symbol of the Ashanti Nationhood "The Golden Stool." The Ashanti live in the finest zone of Central Ghana.

Nuba Plainsmen

The African plainsmen of the Nuba Mountains of Sudan decorate themselves with an intricate pattern of scars. Nuba wrestlers powder their bodies with ashes in the belief that it increases their strength.

African Sculptures

The artistic sculptures of the Ife and Benin peoples date back to the 12th Century, A.D. The technique of brass coating war introduced from the IFE to Benin around 1400. The sculptures were used for palace altars. Unfortunately, some of the Yoruba people's great art heritage was lost when the British colonists burned the city of Benin and confiscated some of the artistic sculptures.

Early Bantus

The present day South Africa area was inhabited many by the original people and not European explorers and colonist who arrived in later years. The African Bantu people crossed the Limpopo River into present day South Africa before A.D.

The Danakil

The East African People who lived in the areas of Ethiopia's Danakil Depressions are called Danakil. However, they refer to themselves as the Afar.

The Malinke

The present day Africans, the Malinke, are descendants of people of the 14th century Mali Empire. Today, the Malinke engage in the occupations of fishing, farming, and trading.

Moslem Heritage

African-Ainericans of Moslem belief today can relate to a heritage of African peoples who adopted Islam and some of them today still pray toward the East. They are the Fulani and Hausa.

African Imports

The following foods were transported into American culture from Africa; black eye peas, watermelon, gumbo stew, okra and coffee." It is believed that coffee is derived from Kaffa and is of Ethiopian origin. The use of kola is an African original. The extract of the kola nut has been used in a popular can soft drink or soda.

Origin Of Columbia Slaves

African slaves who were transported to Columbia came from coastal, West Africa, the areas of Senegal and Gambia. Some of the groups were the Diola, Banan, Balanta, Bran, Biafara, Nalu, and Yalongo.

Djibouti, Home of the Afars and Issas

The former French territory of the Afars and the Issas received its independence on June 27, 1977. The first President of the Republic of Djibouti, President Hassan Aptidon Gouled said, "The star we shall follow in our hope and struggle."

Djibouti is located geographically in the Horn of Africa and its neighbors are Somalia, Ethiopia and Eritrea province or area of Ethiopia. Djibouti was formerly French Somaliland in 1967. The country "overlooks the strait of Babel Mandeb or Gate of Sorrow," where shipping occurs between the Red Sea and the Indian Ocean. The Afars of Djibouti have a historical relation to the "Sultnates of Afars in Ethiopia and Eritrea over the centuries. The Afars are a Somali society group.

The people of Djibouti are mainly sheperds and some are nomads. The government of Djibouti appears very stable. Ironically, eighteen years after independence, President Hassan Aptidon Gouled was pictured at a conference in the Pentagon's Department of Defense. Gouled was conferring with Secretary of Defense Cheney and the Chairman, Joint Chief of Staff, U.S. Military, General Colin L. Powell.

The Beja Of Sudan

The Beja people of southern Sudan are Africans, who inhabited the "eastern desert of Egypt, the Red Sea area province of the former English or Anglo Sudan extending toward Eritrea and Ethiopia. W.E.B. DuBois described the Beja as representative of the "Predynastic Eqyptians", of color.

The Beni Ames, a Beja social group have lived in the Eritrea areas of Ethiopia. They speak "Tigre" rather than their language "Bedawiye or Beja" which is spoken in Sudan. They have been referred to as the "Nomads of Northern Eritrea."

The Kingdom of **Dahomey** had a type of money system prior to the European's invasion of the country. The people of Dahomey used cowrie shells, copper or brass iron.

Tutsi

The tall Tutsi people of East Africa had a system of maintaining pure lines in their lineage. Marriage between the classes were forbidden. Their classes or caste consisted of the Tutsi, Twa, and the Hutu (Iru).

Geography - The Nile River

The Nile River is fed from many rivers, lakes, and has two main branches. The branches are the White Nile, 2,285 miles, and the Blue Nile, 1,080 miles. These branches merge at Khartoun, Sudan. The Nile Delta is a 8,500 square mile triangle between.

Cairo and the Mediterranean Coast. The Nile delta and the narrow Nile valley consist of 3% of Egypt's land. The area from Juba to Khartoun, the White Nile travels 1,100 miles, but falls only 240 feet. A drop about a foot every five miles. The Blue Nile rises in the mountains of Ethiopia.

The Aswan Dam was built in 1971, 600 miles from Cairo to Sudan's frontier. The Nubians in Egypt were relocated in 1960 due to the construction of the Aswan Dam and the creation of Lake Nasser. Some 60, 000 Egyptian Nubians were resettled to land north of Aswan. The Nubians' homes were previously located in a pleasant place with cool houses made from the Nile's mud and the frands (large leaf with divisions) of Palm.

An area of the Nile today between Wadi Halfa and Khartoun is the location of the former ancient kingdom of Kush, near Karima. The kingdom was ruled by the Nubian Pharoahs of color of the 25th Dynasty).

Black Presence 67

The Atabara River joins the Nile after an 800 mile westward journey from the Ethiopian highalnds. The river flows only in season and is the only tributary between Khartoun and the Mediterranean. The source of the Nile is in Southern Burundi. The Nile runs 4,160 miles to the sea.

Geography - Malawi

The country of Malawi located in southern central Africa borded by Tanzania, Mozambique, and Zambia was a former British Proctectorate. The country received its independence on July 6, 1964. The population of Malawi is Chewa, Nyanja, Tumbuko, Yao, Lomwe, Tonga, Ngoni, Asian, and European ethnic groups. The British called the country Nyasaland. The country's present name, Malawi, is derived from the Maravi, a Bantu people that lived in the country around the 13th century. The Chewas are descendants of these people. The Lake Malawi is known for its fish called Cichlids. The lake has some 500 to 1,000 Cichlid species.

The Cichlids are called Mbuna. They live near algae covered rocks and feed an planktons (animal and plant life in the water). Lake Malawi species are very distinctive and are not found in any other area. The food source for Mbuna are fish, larvae, snails, algae, fish, and aquatic plants. The people of Malawi receive over half of their protein from fish. In 1980, the Republic of Malawi established the world's first fresh water, underwater, national park in the lake's southern region with the intention to protect their precious Cichlids.

Geography - U.S. Virgin Islands

The United States' Virgin Islands is comprised of St. Croix, St. Thomas, and St. John. population consist of 74% - West Indies; 8% - Puerto Ricans, and 80% -black, and 5% - white. The Virgin Islands were visited by Christopher Columbus in 1493. The Islands have been ruled by Spain, England, France, Holland, and the Knights of Malta. Denmark occupied the Islands and sold them to the United States for 25 million dollars in

1917. In 1733, slaves working on Danish sugar plantations decided to revolt and their early actions eventually led toward abolition of the slave trade in the Islands in 1848. Columbus named the Islands for the legendary St. Ursula and her 11,000 virgin martyrs. The late Judge William Hastie was the first Afro-American to serve as Governor of the Virgin Islands.

Geography - The Niger River

Africa's third largest river is the Niger and travels some 2,600 miles through West Africa. The river drains a basin of 430,000 square miles. The Niger begins in the tropical highlands of Guinea, approximately 175 miles from the Atlantic Ocean. The path of the Niger River is through the country of Mali's grassland, into the Sahel, an area between the desert and the savanna and travels on southeast into the Republic of Niger, and on to form a boundary between Niger and Dahomey. When the river travels into Nigeria, it moves through jungle and swamps into the Atlantic Ocean. Historically, one can recall that in the eighteenth century explorer Mungo Park was attempting to find the outlet of the Niger River. He was ambushed by some country men near Bussa and drowned while trying to escape. Sometimes the Niger River is called the River of Snow and River of Hope due to its unfortunate seasons of drought in the area. The river's inland delta is a gentle slope, three inches in a mile and stores the Niger's flood and releases it slowly for the 1,500 mile trip to the ocean.

Geography - The Congo River

The Congo River is the third longest river in Africa after the Nile and Niger. It is the sixth largest river in the world. The Congo River winds along and through five of the country's six provinces for 2,900 miles crossing the equator twice before it empties into the Atlantic.

Tanganyika or Tanzania, a country with 381,800 square miles received its independence on December 9, 1961. Julius Nyerere was its first Prime minister. The capital of Tanzania is Dar es Salaam. The country's

Black Presence   **69**

major products are cotton, coffee, diamonds, animal hides and skins. Mount Kilimanjaro is located in Tanzania and it is Africa's largest mountain (over 19,000 feet). The deepest lake in Africa is Lake Tanzania. Some of the peoples of Tanzania are the HA, Nyamuezi, Makonde, Gogo, and Haya.

True Facts About Sierra Leone, Angola, Great Rift Valley Uganda And Zanzibar

Sierra Leone claimed its independence on April 27, 1961. The country was given its name by a Portuguese explorer in 1462. The explorer was Pedro de Sintra. He called the country Sierra Lyoa (lion like) later referred to as Sierra (Spanish) and Leone (Italian). In later years, the capital city, Freetown, received free African-Americans who desired to settle in Africa. Some of the peoples of Sierra Leone include the Timni, Sielima, Mendi, Susic and Fula. The major food crops are cassava and rice. in the 1920's, platinum hematite and gold were found in Sierra Leone. Ginger, oil plant, cocoa and Kola are exported.

The European powers were mainly interested in the wealth of Africa during their "Rape of Africa" in the mid-1800's. They were concerned with the Congo's copper and uranium deposits, South Africans gold mines, Tanzania, an Angola iron ore and Mauritanials and Guinea's bauxite. Phosphates in Senegal cocoa, palm and peanuts oils in Ghana, and the Ivory Coast.

A "geological fracture", the Great Rift Valley, travels through Kenya. Many years ago this large crack was formed in the earth's surface cutting a 4,000-mile path across Africa from Israel to Mozambique. Kenya has an area of 224,960 square miles. The major products are tea, coffee, sisal, gold, sodium, carbonate, silver, salt, wattle bark extract, and timber. The capital of Kenya is Nairobi.

The country of Uganda has an area of 93,9081 square miles and its capital is Kampola (Entebbe). The major products are coffee, cotton, fish, copper, and livestock. Lake Victoria, Lake Albert, Lake Edward, Lake George and Lake Kyoga are in Uganda. Uganda is bordered by the

Republic of the Congo (Zaire) , Sudan, Kenya, Tanzania and Rwanda. The larger groups of people are the Basoga and Iesa and Baganda.

In 1961, the country of Zanzibar (part of Tanzania today, with an area of 1,020 square miles consisted of "240,000 Africans, 40,000 Arabs, 507 Europeans, some Asians, and 335 Somalian and others." The major products are cloves, clove oil, copra, coconut, coconut oil, and marine shells. Slave trading in the early 1700's was very important in the country. In the early 1700's, the country was a very important slave marker. Slavery ceased in 1873 when Great Britain entered in an agreement with the sultan of Zanzibar. A large number of the population are "Africans of mixed descent."

Former French African Protectorates

In 1953 Some former French African Territories voted to become self governing autonomous republics. They obtained their full independence in 1960. These republics are Republic of Chad, Republic of Congo, Republic of Dahomey, Gabon Republic; Republic of the Ivory Coast; Islamic Republic of Mauretania; Republic of Mali, Malgasy Republic; Central African Republic; Republic of Niger, Republic of Senegal, and Voltaic Republic.

West African Ethnic Groups

Some anthropologists, ethnologists, historians, and linguists have grouped the peoples of West Africa in various ethnic groups. However, the African people themselves still refer to their original names. The following are some major ethnic groups of West Africa, the Bambara, Soninke, Songhai, Malinke, Hausa, Bambara, Mossi, Kanuri, Mandingoes, Tukulor, Yoruba, Ibo, Fon, Ewe, Fouta Jallon, Serer, Wolof, Bassa, Tiv, Shuwa, Bagirmi, Nupe, Busa, Gurma, Any; Ashanti Koranko, Gurang Minianka, Kafango, Ibibio, Senuf, and the Dogan.

Black Presence

African Decorative Dress and Jewelry

The rich heritage of craftsmanship and artistic abilities of many African peoples are expressed in their personal customs, traditions, dress, and cultural jewelry.

Kenya - The Masai warrior wears a lions's mane for a ceremonial headdress.

The Turkana people use a wooden head dress to wear while sleeping. They believe it protects their status.

The Rendille people have a bridal gift made of large collars of woven palm fibers bound with cloth indicating the couple's status.

Rendille women who give birth to a first born son wear a hairstyle consisting of mud, animal fat, and ocher (red or yellow iron ore). This arrangement of pigment is called a cockscomb. The Rendille woman wears it until her son receives the circumcision rite or a male relative dies. Her hair has been shaved to wear the cockscomb.

Cameroons - The Western Cameroon Bamileke display decorative architecture using large wooden columns representative of past cultural history. They use bamboo strips that have geometric designs. Cameroon women in some areas use to wear a decorative apron of forged iron pendants.

The Tikar people of the Cameroons sometimes wear a brass chameleon (lizards) pendant.

Ivory Coast - The Baoule group wear gold mask pendants.

South Africa's Zulu - Some Zulu people wear glass beaded necklaces.

Nigeria - The Ibo's wear brass anklet at times as a decorative piece.

Southern Morocco - The Haratin (people of Berber and Negroid descent) women sometimes wear a large amount of jewelry to display her husband's wealth.

<u>Sudan</u> - The Rashaida women wear a veil or burga that is covered with buttons and pendants.

A Toposa woman wears a brass wire that pierces her lower lip and hair style of small pigtails shining with fat. Her cheeks have been scarred and she also wears a coiled iron collar. These all portray that she is married.

ETHIOPIA

We must resurrect in 1997, some facts about ancient Abyssinia and Ethiopia centuries ago. in 500 B.C., Ethiopia was in power in southern Egypt and repulsed the Persian Emperor Cambyses and his military forces. In the 11th century there was a queen called Maqueda who ruled one of the states, Sheba and visited Solomon, King of the Jews. The rulers later assumed the title of Negus Negusti, King of Kings, King of the various smaller kingdoms or provinces. In the 18th century there were some powerful rulers, Yesu, Asfa Nassen and Emperor Theodore III who proclaimed himself not only King of Kings but Emperor of Abyssinia in 1855 and ruled until 1868. He was under the influence of the British and when some disputes occurred, Emperor Theodore imprisoned some Englishmen and in 1867, an English military continent under Sir Robert Napier went to Ethiopia and with internal enemies of Theodore overthrew the emperor who eventually committed suicide. Emperor Theodore was succeeded by Emperor John (reigned from 1868 until 1899, while his young rival, Menelik, who ruled in a smaller state had ambitions to become emperor. Because of England's difficulties in Sudan with the Mahdi, they were not able to overthrow Emperor John at that time. Later the British would continue their interests in Ethiopia under the rule of Emperor Menelik.

During the past twenty-five years, I have had a personal interest in the early history of Ethiopia. Some of the true facts that I have researched

Black Presence 73

and discussed with my world history students over the years are as follows:

> During the classical period of Greece, all the land south of Egypt was called Ethiopia to include Nubia, land of the darker people. The Greeks would use the term to describe the peoples as Aethiops. A city to the south of Egypt was called Meroe, land of the Kush, located in the present day area of Sudan. The city was a major city of African culture and traded with Egypt, Central and West Africa.
>
> When people in 1997 continue the discussions on the racial identity of ancient Egyptians many honorable scholars avoid the true facts of history. There were invasions of Egypt by the Ethiopians of color and Pharaohs appeared who were of black African origin. There were distinctive Negro influences and intermarriages between Egyptians and Ethiopians. This is one historical reason why we can not ignore the truth that Nefertari, 1700 B.C., queen of Aahmes, the Pharaoh of Egypt who founded the 18th dynasty was of African or Negro descent. We must remember that at the death of her husband Aahmes, she shared the rule with her son Amenhotep I who conquered a part of Ethiopia. Amenhotep III was a builder of the Temple of Ammon at Luxor and the Colossi of Memnon. There were blacks in the armies of King Shishkak when he led them against Rehoboam in 971 B.C. They were also in the armies of Xerxes of Sesostris, King of Egypt and Ethiopia. The successors of the ruler Pianki (728-715 B.C.) an Ethiopian have been said to have Negro genes. Pianki ruled Egypt's twenty-fifth dynasty. He was succeeded by Shabaka and then Taharba who was in command of the Ethiopian army which assisted King Hezekiah of Israel against the Assyrians under the command of Sennacherib.
>
> I often pose a question to students how many contemporary ministers of the gospel actually refer to the Ethiopians and Egyptians from a black perspective in their sermons today? I seriously believe that these true facts should be made known to all ethnic groups, especially people of non color. The facts should be in their respective academic curriculums. These facts have been known for years.

The Israelites and Phoenicians traded and were involved in mining and forest operations with Africa. King Solomon and King Hiram of Tyre sent their ships to obtain the produce of the African mines and forests. In recent years, many African Americans have become aware of the black presence in biblical times and have published books and black oriented bibles. However, I believe the facts are necessary to understand the recent awareness of the revelations known to some people. The Queen of Sheba made the journey to visit King Solomon to learn of his wisdom. She brought camels, gold, species, and precious stones. Solomon exchanged presents with her. It has been stated that Abraham, Jacob and Joseph made Egypt their place of asylum. The African converted by Philip in the New Testament story was the Ethiopian of authority under Candace, an Ethiopian Queen who was from Meroe, the capital of the Sudanese Empire. Joseph, the eldest son of Jacob was sold into slavery in Egypt. He saved Egypt from famine and brought his father and brother there. Joseph and army fled to Egypt with the Christ child, Jesus. There were unavoidable contacts and intermingling between the Jewish enslaved people and the black peoples of Egypt and Africa. There may have been Jewish contacts with black Africans. When Assyria attacked Palestine, it was Ethiopia's assistance which prevented its conquest. That was when King Tarharka's Ethiopian army prevented Sennarcherib's army from capturing Jerusalem and carrying the Jewish people into captivity. A late African American scholar once wrote "the Negro soldier of the Sudan saved the Jewish religion." I have stated these incidents in Ethiopian history because we can not avoid the truth that Egypt is in Africa and extends southward into Ethiopia and Sudan. I want young people of all races to understand when they hear that Moses married a black, that it was a woman named Zeporah, daughter of Ravel, an Ethiopian priest.

The following discussion on the Italian, British and French economic interest in Abyssinia or Ethiopia during the late 1800's could provide some serious nutritional reasoning or food for thought about the residual political and economic effects in present day Ethiopia, Eritrea and Somalia. I suggest some questions to my students of world history, first where are the British, French and Italians in 1997 with real serious involvement with financial and military assistance to avoid continued Civil

War among people they exploited some 100 years ago? I will discuss some true facts about foreign interests and eventual annexation of Ethiopian provinces that include tribal and social groups of people who were and their descendants are basically genetically Ethiopians. However in 1997, they are known socially and culturally in their independent states as Somalians and Eritreans.

Italy, England and France Architects

Many current history books especially college texts do not include a detail discussion on the European colonial interest in Abyssinia or Ethiopia in the 1880's. I have used the following discussion in recent years to explain to my college students that Ethiopia has been a country of numerous tribal or social groups who are genetically the same people. However, we refer today to Somalis as people from the country of Somalia and not a distinctive social group of Ethiopians, because from a biological view, miscegenation or race mixing has occurred greatly between Somalis, Arabs and Italians over the years.

In the 1880's, Ethiopia had five kingdoms ruled over by a feudal emperor with his capital at Addis Ababa. The five kingdoms were Tigre in the north adjoining Eritrea, later an Italian possession bounded by the north and eastern section, Godjam in the northwest adjoining Anglo-Egyptian Sudan in the west and Kenya province in the south, Harrar in the southeast adjoining Kenya province and later Italian Somaliland. Abyssinia occupied a central position with the capital and seat of government at Addis Ababa. The feudal kings were not responsible to the emperor. They had their own autocratic government, taxed the people, collected their own customs and levies and had standing armies which they used for conducting war against one another or would lead them into battle against a common enemy in unity with the Emperor in times of foreign invasion.

Italy was interested in establishing a colonial empire in Abyssinia, and started to establish garrisons at various points along the coast, north of Assab. She was interested in preventing France from extending her influence along the Red Sea. In 1885, Italy annexed Massawa and several years later the Eritrean littoral (a coastal region or shore zone between high and low watermarks) was occupied by the Italians. In January 1887, an Italian garrison at Dogali was occupied by the Tigreans. This action caused the Italians to consider some diplomatic options. They decided to take advantage of an internal political dispute in Ethiopia when Menelik, Ras of Shoa was trying to become Negus Negisti (King of Kings) of Ethiopia after the death of Emperor Johannes who was killed in a war against the Dervishes. Italy was interested in annexing the area of Somali or Eritrea. She provided Menelik with 5,000 rifles and supported his cause to become Emperor against the claims of Ras Mangosha, the illegitimate son of Johannes. Italy also gave Menelik a loan of 1 million dollars for the Asmara region. In 1889, Italy and Ethiopia signed the Treaty of Ucciali on May 2, 1889, granting Italy territorial concessions in Eritrea which later would become an Italian Colony, Italian Somaliland. A dispute occurred between King Menelik and Italy over the interpretation of the Amharic version of article 17 of the Treaty. The Amharic's version stated that "*his majesty the King of Kings of Ethiopia may, if he desires to avail himself of the government of his majesty the King of Italy for any negotiations he may enter into with the other powers or governments.*" The Italian versions' the words "may if he desires to" were changed to read that the Emperor consents to avail himself etc. The Italian government had informed the English, French, German and Russian governments that Emperor Menelik was under obligation to use their good offices in any diplomatic dealings with them. When Menelik learned of this, he requested a revocation of the Treaty of Ucciali. Italy resented Ethiopia's action and began to initiate negative actions against Ethiopia. In 1894, Emperor Menelik started a postal service and had a stamp struck with his image. Italy was not consulted and resented this independence of the Emperor. The Italian premier, Count Crispi decided that he would invade Ethiopia and seize as hostages three Ethiopian Princes who were studying in Switzerland. The Italian parliament voted 4 million dollars for the war and organized a military force of 25,000 men under the commands of General, Barateri and Baldisserra.

Ethiopia was fortunate to have received some military support from France who has refused to recognize Italy's claim for a protectorate (superior authority assumed by one power over a dependent power) over Abyssinia. The French dispatched a mission to Ethiopia to train Emperor

Menelik's soldiers and supplied them with weapons and ammunition. It was necessary for Ethiopia to grant a concession to France. A French company, the La Campagne Imperiale was given the rights and privileges to construct the Djibuti, Addis Abba railway which provided an opportunity for France's economic interests to increase in East Africa. When the Italians launched their attack against Ethiopia in 1896, they were probably surprised when thousands of unified Ethiopians were able to win a victorious battle at Adowa. Some six thousand Italians were killed by the Ethiopians and two thousand captured as prisoners to include two general officers. It is unfortunate that some historians who are aware of this victory by an African nation one hundred years ago still will not state the following in their college history lectures.

Emperor Menelik in 1896 became the first known black African ruler in recent history at that time to defeat a major European power. The Treaty of Addis Ababa was signed in October 1896 with Italy paying an indemnity of two million dollars and an official recognition of the independence of Ethiopia.

England and France still had an agenda for Ethiopia in the early 1900's. A tripartite agreement between france, England and Italy was signed to maintain the integrity of Ethiopia. The document defined the respective interest of each country. Great Britain and Egypt was concerned about the Nile Basin, in order to regulate the waters, rivers and its tributaries without prejudice to Italian interests in Ethiopia, namely Eritrea and Somiland. France had a personal interest in her French protectorate on the Somali coast and the hinterlands for the construction of the Djibuti and Addis Ababa railway. These concerns and territorial annexations were actually the division of Ethiopia.

Emperor Menelik had a desire to establish a central government and initiate a change from five kingdoms or feudalism to capitalism. Menelik died in 1913, and his grandson Yasu who later was deposed by his Christian subjects led by Ras Tafari son of Ras Makomen, Menelik's cousin and hereditary Governor of Harar.

The European powers were still negotiating over East Africa interests in 1915. When World War I commenced, Italy was neutral and decided to join the allied powers for a share in the colonial conquests. A London agreement between England and France promised that in event of either power increasing its colonial territory in Africa at the expense of Germany, those two powers agreed in principal that Italy may claim some equitable compensation as regards to the settlement in her favor of the question relating to the frontier of the Italian colonies of Eritrea, Somaliland, Libya and neighboring colonies of France and Great Britain.

In 1924, Britain exerted pressure on Ethiopia and settled a disagreement with Italy by granting her Dijibuti in East Africa, north eastern Africa, boundaries Red Sea to North Gulf of Aden to East Somalia to south east Ethiopia to the southwest and north west. The population in 1996 consists of 60 percent Somali, ethnic groups, Issai and Afar, all of Ethiopian or Abyssinian descent, and also Arab, French and Italian. England wanted to control Lake Tsana and in return she promised Italy's Mussolini to recognize an inclusive Italian economic influence in the west of Abyssia or Ethiopia. The British government also agreed to support Italy in all her demands in all parts of Africa which fell within her sphere of interest.

Ethiopia became a member of the League of Nations in September 1923. France was excluded from the agreement between Italy and Britain and decided to support Ethiopia's protest to the League of Nations. However, England and Italy fearing exposure about their colonial ambitions assured Ethiopia that they had no plans for territorial annexation in Ethiopia. Ethiopia accepted their assurances. Later Britain offered the outlet to the sea through the port Zeila in British Somaliland but the Ethiopians refused the offer. The British also were not happy about Ethiopia being a member of the League of Nations because she had refused to grant England concession to the waters of Lake Tsana.

Ras Tafari was governor of Harar in 1928 and when Empress Zauditu, daughter of Menelik died, Ras Tafari or Haile Selassie was crowned Negus Negisti in 1930. Selassie continued the task of Menelik to establish a central government with uniform laws and a army would be controlled from a central body. Haile Selassie made a decision to appoint a governor in charge of Harar instead of his son and the governor would be

Black Presence

responsible to Addis Ababa. He gained control of the kingdom of Jimma through the marriage of the feudal king to his daughter and changed the king's status to Governor of Jimma and the control would come from Addis Ababa, Emperor Selssie had some difficulty with the kingdom of Godjam and decided to retain the powerful king who descended through an unbroken life of kings over a period of 1,000 years and was reluctant to change. When the king came to Addis Ababa, Selassie detained him for two years. The Italians were tried for treason and imprisoned for life. Eventually Godjam changed from a feudal state to one ruled by a governor directly responsible to Addis Ababa. The King of Tigre whose territory was bounded by the Italian colony required some tact, however Selassie had his crown prince to marry the king of Tigre's daughter and was able to have the king to accept the plan of centralization.

The Europeans were observing Ethiopians attempts to centralize the government especially Italy who possibly had not forgotten their defeat at Adowa and had serious plans to invade Ethiopia. In 1930, Italy had received a concession from the Emperor for a radio station with hook-up in different sections of Ethiopia. The station was constructed at Addis Abba in 1932. Italy also established considerable offices at Godjam in the territory of Ras Hailu and started dissensions between the Emperor and Hailu. The Italians were able to establish mission stations on various parts of the country attacking the Moslem population. They also made a survey of the country without the Emperor's permission using aeroplanes to map the country.

It was stated that Italy had a fleet of 500 aeroplanes and an army combat ready at Eritrea. France did not approve of Mussolini's proposed plans to invade Ethiopia because she was concerned about her railroad. England had made a decision to abandon Ethiopia in 1931 and decided to sell her interests in a bank which was a subsidiary of the Bank of Egypt. She did not prepare the Ethiopians to manage the bank and did not complete all arrangements until 1934.

Italy invaded Ethiopia on October 3, 1935 and Haile Selassie went into exile in England, May 1936. His appeals to the League of Nations were denied. Italy was able to annex Ethiopia to Eritrea and Italian East Africa included the territories of Eritrea, Somaliland and Ethiopia. Emperor Haile

Selassie returned to Ethiopia in 1941 and after World War II, the United Nations developed a plan to have Eritrea annexed to Ethiopia. In 1962, Eritrea was made a province of the Ethiopian Empire again.

I can clearly remember when I was a young child and the "old folk" would talk about a famous African leader who they referred to as the Lion of Judah, Emperor Haile Selasse of Ethiopia. In 1953 while studying at Lincoln University, Jefferson City, Missouri, my math instructor was a Mr. Haile, a native of Ethiopia. When I was visiting the U.S. Army Seoul Korea officers club in 1955, I had the opportunity to meet a major who was assigned to the United Nations contingent from Ethiopia. While assigned at Fort Leavenworth, Kansas as the assistant engineer, United States Army Disciplinary Barracks, I was able to observe on the fort two general officers from Ethiopia who were studying at the U.S. Army General Staff College. I was visiting Rome, Italy in 1967 and as I stopped at a gasoline station, I saw three or four young men standing around a volkswagen car and I told my family there are some colored people or Negro Americans. When I approached the car, one of the young men said hello, are you from Ethiopia? I was conducting some research at the Library of Congress in 1976 and met a very interesting man from Ethiopia who was assigned to the African Research Service. In 1978 while teaching at Northern Virginia Community College, Annandale, Virginia, I became acquainted with a very competent artist who I believed was a relative of Haile Selassee and he possibly completed a painting of the Emperor. I had the opportunity to teach his wife in one of my history classes and she prepared an interesting report on the 1936 Italian invasion of Ethiopia. I also was present at the young couple's wedding reception and observed the guests performing a social group dance of the Galla. I completed a book on the black presence in the American Revolution and needed an artist to draw some pictures of black soldiers in their respective revolutionary uniforms. My Ethiopian friend did an outstanding job. Fortunately that book was published by the Daughters of American Revolution and is in the library of all their chapters. In 1979, I was privileged to be one of the guests at the Independence Celebration of Somali hosted by their Embassy in Washington, D.C. It was a most interesting and informative experience.

In 1991, I was reading the newspaper and listening to the radio, and viewing television about the Somali crisis. On February 17, 1994, I read a newspaper article written by an associated press reporter who was quite aware of some interracial problems of Somalia clan crisis. He wrote from Sagioad, Somalia that people with hard hair suffer the most and that people of Arab descent with soft hair prosper more because of their ethnic roots. The author said the late General Mohammed Rarrah Aided's clan were soft hair. One scholar had stated that those Somalis of distinctive African origin are called Timojeres, hard hairs or Addon slaves. General Siad Barre's regime of 300,000 were Somali Bantu. Some of the Bantu migrated into the area 1,000 years ago and others were brought in by Arab slave traders.

I have mentioned these experiences about Ethiopians as I have passed the way. Unfortunately, I was miseducated earlier about the rich history of these great Africans, but fortunately in 1997, I think I can understand more clearly and logically why Eritrea is independent today and Somali is still confronting many problems of unity and statehood. I also realize that I do not hear about the colonial ghosts or spirits today especially the honorable countries of Italy, Britain and France.

I have included in my discussion on Ethiopia, a profile I prepared in 1991 that will clearly explain some real facts about who the Ethiopian people have been and are today.

ETHIOPIA - A PROFILE

The oldest kingdom, Ethiopia, located in northeast Africa is a county whose inhabitants are representative of different ethnic social groups and physical description (features). The United States has classified its inhabitants as caucasian, black, hispanic, and oriental or Asian. There is no division of ethnicity with the American black. However, in Ethiopia the people have been classified by ethnologists, anthropologists, and linguists, into ethnic and racial groups based mostly on linguistic physical and descriptive features. Sometimes, these professionals will use the terminology "mixed" rather than to state precisely that some of the

Ethiopians over centuries have miscegenated genetically with other races, mainly Arabian and/or Caucasian.

The Ethiopians have been classified as representative of Cushitic - a Mediterranean people, semitized Cushitic and Nilotic Negroid peoples. Their culture is Cushitic and Semitic. It is believed that a group of Semitic people from Southern Arabia invaded ancient Ethiopia around 1000 B.C. to 400 B.C. and over many years developed a heterogeneous miscegenated population of blacks, Cushitics and Semites. These people mated and married and were the founders of the Axumite kingdom. They probably were the ancestors of today's Tigrai people of Eritrea.

Geographically, Ethiopia occupies approximately 457,000 square miles. The countries that border Ethiopia are Somalia and Kenya, northern border; Sudan, western boundary; Red Sea, Djibouti, and Somalia, eastern boundary. There is a northern region of the Rift Plateau where the Kingdom of Axum was located. This is the site of the present capital, Addis Ababa. There is a large seaport along the Ethiopian Coast of the Red Sea called Massawa.

The country of Ethiopia has been divided into twelve provinces and Eritrea, five districts. The provinces were subdivided into subprovinces then districts.

The Ethiopian people have an interesting history of their ancestral ethnic groups. The major ethnic groups are the Amharas, Tigrais, La Gurages, Agau, Falashas, Somalia, Afar (Danakil) Saho, Sidamo, and the Shankellas.

The Amharas and Tigrais people accepted Christianity in 400 A.D. They speak the language Ge'ez. Both are proud of their ancestral background to the Kingdom of Axum and preservers of the Coptic religion. The Tigrais geographical location in the Highlands and Separation from the other ethnic groups could be a significant factor in their desire and determination over the years for political independence and the formation of their own government distinctive from the Amharas. Unfortunately, during the Ethiopian government and Eritrean's recent civil wars, the mass media did not communicate this information to the public. I believe it would have given a better understanding of the country's internal problems that have developed over many years. The Amharas have tried for years to have a centralized government involving all ethnic groups. The Tigrais and Amhara descriptive features are light brown to dark brown complexion, thin lips, "long high bridged noses," medium sized ears, average medium height and curly to wavy hair depending on miscegenation with other ethnic groups (Arabic or Italians). It is believed that because of these physical descriptions and their geographical ancestral home that the Tigrais and Amharas have a genetic heritage from people who are called Caucasians. Today, many Caucasians do not see these Ethiopian ethnic groups as so called true blacks or Negroes, especially many Caucasians in the United States. I can remember as a child that within the African American community, there was a debate as to whether the late Emperor Haile Selassie and his people were Caucasians or black Africans. However, many Afro Americans historically have regarded Ethiopia as an African country that was a role model of black achievements and progress over the centuries. There were early organizations and social groups that would use the name Ethiopian to demonstrate their pride in this African country.

Even though the late Emperor Haile Selassie ruled for many years as an absolute monarch, many African Americans regarded him an their living Emperor of an African kingdom that existed prior to the birth of Christ. The true facts of Ethiopian's history have been some of those missing pages of American History that, "They did not Tell Me."

The Gallas migrated into Ethiopia around the sixteenth century. They are probably of Arabic origin. The Gallas are also known an Oromo. They represent the largest ethnic group in Ethiopia. The Galla people settled in various provinces and areas in Ethiopia. There are the Gallas of Kaffa, Walaga, Central Wallo, Ilubabor, Shoe, Arusi, Gano-Gofa, Sidamo, and Harar provinces. Many Gallas are Moslems and they speak a Cushitic language. Some of the Gallas have miscegenated with other ethnic groups, namely the Amharas, and Afar-Saho (Yaju Gallas).

The Gurages live in the southwestern part of Shoe province. Their religion consists of Islam and Christianity. The Gurages have miscegenated with the Sidamo peoples.

The Gurages physical description consist of some Negroid features and they have some descriptive features similar to the Amhara Tigrai peoples. Some Gurage people were slaves of the Shoe kingdom. They speak several dialects of a Semitic language. Their occupations have been "skilled carpenters, potters, and farmers."

The major social group of the Agau are the Aweya (Kumfel), Bogon, Kelmant, Kayla, Dinder, and the Quarra. They have occupied the areas of Southern Gojam, Lake Tana, Begamder province, Lasta district and the northern part of Eritrea. It is believed that the Agaus miscegenated with the Semitic people and adopted some of their religion, tradition, culture and language. Their physical description is light brown with similar features of the Somalia and Gallas. The religion of the Agaus is Moslem and Christian. The Agau people are the builders of the famous Lalibela churches that were built of rocks.

Recently, the state of Israel extended invitation for the Ethiopian Jews to come to Israel and live. Many of the Falashas people accepted the invitation. The Falashas have been called the "Black Jews of Ethiopia. They have lived in the areas of Semyen, the northern part of Begamder. There are several theories as to the origin of the Falashas. They could have descended from the lineage of Menelik I of Ethiopia, when 10,000 Jews accompanied him back to Ethiopia after a visit to his father, King Solomon. It is also believed that the Agau were converted to Judaism by Jewish missionaries from Yemen in the third or fourth century A.D. They speak an Agau dialect, Amharic and Tigrinya and their writings are in Ge'ez. Their physical features are similar to the Amharas and Bogos of Eritrea.

The Somalis have been a nomadic people moving across the land with their animals, sheep, camels, and goats. Many of the Somalis are Moslems. It is possible that they became Moslems centuries ago during their contacts with the Arabs. They have occupied home sites in the

Black Presence

areas of former French and British Somaliland, northwestern part of Kenya, and provinces in Ethiopia. Somalis have settled in the Ethiopian provinces of Hararge (Ogaden Awraja) and WalWal. The Somalis are represented in cellular groups, nations and divisions. There are two major groups, the northern and southern. The northern units or groups are the Darod, Isaq, and Dir, and they are believed to be descendants of an Arab group who possibly mixed with African peoples years ago. The southern group consist of those Somalis who appear to have a greater African genetic structure. The Sabs are a subgroup of the southern group. The Somalis speak Somali dialects. There have been some Somali groups located on the eastern areas of the Hararge plateau. They are the Gherri-Jarso, and the Gherri-Babile, a miscegenated people of Galla and Somali.

The Somalis physical descriptions are "thin tall people, narrow faces," light brown to dark brown complexion. Some Somalis are similar in features to the Afar (Danakil) and the Masai of Kenya. In 1967, I was visiting Rome, Italy, with my late son, Robert II, and my sister Phyllis Greene McAfee and her two daughters, Michelle and Monica. We were standing on an monument's plaza one evening when suddenly a young man came running toward us and was shouting in a foreign language with a smile on this face. At that moment I was introduced to my Somalian friend when he told me in English that he was from Somalia and was sorry because he thought I was from his country and that was why he was shouting for my attention. This experience has taught me as I reflect back some twenty-five years that African Americans regardless of their descriptive physical features, complexion, or hair all are similar in some physical features to their African brothers and sisters who have also been tainted by other racial groups over the centuries. Geographically, Somalia is located in the horn of Africa. It is situated along the Gulf of Eden and the Indian ocean. It is bounded by Djibouti in the northwest, Ethiopia in the west, and Kenya in the southwest. Two major rivers in Somalia are the Shebelle and Juba. The capital city is Mogadishu. The country's national name is Al Jumhouriya As Somalya al Dimocradia. Some major crops of Somalia are: incense, sugar, bananas, cotton, sorghum, corn, gum, and minerals, iron, tin, gypsum, bauxite and uranium. The overall area of Somalia is 246,300 square miles. The father of Somali nationalism is Abdullah Abdullah. He confronted the British in the early

1900's even though he was defeated, his courageous leadership has made him a national hero.

The city or province of Ogaden in the eastern region of Ethiopia was inhabited by many Somalis. The former Ethiopian regime in 1977 using the assistance of some 11,000 Cuban troops defeated a 32,000 man Somalian army causing some 1.5 million Somalis to flee to Somalia. Later a peace agreement was reached. Recently, there has been civil unrest in Somalia, it is hoped that a peace settlement can be reached by the parties concerned and this historic cultural nation of several ethnic social groups can live in peace, and tranquility in future years.

The Afar are a group that have settled in the areas of the Danakil Depression, located near the Addis Ababa Djibouti railway, the Peninsula on the north, the Red Sea on the east, and the highlands of the Ethiopian plateau to the west. The Amharas and Arabs call the Afar, Danakil, and the Somalis and Harari call the Afar, "Adalis." The Afar speak a Cushitic language.

The Saho are a semi-nomadic group who are mostly Moslems. They have been located in Eritrea. Their largest sub-group is the Asaorta. Some of the Saho are of Afar origin and Tigre speaking people.

There is a Cushitic group who have lived in the Ethiopian highlands. They speak Tigre, a Sametic language similar to Geez. A social group of the Saho are the Beni Amer, a Beja group.

The Sidamos have been classified as part of the Mediterranean race and have some Negroid traits. Their complexion is "dark brown to black." They have seven major groups: the Kaffa-Gibe, Gimara, Janerio, Maji, Bako and ometo. Their average height is 5'5". The Sidamos religion consist of Christianity and Moslem. The western Sidamo had several kingdoms around the fourteenth century.

A group of people who live along the Sudanese-Ethiopian border are called the Shankellas. They were former slaves of some Amharas and Tigrais. The northern Shankellas are the Kunama and the Barya. The

Black Presence   87

word Barya means slave in Arabic. The Amharas and Shankella slaves have miscegenated for many centuries.

Some other groups that live in Ethiopia are the Beni-Sciangul, Baro Salient and the Annuaks.

Ethiopia has some interesting cultural values and traditions. Major Ethiopian folk tales are: The *Tale of the Golden Earth, The Donkey who Sinned, and The Goats Who Killed the leopard.* Major musical instruments are the string-wind instruments, drums, "Nagarat Kabaro," begenna (lyre or harp), single string violin fiddle, masanko, fife, washint shambako and the trumpet, malakat. Some popular dances are the fukara, a boasting dance, hota dance, jump dance, and the esketa and Zafan, a chant.

A dwelling or house in the countryside is called a Tukul. The Ethiopian dress of the Amhara and Tigrai consist of a draped shawl, shamma, in cold weather, a double shawl wrapped around the shoulders is called a Kutta. A cloak worn by women is a barnos. Men wear Jodpurs. The women wear a full length wide sleeved cotton gown called a kamis. Some man carry a walking stick. Some Danakils had a custom of using tattos, the man would have a tatto on their forehead and the women on their abdomen.

An Ethiopian menu could consist of "Teff", grain for bread, barley, sorghum, maize, wheat, cereal grain, beans, lentils, peas, onions, garlic, potatoes, cabbage, pumpkin, red peppers crushed, sweet bread, beef, mutton, chicken, goat milk, taj beverage, honey, vegetable oil, a staple item, injera, sour bread, raw minced beef, berrando, talla, a barley fermented beer, and the Gallas false banana, musa enseti edula.

Ethiopia has had a ruling class of royalty throughout the centuries. Some of the leaders and rulers of the Axum, Abyssinia and Ethiopian kingdoms have been:

King Ezana, Axumite period, fourth century, accepted the religion of Christianity 330-340 *A.D. King Armah* accepted Islam. *Zagwe King Lalibela* was responsible for the monolithic churches at LaLibela. *Emperor Yekuno Amlak* assisted in the destruction of some Moslem states. *Amlak's grandson, Amba Sion*, fourteenth century, was a military leader, reformer and administrator. He helped to spread Christianity and was recognized as a saint in the Ethiopian Orthodox church. *King Zara Yakob* ruled during the period 1434-1468. He was an outstanding administrator and leader in church reform. *King Baselides (Fasladas)* was on the throne in the 1650's. He controlled the Moslem's progress and established a capital at Gondar in Begender. He was succeeded by his son *John I (Yohannes)*. He was confronted with several problems relating to religious doctrine. The ruler of Ethiopia in the late 1600's was *Joshua I (Iyasu)*. In the eighteenth century *King Justus (Yost'os)*, ras of Tegre ascended the throne. This was the beginning of the interruption of the Solomonic line. Later, *David III (Dawir) son of Joshua the Great* came to the throne and he was succeeded by another son of *Joshua the Great*, Asme (Atsme), Giorgis. He was also called Bakaffa (the Inexorable). At his death, *Empress Mentaub* who was of Ethiopian and Portuguese descent came to the throne. She was responsible for increased recognition of the Gallas in the government. She was succeeded by her son *Joshua II*. Joshua II died and the Galla mother of his son, *Joas (Iyo'as)* was responsible for the removal of the Queen Mother. This Galla lady was called *Wobet*. She was instrumental in ending the Solomonic line at that time.

Wobet's son Joas was murdered by the orders of Michael Suhul. Then the throne was occupied by *Joshua the Great's seventy year old son, John II*. Later his son *Sahle Haimanot* ruled until the 1850's. There were several rivals for the imperial throne. They were *Sahll Selassie of Shoa, Ras Ali of Gondar (Begemder), Ras Wuba of Tegre and Ras Hailu* of Gojam. Their continued dissensions erupted into a civil war. The rulers of Gondar and Gojam were killed. Another contender appeared on the scene, he was *Kassa*, a Christian and son of a chief in Kiwara, west of Gondar. Kassa and Ras Ali were able to compromise on their disagreements and intentions to acquire the royal seat. Ras Ali awarded Kassa some responsible territories to supervise and his daughter for a wife. Kassa was an ambitious man whose goal was to become Emperor. Around 1854 he had his father-in-law Ras Ali murdered. Then Kassa became the popular ruler over the provinces of Gondar and Gojam. Kassa was successful in defeating Ras Wuba of Tegre. On February 7, 1855,

Black Presence 89

at the young age of thirty-six, Kassa became Emperor of Ethiopia. He decided to accept the name *Theodore* because a prophecy "that an Emperor Theodore would some day become the country's national hero."

During the period 1855 to 1860, Emperor Theodore was able to make some administrative changes in the operation of the government. He tried to implement reforms in religion, slavery, justice and to support monogamy. He also wanted to contain the Moslems and Gallas.

Emperor Theodore was faced with several problems, the loss of his first wife, Tawabatch, and encounters with the British to include their defeat of Ethiopian forces at a battle at Aroge on April 10, 1868. He committed suicide as the British troops approached the capital city Makedala. Theodore's death created another rivalry for contenders to the throne. They were *Gobayze* ruler of Lasta, and *Kassa*, Ras of Tegre. Kassa was the winner in the confrontation and was crowned *John IV* in 1872 and called King of Kings. His reign was affected by sharing some of his powers with an aggressive and competent leader, Menelik of Shoa. *Menelik* was able to take control of the Gallas and the southern part of Ethiopia. He was able to obtain weapons from a European country.

Emperor John IV designated Menelik as heir apparent to the throne. He also arranged for Menelik's daughter, Zauditu, to marry his son. The Emperor was confronted with a series of problems that eventually led to his death The Egyptians had occupied Harar for ten years. The Italians occupied Assab, Eritrea around 1875. They claimed that a ruler years ago had sold the area to an Italian company. Their was unrest in Gondar and Gojam. The troops of the Mahidi or Mohammed Ahmed ibn Sayyid Abdullah of Dongola approached Ethiopia from Sudan. Emperor John IV was killed in a battle at the border in an area called Matamma. After the Emperor's death, contenders began to argue for the right to the throne. At this time, the Italians took the moment to conquer and seize Massawa and established some control in Eritrea. Eventually, Menelik was able to ascend to the throne as *Emperor Menelik II*.

Emperor Menelik was an outstanding ruler and he was one African leader who stood up and rejected the rape of his country by an European power. He denounced a Treaty of Ucciali which the Italians attempted to use in order to establish Ethiopia as an Italian protectorate. Emperor Menelik and his courageous Ethiopian Army defeated a white European power at the Battle of Adowa in 1896. Adowa was the capital of Tigre. Unfortunately, this true fact of history is not printed in some secondary and college textbooks on European and World History.

In 1893, Menalik moved his capital to Entoto and named it "New Flower." Addis Ababa. This caused some dissention among the people of Tegre. The Italians were successful in taking control of Somaliland after defeating the forces of Mohammed Abdulla of Somalia. Emperor Menelik suffered a series of strokes in 1906, 1907, and 1908. He appointed his nephew, Lij Yassu, as his successor. Yassu was the son of Ras Mikael of Wallo. Ras Tasamma became regent in 1908.

The Shoan nobles decided in 1916 to overthrow Yassu. He was removed from the throne and replaced by Menelik's daughter, Zauditu. Zauditu became Empress and cousin Tafari Makonnen, as regent and heir presumptive. The Empress died in 1930 and Ras Tafari was crowned Haile Selassie I. The following major events occurred during the reign of Emperor Haile Selassie.

Haile Selassie made attempts to centralize government operations. He outlawed slavery, granted a constitution allowing the establishment of a Parliament, Senate, elected Chamber of Deputies, and a court system even though he maintained absolute power. When Italy invaded Ethiopia on October 3, 1935, Selassie went into exile in England, May, 1936. He appealed to the League of Nations to assist him and they refused to give him complete solutions to the problems.

Italy annexed Ethiopia to Eritrea. Then Eritrea, Somaliland, and Ethiopia became the Italian East Africa. In 1941 with the aid of the British and Ethiopian soldiers, Ethiopia was able to make the Italians leave the country. Emperor Haile Selassie returned to Ethiopia in 1941. After World War II, the United Nations developed a plan to have Eritrea annexed to Ethiopia. In 1962, Eritrea was made a province of the Empire again.

A few years after the annexation decisions, some revolutionary movements were formed to oppose the annexation. These movements desired autonomy for their respective territories or provinces. The movements were. The Ethiopian Peoples Revolutionary Democratic Front (EPRDF), it was at one time a Marxist group. The EPROF wanted autonomy for the northern region of the country, Tigre. The Eritrean Peoples Liberation Front (EPLIP) had resisted the annexation of Eritrea to Ethiopia. They desired autonomy for Eritrea. The Ormo (Galla) Liberation Front wanted autonomy for their province. The Ormo's had been the largest ethnic group in the southwest area of the country.

In August 1974, an armed forces committee deposed Haile Selassie, "Lion of Judah" after fifty-eight years as regent and emperor. The parliament was dissolved and the constitution suspended. On August 27, 1975, the world renowned, distinguished monarch, "His Imperial Majesty," Emperor Haile Selassie was reported dead in a small apartment in his former palace at the age of 83 years.

On February 2, 1977, Lieutenant Colonel Mengistu Haile Mariam was named the head of state Ethiopia. Later Mariam was confronted with the problems of Eritrea boldy desiring her independence and resistance from the Somalia guerillas in the southeast region of Ogaden. When the Somali guerillas and Somali's regular armed forces threatened the city of Harar, the Soviet Union and Cuba assisted Mariam in defeating the Somalias and forcing them to return to Somalia. After this incident, Mirian's regime formed a communist group to govern the country on September 10, 1984. From 1984 to February 1991, there was increased and serious, tragic internal unrest in Ethiopia. The country was in a civil war between opposing rebellious liberation fronts and the communist regime of Lieutenant Colonel Mengistu Haile Miriam.

In February 1991, the EPRDF was victorious in their frontal attacks toward the capital city. They seized the capital and Mariam fled into exile. The EPLF were successful in May 1991, in assuming control of the Eastern province. The prayer for peace was answered in July, 1991 when the EPRD and EDLF agreed to have a referendum on Eritrean independence. Eritrea is now an independent state.

Source: *They Did Not Tell Me True Facts About The African American's African Past And American Experience*.

EARLY EXPLORERS

Carter G. Woodson, the late distinguished African American historian, wrote in 1922 "*that Africans could have sighted the shores of America prior to Columbus.* He said, Professor Leo Wiener of Harvard University believed there was early African influence in the American language like canoe, buckra and tobacco and some African fetishes resemble a custom among the American Indian has been considered another reason for believing Africans explored the Americas prior to the 1400s.

It has been stated that two blacks had traveled across Africa between the years 1802-1811. They were Portuguese mulatto traders, Pedro Baptista and Amaro Jose. They traveled also in the areas of present day Mozambique.

In the early years in South America, Padre Antonio Vieira, a mulatto prose writer was a missionary to the Indians. He explored areas of the Amazon, Brazil.

Matthew Alexander Henson

Many school children and adults have heard the name Matthew Alexander Henson and some have visited Arlington National Cemetery where he is buried. His presence in world history should be known to all students of world history because of his outstanding contribution in the field of exploration.

Matthew A. Henson was born on August 8, 1866 in Nanjemoy, Charles County, Maryland. He became an orphan at a young age and later decided to run away and walked without shoes in the cold winter to Washington, D.C. He was able to obtain a job washing dishes at a Miss Janey's lunchroom. He had a great desire to go to sea and become a sailor. He went to Baltimore, Maryland and convinced a ship captain named Childs to hire him as a cabin boy. Henson was given a job and learned some sailors' skills. He learned how to tie sailor knots and also mastered the carpenter's tools. Later he became a seaman and sailed with Captain Childs who taught him how to write and read. Henson sailed on the Katie Hines as a seaman for 5 years and visited the ports of Hong Kong, Russia, West Indies, Africa, Russia, Spain and Japan. When the captain died in 1883, he left the ship and worked briefly as a bellhop, stevedore and watchman. While working as a store clerk in a furrier business, he met Lt. Peary who asked him to be his valet. In 1887, he accompanied Peary on a canal surveying expedition to Nicaragua. When he returned to America, he worked for Peary at the Navy Yard in Philadelphia, Pennsylvania. When Peary asked him to accompany him to Greenland, a navy lieutenant Scapli made a bet that Henson would return with the loss of some of his toes and fingers due to frost bite. During the trip to Greenland, Peary and Henson experienced severe weather where a large iceberg struck the ship's rudder jamming the wheel causing the tiller to strike Peary and break his leg. Henson made a box like cast to hold Peary's broken leg. When they reached Greenland, Henson built a house for their party and used sleds to carry 800 pounds. When he first met the Eskimos, they thought he was an Eskimo and greeted him by saying Innuit (means Eskimo), later they called him Miy Paluk. Henson was able to learn to speak Eskimo language fluently and also learned survival skills for the icy north region.

When Peary's leg was healed the party crossed the northern rim of Greenland and had proven that it was an Island. They returned to the United States. Peary gave lectures in order to raise money for future expeditions and Henson was his assistant. Later, Henson and Peary returned to the north and faced artic storms. One day Henson fell into an icy pit and used his hands to pull himself out.

Henson was able to drive a 28 dog team at one time. When the food supplies were low he would hunt the musk ox. He was able to learn taxidermy procedures and skin the animals. When he returned to America for three years he worked at the American Museum of Natural History, New York assisting the curator and guiding the artists who were painting an Arctic background scene.

Peary and Henson returned to Arctic region in 1896 to continue their exploration. Upon his return home, Henson worked briefly as a railroad pullman porter. He later married a Lucy Ross. When Peary and Henson returned to the north they were determined to continue their search for the North Pole, the northern most point on the earth. The North Pole at latitude 90 north lies in the middle of the Arctic circle.

When they returned to the Arctic and Polar regions, it was necessary for their party to travel 300 miles from their ship. Peary, Henson and Fair Eskimos raveled the last 133 miles. At one time, Peary was attacked by a charging musk ox and his life was saved by Henson. Henson was 35 miles from their destination when he fell into a hole when the thin ice gave in. He was pulled to safety by an Eskimo, Ootah.

Peary was overcome with exhaustion and his feet was frostbitten and he instructed Henson to go ahead the last few miles and said he would follow later. Henson proceeded toward the North Pole and had instructions to complete the final observations and calculations and await Peary's arrival. Forty-five minutes later Peary arrived at the site and Matthew A. Henson had already reached the actual site of the North Pole. Peary then confirmed the discovery on April 6, 1909. A Henson Bay in the N.W. Arctic was named in Henson's honor who became the first man to reach the North Pole. Matthew Henson and his wife were honored at the White House in 1954 by President Eisenhower. Henson died on March 9, 1955. Dillard University in Louisiana named a hall in Henson's honor. The Explorers Club, New York City has a bronze bust dedicated to Henson. A plaque in Henson's memory was unveiled at the State House, Annapolis, Maryland in the 1960's.

Discovery of the Antarctic

A 1996 Almanac states that a British Captain James Cook circumnavigated the area of the antarctica (located on the South Pole and situated almost centrally within the bordered antarctic circle at 66 1/2 S., by South Atlantic, Indian and South Pacific Ocean). Two hundred million years ago, the land was joined to South America, Africa, India, and

Black Presence

Australia in one large continent. Geological changes caused the breakup into separate continents. When Captain Cook made his exploration in 1772-1775, he did not sight land. However, an American, Captain John Davis made the first known landing on the continent on February 7, 1821. The United Kingdom in 1908, became the first nation to claim a part of the continent followed by Claims from new Zealand, 1923, France, 1924, Chile, 1940 and Argenita, 1943. The almanac states that the United States and Russia have never claimed any antarctica territory.

However, an earlier reference has stated that there was an international controversy about the principal claimants to the discovery of the Antarctica. The claimants were Russia, United States and Canada. An Admiral Fabin von Belling Hausen of Alexander I's Imperial Russian Navy said he discovered the Antarctica in 1821. A Captain Nathaniel B. Palmer of Stonington, Connecticut stated that while hunting seals within the Antarctic circle, he sighted the shore of the new continent in November 1820. Captain Palmer's ship was called the Hero. The Hero had a crew of five men and there was a black presence. One crew member was a black man named Peter Harvey who was born in Philadelphia, Pennsylvania in 1789.

Prelude to Partition of Africa

A review of college textbooks in 1996 reveals that there is little mention if any of those early European explorers who actually paved the way for their governments to make decisions to establish trading stations in various parts of Africa and to support efforts to explore the Hinterlands of Africa. Using simple logic, how can a stranger enter an unknown territory and even though they will have the necessary information to begin their explorations, they still must rely on the indigenous population for information, logistical support and in some cases to assure their safety through hostile areas of the country. I have researched the names of some black Africans who are known widely to the average researchers or historian for many reasons, however, I will review their names and accomplishments in supporting and providing assistance to some well known European explorers in the 1800's.

An African bishop, Adjai Crowther was a member of the first Royal Expedition up the Niger River. There were 150 members in the exploration party. There were forty-two whites who died and the remaining 108 were stricken with fever. Crowther's task was to prepare records of the expedition.

When Stanley explored the congo regions he had several African guides and major headmen. There were two brothers, Uledi and Shumari who joined him at Miandeseh.

Livingstone had an African with him named James L. Chuma. He assisted Livingstone in the regions of Lake Nyasa, Lake Tanganyika and Lukuga river.

Joseph Thomson had some blacks with him when he explored many areas of Africa. He gave credit to two blacks, Chuma and Makatubu.

There was an African trader of slaves in the 1880's who was known for his notorious slave trade dealings but sometimes historians and writers do not discuss his valuable assistance to the early explorers such as Henry Stanley, and Cameroon. His name is Tippu Tib or Hamed bin Mohammed. He was a mulatto African Arab. Tippu Tip was a member of Stanley's caravan in the Zanzibar Expedition Force. The Force consisted of nine European officers, 61 Sudanese, 13 Somalia, 620 Zanzibaris and Tippo had 400 men. Stanley paid him 150 dollars per month to serve as the governor of the Stanley Falls district in the Eastern Congo. The Arabs mostly of mixed genes maintained an army of 100,000 men at all times. During Tippo's absence he gave the European rank of District Commissioner to his nephew, Rachel at the Stanley Falls District. Tippo's son, Sefu, was present at a garrison with 10,000 men at Kasongo.

Tippo Tip actually blazed the way for Stanley, Cameroon, White and Livingstone to accomplish their missions in Central Africa. He was regarded by some Europeans as a great Arab captain of the Congo region. The Belgians and British referred to him as Tippo Tip. When the name Zanzibar is mentioned, the name of Tippo Tip has its black presence in world history especially in the Belgium Congo region.

Black Presence

Black Presence with Spanish Explorers

Several African slaves were present with early explorers in North America. One of them, Nuflode de olano, was with Balboa. Balboa also had 30 blacks with him when he explored the Pacific. Hernan Cortes had Negro slaves with him when he explored Cuba. In 1520, Velasquez had two Negroes in the company that was dispatched to discipline Cortes. When Francisco Pizarro entered Peru, he had a contract to take 50 blacks to Peru, free of duty. In 1525, Diego de Almargo landed near the port of Quemado, West Coast of South America. While attempting to explore the countryside, de Almagro was attacked by Indians. He was rescued by his black slave. Later, several Africans helped the Yanacoris Indians in transporting the baggage of Diego de Almagro and his companion along the journey from Cuzeo to Chile. African slaves also accompanied Spanish explorers in Venezuela.

The African slave from Azamor, Morocco, called Estevanico or Estevan distinguished himself as a member of several expeditions in the areas of Texas, New Mexico, and Arizona. Estevan was the slave of Andrews Dorantes de Carranca. Estevan was a captive of the Indians for six years in Texas. He accompanied Cabeza de Vara on a journey across the continent from the Gulf of Mexico through the City of Culiacan to Mexico city. Later, he became the slave of Antonio de Mendoza. Estevan was killed by Pueblo Indians while on an expedition with the Spaniard, Fray Marcos de Niza, a lay brother. Africans were with Francisco de Montejo in the conquest of Yucantan and Pedro de Alvarado in his pacification of Guatemala.

Reference: *They Did Not Tell Me True Facts About the African Americans African Past and American Experiences*

Early Observations and Impressions of Africans by Early Explorers

It is my general thesis that the following accounts of early physical description and characteristics of Africans did have some profound effects in successive impressions of Africans.

When Richard Jobson made a trip to the area of the Gambia River in 1623, he gave an early description of the Fulbies and indicated his lack of knowledge of the genetic diversity of African peoples. He wrote:

"These people are called Fulbies, being a tawny people and have a resemblance right into those we call Egyptians. The women amongst them are straight upright and excellent well bodies, having very good features, with long black hair. Much more loose than the black women have."

When Mungo Park was exploring the Niger River in 1796, he described the Africans as:

"active, powerful and warlike race. The Jaloffs inhabited a great part of that tract which lies between the River Senegal and the Mandingo States on the Gambia. The Jaloffs differ from the Mandingoes, not only in language, but likewise in complexion and features. Their noses are not so much depressed, nor the lips so protuberant as among the generality of Africans. Although their skin is of the deepest black, they are considered by, the white traders as the most sightly Negroes in this part of the continent."

A botanist, Professor Smith, was aboard the Royal Navy ship commanded by Captain James Kingston Tuckey during an exploration of River Zaire (Congo) in 1816. Professor Smith wrote the following impression of Africans in the Congo:

"The people of the Congo would appear, however, to be among the lowest of the Negro tribes. The African black is by nature of a kindly, cheerful, and humane disposition, entirely free from that vengeful, and ferocious temper which distinguishes the savages of the Pacific and South Sea Island, particularly those of New Guinea. "Indolence is the Negroe's bane."

Black Presence

Commander Hugh Clapperton, Royal Navy, and traveler recorded in his *Journal of a Second Expedition Into the Interior of Africa,* the following description of the Songa people of the Cambree who lived between Boussa and Kano:

"These Cambrie people appears to be a lazy, harmless race of Negroes, and as I was informed, inhabit the villages in the woods near the Quora in the states of Boussa, Wawa, and Youre. They are apparently a mild people, in general more tall, more stupid looking than wild, go with little clothing, seldom anything more than a skin around the waist. The young people of both sexes go entirely naked until they have cohabited, when they put on as a skin as their circumstances will afford. They find their unwarlike and mild dispositions often very ill used and imposed upon."

Joseph Corry, an Englishman wrote a book on the *Observations Upon the Windward coast of Africa, the Religion, Character, Customs of the Natives*. His book was designed to portray how the Africans may be civilized. He depicted the people of Africa residing on the coast as more ferocious and barbarians in their customs and manners and more deceitful than the residents in the interior. Corry said the Africans, barbarous condition must be challenged and attempts made to have them adopt civilized habits. He also theorized that the African's muscular body and the procreation of their species is attributed to their infancy and youth where they are happy and mothers treat their offspring with maternal feelings. They are not disturbed by commands or restraints and these things all organize a vigorous manhood and old age. During a visit to the countries bounded by the Rio Pongo and the Gambia Rivers, Corry proceeded toward Teembo, the capital of the King, 270 miles inland from the entrance of the Rio Noonez. He gave a description of the Foolahs.

"The Foolahs are tall, well limbed, robust and courageous, grave in their deportment, well acquainted with commerce and travel over an astonishing space of the country. Their religion is a mixture of Mohammedism, idolatry, and fetishism. The women of the nation are handsome and of a springly (lively) temper, and their countenances (appearance, facial expressions) are more regular than those of common Negroes. The hair in both men and women is much longer and not so

wooly, but they have a most distinguishing custom of forming it into ringlets, bedaubed with oil and grease, which gives them a very barbarous appearance. The Foolah tongue is different from that of the surrounding nations and its accent is more harmonious." Corry further wrote that:

"The Foolahs, the Mandingoes, and the Joliffs, bordering the Senegal, are the most handsome Negroes on this part of Africa. The hair of the Joliffs is more crisped and wooly and their noses are round and their lips are thick. This nation in particular is blacker than nations approximating towards the line, nor are the Negroes in the Krew Coast and towards the Polmas so black as the nation of which I now speak of. This situation may tend to provide that the color of the Africans does not arise from a vertical sun, but from other physical causes yet unknown."

Dr. David Livingstone, the distinguished missionary and physician who made serious attempts to bring Christianity to Africa also offered some healing arts to the sick. Dr. Livingstone did portray some of his social Darwinian views when he wrote the following in his private journal on October 26, 1853:

"I have not met with a beautiful woman among the black people and I have seen many thousands in a great variety of tribes. I have seen a few who might be called possible, but none at all to be compared with the beauty of English servant girls. Some features are said to be found among the Caffres (Amaxhos coastal tribes in South Africa). But many people I have seen I cannot conceive of any European being so capitalized with them as to covet criminal intercourse. The whole of my experience goes towards proving that civilization alone produces beauty and exposure to the weather and other vicissitudes (mutations) tends to the production of deformity and ugliness."

Charles Wheeler was employed by the Royal African Company as a factor (conducts business and transactions) for ten years in Guinea. It is interesting to state that Wheeler admitted that when he first arrived in Guinea he was unacquainted with the nature and dispositions of the

Black Presence

inhabitants and their customs. He said that time and observation did reveal them to him.

Wheeler gave a vivid and detailed description of an African woman that he eventually became sexually involved with. The description will depict how some Europeans would state one thing when initially describing a different people, and another thing after learning about them. Charles Wheeler wrote:

"Accordingly, one of the Captains of the Seraglio, presented me with a young lady in her prime. Her stature was tall, and she was well proportioned and I must acknowledge that the sight of her produced some emotions in me in her favor. The King asked me if I liked her? I answered that I did. His majesty appointed me a house, just by his own palace and allotted us several slaves to attend us during my stay.

During the conversation with my black lady, I could not forebear viewing my fair with an eye. Her hair was done up in a ringlet, set with precious stones and locks of hair loosely played upon her jetty breasts and shoulders. Her neck was adorned with a string of coral beset with rubies. She made me though no despiable (despised) figure and though she was black that was amply recompensed by the softness of her skin. The beautiful proportion and symmerty of her body and the natural, pleasant, and unartificial method of her behavior. She was not forward, nor coy, when I pressed her lovely breasts. My lady, therefore, desired that I would pull off my coat, waist coat and shirt, which I did. Then her ladyship embraces me several times, streaking me from shoulders to waist, both behind and before. At midnight we went to bed and in that situation I soon forgot the complexion of my bed fellow and obeyed the dictates of all powerful nature. I never found during my stay, if paradise is to be found in the enjoyment of a woman. There I was then in the possession of it."

Charles Wheeler's account also showed how an early traveler in Africa expressed his views about African morality. He wrote that during his discussions with his black lady he learned that when an African woman is pregnant, her thoughts are about her developing child and not sexual relations with a man. Wheeler stated that these discussions affirmed his belief that "*among black people there was chastity, true chastity and modesty but among white people there is none.*"

It is quite obvious that Dr. David Livingstone's exposure to some Africans was limited in view of Charles Wheeler's accounts and also that in 1853, some Europeans in America were captivated with Mother Africals comely black daughters.

Reference: *They Did Not Tell Me True Facts About The African American's African Past and American Experience*

SLAVE TRADE AND AMERICAN SOCIETY

Thousands of books, published scholarly articles, films and documentaries, humorous stories and videos have portrayed to the world edited and revised versions of the slave trade and the dehumanizing form of slavery that existed in the United States prior to 1865. I have included in my discussion material that I have researched and obtained concerning the institution of slavery in America from an oral tradition and archival documents.

An overview of the Slave Trade

One must realize that peoples have been enslaved at sometimes during antiquity because slavery did exist in the ancient world. Many slaves were captives from wars. During the Greek era, high price slaves were Greek scholars and phlosophers. Some Greek states were not a democracy and some people were held in servitude and women were not considered a citizen. The great philosopher, Aristotle developed circular reasonsing, especially directed at the Greeks. Once he posed a question, how do you know slaves are inferior? The answer was because they are slaves. Circular reasoning goes back to the days of Aristotle. Some people would say blacks were denied the right to go into the water because they might learn how to swim.

Black Presence

The Roman Catholic church has their early views on slavery. During the middle ages they stated that the Negro has a right to have a soul. Slaves were considered a thing rather than a person. Some years ago, slaves were denied the right to be buried in a Catholic cemetery. One historian stated that as long as barbarians conquered enslaved Christians, than Christians had a right to manumit or free christian slaves. However, barbarians and others had no obligation to free them. But in later years, the Dutch slave owners of the New Netherlands Company would allow limited immersion for some slaves. The Dutch Reformed Church would allow children of some Christian slaves to be baptized.

I believe that it is necessary today to include in humanities, social studies and history curriculums the fact that earlier conquests of people of color has had some residual effects on the tribal or social groups in independent countries of Africa and the Caribbean. We also can not forget the honorable colonial powers, Brazil, Britain, France, Spain, Belguim, Denmark, South Africa, Germany Netherlands and Italy. One must also realize that some of these countries standby today and observe the economic and political disasters of their formal colonial sujects. I would be remiss if I did not say where was the United staes as a mediator or a Bosnia or Haiti like big brother during the recent Liberian Civil War?

It is quite possible that one of the crucial remnants of the institution of slavery and colonial rule has been a division of the people and its country, mentally, economically socially and politically. Actually the destruction of the state and its inhabitants and family structure. The early family of enslaved Africans who were brought to America can be explained in the following true stories:

A Survivor of the Slave Ship Clotilde

The distinguished writer Zara Neale Hurston had interviewed the last survivor of the African slave ship "Clotilde," Cudjo Lewis. She went to Mobile, Alabama, where Lewis was living in 1927 and had a very interesting and descriptive interview with Lewis. During the interview, Lewis discussed in detail his capture; home life in his African home of

Dahomey; the unpleasant voyage of the slave ship, Clotilde; cultural traditions of his homeland, and his eventual freedom.

Cudjo Lewis related to Ms. Hurston that the slave cargo of the Clotilde consisted of Africans Slaves captured by Dahomey warriors (male and female, often referred to as Amazons). Lewis gave Zora Neale Hurston the following descriptive cultural characteristics of his country.
Prior to his capture, the King of Dahomey and his people had raided peaceful social groups and captured slaves. War was made against a community called Togo. The people of Togo were peaceful and engaged in agriculture. They raised hogs, goats, sheep, chickens, and cows. They planted corn, beans, and yams. Bananas and pineapples grew wild. The country's major crop was palm oil obtained from the palm tree. Cord was made from twisting strips of palm leaves. The people made cloth from the fibre and beer from the nuts. There was no hunger and poverty.

Lewis explained the farming procedures of the country. He said that a plot of ground is tilled by the tenant for seven years and then another plot is selected. Yams are produced from the eye of the seed. A melon grows on tall plants and is eaten with salt. The bananas are also used to make beer. The people eat goat flesh, chicken, hogs, deer, and different hunted game. Hurston commented during the interview that the hogs are prepared by using brown sage and burning off the hog's hair and cleaning the skin thoroughly. Normally, the hog would be roasted similar to barbecue. She said this was probably the origin of the barbecue in America, because the word is derived from a native name in Guiana.

Cudjo explained how their houses were constructed. He stated, houses are cylindrical and built of clay being both weather and fire proof. A circular trench is dug and the walls built up about two feet high and eighteen inches thick. This is left to dry and then they add another two feet and let it dry. This is continued until the house is about eight feet high. A series of notches are made at the top to place rafters. A center pole is used and is a straight palm tree. Slight niches are cut in the center piece to receive the rafters, one end is laid through the notches at the top of the wall, and the other fitted into the niches in the center pole and bound with palm cord. Now the ends in the notches are bound and cemented with clay. The roof consists of a long leafy wheat stalk like grass. There are no windows in the house, and the floors are made of beaten clay. The house is lighted by a palm oil lamp.

The dress of his people were described by Cudjo Lewis. He said that men wear a pair of short trousers and on special occasions, a cloak is worn. A large piece of cloth, six feet square, is draped over the left shoulder. Jewelry is worn to include earrings of ivory and bracelets of gold and ivory. The women wear a single garment made from a square of cloth. Nothing was worn above the waist but ornaments such as bracelets from wrist to elbows and numerous shell and ivory necklaces as many as her husband can afford. The earrings and bracelets are made of cowhide and buffalo in sandal style. Cudjo said that all boys over fourteen years were of military age, and the people fought largely in self-defense. His society was polygamous, but a man could only have four wives. The morals of his community were very high and honored. A man did not commit adultery for the punishment was extreme. If a wife committed adultery, she was returned to her parents house and the purchase price was returned to the husband. Illegitimacy was minimal because the man was forced to pay the lady's parents a dowry and he was responsible for raising the child.

Lewis explained that boys were circumcised between seven and eight years and on the fifth day of their circumcision, when the soreness had decreased a feast was held. The village drums beat all day. The small tom-tom, large state drum, and long drum covered at both ends were used. The drums were covered with deer and buffalo hides. The people's religion consisted of worshipping the God Alahra, beliefs in spirits, a spirit of good, Alha-Ahra and a spirit of evil, Ahla-hady-oleelay. Their priest was called Elaha. There was also pagan nature worshippers of the wind, the sun, thunder and lightning. The people would kneel in fear and cross their arms over their breast.

Cudjo's society group was ruled by a king, Adbaku or Iaku. He said that stealing was almost unknown and punishment was very severe. Murder was punished by death, and the guilty person was killed the same way his victim was executed. Court was held in a public square, and all the citizens were equal before the law.

Cudjo Lewis said that one day his village was surrounded at daybreak by Dahomey warriors. The women warriors had on paint and were dressed like men. (Amazons). Men, women and children were attacked and killed. Lewis said he was marched to the coast and could observe the butchered heads of his friends and relatives hanging on poles. Captain Foster, an Englishmen selected 130 slaves to take aboard his ship, the Clotilde. Aboard the ship, Lewis was placed in a hole and remained for 13 days. They reached Mobile Bay, Alabama in August 1859 after a seventy-day trip. The Africans were taken to the Meaher plantation. The area they lived in was called African town or plateau. After the Civil War, the Africans from Dahoney were freed and some were able to purchase small plots of land from the Meaher family. Cudjo Lewis and all of his African friends wanted to return home, but they had no means. Lewis was 19 years old when he was captured. He was around 98 years old when he was interviewed by Zora Neale Hurston.

The interesting descriptive interview conducted by Ms. Hurston contained much valuable information. The 1927 interview with Cudjo Lewis recaptures some historical information about the African past, culture, tradition and high morals that were present in Lewis' African community.

Reference: *They Did Not Tell Me True Facts About the African American's African Past and American Experience*

Views and Impression of Slavery, As told by the White Majority

In 1969 while conducting research on my first manuscript, Black Defenders of America, I visited the Alabama State Archives. A very cordial Causacian lady was kind enough to provide me with some letters and commentaries by former whites who were living on the same plantation with their family's Afro-American slaves.

These following impressions, and statements do reflect the mentality of many white American views in those days of pre- and post slavery about African-Americans. Unfortunately, some of the impressions were handed down to their descendants and without knowing the pros and cons they have developed their present day attitudes based on yesteryears information. These narrations will provide some realistic views of how some white Americans showed their personal caring for blacks even though in many cases they thought of them as subservient and inferior. It is hoped that these stories will reeducate all Americans why some people think the way they do today about African Americans.

Individual Views

"It would be gratifying indeed, had I the power to give forth in language, a minute and faithful description of the many and varied pictures that hang on Memory's walls; pictures that have hung there for over sixty years and are as bright and vivid as the day the scenes passed before me. The Old South, before the beautiful, and historic land was torn and impoverished by the cruel and fratricidal war of sixty one.

The home of my birth and happy childhood; the old southern home with its large rooms, and white columns, the large log fireplace and the glowing fire in winter time around which culture and refinement and modesty cast a charm that hangs to me yet; the bushel basket of big red juicy apples that sat in the corner; the grand old woman into whose face time had written the furrows of age and on whose locks the frost of many winters had settled; grand old woman with lace cap and glasses set on top of her head until needed, the work basket by her side, and her very look demanded the respect of every one white and black, and the master of the whole plantation, stern in demeanor, and positive in command paid that respect to this companion of a long walk in life, which I treasure beyond all measure.

It was my grandmother, glorious grandmother, when joy filled my little heart who smiled in unison with me so sweetly as grandmother, and when trouble came to me and a haven to soothe me was needed whose bosom was so soft and sympathetic as grand mother's. Out of grandmothers window I could see a long line of cabins, and in front a number of little Negroes frolicked, and played in joyous rapture, and how I longed to be with them, and my first ingenuity was spent in devising ways and means to slip around out of the vision of that window, and when I did get with them such joy as I then experienced.

Did you know that there was nothing on this earth that gave a white child of the sixties as much joy as playing with the Negro children? Well that is the truth. Until I was 12 years old I loved Martha, the 15 year old girl that nursed me better than my mother and father. Was I justified? Yes, When I wanted anything Martha gave it with glad hand. When I was in trouble Martha shielded me and protected me, and she would lie for me with the straightest face you could imagine, and she did no wrong for Martha loved me and thought it right to care for me, and that was her duty and her pleasure.

There was Uncle Mack's cabin, and Uncle Austin's cabin, and Aunt Lyza his wife used to keep "cush" ready to serve me when I came, and how I did love to go there.

There was Nelson's and Richard's, and Jacob's cabins, and I was feasted and toasted whenever I made a visit. Then down at the Metcalfe place lived the Negroes that came by my grandmother's and they were the favored ones for they were so religious and good and reliable, and no one was allowed to correct them save the master.

Each head of the family had his own method of control and had a tobacco patch and truck patches, and were given time to cultivate their crop, and they got all the money it brought. Having nothing for which to spend their money, save for luxuries they always had money put away, and a few years ago Uncle Mack spent the day with me, and he had owned a home for many years told me that he always had more money while he was yet a slave than he had ever had since he was freed.

The affection between master and slave as I saw it was beautiful, the confidence the one had in the other was faultless. During those years, the mother and the wife felt as safe when one of the Negro men was left to protect her, as had she been guarded by a patrol, and the Negro was proud of his job of protecting too.

Black Presence 109

Such a thing as an insult of a white woman by a Negro was unheard of and no one ever heard of an attempt on the part of the Negro to rape a white woman.

Such ideas never appeared in the Negro brain until the hate of the North attempted to instill into his brain the fearful and foolish notion that he was the equal of the white man.

Uncle Mack was in my youth my favorite. Do you know why? He was the driver of a six mule team, and was master of the situation, and he would let me ride all day on the off wheel mule, and see him pull hills with a load that seemed impossible. Uncle Mack has a gentle kind disposition. He spoke in a low soft tone and his team was so trained that each one did his duty and I have heard him say that he had pulled a load all the way from Clarksville 18 miles without touching the line of the lead mule, drove all the way simply by talking to his leader and wheelers. It was thrilling and surprising as well when he got on a hard pull, and when he was afraid they would not make it, to see him rise up in his stirrup crack his whip and "cuss" as loud as he could. Then there was exciting times in muledom, for every one would squat and come together, and out they would go, and the smile that then came to Uncle-Mack's face was a joy to my boyish heart.

My life with the Negroes, on that plantation has been a blessing to me as well as a pleasure the Negroes melodies that heard then cannot now be reproduced, and the dances that I saw, had a thrill that none of the 'modern dances can equal. Dinner time down there will always be a pleasant spot in memory. Aunt Rachel weighing about 250 pounds would come out of the kitchen at 11:30 and all was as still as death. The fox hounds asleep in the yard, the hens singing and hunting bugs, and she would pull down on the bell, old bell chord, and with the first stroke of the old bell, pandemonium would break loose. The hounds would set up a howl; the mules plowing in the field commence their loud and long hee-haw, and the Negro plowman commence their joyous shouts. These were good days of plenty, tables for white and black loaded with substantial and not a salad.

One of the old men who was a favorite of mine I shall not fail to mention. Shed Graves was his name, and a Negro trader brought him from Virginia, and stopped at Grandfather's and spent the night. The trader was entertained at the mansion house, and the Negroes he had for trade were sent to the cabins to spend the night. The next morning when the trader was ready to leave, Uncle Shed who was about 21 years of age put at my Grandfather to buy him, and Uncle Shed being a small man, and Grandfather not being anxious to buy, he asked Uncle Shed what he could do. Said Uncle Shed, "You have not got a big nigger on did place dat kin do any more work den I kin, and sides that I can jump dat plank fence, flat footed", Grandfather said, "let me see you do it". Uncle Shed, after years telling me of it, said, "I sho had wings when I went to jump dat fence, and I cleared it easy and Old Master bought me right there, and my wanderings were at an end."

The truth of the matter was he met Aunt Chaney who was a plump girl at 18 and it was love at first sight. In a short time they were married, and lived together for nearly 50 years, Uncle Shed was a banjo picker, and for many years played music for all the barn dances in our country. He could read and write, and when he was sick he read the Bible constantly, and when well he made the walking ring with the music from his banjo.

He never joined a church, and when he was buried, the Negro preacher would not say a word at the grave, owing to the fact that he was a banjo picker, and played for dances and never joined the church. At his burial there was assembled a large crowd of blacks and whites, and when I saw that no one was to say anything, I took off my hat, and walked up to the head of the open grave and preached his funeral myself, and took occasion to state how happy he made others in this world and to the utter astonishment of old audience of Negroes preached him right into heaven. His daughter who was so grieved at her father's death, came and hugged me and never has forgotten me for she said "I knowed that Pappy went to heaven".

When all the scenes I have pictured were going on, down on the plantation, I could hear the mutterings of the storm that broke in my early

Black Presence 111

life. I went to the drill ground, and followed the company, bearing my iron weed gun, Oh! how I wanted to go with them and whip the yankees. I saw the line of gray assemble in the beautiful lawn. I heard the patriotic speeches, and the rebel yell. I saw the mother and sweetheart, bid good bye to the brave boys and I saw for the last time their cause in the air as they went off down the railroad on flat cars, on their way to Virginia, and many of them never to return.

I saw the master and the former slave when the war was over, work side by side to restore the lost fortune; I saw the country merge from the old to the new, and during all my practice of the law for the past 35 years I have defended, more Negroes for nothing than I ever did for pay, and have the first one to prosecute yet.

I must not fail to tell you of the old Red River Church organized in 1791, and all of our people belonged to it, and their salves also belonged to the same church, and had a separate space alloted to them. The minister stood in a pulpit that had decoration of a crude kind and it hid him up to the waist, and he preached never less than two hours, and the members sat and took every word in, and never tired, but I did. My feet lacked nearly a foot of reaching the floor, and I would have passed out and would have given up the ghost, had not my Grandmother been by my side with green calico ridicule, filled with cakes that tempt my appetite to this day. Ah! You should have seen our school houses, and heard the lessons we said Websters blue back speller, McGuffey's readers', and Mitchell's geography, were among the popular school books used at that time. There were no free schools, but the leading men in the community employed the teacher, very largely on his reputation for being an expert with the hickory switch, and his capacity to manage and control larger boys. There were a few ladies teaching but they were employed where the children were small. Usually the teacher took the school for what there was in it and each patron paid so much per month. Every Friday evening was set apart for reception of the parents of the pupils, and all the boys and girls had a recitation, and ended the exhibition with a spelling match.

Little curly locks dressed in a neat little dress, with pantletts, with trimming on the bottom reaching to her shoe tips would get up, and modestly and timidly recite that famous poem, "Mary had a little lamb", and all the while finger each side of her dress while, she recited, but that is a long time ago, and that covering for the, limbs, and that modesty has gone the way of the world. There were higher schools over the country for the grown up boys, and the Greek and Latin scholars that came from them were much more proficient than now, in fact when my father was married at 20, he had mastered a good Greek and Latin education, and was well up in history and literature.

The reconstruction of the country after the Civil war was slow but steady and the Negro who was a slave became a tenant, if not on the former masters farm, then on some other farm in the neighborhood, and this tenantry resulted in a very great depreciation of the land.

Today the Negro farmer has largely taken to the towns and villages. The Negro likes company, and the thrill and excitement of town life. In his natural state, he prefers city and village life to the better and more healthy life on the farm.

When the free school system was inaugurated, the better Negroes were given schools, and have never been discriminated against, and still the whites are paying the tax that goes to educate them.

They have in very rare instances ever taken enough education to write a grammatical letter after 35 years of free school."

It Had To Be True, Because The White Majority Said So

Slave's Living Quarters

1. "As a general thing the houses were built of logs dabbed with mud, the floors were made of rough plank, and very often dirt floors. The chimneys were made of split boards and dabbed with mud inside, and it was very seldom that the huts had a window in them. The sometimes had a little shed in front without galleries. In those days sometimes a whole family stayed in one of these huts, the children

Black Presence

113

ranged from 4-10 in a family. The covering of the shanties were generally of boards."

2. "The man and wife and grown ones slept on the bedstead, good, bad and indifferent, while the children slept on quilt pallets on the floor. In the winter they would sleep near the wide fire place and in the ashes on it. They generally cooked in the fire place and had a rough table and two or three old chairs and wooden benches for seats."

3. "I have to say: My father was the largest slave owner in this (Dekalb) county. The owners of slaves here were generally kind and humane to their colored people who were well fed and comfortably clothed and lived in comfortable and convenient houses."

4. "The construction was plain, but substantial, with windows, doors, chimneys, floors, etc. In fact, all that a human man would give to a valuable animal."

5. "The slaves were required to make their own furniture. This was plain, crude, and consisted mainly of a table, benches, and a few chairs."

Available Food

1. "For their children, according to their age and size, on some plantations they were fed in the kitchen of the white house. It was generally a little bread and syrup for breakfast, pot-licker and bread for dinner, a cup of milk and a piece of cornbread late in the evening for their supper. In some cases the cooking was done for the field hands at the white house by the cook and carried by little boys in buckets to the field. In the wealthy families they had a regular cook, washer and ironer seamstress, from one to two nurses, a carriage driver and a extra man to look after the garden. Sometimes there were as many as two and three colored maids to wait on the white girls of the family."

2. "Their food was 3 1/2 pounds of bacon per head and 1 peck of meal."

3. "The slaves were all fed in one large cabin. One or two long tables reaching clear across the house served for all. Plates were of tin, spoons, knives and forks - there were none, each one ate with their fingers and drank from a large bucket of water which was passed from man to man. This was the cause of many disputes and quarrels which had to be settled by a Negro for that special purpose called "The Judge," making use of his authority."

4. "5 1/4 pounds of meat and one peck of meal a week was allowed, but I never seen any of that, you give them all they could eat. The master always gave them something extra for their Sunday dinner."

5. Their food consisted mainly of bacon, bread, potatoes and peas 3 1/2 to 4 pounds of meat was the allowance per week. They had little 'extra patches' which they worked at odd times and made money to purchase extras. They did their cooking at night for the following day. They generally ate their breakfast at home and carried their dinner to the fields in a little bucket."

Clothing Worn By Slaves

1. "They wore white cotton goods the whole year around, men and women, and were supposed to get a suit every winter. They always got a pair of red brogans every winter. Their clothes and were made by a colored seamstress who sewed for the white people."

2. They wore rough brogan shoes. The men I cotton shirts and jean pants and coats. In the winter they wore woolen shirts. The women wore calicoes and gingham, same kind of shoes. On large plantations a tailor, generally a Negro slave, made the clothes. On others, the women made them."

Black Presence

3. "The slaves were furnished with good warm clothing which was made of jerseys and osnaburg. They were allowed four suits a year. These were made by the white women and the Negro seamstresses on the place. The 'Lady of the White House' superintended the making."

Slave Occupations

1. "All were taught to excel in something. Some as cotton pickers, some as drivers, some as butlers, some as cooks, seamstresses, etc. This to enhance their value in case of a sale. I might say in this connection that all the young ladies of the house were, as soon as they were old enough, taught housekeeping, and in nine cases out of ten were capable of tea always taking charge of an establishment even to cooking. Their teachers being generally slaves."

2. Their work was mainly plowing, hosing, and splitting rails, and any kind of work that would naturally be performed about his plantation. The work hours were from sun-up to sun-down. They were allowed holidays at Christmas and on the 4th of July."

3. "Some were field hands, some carpenters, blacksmiths, wagon makers and plow stockers."

4. "The old men shucked corn, went to the mill, cut splits, and made baskets. The old women looked after children and the sick. There were a number of fairly good mechanics on every plantation, and blacksmiths, carpenters. In the towns much of the mechanical work was done by Negro men."

5. "Corn shucking in the fall were a great gala event with them. A neighbor would invite the Negroes from adjoining farms to come and shuck corn, and they generally attended."

6. "The average-Negro had very little money. Sometimes they were allowed to take watermelons to town and sell them on public days, also cords of wood. They were sometimes-hired out by their masters at $150 per year with clothing and food.

7. "I knew very few slave carpenters or shoemakers who stayed on the farms. There were some, but they were not kept on the farms. The good carpenters among the Negroes (and the majority of the carpenters I knew up to 1860 were Negroes) hired' their time from their owners and worked by contract, or per wages having 3 or 4 apprentice cubs with them at a salary to them of 8 to 10 dollars per month and charged the building owner 25 to 30 dollars per month."

8. "The old and infirm were given such work about the yard and in the garden that would not tax their strength and power of endurance. Some of them spent much of their time gathering vegetables for the cook. However, if they were too old or infirm to work at anything, they were kept from the house but otherwise properly cared for. The little niggers, under 10 years of age, were collected in the morning into a house provided for that purpose, and looked after by a woman set apart and trained for that purpose. Some few Negroes were trained in blacking and accompanying woodwork to keep up the farming tools, and, in a tight spot, do some repair,work for the neighbors."

9. "There are a good many carpenters, blacksmiths, coach workmen, painters, harness and saddie makers. A few of them hired their own time. There were a few colored engineers. only one that I knew of was a locomotive engineer on a passenger train and he ran from Newburn to Selma, Alabama."

Attitudes Toward Emancipation

1. "A good many of my father's slaves said they did not want to be freed, and they remained on the plantation seven years after they were freed; in fact, until my father sold the plantation. I do not recall anyone who was opposed to slavery. I heard that some of the slave holders spoke of gradual emancipation or colonization - I mean during the war. There were no slave insurrections planned or suspected in my region. The only one on record as I know was John Brown at Harper's Ferry, which all are familiar with.

Status of Free Negroes

1. "There was only one free Negro in our community. He made his living by brick masonry. He did not own any slaves. There was no special regulations for free Negroes."

2. "The poor whites here were, as far as my knowledge goes, had of work at fair contented and prosperous. They had wages and, as the luxuries of today were then unknown, they fared very well, particularly as the Negro was not in competition with them, as now. But after the Negro received his freedom, he began competing with white laborers everywhere and in every business. Prior to the war, and for a few years after, white laborers were common and white girls were domestics in almost every house that required servants. Now it is very rare that a white servant is found in any house and hardly any white laborers (unskilled) are employed anywhere."

3. "I knew a man that bought himself a wife and one child for about nine hundred dollars. He was about fifty years old when he bought himself."

4. "Yes, free Negroes, a few scattering ones, they never came to anything. They idled away their time and had no more comfort or means or respectability than the slaves. The only differences being they could move as they pleased from place to place. Under their shiftless, idle habits it took all they could make to provide themselves with those things generally furnished free to slaves by their masters. I never heard of one owning slaves, except an instance or two of a Negro carpenter and barber buying their wives."

5. "There was one family of free Negroes in my section. It was a woman and her daughter. The woman was set free at the death of her old master. The child of this woman was the daughter of this master he left her in a way to get along quite easy. She sold butter, eggs, and milk, raised her own meat and managed to get along very easy. The free Negroes were generally very kind to the slaves."

Lower Income Whites Impressions of Slavery

1. "I remember no instances where the slave wanted to go back into slavery. I knew of a few whites who were opposed to slavery but were afraid to make it known for the colonizing of slaves was very dangerous to be spoken of among whites or blacks."

2. "The non-slave owners respected the slave owners and the slave owners respected the industrious whites. The non-slave holding whites treated the free Negroes and slaves kindly. The poor white people in my community were industrious, and would get aid and work for those who were in good circumstances. I will add that the Negro of today does not live as long as the slaves did. They are not thrifty and do not have regular hours and do not take as good care of themselves as they were by their old masters, which they acknowledge. There is more crime committed by them now. We never knew of a rape case before the Negro was made free."

3. "Before the war, within my range of observation, there were only a few of these. They bought a nigger as soon as they got enough money. There was not as much prejudice on their part against owners of slaves as there is now on the part of the poor against the rich. Negro equality did not trouble or threaten them as they have thought it since the war. It was was a little harder for the very poor to get their heads above the water then than now, but the relations and feelings towards each other was there very much as now. There were some evidences and instances of envy but hardly so much as appears nowadays. One thing is certain, those Southerners who never owned slaves and in proportion to their number have caused more of the race troubles we have experienced during the past 45-50 years than old slave owners. I think this sensitivity, needless for the greater part, is growing out of their descendants."

4. "There were quite a number of persons in this city who were opposed to slavery, but they kept that fact to themselves, as it was very dangerous to express an opinion of that kind."

Black Presence

Slaves' Income

"They had gardens, pigs, made split baskets, raised possum, dogs, chickens and sold them to the homes of white folks or neighbors and so had a little money all the time. Some people had other slave hands, the ablest and best hands, bringing as much as $200 per annum. Most of the Negro carpenters hired their time at 20 to 40 dollars per month from their masters and then took jobs at salaries of $2.00 to $2.50 per day. Barbers did so too. Hezakiah Edwards hired his time from his mistress, Mrs. D. Murphy at $50 per month and built my father's dwelling in 1860-61. (He was architect and boss carpenter).

3. "In regard to passes they were very necessary. They got passes to go to frolics on the neighboring farms and sometimes to church. Those passes were dated for a certain hour in the night and if you didn't get home by that hour the patrollers would give them a whipping. The hour was 9 and 10 o'clock. The passes were written for a certain hour in the day as well as in the night. Around the towns they were captured and locked up in the guard house until morning. The masters were notified and ordered them to whipped a number of thirty-nine licks with a cat-of-nine tails whip and sent home by the marshall of the town. Very often the master gave them another whipping for leaving without a pass. The young masters and the old masters did the whipping and the overseers of the old plantations."

4. I knew of instances where there was talk of punishing slave holders for the cruelty to their slave but I never knew its being carried into courts. I can give very ridiculous relations between female slave and master. I remember of a few cases where slaves murdered one another and as a general thing, they were run out of the state and sold. But as a general thing, when he killed a white man he was hung. Colored families were separated in every direction. Little children from their mothers. The slave owners made arrangements with physician to care for their sick, the sick were fairly cared for considering other things."

5. "They were whipped sometimes for disobeying orders and neglecting their duties. The overseer quietly did the whipping when the master said it was necessary. I never knew my father to whip his slaves. We had one slave owner in our county who was cruel to his slaves by not giving them sufficient food or clothing and he was arrested and brought before the court and was punished according to law."

6. There was no marked devotion between slaves to each other. They were often beautifully devoted to their white masters and friends but not so to their own color."

7. The whipping was generally done by the master but sometimes the overseer in the masters presence. About 10 per cent of slaves were badly treated. I have known of devotions between master and slave. Also I have known a Negro slave to cut the throat of his widowed mistress and the neighbors gathered and took him out in the woods and tied him to a stake, piled pine knots around him, poured turpentine over him and burned him up. The woman recovered and lived to a ripe old age."

8. "Passes were granted for the slave to go from one masters premises to another. This was required all the time but only a few had this priviledge. Where it was required, it was the patrols duty to see that they had their passes, and when they did not they were given a licking - from 12 to 39 licks."

9. "The slaves were whipped for stealing, mostly, and for disobedience, stealing, fighting, etc. The master or overseer did the whipping. Sometimes the Negroes did it."

10. The slaves were punished for crime then as now. When the slave was sentenced to hang, the state reimbursed the owner to the extent the of one-half the value of the criminal.

Slaves' Family Life

Black Presence 121

(Amusements, Morality, Religion, Education)

1. "Most of the teaching that was done, was by the white boys. A few of the slaves could read, but only a very few could write. They were very good at figuring and counting, as they generally had a good memory. The mulattoes were smarter than the blacks, as a rule, though some, of the pure Negroes showed remarkable aptitude."

2. "The religion then was about the same as now. The minister would read out two lines and the congregation would take them up and sing. The Negroes and whites sometimes had separate churches, but often the Negroes used the whites church when they had no services. Also when the whites had preaching, a certain part was set off for the Negroes to use and they attended freely. I have known communities that had Negro preachers in the absence of white ministers. The slaves as a rule had their own Negro preachers, some of them remarkable. They celebrated the rites of baptism and communion. Nearly all of the slaves attended church. There was no Sunday School. They belonged mostly to the Baptist and Methodist church."

3. "They did not have a high sense of morality. They would steal, fight, drink, gamble, etc., whenever a good opportunity presented itself. Only a few of the slave women were virtuous".

4. "Quite a number learned to read and write. They were generally taught by the young white people, boys and girls. Many could figure, count and correctly compute and estimate the amount of merchandise, farm products, etc. The mulattoes seemed smarter than the pure Negroes."

5. "They frequently held religious services attended with much shouting, singing and exhortations. They generally had services in their cabins and in some places they had churches. They celebrated baptisms and communion as much as they could like the whites. Most of them attended church. They were generally Baptist and

Methodist with some Presbyterians in most instances their religion affected their lives."

6. "There were not many instances of stealing, fighting, drinking, accusing, or gambling."

7. "The slaves were allowed to marry slaves of other plantations with the permission of both owners. The children of this marriage, if there were any, were to be equally divided between the two owners."

8. "Holidays consisted of 1/2 of a Saturday once a month in the Spring, the 4th of July with a barbecue and 3 days at Christmas."

9. "This was of an emotional variety. Petty thieving was natural with the darkies and like unchastity with the women, had affected their standing. They all loved whiskey and so did the masters as a rule who gave them a little now and then but very rarely did they have the opportunity to indulge their propensity to intoxication. Slaves, as a rule, did not gamble. Craps came in with freedom."

10. "By law they were not allowed to be educated, though the white children often taught the seamstress and other house servants. Nearly in every instance, the white blood in the mulatto made them intellectually superior to the Negro.

Voices of The Past - Former Slaves

Twenty-two years ago while conducting research in the Library of Congress, Washington, D.C., I read some of the original transcripts interviews with former slaves. The typewritten records called "A Federal History of Slavery In The United States" was prepared by the Federal Writers Project 1936-1938 and assembled by the Library of Congress and the Works Project Administration. I had taken some notes from narratives of former slaves from the states of Alabama, Arkansas, Kentucky, Missouri, Mississippi and Oklahoma. The former slaves discussed some of their memories about the subjects of their birth, family members, former slave masters and mistresses, living conditions, food, clothing, oversee work, church, runaways, funerals, slave activities, children's games celebration of holidays, illness, Civil War, marriage, slave punishment reading and writing, music, (song's, religious and non religious) riddles, and sayings. These interesting interviews are really the voices of those former slaves who were still living in the 1930's and had not forgotten the memories good and bad of their living during the days of American slavery.

In view of all the scholarly research and years of hundreds of volumes of literature written on the subject of slave life, I deeply believe that these accounts of the memories of former slaves provide a more creditable account of the way they were in slavery. Some of the voices of the past of former slaves stated the following:

"Frances Bridges who was born in 1858 stated that the cook on the Oklahoma plantation, Mama Winnie Long used to feed the little black children on the floor just like little pigs with tin cups and wooden spoons."

Phoebe Banks was born in 1858 and was living in Muskogee, Oklahoma in 1938. He said "that on the McIntosh plantation there was a large number of slaves and lots of slave children. The slave men worked in the fields chopping cotton, raising corn, cutting rails for fences, building log cabins and fireplaces."

John Brown of Tulsa, Oklahoma was born in 1851. He gave his version of how slaves were brought from Africa. He told the interviewers that "My grandmother was one of the older slaves on the plantation and she came directly from Africa. She said over in Africa the people lived on fruits and nuts and had never seen white men. One day a big ship stopped off shore and the Africans hid in the bush along the beach." grandmother was there. The ship men sent a little boat to the shore and scattered bright things and trinkets on the beach. The people were curious." Grandmother said, everybody made a rush for them things soon as the boat left." The trinkets were fewer than the people. The next day the white men scattered some more things along the beach and there was another scramble by the people to grab them. The people were less frighten and some walked up to the gang plank to get things on the plank and off the deck. The deck was covered with things like they had found on the beach. There were some two to three hundred Africans on the ship when they felt the ship moving. The people rushed to side but the plank was gone, just dropped in the water when the ship moved away. The folks on the beach were crying and shouting. The people on the boat were wild with fear. Grandmother was one of the ones who they fooled and she said the last thing she saw of her home was the Africans running up and down the beach raising their arms and shouting like they were mad. The boatmen came up from below where they had been hiding and drove the Africans down in the bottom and kept them quiet with whips and clubs. The slave ship landed at Charleston and the town folks were mad cause the blacks were driven through the streets without any clothes on and they drove off the boatmen after the slaves were sold on the market. Most of that load was sold to the Brown plantation in Alabama. Grandmother was one of the bunch. The owners of the plantation were John Barley and Henry Brown of Taloga County, Alabama. The Browns taught their slaves to work, and make clothes for them. They taught the little ones to read and write, said it was good for the Negroes to know about such things."

Eliza Evans was born in 1851 and was living in McAlester, 1938. She stated during an interview that her master was a John Dixon of Selma, Alabama. Eliza Evans recalled the story told her by her grandmother. "My grandmother was a slave from Africa. You know there were white men who went slipping around and would capture black folks and take them to boats and fetch them over here and sell them for slaves. Well, Grandma was a little girl about eight or more years and her parents had sent her out to get wood. They were going to roast something. They captured her and put a stick in her mouth. The stick held her mouth wide open so she would not cry out. When she got to the boat she was so tired and she did not do nothing. There were a lot of more colored people on the boat and when the boat came here, Mr. John Dixon met the boat and bought grandma."

Black Presence

Eliza Evans also talked about how the old slave mistress used to tell them ghost stories. "She would tell us ghost stories after funerals and they would really scare me to death. She would tell of seeing men with no head and see cattle that would suddenly turn to cats and she made us believe that if a fire was close to the cemetery it was coming for a ghost."

Robert R. Grinstead was born on February 17, 1857 in Lawrence County, Mississippi. He was the son of a black mother, Ann and a German father, Elias Grinstead. He stated that "Master went to war. When the Negroes went to church with the white people, they joined the church, a Baptist Church. The white people build a pen in the church in which the Negroes sat and when they would take sacrament, the Negroes would be served after the whites were through. One of the Negroes in the group would pass it around to the others within the pen".

George Kye (Stover) stated that he was born near Van Buren, Arkansas and when the War came the grown men went off to serve because the master was too old to go. But he had to send somebody anyway. "I served as George Stover, but every time the sergeant would call out Abe Stover, my master's name, I would answer, here! They had me driving a mule team wagon that old master furnished and I went with the secession (Confederate) soldiers from Van Buren to Texarkanna and back a dozen times or more. There were eleven boys who served in our regiment for their masters".

Reference: *The Way We Were*

John Newton, Slave Dealer and Composer

How often we hear the beautiful verses and lyrics of music and never question the background of the composer. I believe many people have never asked or cared who was John Newton?

John Newton, a white man, was born in 1725. As a youngster he learned to read the Bible and received religious guidance from his mother who was a devout Christian. His mother died when he was seven years old. After receiving two years of education he joined his father at sea. Newton sailed the sea for eighteen years. Six of these years, he performed duties as the captain of a slave ship. Even though Newton had his Bible with him at sea and studied in the cabin, his morals towards slavery probably had no spiritual meaning. Newton would have prayers with the members of his crew but the unfortunate cramped and inhuman conditions of African slaves had no effect on his religious teachings and compassion for human beings who happened to be slaves of a black skin color. He viewed them as "cattle", Newton did deliver one cargo of slaves to Charleston, South Carolina.

John Newton experienced a spiritual awakening at the age of twenty-three years while aboard ship. He was steering his ship through a gale or strong current of wind when he was about to lose control of the ship, Newton began to pray and asked God to see him through this ordeal.

Later, Newton decided to return to Liverpool, England where he worked for nine years in an office and studied for the ministry. Newton was ordained as curate of a church in Olney in 1764. He remained there for sixteen years. During the period 1780 to 1807, Newton served as rector of St. Mary Woolnoth, London. When he was eighty years of age, he became feeble and his eye sight began to decline. He was unable to read the text and had to resign from his preaching duties. It appeared that Newton's past life was not forgotten in his memories. Because when he was told he should retire, he said *"What shall the old African blasphemer, (one who abuses others) stop while he can speak*! While preaching at Olney, Newton developed a close friendship with William Cowpers, the noted poet. One of the outstanding contributions of the eighteenth century was the development of the English hymnody (hymn writing). There was a collection of hymns during this time that included three hundred and forty-eight hymns. Cowper wrote sixty-eight and Newton wrote two-hundred and eighty.

John Newton composed his epitaph by himself:

Black Presence

"John Newton, Clerk, once an Infidel and Libertine (one who is unrestrained in morality and religious matters was by the rich mercy of our Lord and Savior, Jesus Christ preserved, restored and pardoned, and appointed to preach the faith he had long labored to destroy near 16 years at Olney in Buck's and years in the church."

I have often sat in a church and attended programs where I heard the beautiful lyrics of a song being sung slowly and sweetly. I always think of this particular song as one that reflects our slavery past and the dehumanizing process of our ancestors during those days of injustice. However they were the times of the American experience that our great grandparents and other relatives lived. But somehow the comfort received, and the meditation of smoothness and contentment is present where these words are being sung:

"Amazing grace, how sweet the sound that saved a wretch like me. I once was lost, but now I'm found, was blind, but now I see"

I know that this song has been sung for many years by African Americans and is still a part of our music selection today. But in our American experience we live so many amazing moments. Yes, during my research I was amazed that this beautiful song that some churches of color include in their song books of Zion was composed by an Englishman who at one time was a captain of a slave ship. Yes, the late Reverend John Newton who died in 1807. This is another revelation of America. I wonder did in Charleston, South Grace. I wonder did the descendants of those slaves Newton left in Charleston, South Carolina ever sing the lyrics of "Amazing Grace". I conclude by saying, as I read the words of the song, I feel that John Newton lived the rest of his life asking our Lord Jesus for forgiveness. It is ironical that these beautiful verses would be sung so slow and free with feeling by the descendants of those Africans he once saw as just cattle below his ship decks at sea.

Brazilian Slavery and its Aftermath

The British Empire was probably the largest exporters of slaves. Approximately seventy percent of the slaves sent to North America and the Antilles were brought there by the British slave dealers and the Royal African Company of England. The largest importers of slaves in North America was possibly the country of Brazil. During the period 1500-1800, approximately 10 million slaves were imported to the Americas. Some historians have given a figure of 15 million.

The Portuguese used middle men to obtain their slaves in Africa. They would use blacks or mulattos to go into the hinterland of the country and purchase slaves. They carried messages and information to the slave traders. They were called, "carrier pigeons, hawkers, and Pombeiros." The major ports in Brazil that received the slaves were Bahia, Pernambuco and Rio. The major African parts of departure were Sao Paulo do Loanda, Benguela and Cabinda da Loango. It is believed that seventy-five percent of slaves that arrived in Brazil after 1800 came from East Africa, possibly Angola.

The Spanish royalty assisted the Portuguese, Dutch, French, and English to export slaves from African ports into the Spanish colonies. The Spanish Crown granted the countries a private enterprise or commercial contract called an assiento. However, the slave trade for Brazil was controlled by traders in the Cape Verdes, Guinea and Angola.

Prior to the arrival of slaves in Brazil, the slave traders prepared the slaves for public auctions and private sales. After a forty-five day trip from the areas of Angola to Brazil, many slaves, experienced muscular and joint problems due to the cramped conditions of their quarters. The slave traders would rub the slave's body with palm oil, use root type herbs or medicines to brush their teeth and gums. The slaves were given an opportunity to exercise prior to their arrival in Brazil.

When one thinks of the term mortgage in 1992, the words real estate come to the mind. Prior to 1864, slave masters in Brazil could rent, sell, give, loan, mortgage, or grant interest in a slave.

This is another indication that slavery was an economic business, and that profit was the major factor. The human beings of African descent became the property.

Black Presence

An element of racism or color preference was observed in the early releases or freedom granted to African slaves in Brazil. A large majority of slaves freed were the creoles (black born in Brazil), mulattoes, women and children, and half breeds (a person of mixed white, black, Indian, or oriental genes).

Some slaves in Brazil were freed by their master after considerable years of service, from 20 to 50 years. Many slaves were able to purchase their freedom.

The problem of the "color obsession" was present in Brazil many years before it would become a problem in the United States. Some historians have written that the Spanish conquistadors and slave masters migrated to Brazil in large numbers without their European wife and family. Some were single. Therefore, the original inhabitants, the Indian women and their export property, the African woman became their female sexual mate, mistress and/or spouse. In simple terms, there were no known contraceptives or birth control pills and to avoid that popular term used by many European writers and some Americans, race mixing, I will say a hybrid or offspring was born half African and half European (black and white). Over the years, many words have been given to call them something else other than being a genetic offspring of black and white.

Brazil was confronted with their genetic hybrid that they called the mulatto. In later years, the United States would confront their problem by creating their definition of a genetic hybrid or offspring of an African and Caucasian. America said regardless of how white you look, hair texture, skin color, size of lips, nose, body build, the fact that it is known that you have some black genes (blood), you are a colored, black, Negro or African.

Today, in 1992, there are many Caucasian Americans who are living and will die someday not realizing that because of this so called American definition of ethnic or race, they are descendants of African Americans. I mean descendants of those persons who were able to cross the line and live as white, marry white and have children who think and have thought that they were pure blood white Americans. I make these statements so definitive because as I will state one example without identifying the names of the individuals. I am quite sure other Americans can give hundreds of examples of people that they know are living as white but in the American definition and accepted racial designation, they are African Americans. A lady was born fifty-five years ago to an octoroon Afro American father and a quadroon Afro American mother. At the age of eighteen when I first met her she could pas for a white person. She has married twice to caucasians and lives as a white person. Her children are classified as white and it is believed that they live in a white world today. Her brother is married to a white lady and it is also believed that his family is considered white. They have blended into American white society and have been very successful in their upward mobility goals. That was her desire many years ago to live as white and I respect her for that. Because I often recall the story from the oral tradition that my paternal aunt told me as a child. She said my mulatto grandfather's sister and brother left a plantation in Evergreen, Alabama, in 1871 and disappeared into the white world with their visible caucasian features and hair texture. My grandfather who could have joined them decided to remain with his black skin sister during his one hundred and three years of living, he would always say, my mother was black and my father was white.

Considering this discussion of America's mulatto problems, the Brazilians confronted their problem of color by permitting the mulattoes to have certain privileges thereby preparing some of them for an eventual transition or passing over into the white society of Brazil if their visible features and hair could conceal them from the black population.

Around the 1700's, slaves and freed blacks were told to wear dark clothing. Black freed males could not wear silk. The free mulatto women could wear appropriate dress to include silk. Although there were many restrictions on mulattoes in Brazil, some were able to cross over into the white society and become white.

The ancestral genetic structure of the peoples of Brazil have affected the population in the 1990's. Several popular Almanacs avoid the reporting of the ethnic population statistics of Brazil. One Almanac states that Brazil is made up of the vast majority of Africans and mulattoes. The first

Black Presence

Afro Brazilian Congressman elected to the Brazilian National legislature stated very specifically in 1979 his statistics on the population in Brazil.

Abdias Do Nascimento, a Professor Emeritus, State University of New York at Buffalo said that there is an Afro Brazilian race close to eighty million of blacks and mulattoes in a population of one hundred and fifty million inhabitants. In Brazil some mulattoes are accepted as white because of their wealth and some blacks or Negroes "become white based on their wealth." They are called a "mullato or pardo."

New England

The greatest slave trading colonies in New England were Connecticut, Massachusetts, New Hampshire, Rhode Island, and Vermont. The leading slave ports were Boston and Newport.

Some slaves in New England worked in occupations such as sailors on whaling ships, carpenters, butchers, iron workers, rope makers, tailors, porters, distillers, printers, bakers, spinners, teamsters, common laborers, and assistants to physicians.

An African having been born in slavery, been enslaved either for debt or as punishment for a crime, been prisoner of war or been sold to European slave traders.

During the early nineteenth century, the Dutch, English, and French dominated the slave trade. The shipment of many slaves to Brazil and Cuba occurred in the nineteenth century.

The source of some slave imports to North and South American were as follows:

British

Gambia, Sierra Leone, Gold Coast, Benin, Biafra, Congo, Angola, and Mozambique

Slaves imported to Cuba came from Gambia, Sierra Leone, Gold Coast, Benin, Biafra, Angola, Mozambique and Madagascar. The slaves imported to Brazil came from Gambia, Sierra Leone, Benin, Congo, Angola, and Mozambique. Many slaves were imported to Jamaica, Barbados, St. Vincent, Tobago, Trinidad, Grenada, Saint Dominique, Martinique, Guadeloupe, and French Guiana.

African Slave Trade

During the slave trade, goods manufactured in Europe or India were exchanged for slaves in Africa, and the slaves were exchanged in the colonies for sugar, and the sugar was sold in England for cash. At every stage, a profit was made.

There are more than 700 different languages spoken on the Africa continent. Some of the language are indigenous to the native populations white some were imposed by their past colonial intruders or conquerors. English, French, German, Spanish, Portuguese, Italian, and Dutch dialects can be found throughout African countries. Linguists have attempted to group African languages as follows: Congo - Kordofanian, Nilo Saharari, Afro Asiatic and Khoisan.

There has been discrepancies and differences in the number of slaves who died during the middle passage arid traveled from Africa to America. However, an estimated figure agreed to by many scholars of history is around 15 million.

Guatemala

In the seventeenth century a small number of African slaves were present in Guatanala. According to one observer they worked as laborers on large indigo plantations. There were some slaves who resisted the harsh treatment from their masters and ran away toward the mountains. The Spaniards referred to them as cimarrons or runaway slaves. The slaves would run toward a stronghold in the mountain woods near Sierra de las Minas. It is believed that over the years the descendants of these slaves who became miscegenated or mixed with Spanish and Indian genes blended into the country's population.

Prince Ibrahima - A Former Slave

A slave in Maryland in the early 1730's known as Job Ben Solomon or Ayuba Suleiman Diallo of Bondu wrote a letter to his father in Arabic. The letter was brought to the attention of a linguistic scholar of Oxford University, Dr. Hans Sloane. This letter resulted in the freedom of Job Ben Solomon and his accession to an African throne in Bondu, Senegal. The former slave was also called Ibrahima or Abduhl Rahaman, son of Soro, King of the Fulbe Empire in the area of present day Futa Jalon, the Republic of Guinea. After seven years of meticulous research, Professor Terry Alford, a scholar and historian wrote an interesting and valuable historical novel depicting the life of the African prince. Alford stated that during his early stages of research, he discovered only one published account of Ibrahimals life. This was an article by Charles S. Sydner published in January 1937. However, a distinguished popular historian of color, the late Joel A. Rogers, had included several sentences concerning Abduhl Rahaman in his historian pamphlet, **100 Amazing Facts About the Negro** first published in 1934.

ENLIGHTMENT AND ABSOLUTISM

Peter The Great and Abram Hannibal

The world history standard core curriculums will include a discussion on the noted Tzar of Russia's Imperial Age, Peter I or Peter the Great (1682-1725). Many secondary and college students will be made aware of the following major highlights of his interesting rule and career. Peter the Great was considered as the future ruler of Russia when his half sister staged a royal palace coup. She ruled for seven years as regent for Peter and his half brother, Ivan. Peter was able to assume full control in 1689. He was known as a reformer after visiting countries in western Europe to include Holland. Peter the Great was able to develop his ideas about reforms and innovations that he wanted for Russia. His major goals were the development of strong military, a more centralized government, enforcement of Russia's absolutism, strengthen state police and security, and reforms in the Russia Orthodox church.

Peter the Great was able to raise a standing army of 200,000 men, a special force of 100,000 Cossacks and foreigners. His decisive military victories helped Russia to become a dominant power in the Baltic Sea. He appointed councils, ministers and royal military governors. His noblemen were required to serve in the military or as civil administrators. Peter I established schools and universities. The noblemen had an obligation to study outside of Russia for five years. There was also a merit-based military-civilian bureaucracy for non noble citizens. This assisted them in their upward mobility goals. Peter the Great abolished the Office of Patriarch in the church and had a Holy Synod of Bishops. He even issued a decree establishing dress codes and requesting the men to shave off their mustaches and beards.

Peter the Great established his capitol at St. Petersburg. He was a successful reformer in view of some of his negative actions. Peter the Great died at the age of 43 years in 1725.

I have stated it many times and will continue that it is unfortunate that young people of all ages and ethnic groups are still studying and reading about one perspective of many significant topics of world history. Because of the vast amount of economic equity for the news media and communication sources, the selling commodity is, of course, the sensational and so called profile of peoples of African descent. The following discussion includes some true factor about the black presence in Russia during the reign of Peter the Great, the missing pages of the majority required texts for United States curriculum for World History courses in the black presence. However, in the 1700's, Russia would develop an interest in the Africa slave trade for possibly the purchase and importation of black slaves as servants for the royal court and homes of wealthy noblemen.

Some historians have disagreed on some information concerning Peter the Great's favorite servant, Abram Hannibal. However, very creditable sources have supported these facts and inferences:

Abram Hannibal was possibly born in the area of present day Eritrea (Ethiopia) and the son of a provincial prince. It is believed that he arrived in Russia around 1705 after being purchased from the Dutch East Indian Co. to serve as a slave or servant for the Tsar Peter I. Even though some historians have referred to Hannibal's baptism as a mock ceremony, one did occur. In 1707, he was baptized into the Russian Orthodox church at Vilnius. Peter the Great was his godfather, and Christina, wife of the Polish King Augustus II was his godmother.

Abram Hannibal was an unusual servant for the popular Peter the Great. Peter I provided Hannibal with a very good formal education. Abram studied in Paris for 7 years and later enlisted in the French army. His occupational specialty was military engineering. Hannibal was present in battles against Spain and received a head wound and was captured by the Spanish. Later Hannibal was promoted to the rank of second lieutenant and attended an artillery school at Metz, France. In 1823, he returned to Russia and was assigned at Kronstadt as an engineer instructor and later taught math for a St. Petersburg personal guard unit. Abram was a very educated man, he was knowledgeable of books on Euclid, Machiavelli, Racine and Correille. After Peter's death, Hannibal was assigned to Siberia for three years at Selinginsk in a detention prison. While in prison, Hannibal was given a task to assist in the design and construction of a fortress. Hannibal was released from prison when Anne ascended the throne. Abram returned to the Russian military and received promotions. Abruptly from captain to major in 1730. He requested retirement from the military service in 1733 because of illness. He married the daughter of a Greek sea captain, Eudoxia Dioper, but they were divorced after a long court proceeding. In the meantime, Hannibal married illegally Christina Regina Von Shoberg, the daughter of a Baltic German army officer. They became the parents of eleven children. His first marriage's divorce became final in 1753. However, Christina and Abram were together until his demise. One of Hannibal's sons, Ivan, was a successful military officer in the artillery branch and served as an artillery specialist in the naval fleet of Admiral Spiriclov. Ivan Hannibal was present in the battles involving the conquest of Koron and Navarino and Chesma. Later he was promoted to the ranks of major general of brigadiers 1772, to general of naval artillery, 1776 and appointed a member of the Admiralty College in 1777. It has been stated that General Ivan Hannibal was instructed to build the fortress of Kherson on the Dnieper and was possibly the founder of the city of that name. In 1779, Ivan Hannibal attained the rank of lieutenant general and retired in 1784. He died in St. Petersburg in 1801. Abram Hannibal's sons Peter and Osip served in the Russian military. Osip's daughter Nacdezhda and her husband Pushkin were the parents of Russia's greatest poet, Alexander Pushkin.

The interesting life and times of Abram Hannibal are most significant in the present day curriculum of students because all the stereotypes of people of African descent whether mixed or non mixed could be revisited for their ignorance and replaced with the truth of a people's omitted history.

I believe that it is time for the honorable scholarly revisionist historians and textbook authors to rewrite and include some missing pages about another view of Peter the Great's life, especially Russia and his views on the world famous subject slavery and people of black skin and, of course, the various shades of color.

The young, middle age and senior students of a general education should know that during the enlightment era, the following reforms and suggestions were initiated during the reign of Peter the Great. Some of Peter the Great's reforms did abolish slavery by removing differences between serfdom and slavery. It is possible that the Russians had no major interests in the importation of many slaves to Russia, but were interested in the slave trade in order to obtain some black servants for the royalty and nobility.

In 1818 the Russian government made some proposals to consider the formation of an international court and establish a naval force to really enforce the ban against slavery (1807). Also as early as 1790, Russian people were discussing the pros and cons of slavery.

Black Presence

I sincerely realize that many foreigners over the centuries have studied and learned more about the black presence in world history to include the American black than the children and adults of our so called multiracial color blind society in America the Beautiful.

AMERICAN REVOLUTION

In 1775 a nation was emerging. The citizens of the Massachusetts colony were settling a course for a war that would decide the fate of a nation. Among those concerned citizens was Crispus Attucks, a black man who gave his life for his beliefs. Once the colonies decided to rebel against the oppressive rule of England, many black men joined the militia. They appeared in the handsome uniform of the colonial forces and their names were officially entered on the mister roles. The southern colonies, Virginia, North and South Carolina, Maryland and Georgia were well represented by black soldiers, sailors, drummers and fifers, but all as loyal Americans. The following discussion include some facts that are found in the records and are presented here as a reminder that American blacks were a part of that glorious "spirit of 76".

National and State Policies

Upon assumption of command of the Continental Army, George Washington issued an order dated July 10, 1775, instructing recruiting officers not to enlist blacks but let those currently in the service remain until the end of their enlistment. This general policy was reinforced in November 1775, when General Washington issued an order, dated 12 November 1775 instructing that Negroes and boys were unable to bear arms and old men were not to be enlisted. Many states issued similar policies with references to slaves and freemen.

The Commonwealth of Virginia's General Assembly in 1777 enacted a law that stated recruiting officers would not enlist any black or mulatto until they could present a certificate to prove that they were free men.

General George Washington's policy to exclude blacks from military enlistment was changed when he learned that John Murray, 4th Earl of Dunmore, Royal Governor of Virginia issued a proclamation on November 7, 1775, offering freedom to all slaves who would join the British forces. The news did not reach General Washington until December. After reassessing the situation, Washington wrote to John Hancock, President of Congress, "It has been presented to me, that free Negroes, who have served in this army, are very much dissatisfied at being discarded. As it is to be apprehended that they may seek employ in the Ministerial Army, I have presumed to depart from the resolution respecting them, and have given license for their being enlisted. If this is disapproved of by the Congress, I will put a stop to it." The Congress did not disapprove.

This sudden, strategic, and military policy change by General Washington did provide a nucleus for those states who were enlisting blacks to continue and to enable those states who were excluding blacks to consider their military employment.

Historians have estimated that some 5,000 blacks served in the military during the Revolutionary War. Blacks served in integrated units and some served during the interim period of the active black units. One was from Massachusetts, recruited in Boston and called the "Massoit Guards," and another called the "Bucks of America"; one Connecticut Company called the "Attucks Company"; and the "Rhode Island Black Regiment," Christopher Greene's regiment.

Legal Authorizations for Revolutionary War Pensions

During the Revolutionary War period 1775-1783-blacks had served in the military service as enrolles anticipating freedom at the expiration of enlistment, runaways, persons owned or hired by the government and as substitutes for their masters. At the conclusion of the war, many of these blacks were eligible for pensions and bounty, land. The states of Massachusetts, Connecticut, New Hampshire, New York, New Jersey, Maine, Vermont, and Virginia, implemented Congressional Pension Acts of 1818, 1820 and 1832.

Black Presence

The Commonwealth of Virginia, as an example, paid their recruits in money, in land bounties and pensions. In Virginia, the amount of land granted to a veteran was from one hundred acres for a private to fifteen thousand acres for a Major General. Virginia also provided for the manumission of some slaves who fought in the war.

The veteran's heirs were eligible to claim land or pensions upon the death of the veteran. Many widows in various states applied for pensions and bounty land as evidenced in the pension files. Sons, daughters and cousins were also granted pensions and land when they could prove the actual service of their relatives. The common allowance of pension for most Virginia soldiers and sailors was ninety-six dollars a year.

In order for a veteran or his family member to establish eligibility for the pension, it was necessary that depositions be made in a county or city court and that sworn statements be submitted by individuals who knew of the veteran's service and could also attest to the pensioner's moral character and standing in the local community.

A brief analysis of the pension papers of Prince Hazeltine and Benjamin Simmons will reveal some of the intricate administrative procedures that were required before a veteran could receive a pension.

Prince Hazeltine enlisted in Captain Isaac Warren's and Captain James Means' companies in Colonel Bailey's and Colonel Sprout's 2nd Massachusetts, Regiment. This statement had to be verified: On 22 June 1820 Prince Hazeltine, who was 63 and residing in Upton, Worcester County, appeared in Open Court, Circuit Court of Common Pleas, County of Worcester and made a sworn statement. He stated that he had served under Colonels Bailey and Sprout. He also stated that he was a laborer, owned no property, had a broken shoulder, and no family.

Hazeltine's file included depositions from three persons. Ebenezer Cutter stated that he was a soldier in Captain Means' Company in the 2nd Massachusetts Regiment and Prince Hazeltine was a soldier in the same company.

North Carolina had a brigade with 42 Negroes on its roll in 1778 and in 1779, the Assembly promised freedom to all slaves who had enlisted with the knowledge that they would be free. In 1780 and 1781, the state of Maryland passed laws permitting blacks, free and slave, to be enlisted although Georgia and South Carolina refused to allow blacks to enlist, but blacks from these states did serve in the war.

The states of New York, New Jersey, Connecticut, Massachusetts, New Hampshire and Rhode Island were enlisting blacks in integrated units. However, Rhode Island, possibly because of military manpower needs, enacted laws to raise a regiment of slaves in 1778. Professor Lorenzo J. Greene of Lincoln University of Missouri did some research in 1952 on the Black Regiment of Rhode Island in the American Revolution. He approached the study of the regiment by examining the laws and regulations that established the regiment and the state's necessity for utilizing black troops. He stated, "The act itself was inspired by stark necessity. Never had the patriot cause seemed more hopeless than in the winters of 1777-79."

It has been noted that short enlistments of one to three months were the origin of many misfortunes and debts of the Continental Army. Even though the Continental Congress in 1777 requested 3-year enlistments, many persisted in joining for only three months, Greene revealed in his study:

A total of 395,858 men enlisted, yet the maximum strength of the American Army in field never exceeded 35,000 at one time. Had even half of the enlisted men been available regularly, the Americans should easily have overwhelmed the British, for according to a recent military historian, the latter hd no more than 42,000 soldiers in America.

In regard to this information, 5,000 blacks served in the war, approximately 1 black to 60 whites. However, this figure can be misrepresented when consideration is given to the fact that a large number of blacks served long terms in comparison to the short terms of 3-9 months by many white soldiers. A review of 50 pension files indicated that of these 50 black pensioners, they served an average of

Black Presence

4.5 or 5 years during the American Revolution. The implementation of national and state laws did permit some blacks, slave and free, to make contributions along with those of the white patriots in their revolutionary struggles to defend their rights and independence.

Selected Characteristics of Black Pensioner

The required documentation for a pension application during the period 1818-1855 has been a significant contribution to historical reinterpretations and the rewriting of American history. The correspondence in these pension papers have provided documentary evidence that is essential in restructuring the events of the Revolutionary War period - a post war era.

Historians have made significant efforts to research the black military participation in the American Revolution. As early as 1855, a black author, William C. Nell wrote *The Colored Patriots of the American Revolution.* This book discussed many aspects of black military presence during the war. However there was a statement in his book concerning the heroine of the revolution, Deborah Sampson Gannett who dressed as a man and served during the war. During the past 129 years some historians and authors have assumed that Deborah Gannett was a black heroine. However a thorough examination of Deborah Gannett's pension file and the file of her brother supports the views of some historians that Deborah Gannett was not black.

In 1863, Henry Carey wrote a print on "General Washington and General Jackson on Negro Soldiers."

In 1947, historian Herbert Aptheker published a booklet, "The Negro in the American Revolution." The booklet was a repetition of some frequently mentioned black heroes of the American Revolution. Aptheker's research was based primarily on secondary sources.

Professor John Hope Franklin's *From Slavery to Freedom* includes a representative coverage of events of black military participation in the Revolution. Franklin's book refers to Crispus Attucks, Peter Salem, Prince

Hall, and General George Washington's reversals on the employment of blacks in the military service, and black participation in the naval service. However, Professor Franklin doubts the authenticity of Peter Salem's bravery.

The National Association for the Advancement of Colored People (NAACP) published a booklet, possibly in the 1970's "Black Heroes of the American Revolution, 1775-1783." The booklet mentioned the names of popular black participants such as Lemuel Haynes, Seymour Burr, Joseph Ranger and William Flora.

The Smithsonian Institution and the New York Graphic Society, with the editorial assistance of Sidney Kaplan have produced an outstanding manuscript on *The Black Presence in the Era of the American Revolution.* Kaplan mentions the well known black military participants. This publication has made a unique effort to fill some of the voids and mythical presentations of black military history.

Professor Benjamin Quarles has produced probably the best recommended and scholarly source on blacks in the American Revolution. The book includes many names of black participants during the War. Quarles explained his procedure of selecting a name as a black participant when he wrote: "Only when the source specifically states it or when the source is referring only to Negroes, I make only one assumption: If the first or last name of a person was Negro, he was not likely to be white and although there are certain names largely confined to Negroes, I have not assumed that persons with such names were necessarily colored.

In view of the outstanding research that has been accomplished concerning blacks in the military experience during the Revolution, there is a definite need to examine the common man, slave or free who served in the Revolution. Therefore the primary intent of this book is to address the military and civilian profiles of the black soldier and sailor who served during the war years. The term black pensioner has been used because it is through the documents in the pension files that an authenticated portrayal of selective characteristic life styles of Black Americans 200 years ago can be recaptured and placed within the needed paragraphs of

Black Presence 143

reinterpreted and factual events of the black military and civilian experiences during the period 1775-1855. These dates are used because some widows and other relatives filed for the pension benefits as late as 1853.

An analysis of the "Military Profile-Unit Assigned" has indicated that the selected black pensioners represented ten states and sixteen had applied for pensions from Rhode Island. This number could have been due to the presence of Colonel Christopher Greene's Black Regiment of former slaves. An Army Service Forces Manual has mentioned that South Carolina, North Carolina and Virginia had Negroes fighting in the Revolution at Charleston and Savannah, and that some of these soldiers received ants of freedom and land bounties or pensions as rewards for their service.

Therefore, it is interesting to observe that with the large slave population in the South during the Revolutionary War, there was at least the presence of one known black in the distinctive southern regiments. North Carolina had 6 regiments; South Carolina had 1 regiment; Maryland had 5 regiments; Virginia had 13 regiments.

A thorough perusal of the units in which blacks were present has revealed that the military occupation of some black soldiers was as musician, namely "fifer" and "drummers." The names of Scipio Brown, Nace Butler, Richard Cozzens, Cato Fisk, Francis Herd, and Barzellai Lew are significant and have played a role in revolutionary events.

During the period 1969-1970, the Third United States Infantry Battalion commonly referred to as "The Old Guard," stationed at Fort Myer, Virginia did not have any known blacks assigned to their colonial "Fife and Drum Corps." It was during a conversation between the commanding officer of the infantry battalion and a staff officer assigned to the Office of the Assistant Chief of Staff for Intelligence, Headquarters, Military District of Washington (MDW) that this fact was discussed with positive intentions to consider qualified black soldiers who desired to volunteer for assignment in the prestigious "Fife and Drum Corps."

It was learned that a senior civilian employed by MDW in the Office for the Special Ceremonies and Events, had made an earlier decision that blacks could not be accepted for assignment to the "Fife and Drum Corps" because their presence in the regalia of the Revolutionary War period would not reflect the reenactment of the colonial period and tradition because "Blacks did not serve the colonial forces as fifers and drummers." This decision or opinion by a civilian government employee who was responsible for the supervision and maintenance of plans and operations for White House Medal of Honor Ceremonies and burial activities of past Presidents had been accepted by commanding generals and battalion commanders in MDW prior to 1969-70.

The concerned interest and initiatives of the commanding officer of the U.S. Third Infantry Battalion, Fort Myer, and historical facts provided by the staff officer from MDW prompted the battalion's unit historian to research selected pension files in the National Archives to confirm preliminary information received that would counteract the alleged facts stated by the MDV ceremonial civilian staff member.

The efforts of the commanding officer of the battalion resulted in a detailed letter signed by him forwarded to the commanding general, MDW, with recommendations that in view of currently known and documented facts that blacks did serve in military assignments as fifer and drummers during the Revolutionary War in the Continental and State Militia forces, and that consideration be given to interview qualified blacks for vacant positions in the Fife and Drum Corp.

Military Profile - Combat Wounds

Black Pensioners That Received Combat Wounds

1. *William Anderson* - received broken arm and severe wound in left thigh.

2. *Thomas Camel* - was quite fatigued and very sick at Battle of Monmouth.

Black Presence 145

3. *Primus Coburn* - slight wound in leg.

4. *George Dias* - wounded at Elizabethtown, New Jersey.

5. *Prince Easterbrooks* - wounded at Lexington.

6. *Andrew Ferguson* - received head wounds and wounded in leg at Camden.

7. *Francis Freeman* - In 1820 he stated that he was afflicted with severe pain from the wound he received during the war.

8. *Robert Green* - was wounded in the face by a (musket) ball.

9. *Jamaica James* - received wound in his left arm from a musket ball.

10. *Jabez Jolly* - wounded in June 1780.

11. *Ambrose Lewis* - severely wounded at the Battle of Camden. Lewis received a musket ball through his thigh and bayonet thrusts in different parts of his limbs and body.

12. *Thomas Lively* - lost his right eye at Monmouth and was wounded in the leg in another battle.

13. *Luke Nickelson* - wounded in thigh by a musket ball at surrender of General Burgoyne.

14. *Record Primes* - wounded in the head at Camden.

15. *Richard Rhodes* - received wound in arm by musket ball.

16. *Prince Robinson* - stated that he was lame in lower limbs and blind in one eye from wounds received in the war.

17. *Caesar Shelton* - wounded in the back by a sword thrust and on the shin by a musket ball.

18. *Cuff Slade* - feet were frozen while in service.

19. *Mathew Williams* - wounded in knee by musket ball.

20. *Cato Wood* - discharged in 1779 as a casualty.

Military Profile - Prisoners of War

Black Pensioners Captured as Prisoners of War

1. *Thomas Buckner* - Prisoner at Charleston, South Carolina, for approximately 18 months. Later was shipped to Jamestown, Virginia, and exchanged as a prisoner.

2. *Ison Carter* - Prisoner of war at fall of Charleston to British.

3. *George Dias* - Prisoner at Elizabethtown, New Jersey, and was successful in escaping the same night from the enemy.

4. *Andrew Ferguson* - Was taken prisoner by British and ran away from them to join other Americans who were attached to General Greene's troops.

5. *Ephraim Hearn* - Taken prisoner by British in Charleston for nine months and was carried to New York by the British.

6. *Ambrose Lewis* - Was taken prisoner and confined until the end of the war.

7. *Thomas Lively* - Taken prisoner for fourteen months.

8. *Isaac Perkins* - Taken prisoner at Charleston, S.C. He successfully escaped and returned to North Carolina.

Black Presence

9. *Cuff Whitemore* - Prisoner at the time of General Burgoyne's surrender. He was ordered to take care of the horses and seized the opportunity and made his escape.

Civilian Profile - Civil Status

1. *Jack Anthony* - was a slave for life. He served as a substitute for his master, Eli Dibble, and his son.

2. *Thomas Camel* - "At the time I enlisted I was a slave to Colonel Martin Picket of Virginia who gave me my choice either to remain a slave as I was or go into the artillery with him."

3. *Isom Carter* - "My wife and children are slaves and have no one to support (them)."

4. *Peter Foster* - former slave.

5. *Cato Freedom* - was African by birth and obtained freedom by serving in the Revolutionary War.

6. *Cato Greene* - Was born in Guinea and brought to America and sold as a slave. Greene received his freedom because of his military service.

7. *London Hazard* - was a slave prior to the Revolutionary War.

8. *Titus Kent* - slave of Samuel Kent.

9. *Pomp Liberty* - was a slave when he entered the military service.

10. *Sharp Liberty* - correspondence in his pension application stated that "as the commencement of war, was held as a slave but because of faithful service through the war was emancipated."

11. *Dan Mallory* - was born in Africa and at the age of 5 years was brought to America. He arrived at Saybrook, Connecticut and was sold to a George Stillman of Middletown, Connecticut. He was also sold to Stephen Beck width of Colchester, Connecticut and Aaron Mallory of Woodbury, Litch field County, Connecticut.

12. *Roorback Marlin* - was a slave prior to the Revolutionary War.

13. *Richard Rhodes* - was a slave prior to the Revolutionary War.

14. *Prince Robinson* - was born in Africa and was sold as a slave prior the Revolutionary War.

15. *Caesar Shelton* - correspondence in his pension file stated that "Colored man born at sea while his mother was being brought from Africa. He was a slave of John Shelton of Stratford, Connecticut." Shelton enlisted on the condition that he would receive his freedom. He entered as a substitute for his master's son.

16. *Henry Tabor* - was born in Africa and brought to America at the time of the Revolutionary War. He was the property of Judge Constant Tabor of Newport, Rhode Island.

Civil Profile - The Black Pensioner's Family

1. *Nace Butler* - Correspondence in his pension file states that "When he returned to the neighborhood of his native place he brought with him an Irish woman who he represented as his wife." His wife was Mary Butler, and on 30 July 1840 a Charles Butler requested pension claim for his aunt Mary Butler.

2. *Obed Coffin* - Wife, Violet, 60 years of age, 1820. Their children were Alvin Coffin, born December 2, 1787, and Jeremiah Coffin, born July 4, 1794.

3. *Joshua Dunbar* - Married Lydie Dunbar of Connington, Massachusetts Children born were:

Black Presence

```
"John      born    January 2, 1778
Polly      "       December 4, 1791
Noah       "       June 15, 1795
Ephraim    "       March 7, 1797
Jacob      "       December 27, 1799
Lydia      "       December 9, 1801
Joshua Jr. "       October 1, 1803
Stephen    "       January 1, 1805
```

4. *Prince Duplex* - Married Lament Parker, February 20, 1782. The minister who performed the marriage was Alexander Gillet of a Congregation Church. Prince Duplex and his wife had 4 children: Vashti E. Creed, Arsenio Duplex, George Duplex and Craty Peterson. On 8 March 1855, Vashti Creed signed a statement appointing Charles Robinson, New Haven, the power of attorney to prosecute claim due her mother.

5. *Peter Foster* - Wife's name was Tammy. They had 5 sons and 5 daughters. Some were born before, during and after the war. All of the children were deceased in 1837 except Peter and Chloe. There was one daughter named Sabra and a son named Peter Foster, Jr. who were born in Glastonburg, Connecticut.

6. *Cato Freedom* - had a wife and two children, Charlotte, 15 years old and Aurelia, 13 (weak and sickly).

7. *Call Freeman* - was married to Candis Freeman, their children were Lomans, Cyrus, Mary, Phome and Cynthia, a sick child who was support by town of Sharon.

8. *Chatham Freeman* - wife's name was Maria.

9. *Doss Freeman* - married Sarah Davis, November 14, 1788.

10. *Fortune Freeman* - had one child, Mary who was bound out to service.

11. *Prince Freeman* - had two children, Avis and Prince.

12. *Peter Galloway* - wife's name was Nancy.

13. *Sharper Gardner* - had two sons, Robin and London and one daughter, Patience.

American Revolutionary Navy Veterans

Name	Unit	State
1. Nathaniel Anderson	Virginia	
2. Cato Austin	Frigate	Boston, Massachusetts
3. David Baker	Seaman	Virginia
4. Stephen Bond	Schooner Defence	South Carolina
5. Stephen Bowles		Virginia
6. John Bristol	Armed Boat Franklin	Pennsylvania
7. Scipio Brown	Boston, Navy	Massachusetts
8. William Bush	State Boat Liberty	Virginia
9. Francis Carter	Seaman	Virginia
10. James Causey	Seaman	Virginia
11. Quako Chadwick	Continental Sloop Fire	Pennsylvania
12. George Cooper	Schooner Defence	South Carolina
13. George Day	Seaman	Virginia
14. John De Baptist	Dragon	
15. John Driver	Seaman	Virginia
16. Pompey Effery	Ship Columbus	

"Negro boy died at sea, September 13, 1776."

17. Caesar Fairweather	Frigate-Powder Boy	Boston, Massachusetts
18. James Forten	Royal Louis-Powder Boy	
19. Cuff Freeman	Frigate	Boston
20. John Fyds	Boston Seaman	
21. Samuel George	Liberty	
22. Peter Haws	Seaman	Virginia
23. William Haws	Seaman	Virginia
24. Lewis Hinton	Dragon	Virginia
25. John (Jack) Jones	Continental Sloop	
26. Phillip Wood	Seaman	Virginia
27. Thomas Wood	Seaman	Virginia

"Providence, November 1776, Landsman Jones deserted in August 1776." The newspaper advertisement read "Five pounds reward. Run away from the subscriber living in the borough of Chester, in the beginning of August last. A mulatto man named Jack Jones, upwards of 24 years of age, a cooper by trade, about 5 feet 7 inches high, wears his hair tied in a cue behind, has a hobbling gait when he walks, occasioned by the rheumatism formerly in the hips. This country born, speaks good English, can read, and write a tolerable hand and can play pretty well on a fife, is a sly, smooth tongued fellow, and may probably forge a pass, and pretend to be a freeman. He went on board the Providence privateer, commanded by Captain John Paul Jones, when she lay opposite Chester. . . . On 19 August 1776," John Jones was turned over to the Prize Brig Britannia August 27, 1776.

MUSICIANS

Name	Instrument	State
1. Cesar Black	Drummer	South Carolina
2. Cato Brown	Fifer	Rhode Island
3. Scipio Brown	Drummer	Rhode Island
4. Sipio Brown	Drummer	Rhode Island
5. Nace Butler	Fifer	Maryland
6. Sharpe Champlin	Drummer	Rhode Island
7. Richard Cozzens	Fifer	Rhode Island
8. Prince Downe	Fifer	Massachusetts
9. Cuff Gardner	Fifer	Rhode Island
10. Pomp Jackson	Fifer	Massachusetts
11. Prince Jenks	Drummer	Rhode Island
12. Jabez Jolly	Drummer	Massachusetts
13. Barzillai Lew	Fifer	Massachusetts
14. Cato Moulton	Fifer	New Hampshire

Name	Instrument	State
15. Cato Moulton	Drummer	New York
16. William Nickens	Fifer	Virginia
17. James Northrup	Fifer	
18. Nimrod Perkins	Drummer	Virginia

19. Polydore Redman	Drummer	Pennsylvania
20. Cato Shadrack	Fifer	Massachusetts
21. Cato Shattuck	Drummer	Massachusetts

For further reading, see *Black Courage 1775 - 1783.*

FRENCH REVOLUTION

Jacobins and Reign of Terror

During the era of the French Revolution, there was an organized party in Paris called the Jacobin Club in 1793. France was confronting foreign enemies except Russia. There were some peasants in the west of France who were conducting guerilla war. The Jacobins had to create a new revolutionary tribunal in Paris with an official policy the Reign of Terror which had one sentence, death and verdict guilty. The twelve members of the tribunal used dictatorial power. The peasants of Vendee revolted against national conscription and opposed the national constitution. The Jacobins ruled for one year. Some of their accomplishments were: organized national defense, guaranteed rights to a public education for all and the right of public welfare for the poor. The Jacobins established price controls, divided confiscated property among the poor.

In June 1793, some concerned Frenchmen and free blacks requested emancipation of the slaves. The jacobin convention agreed to the abolition of slavery. However, this was a temporary measure because when Napoleon became First Consul, he restored slavery in the French colonies and forbid interracial marriages.

The Black Presence during the French Revolution and Napoleonic Era.

Some historians have written about instances and events that support the early presence of people of color in eighteenth century France. There

Black Presence

were some black servants who worked for the French bourgeois class and wore fancy uniforms or dress. During the revolutionary era, there was a school in France for Negroes. Black rulers in Africa would send their sons to Paris to obtain an education. Toussaint L'Ouverture of Haiti sent his sons Isaac and Placido to Paris for an education.

Alexandre Davy Dumas and Napoleon I

Alexandre Davy de la Pailleterie was born on March 25, 1762 at Jermie, Saint Domingue, West Indies. He was the son of Marie Cessette Dumas, a Haitian lady and Le Marquis Alexandre de la Pailleterie, a wealthy French colonel and plantation owner. His mother was a slave woman. Alexandre was named Thomas Alexandre Davy de la Pailleterie at birth. He later changed his name to Dumas, his mother's maiden name. Alexandre lived in the West Indies for eight years after his mother's death. He was eighteen years old when his mother died. Dumas was educated in Bordeaux, France. He learned the art of dueling and once won three duels in a day. When his father decided to remarry, he enlisted in the French army against his father's wishes.

Alexandre Davy Dumas enlisted as a common soldier and was promoted very quickly through the ranks and eventually became a commissioned officer. He experienced a spectacular and heroic military career. Private Dumas was assigned to the Queens' Dragons. He was involved in a battle where he was trapped and after opposing thirteen enemy troops, he was able to force their surrender. Later he was promoted to the rank of Sergeant major for bravery. When he was promoted to second lieutenant, he was assigned to the Black Legion regiment West Indian Troops organized by the distinguished musician and composer, Joseph Boulogne Chevalier Saint George. The unit was formerly known as the Corps of Lechevalier St. Georges. After receiving a promotion to Lieutenant Colonel, Dumas decided to marry the daughter of a hotel owner and a National Guard Commander.

Dumas's wife was named Marie Louise Elizabeth Labouret and they were the parents of a son, Alexander Dumas.

Alexandre Davy Dumas elevation to responsible high rank was incredible. He was promoted to brigadier general and within a few months became the commanding general of four difference armies, the Army of the North, Army of the Western Pyrene, Army of the West and the Army of the Alps. The official order for his appointment as commanding general of the Army of the West read:

> *Military orders appointed Commanding General of the Arm of the West By the Order of Robespierre.*
>
> *The committee of Public Safety Decrees.*
> *Signed In the Records*
>
> *Robespierre*

The French army was having difficulties in conquering Mount Cenes in the Alps, Dumas was given the task to conquer the mountain. His detailed tactical strategies included, observing and studying the terrain of his major objective for five days, and considering the enemy's occupation of three sides of the mountain and with many heavy weapons. Dumas and his troops were forced to retreat three times, later they were successful in occupying Little Bernard and then three hundred of his men were able to climb Mt. Cenis and overpowered the enemy and claimed victory upon their conquest of Mt. Cenis. This outstanding military conquest made Dumas a national hero. The National Convention issued a special bulletin stating that *glory to the conquerors of Mt. Cenis and Mt. St. Bernard, glory to the invincible army of the Alps and those who have led them to victory. We do not know how to describe to you Dear Comrades the enthusiasm that has been created by your brilliant feat of arms. We rely upon the energy and genius of General Dumas.*

There was a situation where Dumas and his men were in serious need for fire wood to keep warm on a very cold day. General Dumas had observed some men waiting to be executed because they did not melt their church bells into bullets for the revolutionary war effort. He decided to order the men to be released and then use the guillotine for firewood. The French government ordered Dumas to Paris to face charges of using a village guillotine for firewood. He was supported by the common people for his actions and was acquitted of all charges. He was then assigned to the army of the Sambre et Meuse.

Dumas resigned from the military on October 4, 1795. Later the Directory recalled him to suppress a riot. When he was late in arriving at the location, a young captain was present and had successfully controlled the crowd. The captain was Napoleon Bonaparte I. A year later, October 14, 1796, Dumas was assigned to the area of Milan, Italy and was stationed at Mantua under the command of a promising general officer, Napoleon Bonaparte I. When Dumas was confronting the forces of General Clausen in Austria at Tyrol, he had to defend the Clausen Bridge alone until some of his men arrived and assisted him. This heroic event occurred during the battle of Brixen. When Napoleon heard of General Dumas unusual brave deeds, he called him Horatius Cocles du Tyrol. (A Roman legend states that Horatius Cocles saved Rome by defending a bridge over the Tiber River against an invading Army).

Dumas was receiving medals and commendations for his military performances, however, he also experienced some criticisms and counselling from Napoleon I. When Dumas was participating in a battle area on January 16, 1797, one of Napoleon's favorite major general's of the Grand Army accursed Dumas of not participating in the battle but just observing, Napoleon Bonaparte I ordered Dumas to command a cavalry unit in Tyrol under General Joubert. Dumas was given half of the command and was victorious at the battle of Burk and in 1798 he received orders for Alexandria, Egypt.

Napoleon Bonaparte I was promoted commander in chief of the French Army and had plans to attack Egypt, the colonial empire of Great Britain. General Dumas had some personal concerns about Napoleon's ambitions. However, after assuming the command of the cavalry in Egypt, he participated in the battle of Aboukir, August 1, 1798. When an uprising occurred in Cairo, Egypt, Dumas was able to stop the insurrection.

General Dumas demonstrated his honesty and loyalty when he found an equivalent of two million dollars in the abandon home of a Mameluke chief Bey. The owner had left behind the money when he was fleeing from Napoleon's troops. Dumas wrote a letter to Napoleon Bonaparte and said, *The Leopard never changes its spots nor character and principles. As an honest man, I owe only to you the confidence that I am going to make.* Dumas told Napoleon about the money that was found in the Bey's house

General Dumas wanted to return to France and Napoleon granted him his wish. Unfortunately, while enroute to France his ship was captured by the enemy and Dumas was taken to Tarente and imprisoned for two years. Attempts were made to poison Dumas in prison. When released from prison, Dumas' physical condition had deteriorated. He was lame, deaf in one ear, partially blind, paralyzed and had stomach problems. When Napoleon I became Emperor of France in 1805, he ignored Dumas requests for a pension. General Dumas died at the age of 42 years.

I have read and studied some interesting stories about the French Revolution, however the black presence has been ignored by many scholars and even today this information is possibly not available in many institutions of higher learning in the United States.

Toussaint L'Ouverture and French Revolution

Many people know the story about Christopher Columbus sighting the Island of Hispaniola in 1492, but few people have actually heard of the Island's liberator, Toussaint L'Ouverture. In 1697, the French occupied the western part of the island. Spain had signed the Treaty of Ryswick which recognized French Sovereignty over the western section of the island (present day recognized as France's richest commercial colony. In 1791, a Haitian leader, Toussaint L'Ouverture was influenced by the May Decree of 1791, the Declaration of the Rights and Man. An insurrection occurred in 1791 with some 40,000 whites, 50,000 mulattoes, 500,000 and black slaves. The National Constituent Assembly of France had passed the Declaration of the Rights of Man in 1789 and the decree of May 15, 1791 which granted political equality to the Haitian mulattoes. These acts caused some problems in Haiti.

Black Presence 157

In August 1791, some slave rebelled against their masters. Many mulattoes joined the blacks and some Royalists and mulattoes formed an alliance against the whites. There were some mulattoes, blacks and whites killing each other and plantations were distraught by the slaves. The Royalist and wealthy planters were forced to leave Haiti.

Toussaint was able to have some slaves leave their masters and join his insurgent group. He used his personal funds some 648,000 francs for the insurrections. The rebel leaders, Biassou and Jean Francois believed Toussaint should provide his services as a physician and assume command of some troops.

On April 4. 1792, the Jacobins were in control of the Paris government. The legislative assembly declared that all free Negroes and mulattoes of Haiti should have equal political rights as whites. France tried to enforce the law by sending a Jacobin commission and six thousand troops to Haiti. Toussaint realized that this law did not apply to black Haitians. even though the Jacobin commission tried to prevent riots between whites and mulattoes, they offered freedom to all slaves who joined the French in order to maintain peace. Toussaint and his soldiers opposed the law of 1792, and asked most blacks to refuse military service with the French.

During the period 1793-1794, England and Spain invaded Haiti. The British were in control of Port-au-Prince, they had been invited by the mulattoes and whites to intervene in Toussaint and rebel leader's slave insurrection by opposing them and restoring the plantation and cast systems in Haiti. Toussaint had made a previous alliance with Spanish Santo Domingo to fight the French. However, when he learned of England's plan to enslave Haitians, he severed his military alliance with Spain. Toussaint was successful in suppressing some Spanish troops and led some 4000 trained Haitian soldiers back to Haiti. Eventually the Spanish troops were defeated in Northern Haiti by Toussaint's forces and also the French troops in Haiti. The Treaty of Bales was signed by the Spanish in 1795 and ceded Santo Domingo to France. In 1798, England signed a treaty with Toussaint and withdrew their troops from Haiti. It has been said that yellow fever also contributed to England's defeat. The

British had some early plans to abduct Toussaint's sons who were studying in Paris, France, their efforts failed.

It has been written that Napoleon I had sent agents to Haiti to prepare for the overthrow of Toussaint. Between 1799-1800, the mulatto French military governor Rigoud was guilty of negotiating with French agents against Toussaint. Rigoud was not successful.

On January 26, 1801, Toussaint L'Overture and his generals, Dessaline and Christophe were able to gain control of the island from the French. However, Toussaint had captured Santo Domingo, and Hispaniola, the Western part of the island was ruled by Dessalines and the northern section by another leader. It was necessary for Toussaint to utilize the services of some educated mulattoes and wealthy planters, to hold public offices as judges and administrators.

Toussaint had an assembly of six men to draft a constitution. The constitution was proclaimed on July 7, 1801. The constitution made Toussaint ruler for life and the right to select his successor. The official religion was catholicism, slavery was abolished, but the slave trade was encouraged in order to obtain agricultural workers for the plantations. Toussaint sent a copy of the constitution to the Consul of Republic of France, Napoleon I. Toussaint was concerned about a possible invasion of the island by Napoleon I. He decided to make war preparations by taxing the planters.

In 1801, Napoleon prepared an expeditionary force for an invasion of Haiti in order to destroy Toussaint's power and restore French rule. General Napoleon selected General Charles Victor Emanuel Leclerc as commander of the French forces. Leclerc was married to Napoleon's sister, Pauline Bonaparte. Toussaint had a military force of 20,000 soldiers under the leadership of Christophe. The French were in control of Fort Dauphin, Le Cap and Port-au-Prince.

There was disunity among Toussaint and his generals. In April 1802, General Christophe surrendered 1200 soldiers and weapons to General Leclerc against Toussaint's orders. General Dessalines made arrangements to surrender his troops to the French commander. The surrender of their forces to the French by Toussaint's generals affected the resistance movement in Haiti. On May 6, 1802, Toussaint retired to his plantation in Ennery. General Leclerc disarmed the blacks and some continued to resist the French. Leclerc had instructions to arrest Toussaint. A General Brunet was able to have his troops to apprehend Toussaint and had him imprisoned at Fort de Jeux near the Swiss frontier. Toussaint's family was sent to Bayonne.

Napoleon I had his government pass a decree which deprived the mulattoes of their rights and restored slavery in Haiti. These actions by Napoleon caused some blacks and mulattoes to unite against French oppression. When General Rochambeau was appointed commander of French troops in Haiti, he confronted a strong resistance by the Haitians. The commander in chief of the Haitian army, General Dessalines was able to expel the French from Haiti. They were assisted by a British blockade.

Although Toussaint L'Overture had died in prison in April 1803, his dreams were fulfilled on January 1, 1804 when General Dessalines renounced allegiance to France and declared full independence of Haiti.

ROMANTICISM

Alexandre Dumas II

Alexandre Dumas II was born July 24, 1803, in Villers-Cotterets sur Aisne in France. He used the family name Dumas of his deceased grandmother, Louise Cosette Dumas. He was left destitue by his father. A priest assisted him in receiving an education. Later, he served as a clerk in a law office. When he was 20 years old, he went to Paris and worked as a shipping clerk. The Duke of New Orleans became intersted in him and gave him some assistance.

Dumas became the father of a son who was named, Alexandre Dumas III or Fils. Dumas enrolled in an evening school and completed courses in physics, chemistry and physiology and was taught by a physician, language and literature. He became interested in the theatre and drama.

Some of Dumas' writings were, *Henry III, The Forty-Five, The Viscount of Brageloane, Lady of Monsereau, The Black Tulip, Twenty Years Ago, Christine, Anthony, the Man In the Iron Mask, The Corsican Brothers* and the popular and worldwide writings *the Three Musketeers, and the Count of Monte Crisco*. In 1996, I read an article in a local newspaper about Alexandre Dumas. The author said, "everyone knows the *Three Musketeers.* Hollywood does a remake of the classic every twenty years or more. But how many Americans are acquainted with the sequel to *The Vicomte de Bragelonne*, a novel. *The Three Musketeers* is a worldwide best seller since its first print in 1845 and known as the *Four Inseparables*, published in a children's version. The journalist also said that Dumas made bountiful and creative use of history using his fictional characters with historic persons and not events. He was able to intervene fact and fiction. When remarking about the *Vicomte de Bragelonne*, the critic said the book was about the early years of the reign of the Sun King Louis XIV. Dumas portrayed vivid descriptions. He had a singular gift for creating intense visual scenes long before the advent of motion pictures. Dumas had a film's director eyes.

Alexander Dumas is a renowned author of color. A popular university world history textbook shows Dumas sitting in a chair with other writers present to include George Sands, Rossi, Lizt, Victor Hugo and Paganani. It is quite possible that the readers have no idea that the talented Dumas was a man who had African ancestry and would be categorized in America today as a biracial, mixed person with one drop of black blood and is black or Negro.

It is fortunate that genuis writings of Dumas could serve as an image motivator for many black youngsters who are experiencing low concept characteristics when it comes to expressing themselves in writing. Dumas probably lived an died as a Frenchman and color could make no difference to him.

Alexandre Dumas III was the son of Dumas II and a seamtress, Marie Laboy. He was born on July 17, 1824, in Paris. He became interestd in social reforms, writing and drama. Dumas wrote poetry, and novels. He was interested in the poor. Some of his works were, *Camille, La Dame Auf, Diana de Lys, Le Domimon de, Le Quetion d'Argent, Le Fils Naturel, Le Pere Prodique Les Idees de Madame Le Princess Georges, L'Etrangere, Denis, and Francillon.* His writings showed a strong concern with social and psychological problems. Dumas also wrote four volumes of essays called *Entre Actes*. He was a superb romantic novelist and playwright. Alexandre Dumas III built his own theater in France. He was honored by many admirers of his works. He built a palace estate and called it the Monte Cristo. He wrote the opera, *La Traviata and Camille*. Dumas was elected to the membership in the French Academy and later president of the group. In Paris, France, there are three statutes honoring his grandfather, Thomas Alexandre Dumas, his father Alexandre Dumas II and himself.

Alexander Pushkin was born in Moscow in 1799. He was the son of Nadezhda Osipovous and Sergey Lvovich Pushkin. His mother was the daughter of Osip Hannibal, the son of Ahram Hannibal, an African. His father was a nobleman during the period of Catherine the Great. As a young child, he was greatly influenced by his nurse, Arina Rodionovna. She helped to develop his imaginative nature by telling him fairy tales, legends and would sing to him the folk songs of Russia. She also along with his grandmother, Maria Alexevna taught him to read and write Russian. He was also instructed by French tutors. He would visit his grandfather's library at nine years of age and became interested in the writings of French authors, Voltaire and Rousseau. He wrote his first poems in French. He was sometimes called Sasha. Pushkin acknowledged his African heritage in his writings and as a youngster, he would visit his Hannibal cousins.

Pushkin studied at the Tsarskoe Selo where he assisted in the editing of a journal that included some of his poems. He also entered government service briefly. He was the first Russian to use the Russian language in literature. The French language had been used previously by the Russians. He would also express openly his condemnation against American slavery. It has been stated that Pushkin was not warmly received in the Russian Court because his wife, Natalya Goncharova had been attracted to Nicholas I. However, those allegations have been disputed by his descendant who said Pushkins and his wife were very much in love and that they were the parents of four children.

A duel occurred in 1837 that could have been precipitated by the rumors of a nobleman named d'Anthes, who was alleged to have had an affair with Pushkin's wife, Natalya, even though he was married to her sister Ekaterina Goncharova. A duel between Pushkin and d'Anthes occurred outside of St. Petersburg and Pushkin was opposing a great duelist who attended a French dueling school. Dueling was prohibited in Russia. Pushkin lost the duel and it is believed that he died later in his apartment on the banks of the Moikal Canal. He was buried in Pskov Provine in the Sviatogora Monastery.

I am including some of Pushkin great writings, poems and plays in detail because I believe that his creative and masterful contributions to Russian literature and the world should be known to all especially our polarized multiracial society in our America the Beautiful. As I have stated previously, whether he lived or died as a white person socially and mentally, that is not a problem. Because when our American Society still judges people by the color of their skin, let us resurrect, the creativity of a man who had African genes that he did not deny.

The following are some of Alexander Pushkin's renowned literature that has been shared with the world. He wrote: *Count Nuin, Pultava, The Little House in Kolomna, Peter the Great, the Negro of the Czar,* (it was not completed) *Captain's Daughter, Russalka (The Russian Lorelei), The Banquet* During the Plague, Mozart and Salieri, The Avaricious Knight, The Bronze Rider, The Fisherman and the Fish, The Golden Cockerel (Russian Fairy Tales), Ruslan and Lyudmila, The prisoner in the Caucasus, Bakhchsaray Fountain, The Gypsies, The Robber Brothers, and Evgeni Oneygin.

Pushkin sometimes used the pen name of Ivan Belkin. He was influenced by the great British writer, Byron and wrote a Byronic poem, "Farewell to the Sea". Pushkin's works depicted romantic tales, ancient city of Kiev, scenic landscape, tales of love and vengeance. He read Shakespeare and Goethe. Alexander Pushkin was a genius in literature and prose and yes, he was present so eloquent in the black presence in world history.

SECOND EMPIRE, AND NAPOLEON BONAPARTE III'S, INTEREST IN WEST AFRICA

President of Second Republic (1808-1873), the Second Republic lasted 3 years. Napoleon III later, dissolved the assembly and was proclaimed Napoleon III in 1851.

Napoleon III increased French influence in Indochina, Tahiti and sent a mission into French West Africa.

Achievements of, Napoleon III were the development of policies consistent with the Industrial Revolution, establish credit for business enterprises, financial aid for railways, shipping companies, reduction in tariffs to stimulate trade, increased in French exports with England, Belgium, Switzerland, Sweden, Italy, Spain, Netherlands, and Prussia. He also initiated a universal exposition of 1859, active social policy, mutual aid societies, government owned pawnshops, and improvements in workers' dwellings. Napoleon III's Foreign Policy included the attainment of Nice and Savoy, conquest of Algeria, treaty rights with China, French interests in Syria and established settlements on the African coasts of Senegal, Dahomey (Benin), Guinea and Madagascar. He also had a French protectorate in Cambodia, 1863. Napoleon III was an advocate of the method of diplomacy by conference and at times he served as a mediator for other countries.

Emperor Napoleon Bonaparte III defeat came when France was involved in the Franco Prussian War July, 1870, Bismarck with German armies entered the country of Alsace and Lorraine. Napoleon III was ill but he went to the command at Metz, France and finally surrendered with 173,000 men to the Germans. This was the end of the Second French Empire. The Treaty of Frankfurt was signed in 1871 and the Germany's army of occupation moved into Alsace Lorraine and France paid an indemnity of 5 billion francs.

Napoleon III rose to power and performed some functions of restoring and then destroying powers of the Empire. He offered France both democracy and order, social welfare and social discipline. He promised universal suffrage to the masses and imperial glory to the army.

After World War I, Germany had to agree for France to receive the country of Alsace Lorraine after some 50 years of German occupation and rule.

Napoleon Bonaparte III should also be remembered for his interest in establishing France as a future Colonial Power and her presence is quite evident in Senegal in 1997.

PARTITION AND DOMINATION OF AFRICA

Twenty-fours years ago, I was a graduate student in a class, "The Negro In the Modern World." My distinguished professor gave us a list of his views on the possible retardation of Africa after its many centuries of outstanding productive communities and the early trade with European countries hundred of years ago. Some of the reasons he suggested were: slavery, slave trade to Arab world through Ethiopia, jungles, no contact with the outside world, timber growth not visible for commercial purpose, no local community participation, climate, very hot near equator, rawfall, the rivers flowing increased the presence of the mosquito, the carrier of malaria and languages, different dialects, people were unable to communicate with others. (Lingua Franca, language made up of several different dialects). In later years the following developments would add to Africa's retrogression at times: imperialism, colonialism, the need for black fodder, African troops were sent into battle knowing that they would be killed. In World War II, use of colonial troops were evident and the larget contingent employed were the Senegalese troops from Senegal.

During the period 1885-1914, the Major European Powers had established a strong hold in Africa and had negotiated with others and determined who would possess and control the territories available for conquest. Over the years, historians have presented the reasons of the various countries why they felt justified in the scramble or rape of Africa.

Black Presence

Some of the reasons were: problems in Europe, need for raw materials, excess population, desire for valuable goods such as ivory, tin, rubber and palm oil, gold and diamonds, gave benefits to backward peoples. There were some Europeans who would say they were justified to occupy some African territory because of economic, cultural and Christian motives and of course, "the white man's burden". The European partition and domination of Africa had a great impact on the countries of Africa. The boundaries of previous empires were expanded or receded, the social and political ideas made impressions and influence African thinking. The Europeans suppressed the African's religion and introduced Christianity. (Consider the fact, that there are at least fourteen black Cardinals of the Catholic church in Africa). The Colonial Powers reformed traditional African institutions. The African countries colonized were: Botswana by the (British) in 1880, Burkina Faso (Upper Volta) (British, 1896, Burundi, (German 1899) and (Belgium), in 1916, Central African Republic (French) late 1800's, former Ubangi-Shari, Chad (French) 1900, Congo (French), 1885, Ivory Coast, (French), mid 1800's, Djbouti, (French), 1862, 1900, Equatorial Guinea, ceded to Spain 1778, Guinea (French), 1848-1898, Lesotho, (British), 1868, Mali, (French), 1885, Malawi (British) 1891 Madagascar (French), 1895, Mauritana, (French), 1903, Mozambique (Portugal), 1505, Namiba (Germany), 1890, Niger (British), 1861, Senegal, 1893 (French), Sierra Leone, (British), 1787, Somali, (Italy), late 1800's, Swaziland, (Britain), 1903, Tanzania (Germany), 1885, Rwanda, (Germany and Belgium) later 1800's, Zambia (South Africa), 1889, South Africa and Zimbabewe, 1800's, Togo, (Germany), 1884 and Uganda (British), 1894.

The Partition of Africa by the European nations have been an enormous asset to their economic gains and even in 1997, some of them are experiencing wealth from their investments over 100 years. I do believe one needs to examine the facts that some were there before. Where are they today in assisting the countries?

PARTITION OF AFRICA

When Africa was divided or partitioned by the European Colonials in the 1800's the competing countries made treaties, conventions and agreements to legally ensure their eventual control through a system called protectorates over the conquered African countries. I believe it is necessary to inform students of world history that the African peoples did not say welcome to our countries because we definitely need your presence. The following treaties represents agreements by respective nations to identify and reaffirm their chosen colonial possessions.

TREATIES BETWEEN GREAT BRITAIN AND OTHER COUNTRIES

Year	Date	Treaty etc.	Country area
1814	May 30	Treaty of Paris	Maurituis
1882	June 28	France	Sierra Leone (not ratified)
1884	Feb. 27	South African	Republic
	Sept. 22	German Empire	South West Africa
1885	May 7	German Empire	Cameroons
1886	July	German Empire	Gold Coast
	Aug. 2	German Empire	Cameroons
	Oct. 29 & Nov. 1	German Empire	East Africa
1887	Nov. 11	France	Somalia Coast
1881	Feb. 1	Somalia and Gold Coast	
	Nov. 11	German Empire	Neutral Zone
	June 20	S. Africa Republic	New Republic ceded
1889	Aug. 10	France	Gambia, Sierra Leone and Guinea
1890 Rey	July 1	German Empire	Gold Coast, Rio Del Southwest & East Africa
	Aug. 2	S. Africa Republic	Little Republic ceded
	Aug. 5	France	Niger territories
	Aug. 20	Portugal	Mozamique (not ratified)
	Sept. 14	Portugal	Modus (Vivendi)
1891	Mar. 14	Italy	Somaliland
	Apr. 15	Italy	Egyptian Sudan
Year	Date	Treaty etc.	Country area
	May 28	Portugal	Mozambique

Black Presence

	Date	Parties	Region
	Apr. 14	Germany Empire	Rio del Ray
	May 13	Portugal	Zambesi
	July 13	France	Gold Coast
	July 25	German Empire	East Africa
1778	Mar. 24	Spain and Portugal	Fernado Po Annabom
1869		Portugal and South	Republic
1884	Nov. 5	Germany and Congo State	
1885	Feb. 5	France and Congo State	
	Aug. 1	Declaration of Neutrality by Congo State	
	Nov. 22	France and Congo State	Lower Congo
	Dec. 24	France and German Empire	
1886	May 12	France and Portugal	
		France and Spain (Shara)	
	Dec. 30	German Empire and Portugal	
1887	Apr. 29	France and Congo State	Ubangi to 4 N
1898		France and Spain	Corsica
1891	May 25	Portugal and Congo State	Lunda
1893	January	France and Congo State	(Project only)
		France and Liberia	
1893	Nov. 12	South Africa Republic	Swaziland
	Nov. 15	German Empire	Benue
1894	Mar. 15	France and Germany	
	Mar. 24	Portugal and Congo State	
	May 5	Italy	Somaliland
	May 12	Congo State	Upper Nile and Congo

LATIN AMERICA

Significant Highlights of Afro Cubans

Cuba experienced some serious racial problems in 1908-1912. A group of Afro Cubans organized a political party in 1908 under the leadership of Evaristo Estenoz. The party was called Partido Independents of Color.

The members of the party were demanding better race relations for Cubans of African ancestry in the areas of education, working conditions, judicial reforms and racial discrimination in government jobs. With an increase in membership in 1910, they were intimidated by the government and other political parties. Some of their masters were arrested. The party was disbanded when an amendment excluded political parties of one race. In May 1912, the army confronted Afro Cuban protestors in the Province of Oriente and killed approximately 4,000 thousands Cubans.

It has been that Juan Garirdo was the first who planted and harvested wheat in America. John Cortz a comic actor was living in Mexico prior to his visit to Cuba. Estevanico was possible the real discovery of the seven cities of Cibola.

After the Spanish American War, 1898, the Cuban Revolutionary Army consisted of many blacks and mulattoes. Later they were replaced with a rural guard commanded by a white Cuban officer.

Cuban Music

In the 1930's, there were some energetic and popular Afro Cuban musicians who were instrumental in introducing Afro Cuban music outside of Cuba. Alejandro Garcia Caturla's compositions were played in the United States. Afro Cuban music is an original type of folk music and is a composition of African and Spanish influence. The musicians used many percussion instruments. One dance form that was popular was the bamboula of Africa's origin. The habanera, a Spanish dance possibly was introduced into Cuba from Africa by former slaves. It has been called the contradanza criollo or creole country-dance. The dance music has a short introduction of two parts of eight or sixteen bars of which the first is in a minor key and the second in the major.

Cuban Personalities of Color

Black Presence

Maria Theresa Ramirez-Medina was the daughter of Primitivo Ramirez-Ros, former representative from Matanzas and later secretary of the Special Commissions of the House of Representatives. She succeeded her father upon his death Medina was a law student in the 1930's.

Theodoro Ramos Blanca was born in Havana, Cuba and graduated from the Academy of Painting and Sculpture. He won a commission to execute a monument in honor of General Antonio Maceo's mother, Mariana Grajales.

General Manuel Joe Delgado was a secretary of communication in the cabinet of President Gerado Machado, 1925. He also had served as an Assistant Secretary of Interior. During the Spanish American War, he was a member of General Jose Miguel Gomez's army. After the war, Delgado organized the first Rural Guard of Santa Clara.

Miguel Angel Cespedes-Casado was a lawyer and judge of the Court of Customs Appeals. He was born in 1885 in Puerto Principe (Camaguey). He served as the president and chairman of the Board of the Court of Customs Appeals.

Martin Morua Delgado was born in 1856 in Matanzas Province Cuba. He was the son of Ines Delgado, an African native and Francisco Morua from Spain. He was a journalist, writer, orator and was fluent in several foreign languages. Delgado was elected to the Cuban Constitutional Convention in 1900's. Later he became the first black to be named President of the Cuban Senate. He wrote about the slave condition in Latin America and Africa, miscegenation and the mulatto and African and the mulatto and African culture. The two novels written by Delgado are "Sufia and the Unzuary".

Manuel Velasquez, a person of color was a graduate of the University of Alcala de Henares, Spain. He was a personal friend of Charles V, who wrote from Santiago de Cuba protesting the treatment of slaves. He was instrumental in the founding of one of the first schools. Lorenzo Mendez and Mariano Moya opened some schools. They were members of the battalion of colored men of Habana.

Guillermo Mocada was born in Santiago, Cuba on June 25, 1844. As a young man, he learned carpentry. On November, 1868, he enlisted as a private with Cuban insurgents. Later, he was promoted to captain, colonel and eventual general rank. He was associated with General Antonio Maceo. There were several Cuban stamps issued honoring General Moncada. The stamps were three and five cent stamps.

Cuban Personalities of Color

Herman Cortez had some blacks in his army when he confronted the Aztecs. The first known black librarian of Cuba, descent was Manuel Socorro Rodriguez. He was born at Bayamo in 1958. He worked in Santa Fe de Bogota in Central America. Two women musicians in the earlier years were Theodora and Micaeha Gines. They were bandolin players in an orchestra that performed in the churches of Santiago de Cuba in 1580. Some early Cuban writers were Regina Boti, Ghirardo Jimenz, Regina Pedroso and Micohas Guillen.

Antonio Jose Maceo was a light skinned mulatto born in Santiago, Cuba in 1844. He had nine brothers. On February 24, 1895, Cuba had declared itself independent of Spanish rule. Baracoa General Maceo and other leaders landed at Duaba and Baracoa. On April 11, General Maceo would align with Generals Maximo Gomez and Jose Marti. They formed a plan and Maceo was to remain in the province of Santiago. Gomez would become general in chief of the army. In October 1895, the Cuban revolutionaries were 30,000 in strength in the eastern and western divisions. The Spanish army consisted of 76,000 men under the leadership of Marshall Martinez de Campos. During the summer of 1896, Salvador Cisnero Betancourt became the president of the Cuban Republic. Spain was facing many difficulties in stopping the revolt. On December 7, 1896, Major General Antonio Maceo was killed. Some historian believe that he was betrayed by his own personal physician and friend, Dr. Zertucha. His doctor was with him when he was led into the ambush. The doctor was permitted to surrender. General Gomez' son was killed with Maceo. He was liked by his men and would always set examples for this men by high morales and good living standards. General Maceo believed that whoever tries to conquer Cuba will gain nothing but the dust of her blood soaked soil if he does not push in the struggle. Maceo was able to defeat General Weyler at Guilmaro in 1873. After the death of Maceo, an official anthropological study was made of Maceo's remains. Some scientists believed that mulattos showed inferior traits except when the white genes appears dominant in the miscegenation process of race mixing. The study concluded that Antonio' Maceo's skeleton was of black origin, however, his skull was similar to the Caucasian. These type of absurd and negative racial scientific investigations over the years did contribute greatly to the stereotype views of many people.

LATIN AMERICA BRAZIL

Significant highlights of Brazilians of Color

In 1997, several World Almanacs state the ethnic populations consist of 38% mixed and 6% black. A 1987 almanac states that the ethnic population was African and mulattoes make up the majority ethnic groups in Brazil. In 1996, a magazine of color *Brazil Race* was introduced and stated that 60 percent of Brazil's 152 million citizens are black or of mixed race. The purpose of this new magazine is to raise self esteem among Brazilians of color. The first issue addressed articles on percussions music groups, mixed race marriages and the deities of condomble, an amalgam of Catholicism and the animist religions brought to Brazil by former slaves. The realign is still present among their descendants and some Brazilian whites. It is quite obvious that the race problem is quite alive in the country of Brazil today. An overview of historic facts of the last hundred years ago will reflect why even the official statistics made to the world can be misleading when some people use nice words for themselves as others such as we are a color blind and multiracial society where we all are Brazilians. That would be true today if the following facts did not occur over the years in the country of Brazil. Slavery was introduced in Brazil around 1531. Many of the slaves came from the African countries of Angola, Congo, Mozambique and West Africa. An edict of the King of Portugal stated that slaves should be baptized and accepted by the Catholic church on almost an equal basis with free populations. The church would use Saint Benedicto or Benedict to appease the slave population. The black slaves worked in the mines and sugar plantations. The cities of Rio Janerio and Bahia did have problems of color obsession. A revisit to the past will reveal the early etiology or causes why the Brazilian society today is not color blind and does have a problem of polarization that has necessitated a magazine like Ebony to inform and relate to an almost majority population who would be considered black in the United States regardless how white they physically appear to include straight hair and Caucasian features. One drop of African ancestral genes would make them black and people of color. In the early years in Bahia, the diverse group of people were classified as *"Indian white - Caboclo, Indian Negro, Cabre, Mulatto, Mestico, probably include all admixtures"*. The blacks lived in the areas of Pernambuco, Maranhav, Alagoas, Bahia, Minas Geraes, and Rio de Janiero. Bahia was founded in 1549 and was the principal port of entry for African slaves in the 16th and 17th centuries. In later years, the city would be divided into the upper city where whites and light mulattoes lived on the best streets and the lower class lived in the lower city with dirt roads. There were some racial expressions that reflected the realism of the early racial problem and skin color obsessions. *"A rich Negro is a white man and a poor white man is a Negro"*. The Portuguese had a term *"escapes, he who escapes from being a Negro is white"*. There were some terms used to designate the population, braving whites, pretos, black, pardo, brown, light mixed blood were sand papered, very dark, Negro boy, nails, very black man, black, and slight trace of Negro ancestry, and had a finger in the kitchen". The hair color of a person was more important in classifying a given individual than skin color. That is an individual with straight hair would be classified as white but not an individual with a lighter complexion, and kinky hair". Some other racial expressions heard were similar in some cases heard in America and Puerto Rico, improving the race, cleansing my race, making it whiter, advancing the race, I do not want to go back to Africa and I am not dealing in coal".

Sometimes freedom was given to the slave women and her children based on their white father and Negro women who had ten children were automatically freed and some were freed by will. Some of the following

Black Presence

discussion will depict the early state of the black African and mixed blacks in early Brazil.

SIGNIFICANT HIGHLIGHTS OF BRAZILIANS OF COLOR

Black Resistance In Early Brazilian Slavery

Some African slaves from Guinea who were enslaved in Brazil, in the province of pernambuco by their Portuguese masters carried out a revolt in the seventeenth century. In 1650, forty African slaves ran away with weapons and necessary provisions and settled in an area where the Dutch previously had a black village. This area was referred to as the Village of the Forest or Quilombo of Palmares. They were successful in establishing a strong hold and eventually other runaway slave joined them Their tactics included robbing whites and taking women of all races from plantations. A town was organize and a chief or king was elected. He was called a Zombe and his rule was absolute. Those persons who had obtained their freedom by an means were considered free in the town However, those who were captured while slaves became slaves in the town. At one time, the population was 20,000 and there was a fighting force of 10,000 men. The small city existed for many years. In 1696, the Governor of Pernambuco, Caltano de Millo sent an expedition to conquer the city. The governor's troops were defeated by the blacks of Palmares. Later another expedition consisting of 7,000 men and weapons were dispatched to Palmare. They were successful in securing the city and defeating the Zombe and his troops.

Brazilian-African Related Vocabulary

The following Brazilian vocabulary relates to the former African slaves of Brazil: Candomble, Brazilian folk religion of African background; Macumba, Brazilian folk religion of African background: Mulatto, a person of Caucasian and African parents; Preto, an African with physical characteristics of the African or "True Negro", Quilombo, former colony of runaway slaves; Senzala, slave quarters; and Xango, a Brazilian religion of African background.

African Contributions to Brazil

Some African contributions to Brazilian culture were: "Okra, black beans, red peppers, the wooden spoon, the mortar and pestle and African stories of folktales."

Reference: *They Did Not Tell Me True Facts About The African American's African Past And American Experience"*.

An African Religion Survived Brazilian Slavery

Some Bahia blacks of Brazil did retain some of their African religious culture in spite of many years of exposure to slavery and European imposed culture. As late as 1940, the descendants of Africans from the areas of Nigeria and Sudan were sustaining their cultural heritage.

The religion of the blacks consisted of: The cult of Orishes, cult of Olorum, Great God, Shango, God of Thunder and Lightning. Esu, Carnation of Evil, Gun, the Orisha of War. Their goddesses were Yemanja, Yansan, Anamburucu, and Oshun-Waters, seas, rivers, lakes and wind. There was an Oshose, God of hunting; Shapamma, Orisha of the Smallpox and Ibeji, the twin Gods. The Orishas are worshipped in special temples, called macumbas and candombles. In Africa, the temples are called pegi. The priests are called pae de Santo (father of saints). The priestesses are called maes de Santo (mother of saints). The daughters are called filihas de santo (daughter of saints). When the Catholic Jesuit priests tried to convert the African slaves to Catholicism and believing that they had converted them the Africans had not forsaken their beliefs and faith in their gods.

The Africans of Bahia and some of their descendants changed the name of the Catholic saints to their own Orishes. The Orishala became Jesus Christ; Senhor do Bomfin (Our Lord, in Bahia), the Shango is the African equivalent of Santa Barbara (Catholic patroness of rain).

Black Presence

There were some Africans of the Islamic faith who retained their beliefs and at times rebelled against those who objected them retaining their faith in Mohammendanism.

In many African cities today, African Americans are reviving their cultural roots in gospel and spiritual roots in Catholic masses. Some Protestant churches, the Methodists and Presbyterians have included more gospel and spirituals in their services. The culture and traditions of Africa did not disappear with the worldwide dissemination of her sons and daughters who became genetically altered into hybrids of many ethnic groups. Somehow the dominant genes of "Mother Africa" remains so potent even in years of altered diversity.

African Brazilians Return to the Roots

When the late Alex Haley's best seller book, *Roots* was published that there were some people of African descent in North America who were able to locate their families in Africa. They were able to visit Africa and return or become a permanent resident in Africa. of course, it has been difficult for African Americans to search their roots to Africa, possibly due to the system of slavery that existed in America. There were many prohibitions imposed upon the American slave. They were denied the right to use their native language and read and write.

The Brazilian system of slavery did provide opportunities for some African slaves to retain their native language and cultural traditions. An example is the African Yoruba slaves from Nigeria. When they were transported to Brazil, they were settled in the city of Bahia.

After slavery, some of the descendants of the original Yoruba slaves were able to return to their hometowns. This was made possible when some slaves were permitted prior to abolition to purchase their freedom and return to Africa. There were some freed slaves who would return to Nigeria, Africa and marry and then return to Brazil with their children after abolition. In later years, some former African slaves in Brazil would engage in import/export businesses with Lagos, Nigeria. Slavery was abolished in Brazil in 1888, whereas American slavery and the Civil War was ceased in 1865.

Some examples of descendants of African slaves and former Africa slaves in Brazil returning to Africa are:

"An African salve in Bahia Brazil in 1879, Amaro Marinho purchased his and his wife's freedom. He sailed with her and three children to Nigeria. His children were Andre, 19, Fortunata, 15, and Vicente, 13. He never returned to Brazil. Marinho's daughter, Fortunata, married in Lagos, a Marcos Augusto Jose Cardosa who left Brazil in 1869 with his father. They became the parents of nine children. marcos Cardosa was a skilled mechanic. He learned his trade from an African in Brazil. He is credited for building the first Catholic church in Nigeria in 1880. Cardosa also constructed schools and churches and built the first spiral stairway in Lagos, Nigeria.

Dorothea Manuel Reis was born in Rio de Janerio of African parents who were brought to Brazil as slaves from Abeokuta, Nigeria. Her parents purchased their freedom prior to abolition and returned to nigeria.

Lucia Mendes and his wife were born in Nigeria and came to Bahia as slaves. He obtained his freedom and returned to Nigeria with his wife and a son, Supriane Mendes. His wife died in Nigeria and he died in 1894.

These examples of Brazilian Africans returning to their homeland, Nigeria is evidence that some Africans and their descendants were able to return to their fertile soils of their original roots.

A search of the literature has revealed that there were some people of color in Brazil who distinguished themselves in the disciplines of architecture, sculpture, poetry, military and music. Some of them were: Antonio Francisco Lisboa, interest was religious architecture and sculpture, Joe Joaquim da Rocha established a school of painting and some other celebrated painters were Pedro Americo, Estavo Silva and

Black Presence

Oseas dos Santos. Some poets were Theodora Periera, Manuel Caetano, Azulao Manuel Preto, Jose Antonio Gonzaga, Jose Basilio da Gama, Jose de Natividade Saldanha, Antonio Goncalves Dias, Laurindo Ra bello, Luiz Gama, Gonealves Rabello and Goncalves Crespo. An African Negro general in the war of Independence was Joao Baptisda de Faria. There were some Brazilians of color who distinguished themselves in the war between Brazil and Paraguay. They were Cezario Alvesda Costi, Antonio Francisco de Melo and Andre Reboucas.

Latin America Dance

There have been many dances attributed to its origin in the African communities of Latin American. Some of these dances with an African influence are the rumba, samba, congo, chiba, bamboula, tumba or the nago. Some African influenced dances in Venezuela have been the joropo, in Columbia, the bambuco and in Ecuador, the posillo.

The Black Presence in Uruguay

During the late thirties and the early forties, there were some accomplished black painters in Uruguay. They were Ramon Pereya, Enrique Soto, and Victor Ocampo Velaza.

General San Martin and His Impression of the Black Soldier

It has been stated that General San Martin once remarked that "*the best soldier we have is the Negro and mulatto, where whites are only fit for the cavalry*".

Black Presence In Bueno Aires

In the 1700's, there were many blacks participating in the lifestyles of Rio de la Plata. Blacks were employed as domestics, servants, bull fighters, musicians, soldiers and barbers. Some were slaves and free people of color. It has been said that the private physician of San Martin was black from Lima.

San Martin had blacks in his military units. The regiments were composed of Moreno slaves from Buenos Aires, Cordoba and the provinces of Cayo, crossed the Andes and followed San Martin to Chile and Peru. They also were victims at Chacabuco.

A Historical Note - Simon Bolivar

During my many years of research, I have come across statements that can be very controversial and dubious to many individuals. However, I believe in stating the information and letting the reader use his own logical evaluation of the validity of the material presented, when it is a subject of consternation especially when it relates to the color identity question. Therefore, I am including this information on a distinguished Latin American for the reader to use for their nutritional reasoning or food for thought.

The great liberator Simon Bolivar gave a message to the Congress of Angostura and he was expressing true views of human biological diversity of its simplest form when he wrote, "We must bear in mind or realize that all people are no longer European but a racial mixture of Africa and North America rather than Europeans". He stated so plainly that even Spain has ceased to be European because of her African blood, her institutions, and character. Bolivar then said that it was impossible to determine with any degree of accuracy to which human family we belong, because our Indian population has reduced and Europeans have mixed with Americans and African and Africans mixed with Indian and Europeans. This great emancipator, Bolivar really understood what many people in 1997 might understand but do not care to talk about. They go around using terms such as a color blind and multiracial society then continue to assign prefixes to the word American.

Black Presence

Bolivar said that while we may have the same mother our father can be different in origin and in blood, and all differ visibly as to the color of their skin. A dissimilarity which places upon us an obligation of the greatest importance.

I believe Simon Bolivar summoned it up when he said politically the Democratic Republic offers the only solution because legal equality is indispensable when there is physical inequality to correct to some extent the injustice of nature.

There have been some writers that believe that Bolivar's interest in miscegenation could have been due to his family background. He was raised as an aristocrat on a slave plantation and was a young orphan. He was quite fond of his Negro Nanny who he referred to as Hipolita, his mother. It has been stated that Simon Bolivar's great great grandmother was a mulatto. His biographies over the years, I am sure would deny this inference that Bolivar could have had a drop of black blood flowing in his Vascular system or veins and arteries.

Black of Seville, Spain

There were slaves present in Seville Spain in the 1500's. In 1506, Spain was shipping Christian Negro slaves to Spanish colonies from Sevillo until 1512. When order was received requesting permission to transport slaves directly from Guinea to America. During the reign of Henry III, a black, Juan de Vallado, a porter of the Chamber, commonly Negro or black count was appointed mayor of the Negro village on November 8, 1475. A street in Sevillo, Spain honors his name. An archbishop Gonzalo de Mena founded a hospital and home with a chapel for the members of the Brotherhood of Negroes of Sevillo. Sevillo was the home of Murillo, the painter of Heaven. His slave Sebastian Gomez, known as the mulatto. It is possible that he assisted his master Murillo with some of the famous painting in the Cathedral of Sevillo. Gomez painted several pictures in the cathedral, the "Immaculate Conception" and a picture of Christ. The Brotherhood of Seville in 1573 were granted by the Catholic church authorities, the right to have in their chapel the Holy Sacrament of the Eucharist. Pope Urban VIII heard of other congregation and approved its services and gave them his blessings. On April 29, 1744, Pope Clement XIV issued a bill granting the Brotherhood Congregation's members dispensations and plenary indulgences for many of their religious acts of faith. In 1731, a committee of Negroes along with others of the ministry called on Philip III and the royal family.

The Brotherhood of Seville was a religious order of Negro Christians who were defenders of the Catholic faith. It was the order of the first Christian slaves who arrived in the New World of America. They were actually active as early as the 1400's.

THE WAR OF 1812, 1812-1815

After the signing of the Treaty of 1783, Great Britain appeared reluctant to recognize America's independence. She gave instructions to her naval captains to halt American merchant vessels anywhere on the high seas and search them for any British subjects serving in America's military or marine service. In 1806, the American frigate *Chesapeake* was captured by the British man of war *Leopard*. Three of the four men taken from the Chesapeake were Negroes or blacks.

The captives were carried to Nova Scotia and later (1811) all except the one Englishman were released. This affair and other international complications gradually led America into war in June, 1812.

The battles of the various campaigns of the War of 1812 were fought on sea and land, and many Negroes served abroad naval vessels as well as in the army.

During this period, blacks were enlisted in regular army units and in some cases they were in actual battles where some were taken prisoner.

The records indicate that a Captain William Bezean of the Twenty-sixth U.S. Infantry Regiment enlisted 247 colored recruits at Philadelphia, Pennsylvania from August 30, 1814 to February 15, 1815, some for five years and others for the duration of the war. No specific authority for

Black Presence

this was discovered, although he was at the same time enlisting white men. Some archival records state that Bezean's colored recruits do not appear to have been assigned to active service. In the spring of 1815, they were discharged with the remarks:

"Discharged under an order of War Department directing that soldiers of color be discharged." The register of discharges of military district number 1 (Boston) bears the following remarks:

"Being a Negro is deemed unfit to associate with the American and on account of being a Negro. . . not fit to accompany American soldiers."

Although Captain Bezeans' recruits may not have experienced active service, the register of enlistments of the U.S. Army 1789-1914 (1812-1815 period) indicates that men of color were enlisted, in some cases served until 1817 and some were taken prisoners. Black military men were present at the battles of Lake Erie and New Orleans.

During the War of 1812, American Negroes provided civilian manual labor and served as seamen aboard the war vessels at sea; on land the black soldier fought in some famous battles. Though small in number blacks again contributed to America's defense.

Some of the courageous black soldiers who served during the War of 1812 were:

James Eames, Private, J.R. Bells Co. U.S. Light Artillery Unit. He was born in New Jersey. The records state that his hair was black, his eyes black and his complexion black. The duty roster for February 16, 1815 at Fort Independence, listed him as present.

Private John White was born in Camden, North Carolina and worked as a laborer. He was enlisted by a Captain Henderson in the Marine Corps on May 16, 1813 at Charlestown for a term of five years. The official size roll describes him as having dark eyes, brown hair and a black complexion.

Private Francis Thompson, Eleventh U.S. Infantry Regiment was a native of Bethlehem, Rensselaer County, enlisted in the army in March 1813, at the age of twenty-one. His name appears on the roster of Lieutenant Isaac Clark's company. Thompson was wounded and became a prisoner of war. He is described as having black eyes, hair and complexion.

Private John Scott, Captain Sheldons' Co. Tenth Virginia Regiment was a freeman who served until the end of the War of 1812. He was allowed a pension on his application executed August 13, 1829, when he was living in Hamilton Township, Warren County, Ohio.

Bartholemy Populus was a lieutenant, First Battalion of Free Men of Color (Fortiers), Louisiana Milita. He became the second Negro officer in the battalion when he was appointed adjutant on December 15, 1814. The company muster roll for December 16, 1814 to March 25, 1815, roll dated New Orleans, March 25, 1815, shows the name Populus, Bartholemy, Lieutenant. His date of appointment was December 16, 1814.

Vincent Populus was Second Major, First Battalion of Free Men of Color (Locoste's) Louisiana Militia. Vincent Populus was the ranking Nergo officer of the battalion. According to historian Roland C. McConnell, this was the first recognition by the United States of a colored officer of field grade status. Populus appears with the rank of major on a muster roll of the field staff officers and Band First Battalion of Free Men of Color, Louisiana Militia, for December 16, 1814 to March 25, 1815. A roll dated New Orleans March 25, 1815, indicates that Major Populus was present.

Sergeant Belton Savarie (Savary) was a member of the Second Battalion (D'Aquin's) Free men of Color, Louisiana Militia. Belton Savarie served in combat operations in the War of 1812. The official records state that he was a member of Captain Marcelin Gilot's company of Militia Volunteers of San Domingo and of the battalion commanded by Major D'Aquin. Savarie was mortally wounded and died on January 10, 1815.

Joseph Savory was a member of the Second battalion (D'Aquin's) Free Men of Color, Louisiana Militia. He was a free man of color who came to Louisiana from Santo Domingo and was instrumental in organizing the Second Battalion. He attained the rank of major. Major Savory was present at the famous battle of New Orleans and his leadership and performance of duty were commendable.

Seaman John Bathan Vashon was born in 1792 in Norfolk, Virginia. His mother was mulatto and his father was Captain George Vashon, a caucasian of French ancestry who had served as an Indian agent under General Washington and President Van Buren. In 1812, at the age of twenty, Vashon went to sea on the USS Revenge, as a seaman. He was taken prisoner by the English, with other crew members, in an engagement off the coast of Brazil. Later the prisoners were released in an exchange and Vashon returned to live in his native home Virginia, first in Fredericksburg and later at Dumfries and Leesburg. He was proprietor of a public saloon in Carlisle, Pennsylvania for seven years, but in 1829, he moved his family to Pittsburgh, Pennsylvania and became active in the antislavery movement. Vashon was associated with the abolitionist William Lloyd Garrison and was also a member of Temperance and Moral Reform societies. He was one of the vice president's of the National Convention of Colored Men held at Rochester, New York in July 1853. On January 8, 1812, John Vashon died while attending a National Convention of Soldiers of 1812 in Philadelphia, Pennsylvania. He was a man of courage, and of untiring fidelity to his country and cause of black emancipation.

William Gansey was born in Africa. He was enlisted in December 1814 in the army at the age of thirty at Philadelphia, Pennsylvania. His occupation was a laborer. He was assigned to Captain Begean's Twenty-sixth U.S. Infantry Regiment. He was described as having black eyes, curly hair and a black complexion.

MEXICAN WAR, 1846-1848

The United States in 1845 claimed that it had a legitimate right to controversial land beyond the Nueces and Rio Grande on the Mexican side. The dispute developed into a conflict that lasted from 1846 until

1848. The congress authorized an enlistment of fifty thousand volunteers and black men were among those who answered our country's call. The most participation was mainly in the Navy with an estimated one thousand blacks in naval service during the Mexican War. A review of the Register of Enlistments of the United States Army, 1785- 1914, reveals that Negroes also served in the army in regular and volunteer units. Negroes served as infantrymen and musicians. Some of these most notable servicemen were: Peter Allen, musician, Captain Wyatt's Company. He was a Texas soldier who was massacred with Colonel James Fannin and 300 other men on Palm Sunday, 1836. Allen was a free Negro from Pennsylvania, and in civilian life operated a blacksmith shop. Allen played the flute and banjo.

John Conter served as a fifer in the Thirteenth Infantry, Fourth Regiment. He was a native of Dekalb, Georgia. Conter enlisted in the army in April 1847 in Atlanta, Georgia by F. Kirkpatrick and was discharged on January 9, 1848 at Suole Naturel, Mexico. He worked as a carpenter in civilian life.

Greenberry Logan, a blacksmith of color received his freedom in Kentucky. He came to Texas in 1831, and was one of the blacks who fought for Texas Independence. He was a soldier under Fannin at the Battle of Concepcion and accompanied Ben Milam into San Antonio in December 1835, when the Texas army defeated General Cos. Logan was wounded during the fighting in the vicinity of Main Plaza in the heart of San Antonio, when a ball passed through his right arm, permanently disabling him. He obtained some land from Stephen F. Austin on Chocolate Bayou, in Brazoria County. His wound made it impossible for him to continue in the blacksmith's trade and he opened a boarding house at Brazoria.

Jordan B. Noble was born around 1800 in Georgia. Later he moved to Louisiana and at the age of thirteen, was serving with the Seventh Regiment of General Andrew Jackson's force during the war of 1812. He beat the drums at many famous battles and other events, and on January 8, 1815 played the drums at reverie and before an important engagement. It also has been stated that he served in the Seminole War in Florida in 1836.

Noble served as a principal musician during the Mexican War with the First Regiment, Louisiana volunteers, Colonel Walton commanding. His name appears in the military service record as follows:

"Noble J.B. Company Field and staff, First Louisiana Military Volunteers (Mexican War) Principal Musician, enrolled May 9, 1846 at New Orleans for six months. On roll dated August 1846, Book Mark 970B 1848 Mexican War."

Jordan B. Noble was paid a bounty for his services in the Mexican War.

John Rouse was a drummer boy in the Mexican War. He was in charge of the main door of the House of Representatives for thirty years. He was the youngest veteran of the Mexican War on the House list and served at Vera Cruz, where he lost part of his left arm.

Henry C. Sprague was a native of Brandywine, Ohio who worked as a laborer. He was enlisted in the army on April 19, 1847, at New Orleans by a Captain Lynde. He was discharged at the expiration of his term of service at Newport Barracks on June 20, 1848. Sprague was described as five feet, three inches tall, with black eyes, brown hair and a black complexion.

Joe Travis was a servant to Colonel William Travis. When the Mexican army captured the Alamo and killed Colonel Travis and all of his soldiers they spared his Negro servant Joe, who was not considered a combatant. Joe went to Washington on the Brazos and gave one of the first eye witness accounts of the face of the Alamo to members of the Provisional Government. Joe described the death of Crockett, Bowie and Travis and said that he was taken to General Santa Anna, who questioned him about the Texas army. Joe said he was detained in San Antonio long enough to watch a review of the Mexican troops and was told they numbered eight thousand. He was then permitted to go.

For further reading see Black Defenders of America, 1775-1973.

UNITED STATES CIVIL WAR

The black presence in the blue and gray ranks

When a divided nation sounded the call to arms in 1861, black Americans responded. They were seen on the battlefield in Union blue and Confederate gray; they worked as manual laborers, as body servants and cooks, and followed their masters to battle.

At the beginning of the war Negroes tried to enlist in both the Union and Confederate armies. Their services were refused. In 1862, the Union Army decided to enlist the services of slaves and free Negroes. Under outstanding Caucasian military leaders, a nucleus of superior soldiers was eventually organized. This was the beginning of America's first official recognition of a Negro regiment, the United States Colored Troops. A few Negro officers were commissioned near the end of the war, but very few therefore had leadership experience as officers.

Unfortunately, the accomplishments of these brave men have been excluded from the history texts used in America's public schools, though their deeds were many and in some cases notable. This chapter recounts the heroism, tribulations and accomplishments of black Americans of Civil War days.

The number (twenty-four) of Congressional Medals of Honor awarded to black men during the Civil War is outstanding; the many battlefields of the Civil War stand as a memorial to the veterans, black as well as white, of the conflict between the states.

Ruff Abernathy, Cook, Third Tennessee Infantry Regiment, Confederate Army.

Ruff Abernathy applied for a pension on June 15, 1921, when he was seventy-six years old and living in Aspen Hill, Giles County, Tennessee. His master had been a Tom Abernathy. He stated on his application that he had been a cook for a Captain Barber, Third Tennessee Infantry

Black Presence

Regiment, and that when Captain Barber was killed at the Battle of Resaca, Georgia, he was assigned to work as a servant in the Distributing Hospital in Atlanta. Abernathy was later transferred to a hospital at Alisonia, Alabama. He was released from the Confederate Army in 1865.

Aaron Anderson, Landsman, U.S. Navy.

Aaron Anderson, a black, was born on a farm in Plymouth, North Carolina. He enlisted in the navy on April 17, 1863. On March 17, 1865, while serving on board the *USS Wyandank*, he participated with a boat crew in the clearing of Mattox Creek. Anderson carried out his duties courageously in the face of opposing fire which cut away half the oars, pierced the launch in many places, and cut the barrel off a musket being fired at the enemy. He was awarded the Medal of Honor.

Joe Anderson, Musician, Company G, 109th Regiment, United States Colored Troops, Union Army.

Joe Anderson enlisted at Greensburg, Kentucky, on June 4, 1864, and served until February, 1865.

Frank Mark Welch, First Lieutenant, Company F, Fifty-Fourth Massachusetts Volunteer Infantry Regiment, Union Army.

Frank Welch, a black, was born on October 22, 1841, in Philadelphia, Pennsylvania. He was a single man, and enlisted in the service at West Meriden, Connecticut. He was assigned to Company F and promoted to sergeant and then to first sergeant on May 12, 1863. Welch was commissioned a second lieutenant on April 28, 1865 and mustered on June 3; first lieutenant on June 20, 1865 and mustered July 22. He was wounded at Fort Wagner on July 18, 1863. Welch was discharged on August 20, 1865, at the expiration of his term of service.

Alex Wharton (Big Alex), Body Servant, Company 1, One Hundred and Fifty-Fourth Tennessee Infantry Regiment, Confederate Army.

Alex Wharton, a black man, was born in Macknary County, Tennessee, in 1851. During the Civil War, he served as a body servant to Captain C. R. Wharton. A sworn statement signed by Richard J. P. Wharton reads: Alex Wharton (Big Alex) ... was a servant in the Confederate Army three years. He served me and my brother, Captain C. R. Wharton until 29 July 1864, at Atlanta, Georgia, when both of us were wounded.... At Chickamauga, Mission Ridge, and through the Georgia campaign, he helped care for the wounded in battlefields.

William J. Whipper, Brigadier General, Second Division, State of South Carolina National Guard.

William Whipper, a black man, was born on January 22, 1834, in Morristown, Pennsylvania. In 1866, he moved to Charleston, South Carolina, with his wife and child and opened a law office in the provost court. In 1867, he moved to Beaufort, South Carolina, and became active in the Reconstruction Politics of the Republican party. He held several offices, including judge of the first judicial court of South Carolina. He served in the state House of Representatives from 1868-1872 and 1875-1876. His first wife, Mary Elizabeth, died in 1867 and in 1868 he married Frances Anne Rolleu. Five children were born of this union.

During the Civil War, Whipper joined a regiment of volunteers, but the highlight of his military service to the state came when the governor appointed him to the rank of general in the state militia during the Reconstruction period. A letter commissioning William Whipper brigadier general is preserved in the Christian Fleetwood papers in the Library of Congress.

Blacks Among The Confederate Gray

Throughout the years, there has been considerable doubt as to whether blacks actually served in combat with confederate forces. An official report submitted by Union Scouts on August 11, 1861, stated that the enemy had retired and they talked of having nine thousand men. They

Black Presence

had twenty pieces of artillery among them which was the Richmond howitzer battery manned by Negroes.

During the Civil War, black soldiers from the Confederate Winder and Jackson Hospitals in Richmond engaged in combat during the defense of Richmond in March 1865.

William Emory, musician, Company I. He enlisted in 1861 at Richmond, Virginia. Emory was a free colored man.

The following blacks were soldiers in the First North Carolina Army 10th State Troops Confederate Army.

Eli Dempsey, Private, Company G. Dempsey was captured at Plymouth, North Carolina, October 31, 1864. He was confined at Military Prison Camp, Hamilton, Virginia, November 16, 1864. Dempsey was listed as a cook, colored.

Everett Hayes, Private, Company F. He was listed as a cook, colored.

There were some blacks who served in the Confederate States Naval Brigade. They were: Charles Cleopor, Private, Colored; James Hicks, Private, Colored;
Joe Johnson, Private, Colored.

The Confederate Black

I was invited to be the quest speaker at Winchester, Virginia's Rotary Club luncheon in 1971. The topic of the Confederate Black was discussed. The following are some major true facts and highlights of an address I delivered twenty-two years ago. The question that is often asked, Who was the Confederate Black? The Confederate Black was a slave or free person who performed specific services for the Confederate government during the Civil War as a body servant, military combatant, community resident, and Confederate sympathizers. A body servant was a slave bounded to the master and in most cases very loyal. The military combatant was an enrolled black in the Confederate military service. The community residents were free blacks who lived in the immediate Confederate communities in southern states. They were property owners, business men and heads of families. Some free blacks would take positions concerning their loyalties to either the Confederate or union forces. Many free blacks played the "see-saw" game to survive one day a confederate man, next day a union man.

An act of March 1863 legalized the slave impressment by Confederate authorities. A second impressment act was passed in February 1864. This act was designed to make all free blacks between the ages 18-50 liable to being impressed for labor work in industries, the erection of defensive works and military hospitals. The Confederate government also established a Bureau of Conscription.

A Choctaw County, Alabama Conscription Enrolling office made a contract with slave master, Jesse Taylor. Taylor received an appraisal of the value of two slaves who were contracted or impressed under the provisions of the act of February 17, 1864. The slaves were: Solomon, age, 23, height 5'6, weight 156 pounds, and color copper, value five thousand dollars; and Mack, age 25, height 5'9, 201 pounds, color black, value five thousand dollars.

Body servants performed various duties for the Confederacy during the Civil War. They worked as cooks, wagoners, teamsters, nurses, servants, laborers, blacksmiths, and assisted the Scouts. Some body servants were exposed to combat and followed their master into battle.

Alfred Brown was born in 1844 in Anderson, South Carolina. He was a body servant to Doctor George. Brown was wounded at the battle of Chickamauga. He was wounded twice in one day. A ball was shot through his left thigh and he was wounded in the right leg by a piece of bombshell. Holt Collier was at Vicksburg, Mississippi when he was wounded in the ankle. Collier was a body servant. Frank Lee was a body servant to Lieutenant Waring Lewis, Company F, North Virginia Regiment. He cooked, tended the horses and followed his master into battles. Hutson Longstreet was a body servant to his master, Gilbert Longstreet.

Black Presence

Monroe Jones was a servant to James McAlpine, Company A, First Light Artillery Regiment, Mississippi Confederate. On May 1, 1862, Jones lost both his legs when a shell exploded at Snyders Bluff, Mississippi. Wade Watkins was a body servant to Dr. Willie Meller, Dancyville, Haywood County, Tennessee. In 1932, Watkins requested a servant's or colored man's pension. He stated on his application that he was 85 years old and believed he was 12 or 13 years old when he enlisted in Confederate service. His master was shot and killed by enemy soldiers. Wade was shot at the same time in the right leg. He continued in the Confederate service working for a Colonel Bat Watkins.

The Confederate Black Soldier

There were some blacks who served under the Confederate flag. They enlisted and were officially enrolled on the Confederate rosters. Even though the Confederate government had debated and made a decision not to enlist slaves and free blacks in the military services, there is documented evidence that blacks did serve in various capacities in the Confederate Military service.

The following Afro-Americans were soldiers in the First (McCreary's) South Carolina Infantry, Confederate Army enlisted:

Tobias Dawson, Musician, Colored, Company K, free man, deserted near Fredericksburg, Virginia, in 1863. He enlisted in 1861.

John Graves, Musician, black, Company F. He enlisted in 1862.

Confederate Black Body Servants

The Tennessee State Legislature had passed a Negro Pension Law. The law provided "that the Negroes pensioned must have been actual bona fide residents of this state, three years of their service with the Tennessee Command (during the Civil War) and ten years of their service with a command from any other state. They must have remained with the Army until the close of the war, unless legally relieved from service.

They must be indigent. Unless you come clearly under the law, it is useless to file an application". Some of them were:

Henry Buchanan, Newburn, Tennessee. He was born in March 1845. Henry's master was Tom Buchanan. He served as a body servant to his master during the civil war. He served with the Twelfth Tennessee Infantry.

Ben Davis, Memphis, Tennessee, Shelby Company. Davis served as a personal body servant during the Civil War to General Bedford Forrest. He was given to General Forrest by his master, Hugh Davis of LaGrange, Tennessee.

Turner Earl, Oakland, Tennessee, Fayette Company. Earl was born in Granada County, Mississippi in 1849. His master was John K. Earl. Turner Earl served as a cook and general handy man for his master during the Civil War. He served with the Third Tennessee Confederate Cavalry as a body servant.

Sam Newson, Nashville, Tennessee. He was born on December 8, 1838. He was the servant of William Newson. When his master was killed at the battle of Chickamauga, Sam smuggled through enemy lines and brought him home. Sam Newson lived to be 100 years old.

Booker Hunter, Williamson County, Tennessee. Hunter served as a body servant to Captain H.H. Smith during the civil War.

Rush McNeely, Madison, Tennessee. Rush was born on McNeely's farm near Mefflin, Tennessee, Madison County, Tennessee on August 11, 1824. His master was Frank McNeely. Rush served as a body servant to his master. He served in the Twentieth-Seven Tennessee, Confederate.

John Martin Fitzgerald, Carter's Creek, Tennessee, Maury County. John was born in Maury County in 1846. He was the slave of Aston Fitzgerald. John M. Fitzgerald served as a body servant to Maston Fitzgerald during the Civil War. He served in the Forty-Eight Tennessee Infantry Regiment, Confederate.

Black Presence

The Confederate Black Body Servants

The Confederate black body servants were present with their masters at the following Civil War battlefields and sites:

Antietam	Gettysburg	Snyder Bluff
Big Bethel	Greensboro, S.C.	Vicksburg
Chickamauga	Lynchburg, VA.	Wilderness
Columbia, S.C.	Nashville, TN	Winchester
Decatur, Ala.	New Market	Yorktown
Fair Oaks	Sharpsburg	
lst and 2nd	Manassas	Seven Pines
Five Forks	Shenandoah	

Virginia: Confederate Black Body Servants

The State of Virginia has many Confederate organizations, historians and reactants who pride on reliving and commemorating those good old days as ardent Civil War buffs. There are numerous Civil War magazines, newspapers and journals that include stories of the white confederate experiences. When I became interested in the part played by Afro Americans in the Confederacy during the Civil War, I was appalled at the significant roles and duties performed by blacks. They were not ignorant men who were all subservient to a master. Many of them with limited education did exhibit their fidelity and were loyal to their masters. However, they did assist many of those down trodden, sad and battle worn Confederate veterans as they were fighting their last battle and bravely trying to overcome the increasing defeats by Union Forces.

True Civil War Stories About People of Color

Civil War historians have written volumes of history texts, articles and monthly civil war magazines, and printed serious and humorous stories about the War between the States. However, very few stories are published about the confederate black or sometimes loyal blacks to their masters. On June 24, 1970, my late son Robert II who was eight years old at the time and I visited a senior citizen of Vienna, Virginia, Mr. William West, who was ninety-six years of age. He was blessed to live to the age of 103 years. Mr. West who was born in Vienna, Virginia in 1874 and had attended Howard University for three years, taught school for fourteen years in Cartersville, Odruck Corner and Vienna, Virginia. In 1908, William West began working for the U.S. Government and retired in 1942. He was also a active member in the local NAACP chapter and his church.

I was privileged to listen to Mr. William West 23 years ago relate some true Civil War stories that I seriously believe have never appeared in the popular Civil War books and magazines. These true accounts relate the way we were years ago during the era of slavery and the limitation of our ancestors lives by the dehumanizing system of slavery. The following stories were told by the late William West. A remarkable Vienna, Virginia citizen and a proud gentleman of color.

A Separate Call To Arms

In 1861, the family of Daniel West, father of William Alexander West lived five miles from the Fairfax Court house as slaves on the estate of Major Chichester. There were five boys and two girls in the West family. Just before the Civil War, Major Chichester decided to send three of the boys and one girl to Mississippi but kept Daniel, who was the youngest and had been trained as a house servant, one of his sisters and Henry, an older brother. Whenever Major Chichester had boots made, he would have two pairs, giving one to Henry, who had very small feet, to wear in order to break them in. Henry decided that he was not going to Mississippi, so one day, he put some clothes and two pairs of the major's boots into a sack, saddled a horse and at nightfall rode away. The horse returned the next day, but without Henry, who succeeded in reaching an under ground railroad station and made his way to the state of Connecticut. This did not deter Major Chichester from sending the other children to Mississippi.

Black Presence

In 1861, when the Civil War started, Daniel West, then sixteen, went with his master, Major Chichester, to serve as a body guard. He served with the major throughout the war from Bull Run to Appomattox and Gettysburg. Ironically, Henry had joined the Union Army's in Connecticut and was also at the battle of Gettysburg and must have faced his Confederate brother Daniel from the Union line. Daniel West often told his son, William about his war experiences. He spoke of the musket that he carried to protect his master (my emphasis) and of a fierce three day battle when men were shot in the saddle and were dragged along by their horses, their feet caught in the stirrups.

A Servant's Loyalty

One day in 1863, when the Confederates were firing on a train carrying Union Soldiers from Alexandria, Virginia, a Union officer was killed. It was believed that a captain Franklin Williams of the Mosby Raiders had killed the officer and everyday Union troops went to the Williams estate looking for the captain. If he was at home, he would be hidden. The third day the Union troops came, Simon Alexander, the grandfather of William West, hid his master, Franklin Williams in the horse's manger which was filled with hay. "The horse was standing close by eating and the troops did not suspect that Williams was there. The Union troops burned the house down, but without catching Captain Williams". That was the way some of us were in those days of servitude.

Civil War Veterans, Founders of Lincoln University of Missouri

When the Union Army requested a "Call to Arms" for former slaves and free blacks in Missouri, those black defenders responded and were inducted at Jefferson Barracks, near St. Louis, Missouri. They were assigned to the sixty-second (62nd) United States colored Infantry Regiment in 1863. There recruits were assigned to fighting or combat troops as labor troops. These courageous black men were present in battles and skirmishes at Baton Rouge, Port Hudson, Moganza, Brazas and Santiago. There were approximately 400 casualties in the regiment.

In 1865, the soldiers were mustered out of the service at Camp McIntosh, Texas near the Alamo.

The concerned officers of the regiment had taught the black troops elementary principles of reading, writing and arithmetic, during periods of rest during the battles. Therefore, many of the former slaves at the conclusion of the Civil War were able to write and read. There were several concerned white officers of the colored regiment who wanted to do something about the future education of their men, Lieutenant Aaron M. Adamson and Lieutenant Richard B. Foster made a suggestion to their fellow officers about the regiment giving money to start a school in Missouri. The idea had a snowball effect and the officers, noncommissioned officers and enlisted men of the 62nd U.S. Colored Infantry and the 65th U.S. Colored Infantry had pledged over 6,000 dollars to establish a school in Missouri. Lieutenant Foster assumed the leadership of this gigantic project. The following resolution was adopted by the contributor:

> "Whereas, the freedom of the black race has been achieved by war, and its education is the necessity there of, reserved, that we, the officers and enlisted men of the 62nd United State colored Infantry (organized as the First Missouri Volunteers, African Descent) agree to give the sum annexed to our names to aid in founding an educational institution, on the following conditions: First, the institute will be designed for the special benefit of the freed blacks. Second, it shall be located in the state of Missouri. Third, its fundamental idea shall be to combine study and labor, so that the old habits of those who have always labored, but never studied, shall not be thereby changed and that the emancipated slaves who have neither capital to spend nor time to lose, may obtain an education."

Lieutenants Foster and Adamson and Sergeant Henry Brown went to St. Louis in January, 1866 where a local committee was established

Black Presence

including both black and white men. They visited churches, raised money and selected a location for the school in Jefferson City, Missouri. On September 14, 1866, Lincoln Institute was opened for the new students. In 1870, land was obtained outside of Jefferson city to construct the first building for the school. In 1921, Lincoln Institute was changed to Lincoln University.

Bodyservant of General Robert E. Lee

The Reverend William Mack Lee was a body servant and cook to General Robert E. Lee, Confederate Army. He was born on June 13, 1835 at Westmoreland County, Virginia. He was raised at Arlington Heights, the home of his master, General Lee. William Lee was with the general during the Civil War at the first and second battles of Manassa, the first battle of Bull Run and, on Sunday April 9, 1865 at 9:00 A.M. was at Appomattox when the last gun was fired for the salute of the Confederate surrender. Lee boasted of feeding his master's co-generals at the headquarters in Petersburg, the battles of Decatur, Seven Pines, the Wilderness, on the Plank road between Fredericksburg and Orange County House, at Chancellorsville, the old Yellow Tavern, Five Forks, Cold harbor, Sharpsburg, Bonneville, Gettysburg, New Market, Mine Run, Cedar Mountain, Louisiana Court house, Winchester and Shenandoah Valley. At the close of war, William Mack Lee, although free, decided to remain with his master until his death. William Lee often related to his friends stories concerning the war and his experiences with General Lee.

"I have even see him cry. I never seen him sadder dan dat gloomy mawnin when he tol' me bout how General Stonewall Jackson had been shot by his own men. William he says to me, William, I have lost my right arm. I'm bleeding at the heart William, he says, and I stepped out'n de tent cause he looked liked he wanted to be by himself. A little later I came back and he told me that General Jackson had been shot by one of his own men. The general had told him to shoot anybody going or coming across the line and the general himself put on a federal uniform and scouted across the line, when he came back one of his soldiers raised his gun. Don't shoot, I'm your general, Marse Jackson yelled. They said the sentry was hard of hearing, anyway he shot the

general and killed him. I'm bleeding at the heart, William, Marse Robert kept saying."

William Lee was ordained a Missionary Baptist preacher in 1881. William Mack Lee sold for fifty cents a copy of the history of his life. The cover of the pamphlet stated that he was still living under the protection of the southern states.

An interesting Civil War Saga

The late John Mercer Langston, born free in Virginia and graduated from Oberlin College in 1849. Later he became a lawyer and was elected the first African American Congressman from Virginia. He also was the first black to hold an elective office in the United States. Langston was married to Caroline Wall, an 1856 graduate of Oberlin on October 25, 1854. Caroline was the half sister of Albert Wall, private Co. G, and John Wall, sergeant, Co. G 54th Massachusetts Regiment, Civil War. Langston was a recruiting agent for black troops. He recruited the Wall brothers and also three brothers, Milton, William and James Holland, born in Holland Texas, sons of a slave master named Captain Byrd Holland who was a former Governor of Texas. Prior to the Civil War Captain Holland freed his illegitimate sons, Milton, William and James and sent them to Ohio to receive an education. James and Milton enlisted in the 5th United States Colored Troops (USCT) and William enlisted in the 16th USCT in Nashville, Tennessee. Milton Holland was promoted to sergeant major and was awarded the Congressional Medal of Honor for valor when he assumed command of his company due to the loss of his commanding officer and led the company into battle. After the war, Milton enrolled at Howard University's School of Law and graduated in the class of 1872, receiving an LLB degree. His classmate was Albert Wall's half brother, Orindatus S.B. Wall, a former recruiting officer for black troops.

After the war, William Holland entered post reconstruction politics and was elected to the Texas State Legislature. William introduced a bill that created present day Prairie View State University in Prairie View, Texas.

Black Presence

I realize that sometimes the production of a film or movie requires fan fare, excitement, humor and attention motivators to ensure a box office success. A recently released movie a few years ago on the Fifty-Fourth Massachusetts Regiment and their gallant colonel did not accurately report or depict the true facts about the regiment. Because in actual real life the regiment's sergeant major was not a "grave digger" but Lewis Douglass, born October 9, 1840 in New Bedford, Massachusetts. He was the son of the distinguished abolitionist and statesman, Frederick Douglass. He had served as an editor of a newspaper for people of color.

A gracious Lady, Civil War Era

Harriet Proctor Smith was born in Virginia, 1829, daughter of free parents. Levi, born in 1797 and Hannah, born in 1801. Levi had purchased Hannah from slavery. They were the parents of five mulatto children. Harriet Proctor Smith was related to one of the distinguished first families of the local area, the "Rectors". Harriet was the mother of Faunce, Thomas Sewell, Mary, Turner, Edward, Cecelia, and Dorsey. Faunce, Thomas Sewell and Dorsey had different fathers. Harriet P. Smith was a lady of refinement, industrious and believed in the education of her children. She required that all of her children attend school. When the public school was closed, she enrolled her children in a private school. Harriet was as insistent that the white people in the community should send their children to school as she was that black people should send theirs. Harriet and her daughter, Cecelia worked as midwives in the local community.

During the Civil War, many of the Confederate officers of the Upper Virginia contingent would pass through the mountains near her home. She would cook their meals and at times hide more than a hundred gallons of scotch rye and barley in the stone piles and fences to keep the Confederate officers from over indulgence. Harriet was able to observe some interesting sights as the Union and Confederate troops would confront each other in military actions. On a beautiful Sunday morning Harriet went out to the side of a hill to see if some strawberries were ripe. Suddenly, she heard something flying over her head and in several minutes she heard horses coming up a path in the mountain. There was a rattling of chains and excitement. What Harriet thought was honey bees were minnie balls buzzing over head. The Confederate soldiers were fleeing from some Union troops. Some of the men were wounded and bleeding. Harriet treated some of the wounds with cloth from her loom and juice from her vines to ease their pain. The Confederates were seeking safety in the recesses of the mountain. Harriet was able to see a mile down the mountain where an eighty acre field was covered with what was called General Oliver O. Howard's Union White Horse Cavalry. Harriet had her personal views about John Singleton Mosby and his men. She believed Mosby caused great trouble for the Union soldiers and did not fight fair. She said that he would hide in the mountains and make surprise attacks on unsuspecting groups of Union men as they marched along the road. Harriet once delayed a large contingent of soldiers passing along the old Winchester and Alexandria Pike crossing the mountain at Ashbey's Gap. Harriet Proctor Smith was a very good seamstress. She used her spinning wheel to weave the wool into cloth. The wool was obtained when the sheep left the wool sticking to the briars and when they were killed by the dogs. The wool was washed, carded, spun and woven into cloth. She made clothes for the children.

Her son Thomas Sewell Inborden was a successful educator of color who started his early teaching career for the American Missionary Association in Helena, Arkansas and Albany, Georgia prior to his founding of the Joseph Keasbey Brick Normal School in Enfield, North Carolina in 1895 where he was the principal for many years. Inborden was married to Sarah Jane Evans Inborden of Oberlin, Ohio and a 1890 graduate of Oberlin College. One of their children was Dorothy Viola Inborden Miller who was a graduate of Brick School, North Carolina (founded by her father in 1895), and an honor graduate of Fisk University, class 1919. Dorothy I. Miller taught school at Brick, Winston Salem, North Carolina Teachers College, West Virginia State College and served as the head of the Department of Home Economics Division 10-12, District of Columbia Public Schools. She married Walker D. Miller, graduate of Oberlin Business College and Talladega College, Alabama.

In November 1996, Dorothy Inborden Miller died at the blessed age of 99 years and two months. She had preserved her father's manuscripts,

Black Presence

papers and letters and was responsible for the publication of her father's biography. When I gave some remarks at her farewell victory unto Christ ceremony I said the following:

Mrs. Dorothy Inborden Miller was very fond of her distinguished historical family's history. She was proud to be the granddaughter of Wilson Bruce Evans who migrated from North Carolina in 1855 to Oberlin, Ohio and built his home in 1856 and became the town's carpenter and undertaker. His home has been preserved over the years by Mrs. Miller and is on the Register of National Heritage Homes. Mrs. Miller would often tell you that she was a descendant of General Nathaniel Greene of American Revolutionary War fame.

When Mrs. Miller died, she was the last known immediate relative of her great Uncle Lewis Sheridan Leary and her second cousin, John Anthony Copeland, two of the black men who died with John Brown at Harpers Ferry Raid in 1859. She was also the third cousin of noted poet and writer, Langston Hughes.

As the funeral procession of Mrs. Miller approached the nation's Arlington National Cemetery, I will always wonder was she returning to the paternal homesite of her possible illegitimate grandfather and was she his last immediate grandchild. Mrs. Dorothy Inborden Miller never wanted me to verify whether the following statements are true. After some 15 years of attempting, I still believe that it was more true than it will ever be false. Mrs. Miller's father was born in 1865 in the Blue Ridge Mountains of Upperville, Virginia, the son of a free woman of color, Harriet Proctor Smith. It has been inferred that he was possibly the illegitimate son of General Robert E. Lee or some cultured southern gentleman. When Thomas S. Inborden left the mountains of Virginia at the age of 17 years, he became a pioneer educator of color who lived, toiled and produced results in the education of his people when America was not debating the pros and cons of equal opportunity and affirmative action but suffering a climate of life for people of color of segregation and denial of certain freedoms.

SPANISH AMERICAN WAR - 1898

The Spanish American War of 1898 saw the African American officer take his place as a leader, of his men. The National Guard and state militias were a major part of the country's military force. Several of the black volunteer units were commanded by senior black field grade officers.

During the war, black participation was evident. There were the Ninth and Tenth Cavalry Regiments and the Twenty-fourth and Twenty fifth Infantry Regiments present in Cuba at San Juan Hill and at El Caney making history on the battlefields. The Spanish American War was fertile ground for the growth and development of a new black soldier, a commander and leader of his black troops. The non commissioned officer (NCO) of the four black regular army regiments provided a great resource for the commission of many black officers during the Spanish American War.

Spanish American War Casualties

During the Spanish American war's combat engagements in Cuba, some courageous Buffalo soldiers of the Ninth and Tenth Cavalry regiments and Twenty-fourth and Twenty-fifth Infantry Regiments were killed and wounded in battle. I have included some of the names of these men because I believe it is necessary that we recall the truth and facts that these Black Defenders of America did die in the line of combat operations for "America the Beautiful" some 86 years ago:

Ninth Cavalry Regiment Men Killed

Trumpeter Lewis Fort and Private James Johnson.

Wounded

<u>First Sergeants</u> Charles W. Jefferson, Thomas B. Craig, <u>Corporals</u> James W. Ervine, John Mason,

Black Presence

<u>Privates</u>, Hoyle Irvin, James Gandy, Edward Nelson, Noah Prince, Thomas Sinclair, James Spear, Jacob Tie, Burwell Bullock, Elijah Crippen, Edward Davis, Alfred Wilson, George Warren, and William H. Turner

<u>Corporal</u> W. F. Johnson

<u>Privates</u> John H. Smoot, John H. Dodson, George Stroal, and William H. Slaughter

<u>First Sergeants</u>, A. Houston and Robert Milbrown

<u>Quartermaster Sergeants</u> Smith Johnson, Ed Lane Walker, George Dyers, Willis Hatcher, John L. Taylor, Amos Elliston, Frank Rankin, E.S. Washington, U.G. Gunter

<u>Corporals</u> J.G. Mitchell, Allen Jones, Marcellas Wright

<u>Privates</u> John Arnold, Charles Arthur, John Brown, H.W. Brown, William A. Cooper, John Chinn, J.H. Campbell, Henry Fern, Benjamin Franklin, Isom Taylor, Gilmore Givens, B.F. Gaskins, William Gregory, Luther D. Gould, Wiley Mosher, Benjamin West, Thomas Hardy, Joseph Williams, Charles Hopkins, Richard James, Nathan Wyatt, Wesley Jones, Robert E. Lee, Sprague Lewis, Harry D. Sturgis, Peter Saunderson, John T. Taylor, Henry McArmack, Samuel T. Minor, John Watson, Lewis Marshall, Allen E. White, William Matthews, Houston Riddell, Charles Robinson, Frank Ridgeley and Fred Shacker.

Acts of Bravery

In June 1898, Troop 1, Tenth Cavalry Regiment commanded by Lieutenant R.J. Fleming had some of his men to distinguish themselves in battle by demonstrating "coolness" and gallantry". They were Farrier Sherman Harris, Wagoneer John Boland, and Private Elsie Jones.

The Twenty-fifth Infantry Regiment at El Caney, Cuba

Chaplain Stewart stated in his book *The Colored Regulars in the United States Army, 1903* that an editorial appeared in a religious newspaper and praised the exploits of the Twenty-fifth Infantry Regiment,

"American valor never shone with greater luster than when the Twenty-fifth Infantry Regiment swept up the sizzling hill of El Caney to the rescue of the Roosevelt's Rough Riders, but the bullets was flying like driving hail. The enemy were in trees and ambushes with smokeless powder and the Rough Riders were biting the dusk and were threatened with annihilation".

Twenty-fifth Infantry Regiment Bravery In Combat, Cuba

The commanding officer of the Twenty-fifth Infantry Regiment Lieutenant Colonel A.S. Daggett was concerned about his regiment not receiving recognition for their commendable accomplishments in combat during the Spanish American War. Daggett wrote his higher headquarters and stated that:

"When the Twelfth Infantry in rear of the Fort (Blockhouse) completely sheltered from the enemy's fire received the white flag of the insurgents. However, Privates J. H. Jones, Company D and Thomas C. Butler, Company H, Twenty-fifth Infantry Regiment had entered the Fort at the same time and took possession of the Spanish flag. They were ordered to give the flag to the officer of the 12th U.S. Infantry Regiment. But before releasing the flag, Butler and Jones tore a piece from the flag and kept the torn piece.

Demonstration of Black NCO Leadership

There were instances during the Spanish American War where the white commanders were absent, wounded or killed and the company leadership became the responsibility of the black NCOS. It was reported that during some battle engagements at San Juan, Cuba, units were temporarily under the commands of First Sergeants William H. Givens, Saint Foster and William Rainey.

Black Presence

William H. Givens assumed command of his company on July 1, 1898 when his captain was wounded in action. Givens was a veteran of 32 years having enlisted in 1866. When Lieutenant Roberts was wounded and Lieutenant Smith of the Tenth U.S. Cavalry was killed in action in Cuba, First Sergeant Saint Foster assumed command.

The soldiers of the Twenty-fourth Infantry Regiment were part of the Third Brigade commanded by Colonel Wikoff during the Spanish American War. A group of the Twenty-fourth Infantrymen were patrolling around the foot of San Juan Hill, several officers were wounded. The command of the Company F became the responsibility of First Sergeant William Rainey.

The San Juan Tragedy

Corporal John Walker, Troop D, 10th U.S. Cavalry, wrote the following account of his unit's part in the San Juan tragedy and the death of Lieutenant Jules G. Ord.

"Upon the lst day of July, as the Tenth Cavalry went into battle at San Juan Hill against the Spanish Forces, Troop D deployed to the left and joined Hawkins' brigade in the charge, the Sixth Infantry becoming excited and retreated. They stampeded the entire line, making the charge. Lieutenant Jules G. Ord, of the Sixteenth Infantry and Captain Bigelow of the Tenth Cavalry endeavored to rally the American forces and succeeded by their timely and rave assurances that by standing their ground and continuing the charge up the hill, victory was in store for them. Immediately after which Lieutenant Ord walked down the line toward the road leading to the city of Santiago. Upon seeing the gatling gun detachment selecting a more advantageous position from which to play upon the Spanish lines, and becoming greatly encouraged at this, he hastily retraced his steps down the line saying: "Men, for God's sake raise up and move forward, for our gatling guns are going to open up now. " As the gatling gun opened fire upon the enemy's trenches, the Tenth Cavalry and the Sixteenth Infantry arose from their reclining position and charged forward, commanded by, Captain Bigelow and Lieutenant Ord respectively.

In the charge Captain Bigelow fell pierced by four bullets from the enemy's guns. Upon falling he implored. "Men, don't stop to bother with me, just keep up the charge until you get to the top of the hill. " Captain Bigelow's fall left Lieutenant Ord in command of the front forces in the charge as they ascended San Juan Hill. As we reached the Spanish trenches at the top of the Hill, Lieutenant Ord with two privates of the Sixteenth Infantry and I being the first to reach the crest, and at that time the only ones there captured four Spaniards in their entrenchments one of whom was armed with a side arm [revolver] which I took from him. Lieutenant Ord said, - "Give it to me as I have lost mine, and we will proceed to this blockhouse and capture the rest of the Spanish soldiers. "Taking the revolver from my hand, he and I walked toward the blockhouse. Lieutenant Ord stopped near a large tree, directing his attention to the filing which was coming from the Spaniards who had previously occupied the blockhouse. Just as he tip-toed to see over the high grass, Lieutenant Ord was shot through the throat by a Spanish soldier who lay concealed in the heavy underbrush at the foot of the tree by the side of which he paused to watch the Spanish flying. As Lieutenant Ord fell upon the spot, the Spaniard jumped up and ran toward the already retreating Spanish line.

As he started to run, I shot him twice in the small of the back, killing him, one bullet entering close to the other. I was by Lieutenant Ord's side when he received the mortal wound and he fell at my feet. Without moving out of my tracks, I fired twice at the fleeing Spaniard while standing directly over Lieutenant Ord, and just before he gasped his last, he muttered: "If the rest of the Tenth Cavalry were here, we could capture this whole Spanish Command". Corporal John Walker, Troop D.

Reference: *Black Defenders of America.*

PHILIPPINE INSURRECTION 1900-1901

Black Presence

Black Gallantry in the Philippine Islands

When the United States dispatched military forces during the Philippine Insurrection, there were blacks among the troops. Here again, the black soldier was on the scene, making gallant contributions that in some cases were not reported in the pages of history. A speech in the House of Representatives on Monday, June 8, 1914 by the Honorable Martin B. Madden (Illinois) relates an episode from the outstanding record of Negro troops in the Philippines. Some of the historical data for his speech was researched by a Mr. Daniel Murray, a former assistant librarian, Library of Congress for more than fifty years.

The following account depicts the bravery of American Negro soldiers under the leadership of a capable and heroic commander.

During the Philippine trouble it is related by Dr. Joseph M. Heller, late major and surgeon, United State Army, that during the campaign Captain Batchelor, a North Carolinian by birth and a hero if ever there was one, with 50 colored troopers, a brave and splendidly disciplined little band, marched and fought their way over a distance of 310 miles in one month. The route selected was over roads so difficult as to be almost impossible to travel. In fact, the route did not really deserve the name of roads, but was simply trails, through which the men plodded along, sinking at times to their knees in mud.

The expedition at the time was chasing Aguinaldo through the northern and central portions of Luzon and toward the China Sea. Dr. Heller stated that he never saw men show truer courage than those troops with Captain Batchelor. They were insufficiently clothed for the long march, and without guides in a strange region, but through chilling nights and sweltering days they forded 123 streams and crossed precipices and mountains where the daily average of ascent and descent was not less than 8,000 feet. For three weeks these troops lived on unaccustomed and insufficient foodstuffs and drove the enemy twice from strong position. They captured many of the Natives and set free more than four hundred prisoners. They finally forced the surrender of the commander of the insurrecting forces and made the people of Luzon enthusiastic advocates of American supremacy. No other single command during the

Philippine trouble stood as many hardships or accomplished so much as these Negro soldiers under Captain Batchelor. Such was the report made at the time; and although General Lawton was killed, Captain Batchelor carried out his verbal orders, and died of cholera in the Philippines, thus going to his grave without any further reward or recognition for one of the bravest expeditions ever attempted by soldiers in modern times."

CHINESE BOXER REBELLION - 1900

The Buffalo Soldier's Presence in the Chinese Boxer Rebellion, 1900

After the war between China and Japan 1894, a great dislike for Europeans and foreigners by the Chinese was increasing. There was an emergence of secret anti-foreign societies. An organization known as the "Boxers" were successful in initiating some uprisings in Northern China. They attacked hundreds of Europeans and thousands of Chinese Christians. Some foreign nations became quite concerned about the Boxer's aggressive actions. A unified foreign movement was started to occupy certain areas and provinces in China. England, France, Germany and Russia seized and occupied some areas. The United States became concerned about the Chinese government secretly assisting the Boxer Movement, American residents and their lives and property.

The English had sent a squadron of ships to China and the United States dispatched some vessels along with Germany, Russia, France, Italy, Austria, and Japan war ships to Chinese Ports.

An International Expeditionary Force was organized including the countries of England, France, Germany, Russia, Japan and the United States. This unified forces' mission was to free the foreign citizens who were under seize in foreign legations by the Chinese during the Boxer Rebellion. The American land force under the command of Major General Chaffie arrived in Toku, China on July 28, 1900. The troops assigned to this special task force were the Fourteenth Infantry. Battery of Third U.S. Artillery, Fifth and Seventh Artillery, First and Third U.S. Cavalry.

Black Presence

Unfortunately very few history text books have printed these missing pages.

During the Boxer Rebellion in China in 1900. We were there, people of color, part of the American land forces. There were some members of the following units who were present in China. They were the *Ninth U.S. Cavalry Regiment, Twenty-fourth Infantry Regiment and Twenty-fifth Infantry Regiment.*

HAITI

HAITIAN RULERS 1804-1994
(44 Rulers in 190 Years)

Name	Dates	Fate
Jean-Jacques Dessalines	1804-06	Assassinated
Henri Christophe*	1807-20	Suicide
Alexander Petion*	1807-18	Died in office
Jean-Pierre Boyer	1818-43	Removed from office
Charles Herard	1843-44	Fled
Phillippe Guerrier	1844-45	Died in office
Jean-Louis Pierrot	1845-46	Overthrown
Jean-Baptiste Riche	1846-47	Died in office
Faustin Soulouque	1847-59	Forced from power
Febre Geffrard	1859-67	Forced from power
Sylvain Salnave	1867-69	Forced from power
Nissage Saget	1870-74	Retired
Michel Doningue	1874-76	Fled to Jamaica
Boistond Canal	1876-79	Fled to Jamaica
Louis Foliciti Salomon	1879-88	Fled to France
F. Florvil Hyppoite	1889-96	Died to office
Tiresias Simon Sam	1896-1902	Fled
Nord Alexis	1902-08	Fled to Jamacia
Antoine Simon	1908-11	Fled to Jamaica
Cincinnatus Leconte	1911-12	Blown up by a bomb
Tonere Auguste	1912-13	Poisoned
Michel Oreste	1913-14	Fled to Jamaica
Oreste Zamor	1914	Murdered in jail

J. Davilmar Theodore	1914-15	Fled
J. Vilbrun Guillaume San	1915	Impaled and dismembered
Philippe Dartiguenave**	1915-22	Forced from office
Louis Borno **	1922-30	Forced to resign
Stenio Vincent	1930-41	Pressured to retire
Elie Lescot	1941-46	Ousted
Dumarsais Estime	1946-50	Overthrown: fled to New York
Paul Magloire	1950-56	Overthrown
Joseph Nemours Pierre-Louis	1956-57	Forced to resign
Francois Sylvain	1957	Overthrown
Daniel Fignole	1957	Overthrown
Francois Duvalier	1957-71	Died in office
Jean-Claude Duvalier	1971-86	Fled to France
Henri Namphy	1986-88	Stepped down
Leslie Manigat	1988	Overthrown
Henri Namphy	1988	Overthrown
Prosper Avril	1988-90	Fled to U.S. in military plane
Ertha Pascal-Trouillot	1990	Forced to resign, then jailed
Jean-Bertrand Aristide	1991	Forced to US
Raoul Cadras	1991-94	Fled to Panama
Jean-Bertrand Aristide	1994	Restored to power by U.S. Military

Military Statesman in Haiti

On April 7, 1904, Captain Young was concerned with a war request that he be assigned as the military attache to the United States Legation, Port Au Prince Haiti."

Captain Young assumed his duties a military attache to the United States Legation, Port Au Prince on May 13, 1904. He was accompanied by his bride, the former Ada Bar.

Young wrote one of his closest friends in Ohio while in Haiti. He wrote the well known poet, Paul Lawrence Dunbar on November 30, 1904.

Young expressed his warm friendship for Dunbar and also described briefly life in Haiti. He wrote:

'God bless you, boy you would be in clover down here if you once got on to the informal Creole. Its a wholly unworked field (a tenor cognita) full of surprises, cockroaches, and revolution. Love to your mother, she loves you and will come to you."

Captain Young's duties in Haiti consisted of obtaining essential military information, conduct of land reconnaissance, preparation of maps and collection of specific intelligence information.

The War Department's military information division wrote Captain Young a letter in November, 1905 instructing him that he should use the most extreme caution in securing copies of a map he had prepared. The War Department has received requests from individuals for copies of the maps prepared by Young. Captain Young had prepared a detailed monograph on the Republic of Haiti (consisted of 284 pages) which was of immense value to the military information division, War Department.

In July, 1905, Captain Young prepared a little handbook of French Creole as spoken in Haiti. This handbook was forwarded to the War Department and eventually became a significant intelligence reference.

Captain Young's introduction to the handbook stated the following:

"This dialect or paois of the French is formed upon very simple lines. There is no true gender, no singular and plural; verbs have rarely more, than 6 tenses - sometimes less - and the tense is not indicated by the termination of the verb. There is a remarkable paucity of auxiliaries and in some dialects none whatever, participles are unknown and prepositions and conjunctions few. On the other hand the interjections are many and depending upon their intensity of utterance may be made to mean many different things. Gestures are always in evidence. It is well to remember from the start in learning the Creole that it consists of one half words, one quarter gestures, and one quarter grunts and exclamations they show their slave origin and are relic of the dark days when the Negro dared not express his feelings for the injustice and cruelty received from his master, and when a gesture or an 'oh' varied from a surprise to a prayer or mild protest. The Creole has not lost its charm and forcefulness in this regard after 100 years of freedom. There are many educated and refined Creole women today who pride themselves (my emphasis) on their ability to express every shade of feeling by a single gesture or interjection.

Young explained that the object of this handbook was:

> "To afford the curios and the newcomers among the French Creole speaking people a glance at the principles underlying this dialect of the French - a dialect in many cases so far from the French as to require study of 3 to 6 months by even educated French Priests ... Here it may be remarked that many literary men both from the islands and foreigners have claimed for the Creole a place as a language instead of a dialect; while others have ridiculed it as a kind of monkey-jargon, a make shift of ignorant Negro slaves trying to express themselves in French ...

On November 29, 1905, Captain Young began a horseback reconnaissance of southern Haiti. He returned around December 24, 1905.

The American Minister, H.W. Furness extended numerous invitations to Captain Young to attend official social functions. A formal letter was received by Young on December 28, 1906 inviting him to the Haitian President's reception and also to attend services at the Cathedral on the anniversary of Haiti's Independence.

On October 15, 1906, Captain Young received a formal letter from Minister Furness inviting him to attend the commemoration of the One Hundredth Anniversary of the death of the founder of Haiti on October 17, 1906. Captain Young also accompanied the American minister on various trips. On July 13, 1906, the American minister, W. Furness and Captain Young departed for a 14 day visit to Jamaica.

Captain Young was concerned about whether he would be relieved to join his regiment for another tour to the Philippines. On January 19, 1907, he queried the War Department and he received a reply on February 5, 1907 that he would remain at his present duty station until as signed work was completed."

During the period 1904 to January 1907, Captain Young had enjoyed an eventful and educated assignment in Haiti. Captain and Mrs. Young were the happy parents of a baby in 1907. He was given the name Charles Noel Young.

In February 1907, some of the Haitian people began to accuse Captain Charles Young of sketching Haitian fortifications in the interior and gathering information about the Haitian government. There were some Haitian officials and private citizens that were circulating rumors that Young had been arrested by Haitian soldiers and was mistreated. The American legation considered these reports as merely gossip."

Unfortunately matters did not improve for Young, because on March 1, 1907, the Secretary of State, Eliju Root was informed by Minister Furness that while Captain Young was absent on a trip to Cape Haitian, Port de Paix and areas north, some papers were stolen from his quarters.

Minister Furness explained in his correspondence to the Secretary of State that the papers were possibly sold the Haitian government for $600 by a Charles Stephens, a clerk in the employ of Captain Young. Furness attempted to present the facts that he had and wrote the following:

"Stephens broke into the captain's bedroom, took 4 LOI (letter of instructions) .. and monograph on Santo Domingo ...Recommend that Captain Young had all information to complete his work here. Whatever may be the department's opinions of the matter it is my opinion, after mature deliberation that it would not be wise for him to be ordered home at least for the present, not only because he is still in a position to better furnish whatever information may be necessary that would be a new official. But because his departure would give greater evidence to the idea that our government really has intentions of invading the country at a not distant date."

The United States government was alarmed about diplomatic implications that could possible occur due to the lost of the classified paper. (The papers were classified confidential in 1907) Minister H.W. Furness expressed the government's interest in a letter to Honorable Thomas C. Dawson, American minister, San Domingo City, Dominican Republic, dated March 13, 1907. Furness stated:

> "Charles Stephens, clerk, broke open a drawer and stole certain important documents including a monograph on Santo Domingo, and material of interest to nation conducting military and naval operations against said country . Paper could be used to show that United States had intentions against annexing of Santo Domingo."

Elihu Root, Secretary of State, informed the Secretary of War on March 15, 1907 of his recommendation that Captain Charles Young should be relieved of his military attache duty at Port Au Prince, Haiti.

The Military Information Division, War Department decided on March 26, 1907 that it would be advisable for Captain Charles Young to be withdrawn as military attached in Haiti.

The stolen papers were found in Santo Domingo and were returned to the United States Government. On April 15, 1907. the Army Chief of Staff directed the Adjutant General to issue orders relieving Captain Young of his military attache assignment.

Captain Charles Young departed Haiti on April 28, 1907 and reported to duty with the Second Division, General Staff, Washington on May 7, 1907. He had experienced a successful military assignment in Haiti even though his return was somewhat prompted by the criminal activities of one of his Haitian employees and possible political influences within the Haitian government. However a fair appraisal of his tour of duty in Haiti was expressed by his former classmate. Charles Rhodes in an obituary of Young that was published in the West Point Annual Report, June 13, 1922. Rhodes stated:

"As our attache at Port Au Prince, he ably represented his country and this in the face of difficult conditions which have since rendered occupation of Haiti necessary. While on this duty he made and extended military reconnaissance of the country, and mapped a considerable portion of the terrain, as well as part of the adjoining Republic of Santo Domingo. At that time he foresaw that American occupation might become necessary for the good of the people themselves, and his knowledge of both French and Spanish.

Reference: *Colonel Charles Young Soldier and Diplomat*

An Early Interest in Haiti

In 1915, Haiti was experiencing some revolutions and a financial deficit. A honorable president of the United States, Woodrow Wilson, the one who had ordered segregation in government facilities, sent U.S. Marines to Haiti. The U.S. Government had assumed control of all Haitian custom houses because of their enormous debt. The United States Marines remained in Haiti until 1934.

The United States has been aware of the unfortunate revolutions in Haiti over the years. However, the political remedies for Haiti have been to dispatch Marines, and control the country's custom houses. The recent remedies have been economic blockade and the return of innocent people to Haiti when they attempt to leave the country to survive.

The European remedies over the years have been U.S. dollars, military assistance, and intervention of the United Nations through the U.S. leadership and dollars. I do not believe that our honorable leaders of America are color blind to their "racist" policies toward some African countries to including Liberia and Ethiopia when there are revolutions, and financial problems in these countries. The current situation in East Europe is being treated as a very important problem for the U.S. politically and economically. But where is the power of African American leadership to demand, lobby, and rescue these countries from their problems. I pose the question, is black leadership a myth or a reality? There is an immediate necessity for Afro-Americans so-called leaders to come out of their devisive, and individual circles.

Is black leadership a myth or reality? The Jewish Americans come together as a group and demand what is needed for their homeland, Israel. Lobbyist for various European ethnic groups protect the interests of their ancestral homelands. Ethnicity plays an important part in American politics. How can we account for the thousands of immigrants from Latin America and Cuba who have entered this country in our fight against communism which eventually topple on itself without armed necessities. Where is the black leadership to demand and say it like it is that there are double standards when it comes to black nations and some American diplomatic policies. What are quotas? Ask the Haitians who were not permitted to come to the United States.

There are many plans for African Americans to solve their problems. But are the leaders a myth or a reality? Who is a leader? Do they represent all segments of black America. The time has come for the division's in the black community to form a consortium or one central organization that would include the major fragments of leadership in the black community.

Reference: *They Did Not Tell Me True Facts About the African American's Past and American Experience*

LIBERIA

American Colonization Society Remarks, November 5, 1894

A report on the educational status of the Negro and its relation to his industrial and economic development in 1894 sounds similar to some professional experts remarks on American blacks in 1996.

In 1814, these following remarks were written and reported by a member of the American Colonization Society at Washington, D.C. His name was George Stetson. He stated some of his observations about the southern Negro from his personal experiences during his residence in districts of the south. Stetson said he observed the Negroes' racial character, habits, environment, mental, moral, religions, physical development and idiosyncrasies. He expressed these views at a meeting of the anthropological Society of Washington. He stated in the 1890's what some researchers articulate in 1996, that they are interested in the great majority of the Negro class and not exceptions. Stetson said he will address the unadulterated and uneducated Negro. He said the Negro represents 12 plus percent of the population but is serving out in our prisons and penitentiaries 38 percent of the aggregated sentences of the country. The Negro is sadly deficient in logical, deductive and analytical power - mental defects common in the lack of mechanical and industrial training.

Remember the above remarks were written in 1894, one hundred and two years ago.

Notes of Liberia

In 1893, the Independent State of Liberia decided to start a navy by obtaining its first war vessel for the country. The African Times, January 2, 1893 states:

"The steel cruisers Gorronommah was successfully launched recently by Messrs. M'Illwaine and M'Call at Belfast. The new vessel which is 95 feet long and has an admiralty displacement of 150 tons will be armed fore and aft with Nordenfelt and quick-firing machine guns. She will be stationed at Monrovia."

The American Colonization Society's Bulletin No. 2, February, 1893 listed the names of Liberia's Presidents from 1848 to 1892.

Presidents of Liberia

Joseph Jenkins Roberts	1848 to 1856
Stephen Allen Benson	1856 to 1864

Daniel Dashiel Warner	1864 to 1868
James Sprigg Payne	1868 to 1870
Edward James Roye	1870 to 1872
Joseph Jenkins Roberts	1872 to 1876
James Sprigg Payne	1876 to 1878
Anthony William Garner	1878 to 1884
Hilary Richard Wright Johnson	1884 to 1891
Joseph James Chesseman	1892 -

President Roberts was elected six times, President Benson and President Johnson each four times, President Gardner three times, President Warner and President Chesseman each twice, and President Royen once. The first six Presidents were immigrants from the United States and sometimes referred to as Americo Liberians.

A Dangerous Mission, 1912

Major Charles Young, the third black graduate of the U.S. Military Academy, West Point, class of 1889 was assigned as a military attache in Liberia, 1912. Young was able to develop a rapport with President D.E. Howard. On June 11, 1912, the president of Liberia desired Captain Young to review a proposed plan for the readjustment of the Franco-Liberia boundary which would eliminate the division of tribes.

President Howard wrote Young a letter on November 23, 1912 requesting him to take an expedition to the relief of a Captain Brown who was surrounded by a group of hostile natives. Young was offered some 100 men to accompany him on the mission. Charles Young responded to the president's request on November 24, 1912 by accepting the mission. Young also advised the president to utilize the services of a Captain Stewart and sixty men in order to insure the safety of Captain Browne.

Young and six soldiers departed Monrovia, Liberia on November 25, 1912 in the search for Captain Browne. It was necessary for Young to secure the services of six hammock bearers the next day. The party traveled up the St. Paul River some 20 miles to a town called Millsburg then to a Muhlenberg mission where there was a training school for native boys. Young commented on the beautiful scenery between Millsburg and Arthington and also near the area of Suhen. The second day of the trip, the party traveled through bush country transversing marshy streams to the villages of Morla (Mordee). Charles Young was observant of the agricultural potentials of the traveled areas and often made notes during the trip. He was surprised how well this part of the country was adapted to the cultivation of rice and cocoa. Young felt that the bridges should be constructed on the road from Suhen to Morla. He did not think that this route was the direct passage to the French frontier.

The third day of the trip, November 27, 1912, found Young and his group traveling in a northwest direction over a very dangerous trail. They finally approached a village. The village was called Bombana and the chief spoke some English but was unfriendly and had no love for the Liberian government. Young displayed his statesmanship abilities when he attempted to insure the Chief that the Liberian government wanted nothing free from the village and that the party would pay for food and necessary services. After spending the night in the village, the group proceeded the next day for a town 25 miles away.

On November 28, 1912, Major Young and his men arrived at a town called Borpora, which was very clean and had received assistance from one of the commissioners. However Young was not impressed with the presence of ten indigenous skulls displayed near the entrance of a stockade or jail. He felt the skulls were a reminder to the people of past encounters with the government.

The chiefs at Borpora, Totoquelli and Bellapambo, were hesitant to assist the group when they first arrived. Finally, the chiefs agreed to permit them to spend the night. The next morning (5th day of trip) Young left for the town of Bellapambo, a distance of 30 miles through jungle and large bush. After paying the chief of Bellapambo for rice and other supplies, the group spent the night and the next day departed for Baryar (Baryela). Young was not able to get additional carriers and he was compelled to walk a distance of 25 miles to the town of Gorpor. The reception at Gorpor was warm and supplies and food were obtained. The following day the party proceeded toward the town of Vassly, a distance of 16 miles.

Young arrived at Zorzor, a walled town consisting of approximately 400 houses and garrison buildings for the local frontier force. There was a market place in the town and the Mandingo merchants were present in large groups. Young noticed the French influence in the town, with the French border being only an hour and half from Zorzor using good roads. Young was optimistic of the great potential the town had for the cultivation of raw products, fruit, and vegetables once more roads were opened. Young remained at Zorzor for one week awaiting the arrival of additional troops. On December 9, 1912, Young left Zorzor with a party of ten chiefs and additional men. The party spent the night at Sarraye where chief Gotta Caou hosted the visiting chiefs and Young. The town was clean on the inside and outside. Young was quite impressed with the chief's leadership.

When Major Young departed Sarraye, he journeyed to Bangyea where he received more troops and now had a total of 105 men.

On the morning of December 11, 1912, major Young and his troops left Banqyea for Gangwota. Leaving Gangwota, the party moved down the St. Paul River to a French post at Tinsou. Young observed the indigenous French soldiers constructing earthworks. Major Young showed his courtesy to the French sergeant in charge of the detail and then proceeded to Dineena where they spent the night. During the next few days, Young traveled through the towns of Nama, Ganamow, Nyah, Goinlorycwon, and Gomow.

When Major Young arrived in Dingama, he was welcomed by the indigenous people who were joyously, dancing, singing and stating that Young was the second civilized American to visit the town. These were the Mano people. Young described these people as follows:

> The Manos are a man eating folk and few graves are to
> be seen in or near their towns. These graves are only

that of the buried heads of their chiefs, the bodies of
even these having been eaten.

Major Young displayed his deep concern for the future progress of these people. The suggested that certain measures must be initiated to improve the conditions of these people. Young stated the following:

> They must have (1) a good commissioner (2) troops
> stationed among them (3) a farm school for their
> children. I promised them all of these things as
> a reward for their loyalty to the government. . .

Major Young was now concerned as to whether he was moving in the correct direction. After leaving the Mano's, he decided to move toward the southeast.

On December 17, 1912, he left the village of Klitoma and later arrived at Sanquilly. He was greeted by an elderly man called Dobayiyou who wanted Young to protect his people from the French. A meeting was held and the old gentleman agreed to give land to those chiefs who had been in exile and were present with Young. Major Young realized that this chance to assist in negotiations between the exiled chiefs and the elder chief would be beneficial for the Liberian government.

On the 19th of December, Major Young attempted to make contact with Captain Browne, A messenger was not successful in reaching Browne. The messenger returned and informed Young that the Mandingos were still opposing Browne and his men.

Major Young then decided to leave immediately for Coween. He passed through seven small towns, all loyal to the government and finally reached the area of Taymow. Young described in detail the appearance and mannerisms of the Mandingos when he arrived. He wrote:

> The advance guard marched into the town, and the
> Mandingos, were before a house at the entrance, all in
> a line and dressed in their best clothes, bowing and
> smiling only as those black Jews of Africa can. They

announced how glad they were to see the Liberian troops. They said that they had always been with the Liberian government, while at the same time they had hoisted over their heads, at the entrance of the town, a French flag. I called for an explanation of this. They told me that they had put up the French flag to show that they were French citizens.

Major Young requested that the Mandingos present a trading permit for trading in Liberian territory since the people had stated they were French citizens. They could not produce a permit. An inventory was made of the goods and material and a census of the people present. Major Young explained that he took the following actions:

> I sent the women north over the French lines under the escort of the Mandingo man of their choosing. I cached the goods and left them with the King of Taymow, as a last resort. I needed the four prisoners (men) as carriers for my rice and for the hammocks for myself and the sick, because from Taymow on to Tappe the people are so wild and afraid of soldiers that it is impossible to get carriers.

Upon leaving Taymow, Major Young was threatened with the presence of many warriors with knives and guns viewing his party but fortunately no encounter occurred.

On the 23rd of December, 1912, Young arrived at the town of Maingosha's where he stayed until December 23, 1912. When the party left the town they were led into an ambush where one man and a chief were killed.

December 24, 1912, Christmas Eve, Major Young received his first injury during this expedition. He described the incident as follows:

> The next morning (December 24, 1912) having made a prisoner of an old woman captured in a casada field,

> we put her in a hammock and by hint of threatening to kill her, begging her, promising her and rewarding her if she would lead us to Tappi. She consented and bravely led us wrong. Having run into this ambush, she said that we would have to kill her because she would not go any further. We fought from town to town all that day. Had three men shot and wounded. <u>While leading</u> (my emphasis) the advance guard into the town, I myself was shot in the right arm. At about three o'clock in the afternoon we stopped at a town (name unknown) about fifteen miles from the place where we started from in the morning. I was now convinced that I was going in the wrong direction. I made up my mind to rest and to capture some prisoners.

Young had left Monrovia, Liberia, thirty days ago and now it was December 25, Christmas. The party was lost in the jungle and feared the presence of the man eating Manos. Each man had only 4 clips of ammunition remaining. Eventually they spotted a French town which was named Pawee. At first the people were rebellious to the group and after sharing medicine with them, their confidence was increased. The expedition continued south to the town of Blecna, Gawee and then to Zikki where the party stayed over night.

Young traveled on to Tappi. On December 29, 1912, Major Young had completed a dramatic and daring mission, arriving at Tappi, he found Captain Browne and 78 men.

Young permitted Captain Browne to have 200 men to use to drive out hostile forces in the area. Young also noticed two major problems one was pay for Captain Browne's troop and the other was the overall poor morale of the men because of terrible conditions. Major Young felt that the government should be most appreviative of their welfare, He stated:

> It appears that the government had given credence to petty reports of all kinds with respect to this officer's (Captain Browne) cruelty to his men and cruelty to the

natives, without giving him a chance to be heard, or what would have been better, perhaps, giving him the benefit of the doubt. How he endured surrounded as he was by these warring cannibals who came as far as his stockade, surrounding him by thousands from days into months and still maintained a splendid discipline in his command, is beyond my knowledge and a measure of grit that few men would have displayed.

Charles Young departed Tappi with 125 men, chiefs and prisoners on January 5, 1913 and arrived on January 15, 1913 at Monrovia.

Upon arriving back to Monrovia, Young prepared the detailed report of his expedition and submitted some very sound recommendations for the Liberian government to consider in order to improve relations between the government and indigenous tribes.

On January 19, 1913, Charles Young submitted a preliminary report of the expedition to the Secretary, War College Division, General Staff. He wrote in the cover letter of the report that:

> Field report of this relief expedition will be made as soon as my right arm, which contains a ball received in a four (4) days fight with the tribesmen, sufficiently recovers to permit me to write . . No military attache work in the shape of reports for monograph has been undertaken yet, because the affairs of the country were in a state of transition which depended upon the receivership, which only went into effect November 26, 1912. Intelligent report upon the topographic features and resources depended upon a journey into the interior of the country such as I have just completed.

Charles Young had been assigned to Liberia for approximately one year in 1913 and he had accomplished a most outstanding feat by successfully completing his expedition for the relief of Captain Browne. Unfortunatelly the final complete report that was forwarded to the War College Division,

General Staff, Washington, did not receive the justified appraisal as a commendable and heroic mission that Major Young experienced in the hinterland of the country of Liberia. An action office in the War College Division made a normal simple acknowledgement of the receipt of the report and filed it. This writer viewed more than three copies of the report but no mention of recognition to the major (Young) for his meritorious performance. Later the Liberian government praised and cited Young in a most outstanding manner. However the report of the Browne Relief Expedition became a part of the numerous files of the War Department and was given the usual treatment of "noted and filed". The lengthy narration of Major Young's exciting trip into bush country in Liberia was addressed in this manuscript in order to place the importance and significance of the expedition in its due place of honor in military history and especially the history of forgotten black heroes.

Soldier and Diplomat, 1911-1914 and 1920-1921

The following discussion on Colonel Charles Young's involvement in the internal affairs of the Liberian government reveals some interesting information about the recurring conditions of Liberian and how the country needed more assistance from the United States. Young was discussing social, economic and political conditions of a country that unfortunately would experience a serious and devastating civil war in the mid 1990's. Colonel Young was a prophet in the wilderness whose voice and revelations were not heard or possibly ignored by the state department of America the Beautiful whose interest in Liberia was present as early as the 1800's.

President Howard was evidently quite pleased with Young's first year of duty as military attache to the American Legation. On February 11, 1913, Howard forwarded Young a letter announcing the appointment of Major Young as the military advisor to the War Department of Liberia. The appointment gave Young some very broad powers. These powers were mentioned in the letter of appointment. They were as follows:

> "You are hereby appointed military advisor to the War
> Department of Liberia and as such will be given, by the

Secretary of War, free access and authority in the department to assist in inaugurating and formulating the plans, regulations, and order for the thorough organization of the entire Frontier Force, both as regards to its personnel, assignment and discipline. You are authorized to prescribe all forms to be used in the Force as payrolls, requisitions, etc. and anything else necessary to the perfection of the Frontier Force.

The Honorable W.E. Dennis, Secretary of War and Navy, Liberia, was informed of Major Young's appointment as military advisor. In a letter to Dennis, dated February 11, 1913, President D.E. Howard wrote:

"In order that he (Young) may more effectually perform these duties, I have to request that you grant him free access in the department and that in your absence (at this time W.E. Dennis was recovering from an illness) you instruct Mr. C.E. Cooper, or whoever else you may leave to act for you, that Major Young has been so appointed by me and that all the regulations or instructions he may himself give or request to be given in your name are to be observed and followed, Mr. Cooper will sign officially for you all official documents which the military advisor may deem necessary to be issued, whether for requisitions to the treasury or to the officers in the command, but the forms of these requisitions and orders to the officers, as well as payrolls, etc. are to be under the direct control of Major Young, from whom Mr. Cooper must take recommendations (sic) or instructions. I also desire that, on your return, Major Young shall continue to perform the duties herein enumerated."

Major Young had received from the President of Liberia unusual powers for a military attache and his relations with the host government's War Department, Young was definitely qualified for the tasks and possessed the tact and diplomacy that were requirements for these responsibilities.

Unfortunately Secretary of War Dennis did not cooperate completely with Major Young. Upon his return to work from his illness, Dennis complained to President Howard that Young was exercising excessive authority in the War Department. President Howard had a conference with Dennis. Dennis was not in agreement with the stringent system of accountability of funds that Young had instituted. Young justified this action on the basis of previous gross irregularities and inefficiency in the department. The Secretary of War was not successful in defending and proving his allegations against Young. On March 29, 1913, Secretary of War, W.E. Dennis submitted his resignation to the President. President Howard accepted the resignation:

Major Charles Young's additional duty as military advisor to the Liberian War Department was not completely supported by the United States State Department. The local American legation in Liberia probably agreed to the appointment. However, the State Department had expressed their concern of Young's intervention in the Liberian government's internal affairs in the country, a State Department memorandum to the War Department dated March 22, 1912, stated:

"The Department of State makes the suggestion that the War Department clearly define to Captain Charles Young, recently designated as military attache to the legation at Monrovia, the scope of his new duties, pointing out that his cooperation with the officers employed by the Liberian government in organizing the constabulary of the Republic must be strictly in an advisory capacity and in *no way administrative* (my emphasis), Captain Young should *take no active part whatever in the management of Liberia affairs* (my emphasis) and should carefully refrain from any acts which might be interpreted as *an assumption of duties of an officer of Liberia or an interference in the operation of its government*. (my emphasis).

Major Charles Young suffered a very serious attack of malignant malaria in April, 1913. In West Africa malignant malaria was know as black water fever. It is possible that he could have contracted the malaria while he was conducting the Browne Relief Expedition in December, 1912 and January 19, 1913.

On August 7, 1914, the major European powers, Germany, Austria, Hungary, France, Russia and Great Britain engaged in World War I. They allegedly wanted to satisfy certain individual desires. For example, France wanted to regain the territories of Alsace-Lorraine and England desired to see the destruction of German naval superiority and militarism. In order for some of the powers to satisfy urgent financial commitment, trading and negotiations with small countries like Liberia were curtailed.

Major Young displayed his abilities of the "statesman" and military advisor when he requested from some departments of the Liberian government an assessment of their additional needs because of the European War. On October 10, 1914, the Liberian Secretary of Treasury, John L. Morris replied to Young's request. Morris wrote the following:

"complying with your verbal request on yesterday for a statement of the needs of Liberians growing out of the European War, I have the honor to give the following information for purposes of the cablegram which I understand you are to send to your government.

1. On July 1, the receivership held the balance of $25,685.19 brought from the June quarter. They collected during September quarter $74,314.81 making the total assigned revenues for the quarter to be $90,000.

2. The receivership held the balance paid the government residue in the sum of $9,346.09 for the month of July. The claims for July on account of salaries and other charges were paid by supplementing the aforementioned sum from the internal revenue. No residue has been paid by the government for August and September, and the government is unable to pay its budgetary claims.

3. It is desired that the Department of State at Washington intercede, with the New York Bankers for the advance to the Liberian government of $140,000 secured on the residue of the loan in the hands of the fiscal agents. The residue of the loan

was represented on March 31, 1914 to be: cash on hand $800; unsold bonds on hand at par $142,000.

4. The government of Liberia prefers that the payment of interest and sinking funds be not suspended.

5. Rice, sugar, flour, milk, bacon, slat pork and beef are particularly needed in Sinoe, Marshall and Cape Palmas and quantities of such articles would be welcomed there.

COLONEL CHARLES YOUNG

The African Mission of the Protestant Episcopal Church, U.S.A. also was affected by the European War. Bishop S.D. Ferguson wrote Major Young a letter on October 10, 1914, Bishop Ferguson stated:

"From such information as has reached me I have reason to believe that our missionaries suffer in common with others from the scarcity of foodstuffs and the advance in prices of such as are sold caused by the European War... In answer to your second query, I beg to inform you that the last consignment of rice we received here from Liverpool just before the war (July 15th) cost $3.35 1/4 a cw., all charges included. If we could get that article now at the same rate, if not less, we could run our schools during the war".

After receiving some preliminary reports on condition in Liberia, Young decided to send a message on October 10, 1914 to Colonel McCain, Adjutant General's Office, Washington, D.C. Major Young requested action on some of the financial problems that were stated by the Liberian Secretary of Treasury.

Young made a very sound appraisal of the situation and recommended the following:

"Much produce that might be moved to American markets in American ships in exchange for staples. Good opportunity for (sic) United States merchants. Approximate 1,000 missionaries must be relieved by regulated charity with following food in tons: salt fish or meat, thirty-two; rice, sixty-two; flour, twenty-five; sugar, six; salt, three; soap, one; kerosene, two hundred fifty cases eighty percent. Business controlled by German merchants suspended for lack of stock... American firms should send here financial agent for exchanging goods. Advise see Gravenhart Co., New York, N.Y. McCarthy, Old South Building, Boston and C. Woermann, Hamburg Line for Shipping facilities.

Some of the Liberian officials were quite appreciative of Young's ingenuity and sincere concern about the Liberian problem. Senator Cooper, Maryland County, Republic of Liberia, wrote Young on October 12, 1914. He said:

"... I can assure you that your efforts in this particular matter are very highly appreciated; and to get anything of this nature through will be the means of helping to save Liberia".

On October 13, 1914, Major Young sent a report to Washington indicating the possibilities of American trade with Liberia because of the war in Europe. The report stated that:

"The German Bank has practically suspended operations... Estimates of the total value of imports of the Republic of Liberia for the year 1913.

England	313,886.75
Germany	578,361.27
Holland	14,897.68
U. S. A.	26,730.21
Other Countries	477,360.85

Estimates of the total value exports of the Republic of Liberia for the year 1913.

England	110,821.66
Germany	934,785.16
Holland	18,628.85

U.S.A. <u>312.20</u> (my emphasis)
Other Countries 47,638.56

In December, 1914, Major Young realized that no progress was made in solving the Liberian financial and economic crises due to the European War. He was also aware of the little support that America was offering Liberia. Young wrote a personal letter to a Major Charles Crawford, Secretary War College Division, Washington, on December 31, 1914. Crawford was a West Point classmate of Major Young. Major Young wrote as follows:

> "We are at a stand still here now, or even worse than that since trade is absolutely paralyzed as the result of the war in Europe.

Young was also interested in finding some way to enable the Frontier Force to receive their pay. He said:

> "We have had to reduce the Frontier Force from 1200 to 600 men and the men have not been paid for 3 months. How the subsistence for what we have (which is complete inadequate to the needs of the country) is to be paid for without relief from the U.S., I can't see for the life of me."

Major Young reminded Major Crawford that these problems could have been prevented if the information forward had been evaluated thoroughly and favorable consideration given to the request. He recalled the fact that with the large quantities of produce on hand that the receivership of custom was now bankrupt.

Young also informed Crawford of other conditions in the country and also the status of the Frontier Force. He stated:

> "The bankers (N.Y.) have refused to allow any default in the interest due on the loan, or to make any further advances. The policy seems very short sighted to say the least. The Liberians must have money or ships sent to carry away produce, for their relief. If these do not come, I fear the hostile tribes of the coast and interior seeing their weakness without a trained

soldiery will begin to wage war. If war of this kind comes it will be at a great cost in blood and in money 10 times greater than the advance or relief now needed, it is with regret that I tell you of the death of one of the best of our American officers, Captain Richard Newton, who died on 13th June of this year. Major Ballard has resigned to take effect May 1, 1915. I have been and am still working hard to prepare cadets for commissions to fill these gaps; as I feel that no more American officers can be allowed at this juncture. At the same time I am also personally engaged in using soldiers in constructing a military road from Monrovia up the St. Paul River to the Franco-Liberian hinterland. At a central point on this road we shall construct a station for all reserve troops and thus assure the peace and safety of the country.

A cablegram had been sent to the War Department by Major Young on October 10, 1914. The Chief of Staff, War Department, became concerned on March 27, 1915 about a cost of $387.50 for the dispatch of the message. The Chief of Staff wrote to the Chief War College Division the following:

"Referring to cost of $387.50, Chief of Staff (sic) directs you submit any instruction given to Major Young bearing upon his duties as military attache at Monrovia which would serve to clear up the matter in question.

Brigadier General M.M. Macomb, Chief of War College Division responded to the Chief of Staff's request by writing this:

"Reports and dispatches from Major Young indicate that practically all of his time is taken up in work with the Liberian Frontier Force, which appears to be a police force that upholds the government. The duties performed by him have only very slight value from a professional military stand point. When he was recommended for military attache he was detailed to obtain military information from abroad and designated by the State Department as military attache to the American legation at Monrovia, Major Young's detail having been made primarily at the instance of the Department of the State for the purpose of utilizing his services in connection with the reorganization of the Liberian constabulary and the cablegram sent by him the payment of which is at issue, having no connection whatsoever with the procuring of military information relating Liberia, it is believed that it should be paid from funds of the State Department.

Secretary of War, Lindley M. Garrison wrote an endorsement to the correspondence reference the cablegram. On August 26, 1915 the Secretary of War stated:

"I certify that the cablegram of Major Charles Young, Cavalry, Military Attache to the American Legation and Monrovia, Liberia, dated October 10, 1914 was on official business of the War Department and was a necessity (sic) in the military service."

Major Charles Young's assessment of the Liberian conditions due to the World War I was of interest to non-government institutions that had Christian measures and education organization in Liberia. The librarian of the Boston Athenaeum, Charles Knowles Bolton wrote the secretary of war on May 11, 1915 inquiring about the reliability of Major Charles Young. Bolton had received correspondence from Young and found the information on the conditions in the country quite valuable. He wanted to assure himself and an organization that was known as "Trustees of Donation for Education in Liberia" that Major Young was a reputable officer in the United States Army.

The secretary of war instructed the adjutant general to prepare a reply to Charles K. Bolton's letter. The adjutant general informed Bolton that Major Charles Young was one of the few Negro officers in the regular army and that he had an excellent record and there was no known derogatory information on file concerning Young.

While a cadet at the military academy, West Point, Charles Young had developed a good friendship with one of his classmates. During some of his trials and tribulations, Young would receive understanding and sympathy from Alexander Ross Piper, a native of New York. Piper graduated 29 out of 49 in the West Point class of 1839. He served on the frontier, participated in the Sioux War, 1890-1891 and was professor, Military Science and Tactics, Gordon Institute, Georgia, 1892-1896. Piper was very active in West Point Alumni activities and was President of the Association of Graduates (West Point), 1934-1936. He died in South Salem, New York, November 21, 1952.

On July 26, 1915, Charles Young wrote Alexander Piper a letter. He told Piper that he appreciated the information he had received on the class dinner and reunion at West Point, Young remarked in the letter about his work in Liberia and also how grateful he was for the understanding Piper had shown him at West Point. Major Young stated:

> "We have succeeded in organizing a decent Frontier Force, in making a working system of reports, returns, regulations, a map of the Republic, and when this road of possibly 150 miles is finished with a central military station at its further end, my work that I laid out at the Army War College Before coming over here will be finished. The American officers that I brought with me have been loyal and worked well. The troops are native, not Liberians. They are not one unit inferior in the soldier spirit to our best black troops of our own army, which as you know is saying much. But I set out to thank you all, of the class who remembered me, both while getting up the reunion, during and since. While West Point was pretty hard pulling for me, still the roughness was relieved by the sympathy of many of my classmates, to whom I shall ever be grateful and among (whom) I shall remember you.

In September, 1915, Major Charles Young informed the American Charge d"Affaires, R.C. Bundy of the serious crisis that was present in Liberian affairs and its effect on the future of the Liberian government. Young wrote a letter dated September 26, 1915 and discussed how the Kru tribes at Sinoe were hostile toward civilized people and that there was no means of contact through transportation and telegraph. He also mentioned about foreign influence and plans that affected the stability of Liberia. Young wrote:

> "Also other hostile affairs between the Picanny Cess and Grand Bassa natives are reported. Besides the civilized element at Lower Buchanan having become frightened by reports of the attack at Sinne, in spite of the Frontier Force at that point, turned out its militia which ran amuck and have killed some wholly innocent natives of the Rock Cess Tribe thus bringing about a probable cause for another uprising of this well armed people who were furnished about three years ago with arms and ammunition from secret German sources looking toward wrecking the republic."

Major Young emphasized the possible destruction of foreign merchants and missionaries' properties if the hostile tribes were not controlled. He added that the government had no marine transportation for the Frontier Force and that the force had been reduced from 1200 to 600. Young also remarked how the ammunition supply had been depleted due to mismanagement and theft.

Young concluded his summary of the critical Liberian situation by asserting the following:

> "The ammunition, with the petty wars of the hinterland ... is manufactured in Germany and is for the 8 millimeter mauser carbine. Besides the improbability of being able to purchase it here, we are confronted with the recent sinister order of the English government forbidding its ships to call at Liberian ports in the (sic) future. These also stare us in the face, the fact of search of ships of other nationals and arbitrary seizure and detention of property exercised in African waters by the English. The force of American officers has been reduced to two by the resignation of Major Ballard and Captain Hawkins, who have finished their tours of duty after three and two years contract respectively. I have recommended to the Liberian government the early necessity of replacing them for this reduction coupled with that of the Force mentioned low state

of ammunition and lack of transport have undoubtedly set off the Krus who have never virtually acknowledged the power and authority of the government over them to the extent of paying their customs and taxes. This matter is so grave it should be settled once and for all".

Major Young played an important part in attempting to arouse and impress the American government of the crucial problems that were confronting the government of Liberia. He was convinced and realized that the future of Liberia was in jeopardy. He expressed this interest when he asked Mr. Bundy the following:

"Can't we have the moral support of an American warship at this the most serious juncture in the affairs of the Republic since I have been here? On my side I would advise that we get together, yourself, the General Receiver and I, and *thoroughly acquaint our government with the pressing and sore need of Liberia* (my emphasis) to preserve itself from foes within and without... telling of both just as it appears here".

Major Charles Young had completed three years of duty in Liberia in 1915. The War Department normally assigned attaches to foreign legations for a maximum period of three years. In October, 1915, a decision was made by the War Department to recall Young from Liberia. Young was officially notified on October 16, 1915 of his reassignment and relief from duty to obtain military information abroad.

Prior to his departure from Monrovia, Liberia, Major Young prepared a thorough report on the general condition of Liberia. The report was forwarded to the office of the Chief of Staff, War College Division and the Secretary of State. This detailed analysis of the condition in Liberia presented an unbiased and nonpolitical evaluation of the serious conditions that existed with the central government, provinces and the hinterland of the Republic of Liberia. History has shown that evidently the important warning signals or indications of potential serious results were not considered or acted upon by the American government during Liberia's most decisive and tragic hours of the years 1914-1915.

Major Young explained in his report the impact of the loss of German trade with Liberia. He stated:

> "The condition of Liberia since the outbreak of the war in Europe has been usually hard, because the major position of the trade had been with German merchants carrying the imports and exports of the country in German bottoms. All of this was stopped and the trade virtually fell into the hands of two English and one Dutch firm, all buying their goods in England for the most parts, and carrying them in English ships. The English firms continued more or less openly to buy up and ship to England the produce of the German firms here and with the consent of the English government through its consul-general here. Then the Liberians, many of whom have been factory men and small shop keepers at branch stores of the Germans, were employed by these latter as middlemen to purchase goods for them in England, and thus supply in a small way their stores up and down the coast. This kept the German business going after a fashion and enabled the customer receivership to get enough money to pay the interest on the loan of the Republic and to half-pay the Frontier Force which was to be reduced.. but left nothing for the general government to pay its official personnel and clerks with. Possibly over half the civilized population lives by depending upon the government's chest.

Young further declared in the report that few farm products were being offered for sale in England and that Scandinavia and Germany, the former purchasers, were lost because of the World War. He explained that to offset this problem, the government attempted to impose a head tax upon the population to include the hinterland. However, some of the commissioners were involved in tax scandals and corruption thereby creating additional problems, Young also revealed how the custodian of an arsenal was involved in a major theft of ammunition he wrote:

> "To add to this trouble, the keeper of the arsenal, on Cephas, was a go between to Perry, robbed the government of much ammunition, about 50 cases of which were sold to the

> rebellious Kroos of the Coast. Our Major York took up the case for the government against the thieves. They were released until next term of court o two thousand dollars bond each; but there are many who believe that at this juncture in the affairs of the republic the charge should be treason and not theft, seeing as how gravely important the matter of ammunition is in the country. Consequently, a demand was made upon the government for the arrest and confinement of these two transgressors without bail ... and also for the regulation of the arsenals and the sale of arms and ammunition."

Major Young clearly expressed his opinions, and observations concerning the serious conditions of the Kroos of the Coast area and the Liberian government. Even though primarily assigned to the American legation to collect military information for the War Department, Young demonstrated superior abilities as an unofficial statesman. He was aware of the major internal problems, corruptions in government and the outside influence and personal exploitation of Liberia's weak government at this time by the European powers.

Young discussed the Kroo problems in his report by stating the following:

> "The Kroos of the coast have never fully acknowledged the authority of the Liberian government,. Payment of their (sic) duties has been a bone of contention with them... Again they have not been fairly dealt with in many cases by the Americo-Liberians in the neighborhood of their settlements. The Krooman at best is no angel and even to his own people is a hard, mean, cruel man. During my tour of duty here the Kroos have been set up to make war against the Liberian people by the German merchants, and now things point to their doing the same thing urged on secretly by the English. All with a view to showing the inability of the government to protect life and property of foreigners and to break up the loan agreement and partition the republic. The Kroos themselves at Grand Cess have recently sent a contribution to the English at Sierra Leone

to aid the European War Fund. I saw a copy of the letter of transmittal in the hands of the Secretary of State. There are confessedly other agitators at work among them from the Liberians themselves."

Major Young did not hesitate in stating the names of known alleged corrupters working in the internal structure of the Liberian government. He remarked how the Kroos had objected to a Senator Ross who was known as the Kroos' enemy and oppressor because of the tax situation. Young said:

"The main grievance of the Kroos at Sinoe is said to be against Senator Ross who has been long their enemy and oppressor and is now in this tax squeeze against them. "We want this matter thoroughly (sic) investigated, because this same Ross has a most unsavory reputation all over the republic. Twice charged with forgery (once here and once in the United States), impeached and dismissed from the House of Representatives, openly accused on all sides of incest with his own sister an all-around dangerous and unscrupulous man, a running sore in the body of politics and one whom the government fears.

"If this man is guilty of causing the uprising of the Kroos at Sinoe, knowing as he does the almost defenseless condition of his country, he should after trial be expelled from the republic.

"Indeed an associate justice of the supreme court remarked to me a few days ago that this man Ross has broken every commandment in the decalogue and committed some crimes not named in it."

The Republic of Liberia's interior was administered by a chief commissioner under the Secretary of Interior. There were reported problems in the interior of excessive fines imposed by tribal leaders, slave dealings and possible theft of tax money. Young cited in his report that the Chief Commissioner, M. Massaquoi, could have been responsible for some of the problems that occurred in the interior.

Young's report reveals the intervention of the English in Liberian affairs. He stated:

> "For eighteen months the English Consul-General, Mr. Maugham has been plotting and planning against the Republic, attacking the neutral attitude which the country assumed with respect to the resident Germans here: accusing the Germans now of dealing in contraband, again of making an attempt on his life, again of running secret wireless apparatus and finally of violating the Liberian customs regulations, with possibly ulterior motives. He has done his best to imperil and discredit Liberia with his government. This customer intermeddling was directed upon the American general receiver with a view of showing that the policy of the United States in regard to the loan was not a success. In many of his efforts he has taken ground of questionable honor to say the least and all of them with a view to possible French and English *intervention and final partitioning of the territory between them* (emphasis added). The French have played a tacit but sympathetic and interested part with the English in all this scheme.

It is interesting to note that during 1915, an American army officer had summarized and presented the facts or reliable information concerning the secret interests of England and France to acquire the territories of Liberia. Major Young was fortunate to attend some high level meetings with the president of Liberia and high ranking cabinet officers. He obtained some information that in numerous instances was not known to some American legation officers. Young reported the facts, but questions that can be posed today are: Was the United States earnestly interested in aiding Liberia in its most crucial moments for survival? Did the report of Major Young reach the desks of high ranking government officials or was it just filed as interesting but not relevant. Or was it the indirect intent for Liberia to be eventually saved by submission because of necessity and survival to American business magnates who went to Liberia and profited immensely from her resources and gained an indefinite influence in the internal government of the Republic. Could this have been prevented if the report of a black military attache in 1915 had been thoroughly evaluated and reviewed by decision making statesmen.

Young stressed quite adamantly the reasons why the United States should assist Liberia. He wrote:

> "I submit, as candid opinion, after close contact with both the English and French and also the Germans out here, extending over three years, that neither of three nations undertook the administration of the Liberian customers with the United States in good faith. All three have vied with each other to give trouble to republic to the end showing that the scheme was impracticable and finally of dividing up the territory of the republic. Likewise this would bring the status of the Liberian people down to the level of that of their own colonists; for it must be borne in mind that the Americo-Liberian with all his faults and failings is head and shoulder above his Sierra Leone brother or the German black and even with the liberality of France toward its black population, the Liberian is ahead of the French Guinean in everything that goes to make a self-respecting man. If these nations ever try to assert their authority over Liberia, instead of being a land or promise for the Americo-Liberian and an open door for the American black man, this act will cause these people to seek the United States again for refuge from an intolerable and blighting oppression.

Young was granted two months of leave prior to reporting to his new duty station.

The Republic of Liberia extended its appreciation for the outstanding services that Major Young had rendered. The secretary of state, C. D. B. King wrote a letter to the charge d'affaires, American Legation and expressed his gratitude for Young's contributions to the country.

Richard C. Bundy, Charges d'Affaires and interior, American Legation, Liberia wrote Charles Young a letter on November 20, 1915. Bundy commented about the secretary of state's commendation of Young and also expressed his appreciation of Young's sincerity and devotion to duty. Richard Bundy wrote:

> "The extraordinary zeal and rare devotion you brought to your arduous task in Liberia is the subject of universal commendations justly merited. The actual results of work so well performed through your boundless energy and personal application leaves behind you a testimonial of your true worth far fairer than I can possibly convey in few faltering words of praise. Time cannot fail to enhance the appreciation of your labors here."

Prior to his immediate departure from Liberia, Major Charles Young was honored with a personal letter of commendation from President Howard of Liberia.

The commendations that Major Young received in November, 1915 from the Liberian government; the praise received from the Charge d'Affaires ad interim, and his past outstanding records of service were instrumental in the secretary of state's decision to request the War Department to retain Young in Liberia. However, on December 9, 1915, Secretary of War, Lindley Garrison wrote to Secretary of State the following:

> "In reply to your letter of December 4, with reference to Major Charles Young, United States Cavalry who was relieved from duty as military attache at Monrovia, Liberia, I desire to say that it is gratifying to know that his work has been so satisfactory to the Department of State American Negroes whose hearts are bound up in the welfare of Liberia.

President of Liberia requested Major Young to present his views and advice concerning the serious matters that were confronting the country. Young developed a plan designed to settle disturbance in Sinoe and Bassa counties. They involved imposing martial law in the two counties and stationing a force of soldiers near Greenville, Sinoe to suppress the Kroos uprising.

Major Young concluded his report by appealing to the United States government to assist Liberia. Young also recommended that the American minister should be well qualified and aware of the country's problems. Major wrote the following:

> "I submit that a more active part and firmer stand must be taken by the United States with regard to Liberian matters and the governments that have with America the quasi hegemony over the republic should be made to understand in unmistakable terms that the little republic is not to be harassed nor dismembered; but left as a one last spot where the black man can work out his own nationalism.

Young remarked that the Liberians must be prepared to maintain a sound government void of widespread corruption. He also presented his opinions as to the qualities that the American Minister to Liberia should possess. Young said:

> "This position of Minister to Liberia requires an additional fitness in the shape of knowing the peculiarities of Liberian politics, an intimate acquaintance with the Liberian official class, as opposed to the Liberian people, and the one appointed must have the full confidence of the Liberian government as to his ability to handle its affairs and advise it in time of stress.

The Liberian government was fortunate to have available the services of Major Charles Young for three years and especially during a period of crisis in the country. Young was detailed in 1912 as a military attache to the American Legation. He also served as an advisor and official statesman to the Liberian government.

The Military Diplomat Returns To Liberia 1920-1921

The Department of State requested that the Military Attache to Liberia in 1919, Lieutenant Colonel John E. Green be returned to the United States and that Colonel Charles Young succeed him. It is interesting to recall that the original correspondence did not indicate the racial designation of Lieutenant John E. Green, however it did indicate "colored" for Colonel Young. The request revealed that Young desired to return to Liberia as Military Attach.

In 1920, Charles Young was still displaying his amicable relations with Liberian chief officials. Young often would exchange poetic writings with the current secretary of state in 1921 and later the president of Liberia, Edwin Barclay.

The following writing was from Barclay to Young:

"Human Life"

"Dear Colonel: Apropos of talk yesternight:

A moment of forgetfulness
Between two blank eternities;
A strident should, a cry, a sigh,
Amidst eternal silences;
A shaft of Light no sooner sped
Than quenched within the ocean night:
The glimmer of a falling star against
the crystal veil that screen
The past from what has yet to be;
A moments pause -- a faltering
Along the curve of human woes,
And this, O Young, is all Life
Seems to me.
As youth's blank threshold or
The ivory gate, of satiate age.

       Yours,
       Edwin Barclay, Sept. 27, 1920

Colonel Young had not lost his tact and alertness. He had corresponded with H.F. Worley, Receiver General of Customs, Republic of Liberia, who was residing at 72 Adams Street, Washington D.C. Young and Worley had discussed the Liberian situation and in a letter dated 4 November, 1919, Charles Young wrote that he had decided to accept the Military Attache assignment in Liberia.

When the Secretary of War informed the Secretary of State that Colonel Young had been directed to proceed to Liberia as Military Attache, he stated:

> "Colonel Charles Young, United States Army, (Retired) has been detailed by the War Department to obtain information from abroad in accordance with the provisions of an Act of Congress approved 27 February 1893 and has been directed to proceed to Monrovia, Liberia and report to the American Minister at that capital for such duty under his supervision as may be assigned to him by the War Department."

It is to be noted that there was no mention or instruction for Young that would involve him in the administration and internal affairs of the Liberian Government.

Colonel Charles Young returned to Liberia in 1920. As early as 12 February 1920, the President of Liberia asked Colonel Young to assist him in a problem concerning military and civilian officials. Secretary of State, Edwin Barclay, wrote Young and inquired whether it was possible for him to serve on a commission. The commission was to investigate allegations of outrage committed upon the native population by Liberian Frontier Force and Civil officials. Young accepted the appointment of commission members and prepared an extract from the proceedings of the commission and submitted them to the President for approval. President C.D.B. King of Liberia approved the extract on 4 March 1920.

The commission had investigated reports of theft of native's food, brutal acts inflicted upon natives and cattle illegally used for private use. The major recommendations of the commission was that the general receiver ensure that the troops be paid properly; that divisions of land involving tribal disputes be divided equally; and restitution of unpaid amounts collected July 26, both from superintendent Brewer and Captain Howard.

Colonel Charles Young did not hesitate on 27 April 1920 to write a personal letter to the President of Liberia and adamantly inform him of his displeasure with the commandant of the Frontier Force and the inefficiency of some of the officers. Young did not hesitate to specify names and the major allegation against individuals he thought were incompetent. Charles Young reminded the president that ceratin arrangements had been made without his knowledge or advice. He stated that the president had approved in a cabinet meeting a plan to locate the Frontier Force headquarters and it should be an area that has the largest number of troops. Young had desired to assign two American officers, Captain W.D. Nabors and Captain Henry O. Atwood at stations, Samoquelli and Maryland County. The purpose of these assignments according to Young was to provide discipline and administration of Mano and Gio sections of the country and also in Maryland County and along the Krue Coast. However, the commandant had issued orders placing Captain Whisnant in command of Gio and Captain Smith to command the Krue Coast troops and Captain Boyle was placed in charge of Frontier Office in Monrovia. Young related to the President that these action were "grave" and could jeopardize the welfare of Liberia. He realized that as military advisor his obligation and responsibility to both governments was to discuss the matter with the president.

Charles Young commented that Captain Boyle was once a successful officer but due to a malady of the head, his memory had been impaired and he questioned Boyle's judgment and reason. He had asked the commandant previously not to assign Captain Boyle to the Frontier Headquarters. Young said it was not his intent to offend the concerned officer but it was paramount to make it known that Captain Whisnant and a Lieutenant Potter stationed at Gio would fight but have been proven to be "battle cowards." He said that a Captain Smith was brave and efficient when sober, but he was seldom sober. Young informed the president that Captain Nevins, Supply Officer at Monrovia was allowed to retain his position even though the commandant was aware of his dishonesty and excessive inebriation.

The president was absent from Monrovia when the letter reached his office. Secretary of State, Edwin Barclay, replied to Young's letter.

Barclay apprised Young to submit some evidence to support the charges he had made against the officers. He believed that this would strengthen his allegations and enable the president upon his return to Monrovia to consider the charges as a serious matter.

Colonel Young did not wait for the president to return, he immediately wrote Secretary of State and Acting President Barclay and expressed his opinions about the military attache and advisor's relations to the Liberian government and Frontier Force and his reasons to discuss these problems openly. Young wrote:

"My motive in writing the letter of the 27th incident was not specifically to make accusations or charges against any one ... I wish to state that I understood from the State Department at Washington and also from His Excellency President King both in the U.S. and also in each audience given me (where Secretary of War was present) in which the matter of the Frontier Force was concerned, that such was to be my duty as servant of your government in capacity of military advisor.

Charles Young concluded his letter by making it known to Barclay that the functions of the military advisor should be clarified by the government of Liberia as immediate and he also referred to an executive statement that was given to him during his previous tour which permitted him to be informed of all matters involving the Frontier Force and the War Department. Young wrote, "My sole desire in regard to the government is to be helpful not controversial and not a quibbler over trifles. Nor shall I allow myself to be drawn into quarrels or factions of officers which gets nowhere constructively.

It is quite probable that Charles Young did not receive positive action from the executive branch of the Liberian government in reference to his respective duties as military advisor and also the conditions and inefficiency of the Frontier Force's operations. Because in a report "upon progress" made as military advisor that was sent to Washington, he addressed the problem of the Force and the reasons for the decline in efficiency. Young revealed in this report to the Director of the Military Intelligence Division very candidly why he was present again in Liberia. Young stated:

" Although this report bears at times upon Liberian affairs in general, it treats in the main upon the progress made in my work as military advisor of the republic, chiefly with the Liberian Frontier Force C.L.F.F.I.; for which purpose it was understood the Department of State (U.S.) requested my services here. It may also be important in the connection to add what the present president of Liberia, when president-elect and visiting in the U.S. on more than one occasion in Washington and again at my home in Ohio requesting my coming in this same capacity.

Colonel Young discussed the military force of the republic. He declared that the military force consisted of the Militia and Frontier Force under the control of the secretary of war. The Militia included "Americo-Liberians," "half breeds,' and 11 civilized natives." Young categorized the officers as ignorant to military training and undisciplined. Charles Young wrote that the Liberian Frontier Force was connected with the Receivership of Customs of the Republic and was responsible for maintaining order among the tribes and served as custom guards to prevent smuggling. The enlisted men were from native tribes of the Buzi, Mende, Gbande and Kpwessi people.

Young was not in accord with the excessive number of Liberian officers in the force who were returned by receiving a longevity status as a reward, for bravery. He suggested the awarding of military medals, citations and letters of commendation for outstanding performance and when officers were inefficient, retire them. Colonel Young explained that the Commandant, Major John H. Anderson, a retired staff sergeant of the United States Army was a weak administrator, demonstrated poor judgment and was deficient in military tactics and training.

Military Attache and Advisor remarked that between 1901-1912, Lieutenant Davis was not able to accomplish much with the Frontier Force even though he [got] promises by the government of Liberia to assist him. He also stated that his [Major] Lieutenant Colonel John E. Green was confronted with similar problems. In view of these past situations, Young delayed his return in 1920 long enough to inquire about the conditions of the force and at the request of the president, prepared a plan for the rehabilitation of the force. The cause of the decline of the force in Young's opinion was due to the World War I; inability of the general receivership to finance supplies and pay off the officers and men; and absence of a competent Commandant.

Young, the military diplomat in 1920, was displaying his firm and personal attitudes toward the European countries' consistent desires to intervene in Liberian. He stated:

But for occult political reasons springing possible from secret propaganda now being hatched by the English and French residents against the Americans, both white and colored, the president still remains firm and refuses the American officers both of the Liberian Frontier Force and the Interior Department a status whereby they can accomplish something constructively for the republic.

Charles Young the advisor had emphatically informed the Military Intelligence Division of the internal political and military complexities that existed in the Liberian government. Young had openly criticized the leadership of the country's political body and was attempting to do this in a beneficial and nationalistic interest. Because he displayed these feelings when he said:

> ... Finally only the help of our government can those American Negroes who are here and gradually coming be assured of the repatriation in the <u>land of their forefathers</u> (my emphasis) encouraged and so much wished for by colonization societies and missionaries. The American Negro although he may not come to Liberia for a home still is interested in its possibilities and the idea it holds for his children and their documents. It will be good national policy for the U.S. to hold it.

When civilian American diplomats were reporting in 1915, Minister George W. Buckner and in 1920 Charge d'Affaires Richard C. Bundy about the existence of domestic slavery" within the interim involving the native Liberians, there was also another voice discussing the same subject. Colonel Charles Young mentioned in his report that slavery did exist among the interior natives an investigation (my emphasis) could possibly prove that it was thriving among some of the civilized Liberians. In the conclusion of his report, Young reiterated his concern about the slavery issue. He stated that the Liberian must be protected from the "bond slave" system and that it was the United States that could accomplish this task.

The military diplomat's personal views during his 1920-1922 tour in Liberia did reflect some ideas and recommendations that would be submitted at a later date by Liberian officials and members of the American Legation. Young stressed in his report the immediate need to have competent American advisors to assist the Liberian government in all of its respective departments. This was during President Charles D.B. King's administration and when Edwin Barclay was Secretary of State. It seems as though it was necessary for an International Commission of inquiry and the League of Nations and American statesmen to exert their influence in suggesting principal reforms for Liberia. Because in the 1930's some two years later after a military attache had informed the War Department and the State Department indirectly of his professional analysis of internal discrepancies in the Liberian political and military system, President Barclay made a request for the assistance of specialists in the areas of health and public administration. It is firmly believed that Colonel Young was a prophet crying in the wilderness and within the wilderness his cries were not heard or they were ignored and never entered into the significant agendas concerning Liberia's progress.

On 3 June 1920, Colonel Young had informed the War Department in a report about the inefficiency of an American officer assigned as Commandant, Liberian Frontier Force, Major John H. Anderson, it has been stated consistently throughout this paper that Charles Young actually went beyond the expectations of his military assignments and became deeply concerned about internal problems and incompetence in military and civilian areas of the government. An extract from a Liberian newspaper in December 1920, supports the validity of Young's appraisal of Major John H. Anderson:

The newspaper published the following in reference to Major Anderson:

> "...Our attention has several times been called to the gross neglect of Camp Johnson, the Military Training Station near the city of Monrovia, under the direct control of Major J.H. Anderson and which is intended for a training school for native aborigines and Americo-Liberian youth in the science of modern warfare and military discipline. We are surprised when we were told that for nearly twelve months there has not been a flag of any kind seen flying at Camp Johnson, which is situated on a slight promontory projecting into the sea, and can be clearly seen by vessels passing from North to South and vice versa ... Who is the Liberian Force at Camp Johnson? Is he a military trained man; for how can a man who has been trained in any military academy in the United States or in any other foreign country commit such flagrant neglect, especially in a training school by omitting to fly daily the nation flag of the country?... We earnestly contend that since the United States government has consented to send men to train the Liberians in that particular line for which they have been sent, but not men who are intellectually physically, morally and socially inferior to the Liberians generally..."

In view of the fact that the editorial was centered around Anderson not hoisting the Liberian national colors daily, there could have been other allegations that precipitated the article.

The internal conditions of Liberia and its government were of constant importance to the War Department and State Department. On 8 February 1921, Colonel Charles Young sent a confidential document to the

Director, Military Information Division, War College Division, Washington. The document had been written by an American that had worked as an assistant for approximately four years in the Liberian government. When he resigned, the confidential expose was made available to the military attache.

Charles Young stated in his cover letter that the information contained in the document had the sanction of most American assistants and the contents have been known to the Legation and some parts were included in reports to the Department of State. Young wrote that:

> "By this Expose it is self evident that without the strong arm of the United States to set the government right, it must collapse and possibly involve our country in work, expense, and trouble with England and France, who at present are straighten out the tangle".

The anonymous author of the document cited his reasons for the document as to show how England and France had desires to dominate Liberian affairs and possibly partition Liberia among themselves; to reemphasize the facts that increasing interest in Liberia by Negro Americans and their race consciousness since World War I should serve as a valid reason for their country the United States to assist Liberia and at the same time provide Liberia as a possible "haven" from their oppression present to the Liberian government. The challenges that they faced during this first tour 1912-1915 were also repeaters or still stagnant upon his return for a second tour of duty as military attache to the American Legation, 1920-1922.

Immediately upon his arrival in 1912, Young was beginning to perform additional duties in the form of advising the President of Liberia and leading an expedition into the interior at the request of the President. He developed an unusual interest for a career military man in the political and economic affairs of the country. One conclusion can be reached and that is Charles Young's personal feeling of racial pride and African Nationalism could have been a compelling stimulus for him to regard his brother's country as his country that needed his offerings in talent and experience.

His striking rapport with the American Minister at times and his fitness in conferring with the President of Liberia and his cabinet members all contributed to his successes as a soldier and diplomat.

There is a reason for the critic and layman to weigh Colonel Young's intervention in Liberian affairs as minimal and probably insignificant. However, this chapter has only presented some available facts that portray this attache's knowledge of the conditions of the civilian and military climate of the country and also quite aware of the European colonial powers who were attempting to encroach upon and eventually dominate the government of Liberia. Some years after Young had departed Liberia due to demise, American and Liberian diplomats were discussing the "Prophetic Warnings" of the Soldier-Diplomat. The 1930 slave labor controversy had previously been discussed in official channels by Charles Young, but it is believed that his verbal expressions were just conversations that were lost with the passing tides.

Charles Young's very detailed impressions of the economic conditions and political unrest and corruption in Liberia was presented to officials prior to 1915 and it was not until the United States became concerned about Liberia's possible continuation of diplomatic ties with Germany that a pledge that was not fulfilled was made to Liberia and she quite gracefully requested American assistance. It can be concluded in respect to this matter that the official reports of Young were staffed, reviewed and staff action officers comments made and a disinterested one hundred percent military oriented general or colonel completed final endorsement and could not understand what Colonel Young was echoing from the wilderness. The United States State Department received dispatches from their Liberian Legations and also copies of the Secretary of War's reports from Young. In view of the fact that a black career qualified officer was providing sufficient information not necessarily military strategic intelligence but political information of Liberia, that some honorable and astute military and civilian officials could not place the critical significance upon his recommendations.

During the period 1917-1922, the American government in this writers' analysis procrastinated, whether it was for political or urgently diplomatic foreign relations reasons they did not consider it feasible or in reality in the best economic interests of America to approve a $5,000,000 loan to the Republic of Liberia. It could be concluded that Colonel Young's documented reports and monographs on Liberia could have played an intentional or unintentional source input to alter or support the attitudes of some American Congressional leaders toward their votes for or against the loan to Liberia.

Through the years many historians and writers have characterized countries similar to Liberia as having experienced the various economic problems and political immaturity with numerous sociological and glorifying financial justifications. But the characterization based on American and European personal interests, economic potentials and possibly first not last, the ever presence of racial and paternal superiority over people of color.

The title soldier and diplomat is relevant to Charles Young because of his recurring efforts to expose American as well as Liberians who were contributing to the inefficient operation of the Liberian Frontier Force.

It can also be concluded that the War Department and State Department were definitely aware of Colonel Young's outward intentions in the affairs of Liberia as evidenced by several informal warnings to remind him of his respective military missions.

Some mention should be made of the fact that Colonel Young did not maintain a constant cordiality with all members of the American. Legation and also the Americo-Liberians of the Liberian government, some commissioners and officers of the Liberian Frontier Force. At times Young had a very promising and beneficial relationship with the presidents and secretaries of state of Liberia. This of course can be substantiated by the President requesting him to accept the position of military attache in 1919. The articles in the Crisis Journal and Liberian newspapers concerning his cartographic work in Haiti did not improve his image among his opposition.

Colonel Charles Young has left a rich legacy in the annals of the diplomatic history of Liberia. This legacy might not be visible in the

Black Presence

context of the scholar's ground rules of acceptance for a diplomat's laurel. However, this legacy is present today when one reviews what did occur and did not occur during those hours, days, months and years of Liberia's struggles for a self-sustaining Independence. A simple tribute that can be given to Colonel Charles Young is written in a verse of a poem by Contee Cullen, "In Memory of Colonel Charles Young:

> "No lie is strong enough to kill
> The roots that work below;
> From your rich dust and
> Slaughtered will
> A tree with tongues will grow.

Additional information on Colonel Young and Liberia can be found in my manuscript, Colonel Charles Young Soldier and Diplomat

PUNITIVE EXPEDITION - MEXICO

Tenth Cavalry Regiment, The Truth About Carrizal

On June 21, 1916, newspapers throughout America carried the tragic news concerning a small-scale American massacre at Carrizal, Mexico. Though the only participants were three American white army cavalry officers and black troopers of Troops C and K, Tenth U.S. Cavalry, the nation was stunned and concerned. The black press and community were saddened by the incident and for some time were not made aware of the actual facts. The following account of the Carrizal incident has been summarized from official correspondence between the investigating officer of the incident, Commanding General, Punitive Expedition, U.S. Army, Mexico, and Commanding General, Southern Department, Fort Sam Houston, Texas around June to September, 1916.

A Lieutenant Colonel George O. Cress, Inspector General's Department stated the following in his report to General Pershing, Commanding General, Punitive Expedition, U.S. Army, Dublan, Mexico:

Captain Charles T. Boyd, Troop C, Tenth Cavalry, and Captain L. S. Morey, Troop K, Tenth Cavalry were each ordered by the Commanding

General, Punitive Expedition, to make reconnaissance, from their respective stations, in the direction of Ahumada. There was no cooperation between these troops ordered by the Commanding General, Punitive Expedition [Cooperation by Commanders].

When Captain Boyd arrived at a Santa Domingo ranch on June 20, 1916, he decided to assume responsibility for both troops, with Captain Morey as his subordinate. Carrizal was approximately eight miles from the Santa Domingo ranch. Ahumada was some twenty miles away. Boyd decided to pass through the town. After several conferences with Mexican officers (Lieutenant Colonel Rivas, and General Gomez), he was informed that American troops could not pass east, west or south of the area. During these conferences, the American troops had advanced east across an open flat toward the southwest edge of Carrizal, where Mexican troops were formed. As the American troops decided to advance forward in a line of platoon column, Captain Boyd ordered Captain Morey and a Lieutenant Adair to defend their flanks. The Tenth Cavalry were facing 315 Mexican soldiers, mounted and dismounted.

The inspecting officer of the incident stated:
Captain Boyd appeared to be of the opinion that his orders required him to pass through the town of Carrizal . . Lieutenant Adair appeared to hold the same view. Captain Morey differed with Captain Boyd. . .

Finally Captain Boyd decided to go through the town according to a sworn statement by Quartermaster Sergeant Dalley Farrior, Troop C, Tenth Cavalry. Farrior said:

When we arrived near Carrizal, the captain had us load our rifles and pistols. We halted and sent a messenger in to ask permission to pass through the town. When the messenger returned, several Mexicans came with him and they halted at our point. The captain went forward and talked to them. He returned to us and said that it looked favorable but we could only go north. He said his orders were to go east and he meant to go that way. By this time, the General of the Carrizal Troops had come out and the captain went forward to talk to him. When he turned he said the general had given us permission to go through the town, but we would go through as foragers. As we formed lines of foragers the general called him back again. When he returned he said he would execute fight on foot and advance in that formation. We did this and ordered no man to fire until fired upon. As we moved forward Troop K was on the right and Troop C on the left. The captain cautioned Sergeant Winrow, who commanded the right of Troop C to keep his men on a zig zag line.

The Mexicans during this time had formed a line to our front about 200 yards away and opened fire on us. We laid down and fired back... Then we advanced by rushes. On the second rush I was wounded in the right arm and stood where I was. The line had been moving forward. On their third rush they reached the Mexican's first line of defense, where there were two machine guns. By this time, Captain Boyd had been shot in the hand and shoulder... The captain tried to get Troop K, which was in our rear to move up to us. He was shot and killed at that time. Lieutenant Adair had gone with his men and was out of sight. Captain Morey said to assemble Troop K on him and we would all surrender. But several men of Troop C remonstrated with Captain Morey and induced him to make towards an adobe house in our left rear, where we could make a stand. Captain Morey was very weak from loss of blood and fainted once. From here, I finally made my way to the Santa Domingo ranch.

Lieutenant Colonel Cress's conclusions of his investigation were:

That in carrying out his mission Captain Charles T. Boyd, Tenth Cavalry, did not obey the instructions given him by the Commanding General, Punitive Expedition, and that in failing to do so and in assuming command of Troop K, Tenth Cavalry, he became responsible for the encounter between the American troops and the forces of the de facto government at Carrizal, June 21, 1916.

There was not further action recommended due to the peculiar conditions at the time.

General Pershing stated in his endorsement that:

Under the circumstances, unfortunate as they were, it is not believed that any disciplinary action is indicated as advisable. There is no reliable *evidence obtainable to sustain charges against any individual or group of these men for their conduct. Notwithstanding the disaster resulting from this encounter, it must be said to the credit of this little body of men that they fought well as long as their officers remained alive to lead them and for some time after...*

The Mexicans sustained a loss of forty-two killed and fifty-one wounded. The following Tenth Cavalry soldiers gave their lives in the line of active combat duty at Carrizal.

Captain Charles T. Boyd, Lieutenant Henry R. Adair, Private De Witt Rucker, Troop K, Private Charles Matthews, Troop K, Sergeant Will Hines, Troop C, Lance Corporal William Roberts, Troop C, Private James E. Day, Troop K, and Private Walter Gleeton, Troop C.

Reference: Black Defenders of America 1775-1973

The Ninth Cavalry and Biogenetic Diversity In The Philippines, In 1922

"What About The Mothers and Children"

The United States Military has stationed troops in many areas of the world. Sometimes these troops remain for a number of years. A problem that is often addressed by military and civilians of the host countries is the fraternization of servicemen with ladies of the respective countries. Often a relationship develops into marriage and/or the birth of children out of wedlock. This has occurred since the 1900's and the military has dealt with these situations in World Wars I and II, Korean War and the Vietnam War. There are many happy and long relations in marriage between military men of all services with foreign women from Asia and Europe. Their children in the majority of cases have adjusted into the American way of life as another American child of military or former military parents.

There is a problem that the U.S. Military has had to address in World War I and II, Korea and Vietnam Wars, especially World War II, with the coming home of African American soldiers from Europe with their French English and Italian brides.

After the wars or conflicts, the countries were left with some brides and/or girl friends who had children fathered by white and black servicemen. In some countries there were no problems in locating orphanages and adoption centers to accept the children of white Americans. However, that problem of skin color did exist when the miscegenated or mixed babies/children of African American fathers were present. A question that has often been asked, where are the mixed children of African American fathers and their mothers of Korea and Vietnam? Also how many children of African fathers actually boarded that mass airlift of young children from Vietnam at the end of the conflict. Today America has a serious problem of having babies of black parents being adopted by blacks and of course non blacks. Therefore, there would also exist a problem of adopting biogenetic diverse children from foreign mothers.

The problems of the disposition of children born to foreign mothers and African American men did not originate in 1945. There was some concern as early as 1922. A concerned and thoughtful post commander developed a plan for the disposition of 207 Filipino women and 72 children of the 9th Cavalry and other "colored soldiers". The post commander of headquarters at Camp Stotsenburg, Pampanga, Philippine Islands (P.I.) submitted his plan and recommendations to the commanding general, Philippine Department, Manila (P.I.). The plan classified the wives and non wives and children into four categories:

"<u>First</u>. 37 Filipino women legally married to soldiers, having 56 children by them.

<u>Second</u>. 9 Filipino women not legally married to soldiers but living openly with them, and having 16 children by them.

<u>Third</u>. 95 Filipino women legally married to soldiers but having no children by them.

<u>Fourth</u>. 66 Filipino women and one Japanese not legally married to soldiers but living openly with them and having no children."

The Post Commander viewed the first category as presenting great difficulty. He believed the U.S. Military should not compel, encourage or allow these soldiers to abandon their lawful wives and children. He wrote, *"This should not occur merely for the purpose of conforming to a change of policy based on some minor economy or convenience to the government. On the other hand, it seemed to be impracticable to take these 37 families to the United States. Transportation having been provided as far as San Francisco, very few soldiers would have the money to pay railroad fare to Fort Riley or Fort Huachuca, and even if they were taken on troop trains no quarters would be provided for them after arrival. Climatic conditions would not suit them, and if their husbands, at some future time, failed to reenlist or were otherwise discharged, these native women and children would be a charge upon the United States".* The commander also addressed government policies. He said, *"It seems inconsistent with the policy of a generous government to discharge these men for its own convenience without making any provision, or allowing them any opportunity for securing proper employment. I cannot believe that if the facts were understood, the War Department or higher authority on account of color would compel the immediate discharge of high type, faithful and efficient soldiers of long service in such numbers as to embarrass the local labor market and impose an enormous hardship upon them without even giving them an opportunity to complete their current enlistment. Besides this, the insular government would probably object to such a procedure, as a number of such discharged soldiers are already open to the charge of vagrancy".*

The post commander saw the third category presented a similar difficulty but to a lesser degree. His reason was that 95 women without children that were easier to handle than the 37 women with children. The 9 women and 16 children of the class two presented a different problem, because these women could not be taken to the United States, unless the men married them and then they could be placed in class one. They would have to provide for them in the P.I.

The commander also believed that the only problem presented by the women in the category four was to get rid of them from the neighborhood, unless the men would marry them and place them in class three.

The commander had to address his views of the "so called paternal slave master when he said, "*We cannot assume that the heart of a colored man is any less sensitive to the destruction of his black family ties than that of a white man. No decent slave owner in the old south, would consent to the breaking up of families (the slave owner broke up families when he separated them by selling slaves from families), and the whole world was sickened by the sight of Germany's disregard of family ties in Belgium. It is inconceivable that these families should be broken up and abandoned merely to carry out some little unimportant detail of the policy, that can be changed by the stroke of a pen, along with hundreds of other changes being made every time a new man gets into a new position*".

The commander decided upon his solution. He said they were based upon the following principles:

"*First*. *We must be governed by the ordering principle of humanity.*

Second. *We must be fair in our treatment of soldiers who have rendered honorable and faithful service.*

Third. *Our plan must be acceptable to the government general in so far as it affects the civil community.*

Fourth. *The efficiency of the army must not be sacrificed*

Fifth. *The plan must be such as to minimize subsequent controversy.*

The post commander solutions were:

A. Many of the women and children be sent to the United States as can be properly cared for and that the soldier responsibility for the rest of them be retained in the service in the P.I. until they can be otherwise disposed of.

B. That a cable be sent to the War Department requesting information as to whether in the case of soldiers without necessary funds, the women and children in category one and the women of category three shall be sent to the United States (U.S.) with the troops and if so that proper arrangements be made for their transportation to the new stations and their accommodations after arrival.

C. That a careful canvass should be conducted to determine those men who desire to be discharged and who are prepared to take care of their families in the P.I. These men to be so discharged. A canvass should also determine the native women who are willing to give up their husband and who consent to their husbands return to the U.S. without them. Affidavit to be secured from these women to this effect and the men so returned.

D. That all men of categories one, two and three not disposed of a,b and c above, be retained in the military service in the Philippines and gradually discharged for the convenience of the government as rapidly as they can obtain suitable employment, or otherwise make their own arrangements for the proper disposition of their family ties. The following assignments are suggested for these men while being retained in the service. A certain number preferably the older non commissioned officers (NCO) could be retained as instructors in the new 26th Cavalry regiment. Of the balance some could be transferred to the medical department, some to the quartermaster corps and others formed into labor detachments. They could be used as teamsters, orderlies, messengers, mounted military police and on other necessary duty.

E. That the disposition of the 67 women in category four be held in abeyance until some policy is outlined for the dispositions of others. But that a careful investigation be made of each case with a view to obtaining a release of the man and to adjust all *differences as to debts, ownership of property, etc. Then the soldier, could be returned to the United States."*

The commander also stated that the whole question was more or less a local problem and the commanding general must expect to bear the burden of it and work out the details. Therefore the commander made a request for approval as submitted.

The Commanding General, Philippine Department, Fort William McKinley, Rizal, approved the plan. He stated that he had discussed the plan with the governor general who seemed satisfied with the plan.

There is evidence that some parts of the plan were executed because a memorandum to the commanding officer, Fort Riley Kansas from the office of the post commander, headquarters Camp Stotsenburg, P.I., dated October 8, 1922 was received. The subject of the memorandum was *"Relation of certain soldiers of the Ninth Cavalry to native women."*

There were listed on the memorandum the names of one first sergeant who was released from all obligations to a Filipino woman with no children. A staff sergeant was also released from obligations and the Filipino woman with no children would remain in the islands. Two privates were released from all obligations when the Filipino woman signed the affidavits. One of the privates was married and had no children and his wife decided to remain in the P.I. There were two privates who were married and their Filipino wives accompanied them to the United States.

A corporal's Filipino woman friend, not married and no children signed an affidavit refusing to release the soldier from obligations. A sergeant who was not married to a Filipino woman would remain in the P.I. with their one minor three month old child. The sergeant was unable to make an allotment for the Filipino woman because he had an allotment of fifty (50) dollars a month to a wife in the United States. The soldier agreed in writing to send ten (10) dollars a month until April 1924 for support of the child.

There are many inferences that can be made concerning the Ninth Cavalry soldiers and their Filipino wives and friends in 1922. The military viewed the situation as a problem. They were concerned about the welfare of the child and mother and also obligations that the soldiers could confront. There was no discernible instances of racial factors involved in correspondence reviewed. However, one must be realistic in the view of the climate of racial segregation in America and the white majority in power enforced all facets of segregation where possible from a legal justification. Therefore, I infer that the problem was not a racial one. Because from a biological perspective, the military authorities were concerned with two peoples of similar skin color in many cases, simply "people of color". Of course, that can be debatable in America because unfortunately people are classified by sight and descriptions such as "hair, lips and skin color". I ask the question, why weren't some of the procedures used by the military in 1922 considered in relations to those brown babies in France, Germany, England, Korea and Vietnam. Whatever the answer may be, I deeply believe that many citizens of the Filipinos in 1922 probably would have said, a person can be accepted by their character, sincerity, morality and honesty and not be so concerned about one's skin color. I salute the concerned white post commander and his superiors who concurred with his recommendations because they were ahead of their time when concerned about the family and not just welfare and who pays for it.

WORLD WAR I

African American Presence

During the period 1900-1917, the four regular Negro regiments and two volunteer units (Forty-eighth and Forty-ninth) were ordered to the Philippines, where they served during the insurrection. At the beginning of World War I, the black Americans were again summoned to service. Negro National Guard units were the nucleus of the Ninety-third Provisional Division, designated primarily for purposes of administration. A second division was organized, the Ninety-second, which ought with the American armies while the Ninety-third were among the first

Black Presence

American combat troops to arrive in France. The Three Hundred and Seventy-Second Infantry regiments compiled an outstanding record while serving abroad. Some Negro units also served as supply troops during the war.

Negro troops participated in the battles of Argonne, Chateau Thierry, St. Mihiel, Champagne, Vosges, and Metz. Nearly four hundred thousand Negroes served during World War I, according to Emment Scott, former civilian aide to the Secretary of War and their accomplishments were numerous. The Croix de Guerre was awarded to 171 Negro troops. Two outstanding black heroes of the war, Henry Johnson of Albany, New York, and Needham Roberts of Trenton, New Jersey. Negro troops also served as pioneers in labor battalions, butchery, companies and engineer service battalions.

Although the Negro draftees' overall training and educational background were quite low during World War I, black soldiers overcame many obstacles and their list of achievements and honors is futher proof of their ability on the battle field.

Hannibal Lloyd Davis was a member of the HQ 369th Infantry during World War I. He was promoted to Sergeant. He also served as acting sergeant of the unit. Davis served with an excellent record and his unit was under fire for 191 days. His brothers also served during World War I. They were Edward A. Davis, William H. Davis and Arthur P. Davis.

James Reese Europe was a first lieutenant in the 369th U.S. Infantry (former 15th New York National Guard). While serving in France, he participated in band concerts and served as a band conductor. He also served in the trenches as a machine gunner. After a long period of combat, he was gassed and after his recovery he returned to the unit's band. His band was also called Europe's Society Orchestra. He is buried in Arlington National Cemetery.

Neeham Roberts served as a private in the 369th U.S. Infantry Regiment. His unit was assigned with the French troops. In May 1918, Roberts while on guard duty was attacked by the enemy. He received serious wounds in his leg, but he continued to resist the advancing enemy, throwing hand grenades from a prone position until the enemy retreated. Following the action Private Roberts was one of the first Americans to be awarded the French Croix de Guerre during World War I.

Kenneth Lewis was a private in the First Separate Battalion District of Columbia National Guard. He was a native of Washington, D.C. and volunteered at the age of 18 years. He was killed in combat while serving in France. He was awarded the French Medaille Militaire.

Henry Johnson served as a private in the 369th U.S. Infantry Regiment during World War I. While fighting in a combat situation in May, 1928. Johnson confronted at least a dozen German soldiers. He shot and wounded several of them. He then ran to the assistance of a wounded conrade who was about to be taken prisoner. Johnson continued to resist until the Germans retreated. Private Johnson was awarded the French Croix de Guerre for his bravery.

Lieutenant Robert S. Campbell, a member of 369th U.S. Infantry was awarded the Distinguished Service Cross (DSC) during World War I in the Argonne Forest.

The presence of black physicians during World War I was quite significant because the black troops who were sent overseas could not serve with the all white American units and had to be brigaded with the French Troops who also had employed their colonial Senegalese troops during World War I. In 1917, black military surgeons were on duty with the all black units of the 365th, 366th, 367th and 368th field hospital and ambulance companies, the division supply train and the military police units. It should be noted that the regimental surgeons and commanding officers of the field hospitals were white physicians. However, the 93rd division's regimental surgeon was black and African American physicians served with the French units at the front lines. An article from the official publication of the chief surgeon's office of the American Expeditionary Forces, dated November 25, 1918 indicated how the black doctor used precaution and applied good antiseptic techniques in reducing the spread of influenza among the medical personnel and patients. The article stated

Black Presence

that "Effective cubicle isolation was practiced in the 366th field, and 357th hospitals, 92nd Division". A sheet cubicle system was used about the beds and masks for patients and attendants, doctors or orderlies were used so consistently and thoroughly that none of the attendants, doctors or orderlies acquired influenza or pneumonia, although the wards were full of both diseases. That was the way we were seventy eight years ago practicing good hygienic measures demonstrating the efficient and capable attributes of our medical doctors and commanders.

The prestigious French Medal, the Croix de Guerre citations were awarded to first lieutenant, Clarence S. Jennifer, medical corps. He was from 172 Parker Street, Newark, New Jersey, Lieutenant Urbane S. Bass, medical corps from Fredericksburg, Virginia received the American Distinguished Service Cross. **Major James R. White**, medical corps received the French Croix de Guerre. White was from 5158 Michigan Avenue, Chicago, Illinois. The three officers were assigned to the 372nd Infantry Regiment.

J. Leoidas Leach served with the 349th Machine Gun Battalion and Ammunition Train in France. He was commissioned as First Lieutenant, Medical Corps, U.S. Army in World War I.

I believe that a historian's delight is to obtain real primary source material. In November 1996, I attended the burial of the late Dorothy Inborden Miller at Arlington National Cemetery. The military chaplain remarked, you know sir, her husband died in 1936 and his grave has been opened after 60 years for his widow, who is 99 years old. Mrs. Miller's husband was Sergeant First Class Walker D. Miller, 92nd Division U.S. Army. He was a graduate of Oberlin Business College and Talledega College, Alabama.

I have in my personal library a copy of a pocket size French Dictionary.

"Dictionnaire Francais - Anglais dated 1918. I also have several sets of post cards or cartes postales describing pictorial scenes of the areas of Aix-les-Bains, Brest Chambery et ser Environs, and Paris. Sergeant Miller purchased a map of France, Carte de Francaise. He wrote on the

back of the map, *"Walker D. Miller, Sergeant lst class, Quartermaster Corps, Finance and Accounting Division, Allied Expeditionary Forces"*

An examination of the map revealed some very interesting information. The map included topographical information of Paris and French cities and towns and areas of Germany and Brussels. The heading in French read *Nouvelle Carte France, Belgiue, Bords Du Rhin, Suisse, etc.* This French map also included the French colonies, *Colonies Francaises, Algiers and Tunisa, Algerie et Tunsisie*. The map included the African colonies of French Niger, Guinea, Senegal, Somalia, Congo, Chad, Guadeloupe, Martinique and Guyana were also included.

Sergeant Miller had in his papers a brochure for a leave area. The brochure had the following information. *"Leave area of Savoir, the Play Ground of Europe, pictures of Old Roman Arch and Aix-les-Bains and Lake Bourget."*

The brochure stated the Savoie region has been known as the resort of kings and milionaires, yet, this is where the soldiers of the American Expeditionary Forces will spend their leave. There were three principal resorts where the soldiers stayed along the French Alps and not far from the Italian border. They were Ax-les-Bains, Chambery and Challes-les Eaux. The area of Chambery is the capitol city of Savoie. A castle was built there in the thirteenth century and in 1918 was known as the birth place of the present house of the kings of Italy. There was a catheral dating back to the fourteenth century. The district was settled by the Romans hundreds of years before the birth of Christ. The Roman Arch and the remains of a temple of Diana prove the early settlement of the district. The baths located at Aix were built by the Romans 122 years B.C.

The brochure stated that the soldiers would have access to the following activities and recreation: football, baseball, rowing, canoeing, swimming, aquatic sports and gold. Activities available were movies, casinos, game rooms, library and boat rides. There were also restaurants available and hotels available in the town. The brochure said that celebrated guests have been among the regular summer clients. Some of

Black Presence 269

them were Queen Victoria, the King of Greece, Queen of Holland, Andrew J. Carnegie and J. Pierpont Morgan. A paragraph in the brochure stated that the hotel rooms vary according to the their class of accommodations. The meals will be the same at every hotel. For an eight days stay the cost, including a 10 percent tip, will vary from 96 to 149 francs. Hotel accommodations will be assigned by lot, care should be taken to bring suficient fund for the most expensive class if such assignment should be made. Sergeant Miller had scratched out that paragraph on the cost and then wrote below it *"the government paying hotel expense.*

I have included the above detailed information about the procedure, because I would like to inform or educate the reader that these first class facilities were available to black soldiers in 1918 in France and paid for by the military. I will not argue the point whether the facillities were segregated or not. However, I will state the facts that those soldiers of color could not fight side by side with their American white brothers in the Expedtionary Force, but they were allowed to fight with the French Army and also near their Colonial Senegalese troops. I do not believe that those facilities that were available to black soldiers in France in 1918 would have been available in America the beautiful.

I must assume that Sergeant Miller did visit that recreation area and the memorabilia that I found in his papers is actual proof that those courageous soldiers of color in World War I and were present not only on the battle field of France and some later in the military cemeteries, but also were able to enjoy some social and recreational life in France that was far more superior than a segregated United States could provide. I repeat, the young, middle age and senior citizen of all races in America should learn about the black presence in world history, especially the experience of ordinary people of color, who visited Europe as soldiers, some 80 years ago.

When Sergeant Miller departed France for "Home Sweet Home" in 1919, he kept a small card that is my primary source along with his military paper that he did cross the waters and did return. Because the card's front cover has a picture at sea and a picture of a man in the upper left hand corner with the name Willem Van d Velde and at the bottom of the cover, an inscription, the cannon shot. The back cover of the card shows a ship at sea with the inscription, S.S. Nieuw Amsterdam Holland - American Line. The right inside of the card has "*S.S. Rotterdam left Brest, (France) 10:00 AM, Saturday, Febr. 8th, arrived at New York Monday, February 17, 1919, Walker D. Miller, Sergeant lst Class QMC, 92nd Division, U.S. Army*". The right inside of the card listed the 92nd Division's major battles, St Die Sector Vosges, 23 August 1918 to 1920 September 18, Meuse-Argonne offensive 25 September to 30 September 1918. In reserve 38th AC (French) 30th September to 4 October 1918 Marbache Sector 9, October 18 to 11th November 1918. Offensive operations 2nd Army 10-11 November 18 attacking direction Corny.

There are many documents memorabilia, letters and papers of African American's rich family heritage that have been discarded in the trash or were burned in fires. I cherish the rich memorabilia of Sergeant Miller because as a historian and biologist, I realize that when his widow, Dorothy Inborden Miller was buried with him at Arlington National Cemetery in November, 1996 that his graceful wife had preserved his papers during her 60 years of marriage and I have been able to write a personal story about a noncommissioned officer of color who was "*over there*" 79 years ago and becoming a part of the black presence in World History.

They Did Not Tell Me That

The 805th Pioneer Regiment that was deployed to France consisted of 3,000 men and 99 officers. They included 25 regular army officers 38 mechanics from Praire View College, 20 horse shoers from Tuskegee Institute (University), and 8 carpenters from Howard University. The Regiment arrived in France in October 1918. They were given labor missions to repair French road arteries in the areas of Clermont Neuvilly and Auzeville. They constructed ammunition dumps and repaired railroads. They were also involved in a salvage redistribution program where they were responsible for the salvaging of enemy weapons and military equipment. The 805th Regiment assisted filling trenches in order to improve the French farm lands.

Black Presence

The 93rd black division in the American Expeditionary Force was the first black unit to arrive in France. The division consisted mostly of National Guard units from the states of Illinois, New York, District of Columbia, Maryland, Ohio, Tennessee and Masschusetts. They were brigaded with French troops.

The 369th Infantry Regiment arrived in France on January 1, 1918 and participated in the second battle of the Marine in July. They were present east of Verdun near the Ville - Sur-Turbe. It is believed that they were the first black American unit in combat. The unit received over 170 citations for bravery, the French Croix de Guerre and the Distinguished Service Cross (DSC). The regiment was the first unit of the allied armies to reach the Rhine river on November 12, 1918 with the Second French Army.

The 371st Infantry Regiment's soldiers were drafted from South Carolina with southern white officers at first. They brigaded in France with the 157th French Division, 13th Army Corps and remained on the battle line and were later in reserve until the Armistice was signed.

The 372nd Infantry Regiment consisted of units from the District of Columbia (First Separate Battalion Infantry), Ohio (Ninth Battalion Infantry), Massachusetts (Sixth Batallion Infantry), and one company each from Maryland, Tennessee and Connecticut. The 370th Infantry Regiment was with the 34th French Division at St. Mihel, 36th French Division at Argonne and at Soissons with the 59th French Division. While fighting in the Vauxaillion area, the units captured Mount Dessinges and the adjacent woods. They also held a sector on the Canal L'oise et Aisne.

A colonel, major, eight captains seventeen lieutenants, eight noncommissioned officer and twenty-sixth enlisted men all of color and members of the 370 Infantry Regiment received the French Croix de Guerre. They distinguished themselves in the battles of Chavigny, Leary, Bois de Beaumont, Val St. Pierre, Auberton and Logny.

The 371, and 372 Infantry regiments fought in battles while brigaded with the French 157th Infantry (Red Hand). Some of those battles were

Champagne, and the heroic charges up an observatory ridge near the plains of Monthois.

Prior to the 371st and 372nd Regiments departing France, a French commander, General Vincenden wrote his sincere appreication in a general order No. 245. *"For seven months we lived as brothers-at-arms, partaking of the same activities, sharing the same hardships and the same dangers. I respectfully salute our glorious commander who has fallen and I bow to your colors side by side with this the flag of the 333rd Regiment of Infantry (French). They have shown us the way to victory."*

The 92nd Infantry Division was planned as a black division with black officers. Unfortunately, their division commander was considered a person who believed that black troops possessed some inferior qualities and were not efficient for combat duty. He also believed that black officers were not competent to perform their duties and he would only suggest the use of company grade officers in the rank of lieutenant and captain. Without devoting considerable paragraphs to this commander, I believe the following quote from a speech he delivered to the men of the 92nd division in an area called Pompey, France will provide the reader something to consider if they desire to assess the General's views on black soldiers. *"They were cowards, they had failed and they did not have the guts that made brave men"*

One distinguished black historian said that there was a concerted effort on the part of white officers in France to discredit the accomplishment of black troops in France during World War I, especially in the 92nd division under a commanding general who possibly had developed his perceptions of blacks as soldiers.

I understand more clearly now why President Bush awarded a black soldier from World War I and the only black soldier, the Medal of Honor posthumously to his two sisters Mary Bowens, Greenville, South Carolina and Georginia Palmer, Richard, California. The soldier was Corporal Freddie Stowers of Anderson County, South Carolina.

Black Presence

Those courageous black soldiers of World War I did fight bravely in France and its is unfortunately, that over the years the news media, and magazine columnists like to remind us of the negative sides of being black in a society of America that still faces the problem now of the 21st century, the color problem. A recent magazine article on the black soldiers in World War I stated that a single incident was used to evalute the black soldiers who were exposed to combat. He was referring to 368th Infantry's performance during the Meuse-Argonne offensive in September 1918. This author does not state in his article that some of the problems of the 368th were due to the following facts stated in interviews with a competent historian and scholar some 80 years ago. The distinguished historian said that it was told to him point by point by those who were actually on the spot. They were earnest able men. Mostly lieutenants and captains and one could not doubt their "absolute conscientiousness and frankness" during the interview in their tents at LeMans.

The interview basically said that the 368th Regiment went into the Argonne September 24 and was ordered into battle on the morning of the 26th. Their duty was "combat liaison", with the French 37th Division and the 77th (white) division of Americans. The regiment was not ready for combat duty. It had no artillery support until the sixth day of battle, it had no grenades, no trench fires, or signal flares, no airplane panels for signaling and no shears for the German type barbed wire and no maps and were at no time given definite objectives. The men told the historian that the Second Battalion of the 368th Regiment entered battle on the morning of September 26, with a white major in command and all the company grade officers were black.

There were some white field grade officers whose leaderhip could have been questioned and could have been responsible for the court martial of some black officers who were charged with cowardice and abandonment of positions. It was reported that several white commanders left their troops and returned to the dugouts. The above remarks were mentioned in 1918.

The following excerpts from a declassified document of World War I reflects the climate of racism that existed in the United States military in

World War I and how the policies and decisions of so called honorable men in authority would parallel the thoughts of America as far as the divisions of black and white people in the land of the free where soldiers of black skin had been drafted and volunteered to fight and save the world for democracy. Again, I write that it is unfortunate that youth in our schools today are not given an opportunity to evaluate both side of the problem when they still reads books and magazine that do not always tell all of the facts.

The late Dr. W.E.B. Dubois was able to publish the excerpts from a then classified document that American officials had issued to the French government and advise them to publish it for their troops. The background in 1917 was the first social contact with the first American Negro regiments to go into action. The regiments were brigaded with French white regiments. During the period of 1917-1918 was the genesis of some unfavorable European impressions of the black American racism towards black servicemen in Europe. According to a copy of the published French directive, the following excerpts were addressed to the French troops. The directive was requested by some Americans.

"The increasing number of Negroes in the United States (about 15 million) would create for the white race in the republic a menace of degeneracy were it not that an impossible gulf has been made between them. As this danger does exist for the French people, the French public has become accustomed to treating the Negro with familiarity and indulgence. This indulgence and this familiarity are matters of grievant concern to the American. It is of the utmost importance that every effort be made to avoid profoundly discussing American opinion.

Although a citizen of the United States, the black man is regarded by the white American as an inferior being with whom relations or business or services only are possible. The black is constantly being censured for his want of intelligence and discretion, his lack of civic and professional conscience and for his tendency towards undue familiarity.

The voices of the Negro are a constant menace to the American who has to repress them sternly. For instance, the black American troops in France, have by themselves, given rise to many complaints for attempted rape as all the Army. And yet, the black soldier sent us have been the choicest with respect to physical and morals for the number disqualified was enormous.

We must prevent the use of any pronounced degree of intimacy between French officers and black officers. We may be courteous and amiable with these people, but we cannot deal with them on the same plane as with the white American officers without deeply wounding the latter. We must not eat with the blacks, we must not shake hands or seek to talk or meet with them outside of the regiments of military service. We must not commend too highly the black American troops, particularly in the presence of white American. White men become greatly incensed at any public expression of intimacy between white women with black men."

Racism in America did not start in recent years but many years ago. Therefore, how can anyone logically say it can end today.

The African Presence

Colonel Helidore Mortenol a native of Guadeloupe had commanded a fleet of torpedo boats in the China Sea and also at Cherbourg and Toulon, France during the period 1892-1900. In 1907, he was recipient of an award for his fleet of torepedo boats superb performance in a Navy arms contest. Mortenol served as the coordinators of target practice for the French Navy and commanded the ships *Suffren, Redoubtable, and Admiral Deperra*.

During World War I Mortenol commanded the Air Defense Command in Paris with 10,000 men and 205 airplanes. It was during the 1901, Boxer Rebellion of China that he was decorated with the Order of the Crown of Prussia by Kaiser Wilhelm of Prussia for bravery in the rescue of a German Torpedo boat destroyer and its crew. His other decorations included the commander of the Legion of Honor, an officer of the Order of the Dragon of Annam, officer of the order of Anjouan, Gold Medal of Cambodia, and the Merit Medal of Madagascar.

The foreign allied powers did employ African soldiers during World War I. There were thousands of Sengalese soldiers who were victorious in repulsing the German troops at Marne and Oureq. There were also the Belgium's Congolese soldiers and England's Black West Indian soldiers who contributed to the first victory of the allies. The Spanis, the Negroid Algerians were present at Salmica.

On December 29, 1918, the French Colonial League held an awards ceremony in the Trocadero, Paris. The celebration was in honor of the native troops who had fought for France during world war I. Some of the people present were M. Henry Simon, Colonial Minister, Eugene Etienne, President of the French Colonial League, and one of the seven black deputies in France's House of Deputies, Blaise Diagne who was appointed Commissioner General of Colonial Affairs in the Cabinet of Clemencea.

THE LEAGUE OF NATIONS AND MANDATES

The League of Nations

The League of Nation's idea had developed in Britain during World War I. A League of Nations society was organized in Great Britain to enforce peace. In 1916, President Woodrow Wilson suggested a Concert of Nations: Pope Benedict IV pleaded for an institution of arbitration. The French Chamber debated a league in 1917 and the British Imperial War Cabinet discussed the possibilities of a peace organization.

President Wilson suggested on June 9, 1918, his fourteen points for peace. He believed a general association of nations should be forced under special covenants for the purpose of mutual guarantees of political independence with territorial integrity to great and small states alike.

A draft covenant of the League of Nations was adopted on April 28, 1919 and its main composers were Americans. David Hunter Miller and Englishman, Sir Cecil Hurst. The American experts contributed the principles and the British the legal framework. The highlights of the preamble were not to resort to war, respect all treaty obligations and agree to the covenant of the league. The assembly was the league's parliament and consisted of representatives of all members of the league. The council was the league's cabinet and consisted of representatives of four other powers selected, by the assembly from time to time. There was a secretary general and staff secretariat. The seat of the league was Geneva. The Mandate Commission, The International Labor Organization and the World Court were associated with the league.

The first assembly was held in November 1920 and there were 42 original members signatures of the Treaty of Versailles and neutrals. China had refused to sign at Versailles, but joined the league in 1920. The United States did not ratify and never became a member. Germany became a member in 1926 and Russia in 1934. In 1936, 19 additional states joined and six including Japan, Germany and Italy had seceded: The Soviet Union was expelled in 1939. The last assembly of the League was conducted in 1946.

Articles 1-7 of the covenant related to membership, powers and functions of the assembly and council. Article 16 referred to specified sanctions to be applied to members resorting to war. Article 18 consisted of the fourteen points demanding open covenants of peace and provided for the registration and publication of all treaties and international engagements entered into by member states. Article 19 provided for reconsideration of treaties. Article 21 made an exception of regional understandings like the Monroe Doctrine for ensuring peace.

It seemed as though each member entered the league for some purpose. France saw the league as an instrument to suppress Germany. Italy saw the league as an obstacle to her expansion especially in East Africa and decided to leave the league and possibly felt free to invade Ethiopia in 1936. Germany viewed the league as an assistance to minimize some of her sanctions from World War I. Great Britain more or less observed the functions of the league.

A very significant article was Article 22 of the covenant which allowed for a Mandate System and its provisions in some of the classes (A.B. or C) did affect the future of African countries. This article provided for the political justification to continue the domination of African nations by European powers.

The Mandates

1. Article 22 of the league convenant. The Mandate Article provided for the disposal and distribution of the foreign and overseas territories of Germany and the Ottoman Empire "by reason of their defeat and deplorable records as ruler of subject races." Those Victor Allies believed the territories inhabited (consisted) by the modern world could not be expected to exist without the tutelage of advanced nations.

2. Under the Mandates System, the territories would be granted to colonial powers (Allied Powers) which had occupied the territory during the World War I. The territories would be held in trust on behalf of the League and abuses of imperialism would be avoided. The Mandate would require respect, freedom of religion, prohibition of slave trade, prevention of building of fortifications, and military training of natives and render to the council annual reports.

3. Three Classes of Mandates: "A, B, C"

   <u>Class A</u> - former possessions of Ottoman Empire inhabited by liberated peoples who became independent (Mesopotamia, Palestine allotted to Britain as Mandatory Power and Syria and Lebanon to France).

   <u>Class B</u> - former central and East African possessions of Ottomon Empire <u>inhabited by people who were not expected to becoome independent</u>. Of these possession, the greater part of Tanganyika alloted to Britain, the remainder to Belgium and Togoland and Cameroons were divided between Britian and France.

Black Presence

<u>Class C</u> - former central and East African possessions <u>of Germany inhabited by people who were not expected to become independent</u>. Passed under laws of mandatory as integral portions of its territory (German Southwest Africa) allotted to Union of South Africa. However, the former German islands in the Pacific north of the equator were allotted to Japan and those south of the equator to Australia and New Zealand. In 1932, Iraq (Mesopotamia) was the first state to be emancipated from its mandatory status to an independent kingdom.

4. General Jan Smuts, famous Boer leader and former Prime Minister of Union of South Africa is "frequently called the Father of the Mandate System." Three fundamental ideas of the system were international control, open door and trusteeship.

In 1921, the second Pan African congress convened in London, Brussels and Paris. There were representatives of African descent from the countries of British Nigeria, Gold Coast and Sierra Leone, the Egyptian Sudan, British East Africa, former German East Africa, French Senegal, the French Congo and Madasgascar, Belgian Congo, Portuguese St. Thomas, Angola and Mozambique and Guadeloup, British Guiana, the United States of America, and blacks who were residing in England, France, Belgium and Portugal and there were some non blacks visiting from India, Morocco, Philippines and Annam. Even though the Congress knew that the League of Nations would have little power to correct their challenges to the Mandates that involved the African countries, they decided to submit some resolutions to the League. They requested that in the International Bureau of Labor a section be set aside to deal with the conducting and needs of the native black labor in Africa and in the Islands. A resolution arrived that there be a movement toward self government as an ultimate aim of the World Peace Organization and also a black person should be appointed as a member of the Mandate Commission. Another resolution asked the League of Nations to seriously observe the conditions of civilized black people throughout the world.

There must be an awareness in 1997 that in regard to continuing political and economic problems in African countries today that 75 years ago African and American blacks have been trying very diligently to help to solve their problems and have requested the European powers to realize some of the negative residual effects that they created when decisions were made after a World War I to determine the future of peoples of African descent. Students in the academic arena must be reeducated today to understand what really occurred that adds to some of the political, tribal and economic conditions of many Africans countries. How many people who are educated in the world today through courses in European or world history actually have been told the following facts.

The League of Nations Mandate B and C affected the following African countries. I will name the country and its former so called "protector". Tanganyika (Tanzania), parts of the Cameroons and Togoland, (Britain), remaining sections of Germany's former colonies in East Africa (France), and Rwanda Urundi (Belgium) and German South West Africa to South Africa.

Now it should be known that after World War II, 1945 a new idea was born and that was the new Peace Body the United Nations Organization with its headquarters in New York City, U.S.A. Many of the great European powers had suggested that the League of Nations Mandate System be transferred to the UN's trusteeship council which would replace the League of Nation's Mandates Commission. There were no definitive plans for African Independence in 1945. The idea of trusteeship was really no new formula to address the problems of the Mandate System. Because in 1885 at Berlin Congress, it was stated that developing trade and civilizations in certain regions of Africa would further the material and moral well being of the native Africans. Similar declarations of trusteeship were included in the Brussels Acts of 1890 in which the parties agreed to protect the aboriginal" people of Africa. Then the concept of a trusteeship formula surfaced in the Algeciras Act of 1906 whereas Britain, France and Spain would submit annual reports and permit representative from Switzerland to visit Morocco and investigate the implementation of the agreements of the act.

The initial concept of the UN Trusteeship Council in 1945 was that membership in the Trusteeship council would be equally divided between states administering trust territories and other states and members would represent their respective governments. The Trusteeship Council would be responsible to the General Assembly and would provide for visits of inspection to trust territories. However, these visits must be arranged for times agreed upon with administering authority. The United Nations Charter provided that the administering authorities may make use of volunteer forces, facilities and assistance from a trust territory in carrying out their obligations towards the Security Council as well as for local defense and the maintenance of law and order in the trust territory. It should be noted that the United States diplomat and former Secretary of State, John Foster Dulles did suggest that members of the United Nations be responsible for non self governing territories aiming at developing independence as an addition or alternative to self government. Now consider this, he was flatly opposed by the country of Belgium's representative who said the "*word independence would be like flaunting a red flag before a bull.*" History has recorded the facts that General Patton's Third U.S. Army traveled into Belgium especially Brussels in World War II to ensure their safety and independence from Germany's provocations, my primary source is that my late brother, Arthur A. Greene Jr., was a member of Patton's Third Army segregated medical unit that went into Belgium on its way to France and Germany. Yes, soldiers of African descent were assisting Belgium and some of their leaders still possessed the mentality of superiority versus inferiority in reference to their subjugated colonial subjects in the Belgium Congo. Yes, misinformation is negligible but real information is so powerful when you are reeducated to what was and its logical significance to what is in 1997.

A study of the Mandate System and its so called legal justification for the trusteeship of many African nations should help the student in understanding some of the internal problems of the continuing developing nations of Africa who actually received their full independence from European control in the years of 1960, 1970, and even 1990.

WORLD WAR II

African American Presence

The employment of black soldiers during World II in combat operation and the establishment of Negro pilot training opened avenues towards advancement and eventual equality for the blacks in America's military services. Black men were drafted and in some cases volunteered at the beginning of the war. Those with minimal education were assigned to quartermaster, labor and engineer service battalions. Various branches of the three services excluded Negro participation, but due to the administrative and personal effort of civilian aides to the Secretary of War such as Judge William Hastie and Truman Gibson, blacks made great strides towards recognition and equality of assignments.

Black soldiers began to emerge from confinement of labor details and assignments to find opportunities as infantrymen, tankers, parachutists, as officers leading patrols on tactical missions, as pilots, nurses and doctors. The pattern of exclusion because of the skin color was beginning to lose its uniformity and strength.

Although the war was nearing its end when combat forces were integrated, black soldiers no less than their white comrades proved themselves worthy of distinguished honors. Black soldiers served in African and in the Pacific and European theaters of war. Although often used in menial and supply functions, their contributions to the overall tactical successes were praised by many senior commanders. When black Americans went into combat in Normandy, in the hills of Italy, and in the Pacific jungles, they established a record of pride and achievement.

Black officers and noncommissioned officers assumed greater responsibilities during World War II. Senior officers serving today received their rudimentary background and training on a wider basis than ever before as black men and women served on land, sea and in the air for the first time in America's history. For the first time the achievements of blacks in military endeavor were documented and accepted without debate in the desire to suppress unwelcome information.

BLACK MILITARY MILESTONES

Generals Praise the Black Tankers of World War II

During World War II, the employment of American Negro Troops in combat operations was slight and when they were committed there was constant controversy concerning their performance of duty. The Negro press during this period took the lead in attempting to report the truth concerning the Negro's abilities as a soldier and his performances at the front. Even today many persons question the validity of the news coverage during this period; however, the following quotes from two heroic World War II generals should satisfy dubious reader's impression, of Negro press coverage during World War II.

The Ninety-Second jumped into La Spezia and other Fifth Army Units took Bologna. Then they moved into Geona and took it, much to the surprise of the enemy and headquarters. I needed the Ninety-Second and if anyone had tried to take it from me, I would have protested loudly.... they were glorious--General Mark Clark. Commander, Fifth United States Army.

The Negro tank battalion attached to my command fought bravely in the critical battle, of Bastogne.. the Negro soldiers were damn good soldiers, of which the nation could be mighty proud.--General George S. Patton, Commander Third U.S. Army on the Western front."

Black Navy Seabees

Throughout the military services the Negro-American has used his skills and labors in the construction of fortifications, buildings, roads, air fields, and housing. Although to some these tasks may seem menial, the commander knows that they most be accomplished and their completion will determine the potentials of planned combat operations and successes in many instances. During World War II the Negroes were extensively employed on construction projects; however the navy's experienced Seabees also used Negroes.

Army Nurse Corps, Black Angels of Mercy

The American Negro female has played an outstanding role in the military services of this country. During World War I, Negro women assisted in the war effort as members of the Red Cross Society, Women's Auxiliaries of Military Units, Loan Drives, Young Women's Christian Association Hostesses' Program, and Red Cross Registered Nursing Service and Canteen War Workers.

The advent of World War II saw the introduction of the Negro female into the Armed Services Nurse Corps. After considerable debate and requests by Negro leaders, the Negro woman was accepted into the Army Nurse Corps. Because of the military policies at that time, Negro doctors and nurses were not integrated with white professional personnel in the operation of hospitals treating white patients. Therefore, all-Negro hospitals and wards were established. In 1942, an all-Negro station hospital was organized at Fort Huachuca, Arizona, at a post it which Negro troops were being treated. Negro nurses on duty with the army increased from 218 in December 1943, to 512 by July 1945. Some of the nurses continued to serve with all-Negro hospitals in this country and others were used on a nonsegregated basis in four general hospitals, three regional hospitals, and at least nine station hospitals in the United States.

In May 1944, the surgeon general appealed personally to the chief surgeon of the European Theater to use Negro nurses in at least one hospital. The chief surgeon agreed and in July 1944, sixty-three Negro nurses among whom were some who had formly served with the 25th Station Hospital in Africa and had been returned to the United States at the end of 1943, arrived in the European Theater. After a period of training, these nurses were assigned on September 16, 1944, to replace white nurses in the 168th Station Hospital located in England. Until December 4, 1944, the station hospital was used as a prisoner of war hospital. A plea was made by the present 128th Station hospitals staff, to put new nurses under white supervision and the chief nurse, the operating room supervisor and two section supervisors were mentioned. The chief nurse and the operating room supervisor were permitted to retrain. Since the Korean War and integration in the military services, the army Negro nurse has benefited professionally from the equal opportunities that are offered. The Negro nurse performed outstandingly during the segregated period and today in an integrated society, she continues to pursue a path to success.

The Seven Hundred and Sixty-First Battalion, World War II

The 761st Tank Battalion was activated on April 1, 1942. The battalion received its early training at Camp Hood, Texas (later Fort Hood, Texas). They had received praise from the Second Army Commander Lieutenant General Ben Lear and Lieutenant General Lesley J. McNair.

The morale of the unit was quite high. Brigadier General Ernest J. Dawley addressed the men of the 761st on three occasions. On one occasion he told them that some things will happen during a war for which there would be no obvious explanation but which must be laid to the "fog of war." He concluded: "When you get in there put in an extra round of ammuinition and fire it for General Dawley!" This speech made a lasting impression on the men of the 761st. When the unit entered combat in Europe during World War II, one of their tanks was named "The Fog of War" and to top it off several rounds of ammunition were put into it and fired for General Dawley according to the Unit's historian.

The reputation of this unit was so high that when men of the battalion who were hospitalized subsuquently transferred, they attempted to return to the 761st Tank Battalion.

Military historian U.S. Lee stated that "The Negro armored units, by virtue of their use in task forces and the attachment of their companies and platoons to infantry, had closer continuing contacts with the main stream of battle than most other small supporting black units."

The 761st Tank Battalion was the first black Negro armored unit to be committed to combat. The unit landed at Omaha Beach on October 10, 1944 after brief garrison duty in England. The unit had 6 white and 30 black officers and 676 enlisted men.

The men of the 761st received praise from General George S. Patton Jr. on November 2, 1944. Patton remarked: "Men, you are the first Negro tankers to ever fight in the American army. I would have never asked for you if you were not good. I have nothing, but the best in my army. I don't care what color you are, so long as you go up there and kill those Kraut sonsabitches. Everyone has their eyes on you and is expecting great things from you. Most of all, your race is looking forward to you. Don't let them down; don't let me down."

The unit spent 183 days in action. While fighting with the Third U.S. Army, the 761st Tank Battalion was attached to the 26th, 71st and 87th Division, 17th Airborne Division, 17th Armored Group.

They were also assigned to the 9th Army, 90th and 79th Division and XVI Corps, 7th Army, 103rd and 71st Divisions. The unit fought with larger units in Belgium, Holland, Luxembourg, Germany and Austria.

On November 8, 1944, the 761st Tank Battalion was attached to elements of the 26th Division and placed in special task forces at Athainville east of Nancy. Company A of the 761st was attached to the 328th Infantry Provisional Task force A contained Company K of the 101st Infantry Engineers, the 602nd Tank Destroyer Battalion and the remainder of the 761st Tank Battalion (excepting its mortar, assault gun and reconnaissance platoons in reserved.) All of these units were under the command of a Lieutenant Colonel Peter J. Kopcsak, Commander of the 602nd Tank Destroyer Battalion.

Later a Lieutenant Colonel Hollis E. Hunt, Seventeenth Armored Group, was assigned to assist Lieutenant Colonel Kopcsak. Both commanders were wounded by shell fire. After Colonel Kopcsak was evacuated, Colonel Hunt, though wounded, assumed command of the task force.

The heroic exploits of this outstanding black tank battalion during World War II have not been properly credited in the current military literature. This is attested by the fact that a motion picture company within the last several years produced a movie highlighting the life of General George S. Patton Jr. and his triumphant military, tactics and achievements in Europe

Black Presence

during World War II. The script of the movie did not concern itself with black tank participation with Patton's Third Army. Some concerned black citizens questioned why the producers and directors mentioned only General Patton's black enlisted military aide. Unfortunately, there was a negative response. Were blacks really there as tankers? The American military newspaper, *The Stars and Stripes* of November 14, 1944, answered the question positively with the following headline and news coverage:

Negro Tankers Cut Deep into German Lines

With U.S. Third Army Forces east of Chateau-Silins, Nov. 13.--Negro tank forces, "making their combat debut with Gen. Patton's troops sweeping northward across the Seille River and toward the Siegfried defenses, have figured in the successful U.S. breakthrough launched in this sector.

Early last Wednesday (Nov. 8) two companies of a Negro tank battalion started fighting in the vicinity of Bezange and Moncourt as H-hour of the first round of the offensive struck.

But the main and sternest mission of the tankers began early Thursday morning when the unit spearheaded an important task force whose objective lay deep in German-held territory.

Commanded by Lt. Col. Peter J. Kopcsak, a TD battalion C.O. from Pittsburgh, the task force included tanks, TDs, combat engineers and assault infantry men, who rode the Sherman [tanks].

Crossing the rain-swollen Seille, just north of the recently taken town of Morville-les-Vic, was the real testing of the tankers. Furious shelling met them at the crossroads, six hundred yards from the town. Tank-infantry teams moved down on the town from three directions and the battle was joined at once.

Within ninety minutes of the start of the push, Nazi prisoners were being sent rearwards by the first Negro tank troops ever committed to combat operations.

...tankers suffered their heaviest loses in a running three-hour fight with German AT guns concealed woods capping a high hill northeast of Morville.

"Home Front War Efforts"

In cooperation with the Governmental Defense Agencies and the WPA Adult Education project, there were special weekly events for black servicemen stationed in the Washington, D.C. area. The black community provided exceptional support for the military men of color. There were events at the Phyllis Wheatley Y.W.C.A. They had programs to include pin pong, badminton, hobbies, handicrafts, shuffle board and music. The YWCA also scheduled Fun Night and Soldiers' Night. They also scheduled a Draftee dance in the soldiers blue at Fort Belvoir, Virginia and provided hostesses from the Phyllis Wheatley YWCA on 901 Rhode Island Avenue, Washington, D.C.

The Young Men's Christian Association (YMCA) also had an active program for the soldiers. They conducted recreational activities at Fort Belvoir with assistance from the Young Women's Christian Association (YWCA) and the Community Center and Playgrounds Department of the District of Columbia.

The YMCA had their post opened on Sundays and had an escort service to accompany the soldiers to church services. The YMCA offered a program for the servicemen on Saturdays that included swimming pool privileges, billiards, basketball, and checkers. There were also scheduled dances. There were some city churches who opened their doors to the servicemen. Dinners were provided by the Mt. Carmel Baptist Church at 3rd and Eyes Street, N.W. and the Wesley Union Church, 1107 23rd Street. They were coordinated by the American Legion Post.

Soldiers were given tickets by the Management of Howard Theatre to attend their professional weekly stage shows.

Reference: Primary Source document, *"Special Weekly Events For Colored Men, December 24, 1941 - January 2, 1942"*.

These activities were coordinated by a unified black community during the era of a segregated army, and city in the Nations Capitol.

Ollie Stewart

The late outstanding journalist and war correspondent Ollie Stewart was present at the famous Casablanca, Morocco Conference where President Franklin Delano Roosevelt of the United States and Prime Minister, Winston Churchill of Great Britain discussed the allied war situation for ten days. President Roosevelt was accompanied by statesmen, Harry Hopkins and Averell Harriman. Churchill was with Lord Leathers, British Prime Minister of Transport. Stewart stated that he, with twenty-five other newsmen, greeted Roosevelt and Prime Minister Churchill at the Press Conference. Ollie Stewart said a company of black soldiers flanked the road during the leaders review of troops. The visit was the first time that a wartime president had left the continental limits of the United States to visit a foreign battle zone. Stewart lived in Paris, France after the war. I had the opportunity to meet Ollie Stewart in Paris, France in 1965.

"True Facts They Did Not Tell Me"

There are hundreds of books in print on the courageous performances and events about people of color during World War II, especially African Americans. I have researched some interesting facts about the black presence and they were included in my book, *Black Defenders of America 1775-1973*. They were facts that they did not tell me in my earlier education and also college experiences. They Did Not Tell Me that:

Brigadier General Benjamin O. Davis, Sr. was the first African American General officer in the regular U.S. Army. He was on active duty in World War II.

The Navy promoted their first black officers in 1949, 12 Naval officers as Ensign and one Warrant officer.

Mess Attendant Second Class Dorie Miller was a hero in World War II. He received the Navy Cross for bravery at Pearl Harbor where he was manning a machine gun. Miller served aboard the USS West Virginia.

Sergeant Joe Louis, the heavy weight champion of the world presented his fight purse of $89,000 to the World War II war effort.

The Great Lakes Naval Center had a varsity baseball team in 1944 and one of the team's player was Larry Doby. Later he became an outstanding professional baseball player.

Many visitors come to Washington, D.C. and visit the famous Iwo Jima Memorial, and of course, there is no indication that black marines were on the beach during World War II. Black soldiers were stationed at Iwo Jima beach.

The first black graduates of the U.S. Navy Academy was Commander Wesley Brown, class of 1949.

William Baldwin, a native of Washington, D.C., was the first black recruit inducted into the U.S. Navy Reserve during World War II. He received his oath of office from Navy Secretary, Frank Knox.

John Walter Bowman of Lafayette, Louisiana was the first known black Catholic Chaplain appointed to the Chaplain Corps during World War II. He was a graduate of St. Augustine's Seminary Bay, St. Louis, Louisiana and parish pastor of the church of the Immaculate Heart of Mary, Lafayette, Louisiana.

Black Presence

Robert H. Brooks was born in Tennessee. While serving in the Pacific Theater during World War II, he was assigned to an armored unit and was killed near Fort Stotsenburg, Philippine Islands on December 8, 1941. It is believed that Private Brooks was the first American soldier of the armored force to be killed in the Pacific Theater while engaged in combat operations. The main parade ground at the armor center at Fort Knox, Kentucky has been named Brooks Field in his honor.

Phyllis Daley was the first Negro nurse to be commissioned in the Navy Nurse Corps during World War II.

Ruth C. Isaacs, Katherine Horton and Inez Patterson, the first black waves to enter the Navy's Hospital Corps.

Harriet Ida Parks and Ensign Frances Wills were the first black waves commissioned in the U.S. Navy.

Alexander Palmer Haley was born in Ithaca, New York on August 11, 1921 and attended State Teachers College, Elizabeth City, North Carolina, from 1937-1939. He enlisted in the U.S. Coast Guard as a mess attendant in 1939. He served as the editor of the ship's paper aboard a pacific supply vessel where one of his editorials was widely reprinted. Haley returned to the United States on a service magazine assignment in 1944 and was reassigned to edit our *Out Post* the official Coast Guard publication. He became the first chief journalist in the Coast Guard in 1949. The late Alexander P. Haley was acclaimed and praised for his outstanding book *Roots*.

Lieutenant Edward Swain Hope was the first Negro to obtain the rank of lieutenant in the U.S. Navy when he was commissioned on May 15, 1944, in the Civil Engineer Corps of the U.S. Naval Reserve. Before his commission, he was employed at Howard University, Washington, D.C. His primary assignment was at U.S. Naval Construction Training Center, Davisville, Rhode Island

Joseph Jenkins graduated from officers training school on August 14, 1942. He was assigned as an engineering officer in Baton, Massachusetts, and it is believed that he commanded an integrated unit.

Ensign Jenkins was one of the few black officers commissioned in the U.S. Coast Guard during World War II.

During World War II, there were some outstanding African American War correspondents. Some of them were: Ollie Stewart, Arthur Carter, Vincent Tubs, Elizabeth Phillips (she was the first black woman overseas war correspondent), Max Johnson and Herbet Frisby. Ulysses Lee was a native of Washington, D.C. He was a honor graduate of Howard University and was a Rosenwald Fellow at the University of Chicago. Lee was a teacher for nearly thirty years at Lincoln University, Missouri, at Morgan State University and a visiting lecturer at the University of Pennsylvania. Dr. Lee was a staff member at the office of the chief of military history from 1946-1952. He also served as an education officer in the field and at the headquarters of Army Service Forces. He was considered the leading authority on the history of Negroes in the army and his book, *The Employment of Negro Troops (World War II)*, was published in 1966. Dr. Lee was co-editor of the *Negro Caravan* an anthology of writings by African Americans and was associate editor of the Midwest Journal of the College Language Association. He died in 1960 and will always be remembered as a veteran of some years of military service (Major), a renowned scholar and a teacher.

Hazel. P. McCree was a member of the Navy's Nurse Corp in World War I. She became the first black woman appointed commander in the Nurse Corps.

Lieutenant Colonel Henry Morgan was a member of the Seven Hundred and Fifty-Eighth Tank Battalion, Company A. While serving as a captain, he displayed unusual bravery at the Cinqualle Canal Crossing north of Viareggio, Italy. He was awarded the Silver Star medal.

Howard D. Perry was the first black to enlist in the Marine Corps in World War II. He was also a member of the first class of twelve hundred black volunteers who trained at Camp LeJeune, North Carolina.

Captain Wendell O. Pruitt was a flight instructor and veteran combat pilot, Thirty-Second Fighter Squadron U.S. Army Air Force. He was born in St. Louis, Missouri and was educated at Charles Sumner High School, Stowe Teachers College and Lincoln University of Missouri. Pruitt was commissioned on December 13, 1942. He was credited with destroying three enemy planes in the air, eight on the ground and sinking a German destroyer. He was awarded the Distinguished Flying Cross, Air Medal with seven oak leaf clusters. In December 1945, while on a routine local flight near Tuskegee, Alabama, his plane crashed and he was killed.

First Sergeant Mark Matthews was born on August 7, 1894 in Greenville, Alabama. He enlisted in the Tenth U.S. Cavalry in 1916. During his military career, he served at Fort Huachuca, Fort Myers, Fort Riley, McCoy Field, North Carolina and the South Pacific. He served as a saddler and a border guard with the U.S. Immigration Service at Naco, Arizona and New Mexico.

While assigned at Ft. Myer, Virginia his additional duties included being a member of the Firing Squad who fired volleys for funerals at Arlington National Cemetery. Matthews said the cemetery was segregated in the 1930's but his unit were still detailed to fire the volley for all funeral processions, black or white. He stated that the bugler and poll bearers were white. Matthews said he was a bugler for seven years. He could play taps and all the calls.

Matthews related to me in a personal interview that his unit performed for the late Emperor Haile Selassie of Ethiopia. On one visit where they were scheduled to perform, the Emperor was ill and they performed for his nephew, Ras Desta in the Fort Myer large riding hall. They also performed for Queen Mary of England. They escorted her from the Washington Union Station to the White House. Matthews was assigned to Fort Leavenworth, Kansas in 1939. He was assigned as a stable sergeant. When World War II commenced, First Sergeant Matthews was assigned to Camp Funston near Fort Riley, Kansas. Later he was assigned to the Twenty-fourth Infantry Regiment at Saipan. Mark Matthews retired from the military service in 1947 after 30 years of outstanding service. First Sergeant Matthews was also a member of the Rifle-Pistol team and participated in competitions. He was an expert marksman. Matthews told me when he marched in President Franklin D.

Roosevelt's parade on February 2, 1939, that when he reported to Fort Leavenworth and received his horse, he named it "Franklin D".

In 1944, I had the distinguished pleasure of meeting and interviewing a *"Real Buffalo Soldier"*. His reflexes and swiftness was an experience to witness, especially for a man who was 100 years old.

Reference: *Who Were The Real Buffalo Soldiers?*

During World War II, the black military surgeon made an outstanding contribution while serving in the U.S. Army and Air Force Medical Corps. Some of those courageous physicians and surgeons were:

Barnett Milton Rhetta Jr. was assigned as a first lieutenant, 876th Engineer Aviation battalion and the 268th Station Hospital, Australia.

Arthur Hugh Simmons was a major and served as the commanding officer, 268th Hospital, Australia.

Wilbur Hughes Strickland was assigned as a major to the 335th Station Hospital, India Burna Theater of Operations.

Theodore D. Phifer was assigned as a major, U.S. Army medical Corps, 93rd Division. His specialty was psychiatry.

Allison B. Henderson served as a military surgeon during World War II as a major and was assigned to Liberia.

Arthur Harold Thomas was the director of general surgery, U.S. Army, Fort Huachuca, Arizona. He was also the chief, Department of Surgery, 268th Station Hospital, Asiatic Pacific Theater of Operations, 1941-1946.

Bascom S. Waugh served during World War II as a squadron flight surgeon, 332nd Field Hospital.

Colonel John F. Hanes served as a regimental surgeon in the 366th Engineer Regiment during World War II.

Lieutenant Colonel Norman E. Robinson served during World War II at Fort Devins, Massachusetts and served in Oran, Algiers, North Africa.

Reference: *Physicians and Surgeons of Color Real Image Models for Youth and Adults.*

"Seven Image Models of Bravery"

There have been some specific instances that established the climate for lower military commanders not to consider or recommend African Americans in World War II for the Congressional Medal of Honors. When a soldier performs honorably in a combat situation and is deserving of the Congressional medal of Honor, his immediate commander must recommend him and also the higher echelons of command, must approve the award. However, if there were preconceived impressions of the black soldier by top commanders sometimes these views served as a basis to justify the lower commander opinions and personal reasons of not recommending the soldier and not suggesting the silver star or distinguished service cross awards.

Although some very competent and qualified persons in 1997 will say racism was not involved, I suggest that they reeducate themselves and ask who are minorities today other than African Americans? Because in World War II, there were two minorities who served in white units and were designated officially as white and not Hispanics or native Americans. There were at least ten known medal of honor awards presented to Hispanics during World War II. There was one Asian soldier or Japanese American who served in a segregated Asian unit, the 442nd Regiment, who was awarded the medal of honor for his exemplary bravery.

I believe that some distinguished and honorable military commanders did not have negative or statistically analyzed impressions of the Hispanics, Native Americans and Asians in the 1940's

When the late military commander and former President of the United States Dwight Eisenhower testified before the Senate Armed Forces Committee on April 3, 1948 concerning integration in the Armed Services he said: *"In the war when we became so desperate for infantry replacements in the fall of 1944, we did not make the best use of our Negro manpower. We had some 600,000 in Europe. We told the Negroes we would take volunteers for service in the line, in the front lines. 2,400 were organized as platoons. I personally, have always stood since that time for organizing Negroes down to include units no larger than platoons. It does create social problems on a post, because you always have men that do not like to mingle freely between the races, and therefore, if you have dances for your soldiers you have a problem. But I believe these things can be handled. Now if you are going to go further; here is the problem you run into, Senator (Saltonstall), In general, the Negro is less well educated than his brother citizen that is white, and if you make a complete amalgamation, what you have is in every company the Negro is going to be relegated to the minor jobs, because the competition is tough."*

One of the first official acts of the President of the United States in the new year of 1997 was the presentation of long due recognition to seven black American veterans of World War II who distinguished themselves conspicuously by gallantry and intrepidity at the risk of their lives and beyond the call of duty while engaging the enemy in action. On January 13, 1997, the nation and the world witnessed through the news media the awarding of seven medal of honors to African American veterans of World War II, one is still living and six are deceased. First Lieutenant Vernon J. Baker received his medal of honor from President Clinton. The other six men's medals were presented to their respective family members. The award ceremony should be an awakening and an education to all Americans and the world that there must be a continual effort by people of color to be recognized for their sincere contributions to the American experience whether it is military or civilian. How can one seriously believe that the second class citizenship status of African Americans in recent years can be eradicated in civil rights measures in 35 years whereas it has taken 52 years to officially recognize and award seven black soldiers whereas some 433 white, Hispanic and an Asian were honored in the 1940's because they were considered non black soldiers. As the late James C. Evans, former counselor to the Secretary of Defense quoted Goethe Faust, I will use the quote to say my factual views are *"Das werke loben den meister"* or *"The proof of the pudding"*. There will be many articles, commentaries, possible television documentaries and books on these courageous men of color.

Since I wrote biographical sketches on four of these men in my book, *Black Defenders of America, 1775-1973*, I have updated their sketches and written sketches on the other men. Hundreds of books, articles and even comic book material have been written on the medal of honor recipients. There have been very few accounts that have told the true story of black military exceptional superb performances as the following biographical sketches will reveal.

First Lieutenant Vernon J. Baker was a member of Company C, First Battalion, 370th U.S. Infantry Regiment, 92nd Division during World War II. On April 5, 1945, the 92nd Division was launching a diversionary attack prior to the Fifth Army's main attack toward Bologna, Italy. The immediate objective for the 92nd's diversionary attack was Massa. The 370th's lead company, C Company, had advanced toward the vicinity of its battalion objective, Castle Aghinolfi. Mortar and heavy fir caused considerable casualties as the Regiment continued its advance in the area when Baker and his 25 man platoon had reached the south side of a draw 250 yards from the castle very early in the morning. He saw a telescope pointing out of a slit in a bunker at the edge of the hill. Lt. Baker placed his M-1 rifle into the slit, fired continuously and then looked inside. He saw two German soldiers he had killed and one was still slumped in his chair in the observation post. Baker came across a camouflaged machine gun position or nest killing their German occupants. (Historian Ulysses Lee stated in his book that there were eight German occupants). While talking to his company commander, Captain Runyon, a German soldier suddenly appeared and threw a hand grenade that hit Runyon's helmet, bounced off and failed to explode. Lt. Baker immediately shot and killed the German as he was fleeing.

Captain John Runyon had assessed the current tactical situation at the time and realized that company C's radio man and its artillery observer were both wounded and of the twenty-five enlisted men in Baker's platoon (the advance party) only eight were not wounded or killed. Runyon also had two officers wounded. Captain Runyon then made a decision to withdraw to battalion lines. Baker protested about the immediate withdrawal, however, Runyon ordered the withdrawal and told Baker that he would get reinforcements which never appeared.

Lieutenant Baker decided to make a courageous decision and volunteered to remain and cover the withdrawal of the first group, that included most of the walking or ambulatory wounded men. He was staying to assist the more severely wounded. Lee reported in his book, *The Employment of Negro Troops* that eight men and the wounded artillery observer stayed with him. Baker guarded the rear and left after destroying equipment left by the killed and wounded. During the withdrawal, four different enemy machine gun crews had been destroyed by the first group. As Baker's party followed, they lost two men, one wounded by mortar fire and their own medic, killed by sniper fire. The group's Private James Thomas was able to locate the sniper and killed him. Baker and his group then encountered two machine gun nests that were bypassed during the morning attack. Thomas provided cover for Baker and he was able to crawl up to the machine gun positions and destroy them with hand grenades. Lt. Baker and his small party were finally able to evacuate its casualties. The following night, this unknown hero to many until 1997, led a battalion advance through heavy mine fields and heavy fire and was awarded the Distinguished Service Cross.

I am sure that others have agreed with the statement that I wrote 25 years ago in my book *Black Defenders of America 1775-1973*, "From the following account of Lieutenant Baker heroic conduct on April 5-6, 1945, he would appear to have deserved serious consideration for a medal of honor award. However, there were no such awards to black soldiers in World War II".

Black Presence

299

This demonstrates the outstanding performance of duty of Lieutenant Baker on April 5, 1945, who served in a segregated U.S. Army with restrictions, quotas and no debate on Affirmative action and no created terms of political correct, race cards, and racially sensitive. This hero has at last been officially recognized and his courage is now known to the world. I believe that Lt. Vernon J. Baker has been blessed with his 77 years of life and is now able to enjoy those fruits of labor when so many other Americans of all color will understand his patriotism to a country that still needs Affirmative measures to eradicate the vestiges of years ago. I personally salute you, Lt. Baker and may you be an image model for all and you are a superb Black Defender of America.

Staff Sergeant Edward A. Carter Jr. was a member of the Seventh Army Provisional Infantry Company I, Fifty-Sixth Armored Infantry Battalion, He was awarded a Distinguished Service Cross for bravery in action on March 23, 1945, when he was with the detachment of the Seventh Army Provisional Company riding on a tank near Speyar, Germany. His tank was confronted with heavy bazooka and small arms fire from a large warehouse. Carter voluntarily attempted to lead a three-man group across 150 years of open field to check out the warehouse. Within a short time, two of his men were killed and the other wounded and the third seriously wounded before they could reach cover. Carter continued toward the enemy emplacement alone. He was wounded five times, three bullets in his left leg, one in the arm, and one through his hand. Carter took cover behind an earthen barn near the warehouse. Two hours later, eight German soldiers attempted to capture Carter. He was able to kill six of the German riflemen and captured the remaining two. He then used the two prisoners as a shield as he returned across the field. He was able to obtain from them valuable information about the disposition of enemy troops. Staff Sergeant Carter of Los Angeles, California died in 1962. He was awarded the Congressional medal of honor posthumously.

First Lieutenant Charles L. Thomas of Detroit, Michigan was a member of Company C, Six Hundred and Fourteenth Tank Destroyer Battalion attached to the 103rd Division. He was awarded the Distinguished Service Cross for gallantry while serving as Company C, tank commander in combat near Climbach, France during World War II.

Company A had been attached to Task Force Forest, made up of the 103rd Reconnaissance Troop, a company of the 756th tank battalion and a company of the 409th Infantry. Company C was attached to the 411th Infantry. The leadership of L. Thomas was demonstrated on December 8, 1944 when his company knocked out an observation post in a church steeple and destroyed a machine gun emplacement and delivered harassing fire on the German troops.

On December 14, 1944, Lt. Thomas and the task force had left Prueschdorf on a foggy cold morning. The visibility was less than 300 yards. Thomas was in the lead armored scout car proceeding through enemy territory slowly toward the town of Climback, France five miles from the German border. The Germans had waited until the platoon was well advanced before they opened up with small arms, automatic weapons, mortar and artillery fire. When within a thousand yards of Climback, Lt. Thomas' M-20 scout car was hit, shattering the window and spraying Thomas with glass and metal sharks. Another round blew the tires off the car. Thomas, though wounded, dismounted from the wrecked car and scrambled on top of the vehicle, grabbed a .50 caliber machine gun and kept firing at the Germans, although he was wounded in his arms, chests and legs. Lt. Thomas instructed his men to proceed up the road and go into firing positions. He ordered the dispersion and displacement of two of his tank destroyers. Only when he was in full control of the situation did he permit himself to be evacuated. Later he was promoted to the rank of major.

Major Charles L. Thomas died in 1980. He was awarded the Congressional medal of honor posthumously.

Private Willy F. James Jr., of Kansas City, Missouri was a member of Company G, 413rd Infantry Regiment, 104th Division in World War II. He was killed in action on April 7, 1945 in Germany. James was awarded the Distinguished Service Cross for bravery posthumously.

After the 413th Infantry had established a bridgehead across Germany's Weser River and secured the vital crossing, they were ordered to capture the town of Lippoldsberg. Private Jones was scouting ahead of

Black Presence 301

his platoon and had volunteered to move forward another 200 yards to observe the German positions, and obtain a report. He walked into an immediate assault and his platoon leader was wounded. James went to his aid and was suddenly killed.

The heroic efforts and a personal concern to help others were incidental to Private Willy F. James Jr.'s ultimate sacrifice of life. He died in 1945 and at last his country who he showed his great patriotism for, has recognized him posthumously again, but this time with the medal of honor.

Private George Watson of Birmingham, Alabama was a member of the 29th Quartermaster Regiment. On March 8, 1943, he was on a ship near Porloch's Harbor, New Guinea. Japanese bomber aircraft approached his ship and afflicted it so seriously that all of its occupants were ordered to abandon the ship. There were some men who could not swim and Pvt. Watson remained in the water to assist them to the life rafts. Watson became very exhausted and was not able to get clear of the turbulence when the ship went down, and he disappeared beneath the waves. His body was never recovered. When Private Watson was awarded the Distinguished Service Cross posthumously, he became the first known black American to be awarded the medal in World War II. He was 28 years old when he was drafted. Private Watson has been remembered on a Memorial at American Cemetery and in Manila, Philippines. There is also a George Watson Memorial Field at Fort Benning, Georgia. In January 1997, some 54 years later after his heroic acts of bravery, Pvt. George Watson was awarded the Medal of Honor posthumously.

First Lieutenant John R. Fox of Boston, Massachusetts was a member of the 366th Infantry Regiment's Cannon Company, 92nd Division. In December 1944, the Fifth Army headquarters made a decision to deploy the 92nd Division in the Serchio Valley Counter attack for a proposed offensive toward Bologna, Italy. The 370th Infantry had the 2nd battalion, 366th attached. The day after Christmas, December 26, a major attack commenced. When the 370th's 1st battalion moved toward their objective, a small garrison at Sommocolonia, they came under small arms fire and artillery. Later the town was under attack by enemy troops consisting of Germans, Austrians and Italians and the situation at Sommocolonia worsened. Lt. Fox who had volunteered to serve as an artillery forward observer in the village of Sommocolonia in the Serchio valley selected the second floor of a house to use as his observation post. However, on the early morning on December 26, 1944, Fox and his men woke to find themselves overrun and the enemy were trying to break into the house where they had established their observation post. At this time, Lt. Fox got on his radio and requested artillery fire on his own observation post and also called for smoke screen to cover the withdrawal of the remaining troops. He repeated his request to the fire direction control command post of the 598th Artillery unit, 92nd division.

It has been learned that Lt. Fox's procedural request to call fire on his own position even though he was under life and death situations was odd, the artillery battalion commander and his subordinates were questioning and trying to clarify the request. They went all the way through the chain of command to obtain approval. Once approval was obtained, a decision was made to have an artillery battle to use four guns to fire toward the post. Unfortunately, later they obtained the shattered body of Lieutenant Fox. Lt. John Fox's act of heroism would earn him the Congressional medal of honor in 1997 posthumously. It should be noted that Lt. Fox was recommended for the Distinguished Service Cross and it was not approved until April 15, 1982, possibly due to administrative problems.

Staff Sergeant Reuben Rivers of Tecumseh, Oklahoma was a member of the 761st tank battalion 104th Infantry Regiment, 26th Infantry Division. Sgt. Rivers was awarded the Silver Star medal for alertness and intrepid deeds on November 7, 1944, in the area of Vicsur-Seille, France. Sergeant Rivers was riding in a lead tank in Company A which ran into a road block obstructing the tank column. He dismounted under small arms fire, attached a cable to the road block and moved it off the road. His heroic action allowed the infantry tank team to continue their mission. His white tank commander recommended Rivers for the silver star on November 8, 1944.

On November 16, 1944, Sgt. Rivers tank struck a German mine at a railroad crossing outside Guebling, France. He suffered injuries on his right leg and refused immediate medical attention and also evacuation. He later assumed command of another tank in the front of the formation. Then on November 19, Sgt River's battalion was attacking toward the town of Bourgaltroff when its lead tank was hit by a 88 mm antitank round. Rivers was ordered to pull back, but he radioed that he had spotted the enemy's positions and that they would move forward and engage them in a battle which ended when a German shell hit Rivers' tank's turret and killed him. After 52 years of heroic acts, Sergeant Reuben Rivers' personal sacrifice of his life and devotion to duty has been recognized by the awarding of the Congressional Medal of Honor posthumously.

In 1974, while traveling to Paris, France, I decided to stop briefly in the most beautiful and well preserved American military cemetery at St. Avold, France near the town of Lorraine. I immediately went to the administration building and I was able to meet the Assistant Superintendent who was quite cordial and offered his assistance to me. I asked if any black soldiers from World War II were buried there. The gentlemen politely and adamantly replied all of the soldiers buried here are American soldiers. I then asked if I provided a name could he locate the grave site. He took the name I gave him and within minutes my family and I were standing within the beautiful and spacious grave areas of the cemetery. I was at the grave site of an American soldier of color who was a member of the 761st Tank battalion. I stood somberly and proudly over the grave site of this soldier, and saluted the remains of Sergeant Reuben Rivers. I realized that he was buried among many soldiers of color in the military cemetery at Lorraine and was unknown in physical identity, but naturally known to his immediate family. I believe that the awarding of Sergeant Reuben Rivers the Medal of Honor in 1997 posthumously has a personal place in my heart and mind. Because in 1974, eight months after the publication of my book, I selected a name and was able to visit the grave site of a brave soldier who I had researched his name for my manuscript. I am most happy for his family because I know now that this country and the world can also salute and praise the name of a World War II hero and I will always cherish the memory of saluting him as he rests among many known, and unknown, in a beautiful cemetery in France. Yes, Sergeant Reuben Rivers is my personal image model of a courageous American whose patriotism has finally been honored and now will be preserved in the annals of history after 52 years since his heroism was proven on the battle fields of France. Where our people of color defended freedom for others in 1918 and again in 1944.

There is a serious need for all Americans and the world to be aware of some positive attributes of African Americans. The recent White House Medal of Honor Ceremony should be an awareness to all people that for many years blacks had to perform most exceptionally in order to earn the medal of honor through the years. The official records will reflect that blacks were awarded the following numbers of medals in military wars and campaigns. During the Civil War 24 medals out of 239, Indian Campaigns, 14 medals to members of the four black regiments and four medals to the Seminole Negro Indians Scouts, a total of 18 out of approximately 400. (Ironically, a black recipient of the Indian Wars, Sergeant Thomas Shaw, Troop B. Ninth U.S. Calvary regiment has a descendant in 1997 who is an outstanding military surgeon and a successful civilian physician. Colonel Dr. John W. Huguley III is the former chief outpatient medical clinic, Walter Reed Army Medical Center, Washington, D.C.). There were six medal recipients in the Spanish American War out of 109, 1 recipient, World War I, 1 out of 124, 2 recipients, Korean War, 2 out of 131, 7 for World War II, 7 out of 433 and 20 recipients, Vietnam War 20 out of 239 (There were more black servicemen committed to combat situations).

The progress of the African American in the United States military services since 1775 has been most commendable and as I have stated before the undaunting military pride and attention to duty with outstanding heroic results such as those seven men of color in World War II helped to show the majority white Americans that those who have proven themselves admirably in the late decade of this twentieth century could perform as well as or better than anyone else who call themselves an American. That has been attested to through the living proof of what I call the military miracle, General Colin Powell.

African Presence

When the allied colonial powers entered World War II, they made a decision to employ their colonial subjects as "black cannon fodder" to assist in satisfying their personal war plans and their efforts to the allied victory over many in Italy and Japan. The following African nations did provide military service toward the ultimate victory for the allied forces. Some African civilians also made their personal contributions. Their loyalty to their colonial protectors or colonial rulers is a significant part of the African presence in World History. There were also some Africans who were possibly forced to provide their services to Italy and Germany.

The Netherlands had Dutch Colonial soldiers from Guiana, Surinam and some were manning coastal defense posts near the county of Paramaribo, Dutch Guiana. Some were anti aircraft gunners who would manned positions near Fort Amsterdam.

East African soldiers were assigned to military duties in Burma and Ceylon during World War II. They were members of the East African Pioneer Corps and there was also the Royal West African Frontier. There was a division stationed in the Arakan jungle, Burma, known as the 81st West African Division. They were excellent soldiers in jungle warfare. The West Africans demonstrated their abilities to fight a long and bitter campaign in the Arakan in clearing the coastal sector north of Akyab. When the British were fighting the Japanese in the eastern part of Burma they employed thousands of African Troops. It has been said that prior to World War II that no troops from the West African colonies had ever left Africa for an overseas theatre of war. The troops had previously been used in Ethiopia and the Middle East. The Belgium had a Belgium Colonial Infantry. The men were from the Congo. Their uniforms included a headgear that was a red fez with a neck cloth attached. They used Belgian rifles.

Gaston Monnerville was born in French Guiana in 1897. He received a scholarship to the University of Toulouse and graduated with a law degree in 1922. In 1928, he represented some of his fellow citizens who had been accused of participating in a political riot in Guiana. They were acquitted and this legal case made Monnerville a hero among the people.

Later he was elected to the French Chamber of Deputies in 1932. He was appointed to serve as Secretary of State for Colonies. During World War II, he joined the French Navy and assisted in the organization of French resistance movements against the Germans. After World War II, he returned to the House of Deputies and in 1947 was elected President of the Council of the Republic. When President DeGaule of France founded the Fifth Republic, Monnerville supported him. However, they disagreed over democratic procedures and Monnerville said the constitution is openly violated and warned that France was headed for a dictotorship. DeGaule insisted on his politial views, but Monnerville sustained his position.

In later years, Monnerville was elected President of the French Senate and had DeGaule resigned or died in office while Monnerville was President of the Senate, then France would have had a President of color.

Africans Support The War Efforts

During World War II, citizens of Nigeria and the Gold Coast gave full support to the war efforts. Some West African troops did engage the Italian soldiers in East Africa. Africans were purchasing war saving stamps. They also donated approximately $100,000.000 in contributions to the war effort. In Nigeria and the Gold Coast there were twenty-eight fund groups organized to collect money for World War II. Some of them were mine sweepers fun, British Red Cross Fund, Lord Majors Fund, Naval Charities Fund, Prisoner of War Fund, St. Dunston Fund, Seamans Orphanage Fund, Overseas Cigarette Fund, Kings Fund, Childs Evacuee Fund, and Mrs. Churchill's Aid to Russia Fund.

There were some African students living in London who served as air raid wardens. Some of them would broadcast to Nigeria and other West African countries by short wave radio. Some West Africans did serve in the Royal Air Force.

KOREAN WAR

The year was 1955, two years after an armistice was signed in Korea. I can remember the beautiful sunny day when I arrived in Korea, the land of the "morning calm" and reported to the 24th Infantry division replacement depot in Seoul Korea. It would be some sixteen years later that I would write about the Black Defenders of America during the Korean War 1950-1953. I was very proud to be an engineer officer in the 3rd Engineer Battalion and assigned to Company A, located near a small Korean village WillSan N. Yes, I was stationed toward the north and knew that over the spacious mountains was North Korea and the line of demarcation, the demilitarized Zone (DMZ). I finally realized that I was the only black commissioned officer assigned to the Engineer battalion. There was one black warrant officer. I really believe the black soldiers were glad to see me and I tried very diligently to become an outstanding officer that they would feel pleased to have in their "A" company. It just happen that my third platoon was the best in the company. The black soldiers and even some whites would leave the dining hall or mess hall with their deserts in their hands and sit around on the hill to observe my inspection of the guards before they would report to their guard posts. I enjoyed serving as an officer of the day and would very seriously perform an outstanding inspection in the ranks of the soldiers who reported for guard duty. I had learned to twice twirl the M-1 rifle and abruptly return it to the soldier with precision.

One day while working near the site of the United Nations unit, the Sixth Turkish Brigade, one of their officers invited me to visit their compound and I enjoyed some very hot and delicious baked Turkish bread. To my amazement, my host introduced me to a Turkish officer who was the brigade's pharmacist and I was told that his father was Turkish and his mother was a West African. He did not speak English only Turkish. I believe that was an early experience in my young life to see the black presence in the world and that he was accepted by his comrades from Turkey whereas America the Beautiful was unknowingly preparing for a civil rights revolution. I also recall a moment of an immediate challenge to my leadership abilities on the cold night of 5 December 1956. My commanding officer, Lieutenant Colonel Zitzer expressed his appreciation. He wrote a letter of appreciation, without the "soldiers medal" for my immediate actions. The letter read: *Your response to a call for assistance in rescuing six enlisted men lost in the Imjin River on the evening of 5 December 1956 is commendable. In spite of the intense cold, your supervision and assistance in launching and operating the power boat which effected the rescue was of such a nature as to prove you to be a competent, capable officer. I am proud to have you in my organization.*

In later years I would learn that the location of our battalion headquarters would become a famous background area for a popular television program. I can remember looking across the road at the 44th Military Army Surgical Hospital where some creative person would develop a movie script about the field hospital and it would be called "MASH".

I would be assigned to Korea in later years, 1971 and served as a logistical plans staff officer for the Korean Support Command, Eighth U.S. Army in Taegu and Seoul, Korea. In 1996, I know many of the Koreans in the United States have heard about those courageous soldiers of color who preceded me and were part of the U.S. military command that came to the assistance of the South Koreans when they were attacked by the North Koreans in 1950. Who were those brave black soldiers who were wounded and some died and others returned home safe. They were the black defenders of the Korean War who played a significant role during the Korean conflict.

On June 25, 1950, South Korea was attacked by North Korean troops along the Onjin peninsula northwest of Seoul, the South Korean capital. Seoul was taken on June 29, and on June 30, the first U.S. ground forces entered the conflict as part of a United Nations "police action" to force North Korean troops back to beyond the thirty-eighth patrolled. Black soldiers were part of the war, first in the segregated regiments, among them the First, Second and Third Battalions of the Twenty-fourth Infantry Regiment, Twenty-fifth Infantry Division and, after October 1, 1951 when the U.S. Army started to implement President Truman's order to integrate the armed forces, distributed throughout the military in an attempt to integrate all units as quickly as possible.

Various accounts have been given of the performance of black soldiers during the Korean conflict. Unfavorable reports have been magnified and allowed to remain unmodified by more creditable actions. There have been reports of individual actions of which black people and others can be proud.

On July 22, 1950, the Second Battalion of the Twenty-fourth with elements of the Republic of Korea Seventeenth Regiment were advancing into mountains near Sangfu. One of the Twenty-fourth's companies was fired on and some men began to disperse in a disorderly manner and to show signs of panic. On August 12, 1950, the Third Battalion of the Twenty-fourth were unreliable in their performance and later on August 15, when the Second Battalion was attempting to occupy the Obong-san mountain ridge west of Battle Mountain, the battalion broke contact with the enemy and withdrew to Battle Mountain and the ridge west of Hamon. Some men abandoned their positions. The area of Battle Mountain changed hand several times and in September 1950 on meeting the enemy south of Hamon, some members of the First Battalion were reported to have fled to the rear. The commanding general of the Twenty-fourth Infantry recommended to the commanding general of the Eighth Army that the Twenty-fourth Regiment be removed from combat because of their demonstrated inefficiency. However, the Eighth Army commanding general did not concur in this recommendation and the Twenty-fourth Infantry continued to serve with the Eighth Army until the regiment was dispersed in the integration process which was initiated in 1951.

More favorable reports were made about the performance of Negro soldiers in the following combat operations: Task Force Kean near Hamon when Private William Thompson of the Heavy Weapons Company set up his machine gun and fired at the enemy until he was killed by grenades). Task Force Matthews which involved the Twenty-fourth Infantry and Dolvin's Combat operations near Chonju and Kanggyong in September, 1950.

The reports about the Twenty-fourth Infantry Regiment should not be given too much weight in assessing the performance of Negro soldiers in combat; their illustrious resource in previous wars, the heroism displayed by many in the Korean War, and their record in Vietnam should more than discount this one episode.

Some heroic performances were accomplished by the following individuals: Sergeant Cornelius H. Charlton Co. C Twenty-fourth Infantry Regiment was born in East Gulf, West Virginia. He distinguished himself on June 2, 1951 at Chipo-si, Korea, by a heroic performance beyond the call of duty for which he was awarded the medal of honor.

Private First Class William Thompson, Co. M, Twenty-fourth Infantry regiment was born in New York City. He displayed great bravery near Hamon, Korea, where he was mortally wounded. Private Thompson was awarded the medal of honor posthumously for his courage and self sacrifice.

First Lieutenant Ellison Wynn, Co. B, Ninth Infantry Regiment was engaged in a combat operation that displayed his heroic abilities and for which he was awarded the Distinguished Service Cross. Lieutenant Wynn led his troops in an assault on an enemy position near Kuni-si. During a counter attack the machine gunner was killed. Lt. Wynn remained at his post throwing grenades until his men could rejoin him in defending his position. Although bleeding from wounds, he directed a withdrawal.

Lieutenant Colonel Luther McManus was awarded the Distinguished Service Cross for gallantry in action inspiring his troops with his personal fearlessness and calling them to fix their bayonets as he led them in a determined charge against a hostile position near Wolbon-ni on October 18, 1951.

Master Sergeant Levy H. Hollis of Texas was assigned to Hamon, Korea, during the war and was awarded the Distinguished Service Cross for heroic performance of duty.

AFRICAN NATIONALISM AND INDEPENDENCE

History has recorded the facts, but are they known in 1997 in the social studies curriculums on the secondary and college levels? Are students really aware that many of the present day independent African nations did not receive their independence on a "silver platter", but through years of planning, individual sacrifices, and the organizing of revolutionary movements. Some of those revolutionary groups that eventually brought independence to their countries must not be forgotten.

There are many courses and reasons why independence came to the African nations in the 1950's and 1960's. Some views of historians are: an increase in African nationalism and imperialists motives, some Africans were observing gains of Indian Nationalists, early initiatives by the countries of Ghana, Kenya and Senegal, the African Nationalist Congress in South Africa was demonstrating their resistance, the impact on African thought and goals from the Pan Africanists. They held a Conference in London in 1921 and other sessions in Paris, and Brussels. Some of the participants were Ojo Olaribigde, a physician from Sierra Leone, Dr. Vitallian, former physician to Haile Selassie, Ethiopia, Helen Curtis, Liberian Consul to Brussels, M. Dantes Bellegarde, Haiti, Jose de Magalhes of Angola, deputy for SAO Thome in the Portuguese Parliment and president of an African group, Liga Africana He was also a professor at the London School of Tropical Medicine. Others present were Santos-Pinto, Sao Thome, M.P. Panda, leader of Union Congolaise, Belgium, M. Gratien Candace, M. Issac Beton, Guadeloupe, and Americans W.E.B. Dubois, Walter White, Jessie Fauset. There were African groups that included students studying abroad, union leaders and future politicians whose names would become known to the world. The following groups and organizations played an important role in establishing the climate for independence in African countries. They were the West African Students Union (WASU), International Africa Service Bureau (some of the members were T. Ras Makonnen, George Padmore, Jomo Kenyatta, N. Azikiwe, and Max Yeargan.) Other groups were Negro Welfare Association, pan African Federation, African Union, Friends of African Freedom Society, Gold Coast, Kimuyu Central Association (Venga) Negro Association, United Committee of Colored Peoples.

In the West Indies, there was also a great nationalist awareness from an economic view. This was being expressed by the former Prime Minister of Trindad, Tobago, Eric Williams in his book, *The Negro in the Caribbean, 1945.* There was a League of Colored People organized by Jamaican Harold A. Moody.

The self governing states of Africa met in Accra Ghana, 1958 and they were hosted by Prime Minister Kwame Nkrumah. There were representatives from Egypt, Ethiopia, Ghana, Liberia, Libya, Morocco, Sudan and Tunisa. They discussed political, economic, social and cultural matters. An All African Peoples Conference was concerned in Accra in December 1958. Representatives present were from Ghana, Nigeria, Egypt, Somaliland and Morocco. The delegates represented nationalist groups to include the Union of the Peoples Congress of Cameroons, and Basutoland Congress Party Trade Unionist. The black Americans present were Dr. Horace Bond, former President, Lincoln university, Pennsylvania and Marguerite Cartwright, author and journalist. There were some Soviet writers and observers who brought greetings from Nikta Khruschev and China's Chou En-Lai, Tom Mboya of Kenya read a paper on *the Cold War and Africa.* Dr. W.E.B. Dubois was ill and his wife read a prepared statement from Dubois. He wrote: *"If Africa unites, it will be because each part, each nation, each tribe gives a part of their heritage for the good of the whole. That is what union means, and that is what Pan Africa means".* Also present at the meeting was an Zaire hero and revolutionary leader for independence, Patrice Lumumba from the Belgian Congo.

Prior to the Accura Conference there was a meeting and formation of an All African Peoples Conference (AAPC).

African leaders Kwame Nkrumah and Sekou Toure of Guinea had early ideas that all independent nations should be under one flag, with colors red, gold and green and have an anthem and motto. After many meetings and discussions, some African leaders decided to meet in Addis Ababa, Ethiopia. Emperor Haile Selassie had decided to change Ethiopia's policy of isolationalism and become more active in the Pan African Movement. He sent a representative to the first meeting of the Indepenent States of

Africa in Accra in 1958. The Emperor was instrumental in the establishment and funding of an African Development Bank and the creation of the Economic Commission for Africa (ECA) by the United Nations. The headaquarters of E.C.A. was located in Africa Hall in Addis Ababa, Ethiopia. At the inauguration of the E.C.A., Emperor Haile Selassie demonsrated his sincere interest in the Pan-African Movements' ideaologies when he stated, *"The African peoples too can cooperate effectively for the common good, for their own good and for that of all men"*. He also established scholarships for students of African states to study at the Haile Selassie I University in Ethiopia. In 1962, Haile Selassie attended a meeting of African states in Lagos, Nigeria. He told members of that group that "Ethiopia was a member of one group only. The African Group. On May 22, 1963, this great African Monarch and his country hosted heads of states from 36 countries who settled their compromises and differences and their successful meeting was concluded with the birth of the "Organization of African Unity" (OAU).

When I researched and learned about this rich information about Africa some years ago, I realized as I do today that as long as we have children, youth and adults of all races attending private and public schools with students representing 98 percent of their ethnic heritage, then the real truth of African past and present problems for political, social and economic independence and upward mobility strides will never be understood by the masses. Then education will continue to be the newspapers, magazines, documentaries and films highlighting the sensational events that will charactize the weaknesses of a people and never will they be reeducated on the other side of the coin or the true facts and now residual effects of African Nationalism and Independence.

I believe that young college and older students should be taught about the revolutionary groups that were formed and were most instrumental in the ultimate goal of freedom and independence through self rule. I tell my college students that using the simple to complex method, just realize the struggles of Portugual's Colonies for independence when they finally received their independence in 1975 after some 500 years of Portugese rule and influence.

These revolutionary groups represent some of them that were needed for a mental awakening to their colonial rulers at that time who did not want to release their economic and political prizes of Africa: Guinea Bessau, Portuguese West African nation's African Party for Independence (Guinea and Cape Verde), the PAIGC. In Angola, there were the Popular Movement for Liberation, a political party founded in 1956 and began their guerilla offensive in 1961. There were the Union of Angolian Populations, known as GRAE, Revolutionary Government Angela and the Union of Total Independence of Angola (UNITA). In Mozambique the Mozambique Liberation Party.

African-Americans played a significant role in assisting their brothers and sisters in Africa to move toward their eventual freedom after World War II. When the late President Franklin Roosevelt and the late Prime Minister Churchill of Great Britain agreed to the signing of the "Atlanta Charter in August 1941 (later agreed to by the United Nations, 1942) there was a point three. Point three stated, the right of all peoples to choose the form of government under which they will live should be allowed. Some historians believed Roosevelt interpreted this point to include Africans, however, Churchill did not. Many Afro-Americans saw point three of the charter as an avenue for Africans to work toward eventual independence from their colonial rulers. There was a "Phelps-Stokes Fund Committee on Africa, the War and Peace Aims, 1941-1942. The committee was responsible for making many African Americans aware and supportive of assiting Africans to improve their situations. Afro-Americans who were member of the committee included Dr. Ralph J. Bunche, former Undersecretary of United Nations and recipient of the Nobel Peace Prize; Dr. Charles S. Johnson, former President of Fisk University and noted sociologist, and Dr. Channing Tobias, senior YMCA executive.

Significant Highlights of African Independence

Between 1957 and 1975 there were 51 new Independent Africa nations. In May 1963, representives of 32 new African states met in Addis Ababa, Ethiopia to establish the Organization of African Unity (OAU). In 1964, Tanganyika, a former German East Africa protectorate and Zanzibar which was under British rule united in 1964 to form the country of Tanzania.

After World War I, the Cameroons, former German colony was divided by the League of Nations' Mandate between the British and French. On January 1, 1960, the French Cameroons (eastern section) received its independence. In 1961, the northern section of the British Cameroons joined Nigeria and the southern section joined with the French Cameroons to form the Fedeal Republic of the Cameroons. Geographically the Cameroons are located on the West Cost of Africa. When the Portugese navigator Fernado Po observed many shell fish, the Portuguese name for shrimp, camaroes, he named the country Cameroons. The spelling varies in other languages, German Kamerun, French, Cameroun and English, Cameroon.

France was aggresive in allowing some of her colonial countries to be represented in government by their own representatives. Some of them were members of Frances, House of Deputies, Blaise Diagne, Gratien Candace, Diouf, Aime Cesaire, Leopold-Sedan Senghor, and Madame Eugenie Eboue. Felix Sylvestre Eboue of Guadeloupe served in the prestigious positions of governor, acting governor of Martinique and acting lieutenant-governor of the French Sudan.

The Sudanese people had some courageous leaders who were instrumental in organizing early nationalist movements in Sudan and resisted treaty negotiations that the British were proposing in 1946. These nationalist were members of the UMMA (Peoples) Party and the Sudan Independence Front. Ya Goub was a representative of the UMMA party in London and he was the editor of a paper that supported UMMA. The paper was the *Sudanese Daily, El Nil*. M.A. Mahgoub was the secretary and representative of the Sudan Independence Front in London. Brigadier General Abdula Bey Khalil of the Sudan Defense Force was the secretary general of the UMMA and he was one of the founders of the party in 1945. He studied engineering at Gordon College, Khartoum and also at a military school. Khalil joined the Egyptian Army in 1910. He served in the Gallipoli campaign and when the Egyptian army was evacuated from the Sudan in 1924, he transferred to the Sudan Defense Force.

The Second Pan-African Congress that met in Europe during the early 1920's had among its 110 delegates some distinguished Americans of color whose names I can recall from my childhool awareness and also in young adult years. Yes, I heard the names of Reverend W.H. Jernagin, Jessie Fauset, Bishop John Hurst, Richard R. Wright, Captain and Mrs. N.B. Marshall, Walter White, Roland Hayes, Ida Gibbs Hunt, Rayford Logan, and Ida Barr Young (wife of Colonel Charles Young). As a youngster, I had no idea that some of these people were really interested in addressing their racial problems in America along with their African brothers and sisters who were also experiencing similar treatment.

Many African Americans in 1997 have a wonderful awareness and appreciation of their African heritage. They have shown a great interest in cultural features such as hairstyle, dress, music, dance, poetry, literature, storytelling for youngsters, artifacts, art, sculpture and language. I applaud this long overdue awareness and the initiative of African Americans to recapture their past. However, as a historian who minored in African history and studied the geography, economics, political system and the life styles of some countries, I am concerned that more African Americans need to study some of these aspects about these countries and especially when we must rely entirely on the news media, interest and other means of communication today about Africa. I state these views so emphatically because my experience with students and communicating with people who tell me that they are very African oriented, in many cases they are not knowledge about Africa. This is why I am a supporter of African Americans, Hispanics, Asians, whites and others to learn more about the black presence in world history to include Africa from a more scholarly and educational perspective, especially when the knowledge is not included in most course curriculums in our multicultural society. I tell my students about these leaders because even though some of them are no longer with us, their contributions to African nationalism and independence must be a part of the long struggle by Africans world wide. Lest we forget these who paved the way, namely: Jomo Kenyatta, Kenya, Leopold Senghor, Senegal, Kwame Nkrumah, Ghana, Benjamin Azikiwe, Nigeria, Sekou Toure, French Guinea, Patrice Lumumba, (Leader for Independence in the Belgian congo, later murdered). Joseph Mobutu, Belgian Congo, Robert

Mugabe, Zimbabwe (formerly Rhodesia) Samora Machel (socialist leader, Mozambique, had confronted rebels leaders supported by the United States). Julius Nyerere, Tanzania, Kenneth Kaunda, Zambia and Nelson Mandela, South Africa.

When the serious Rwanda crisis occurred in 1995 and 1996, I gave brief lectures to my students about some historical realities about the country of Rwanda. I told them that the country has had a historical social structure that evolved one group being superior over a designated inferior group. The early royal clan of Hamitic pastororalists dominated the Bantu agriculturalists. A nuclear kingdom emerged where the Tutsi expansions started under the ruler of Ruganza Bwimbu in the 15th century. In the early 16th century areas of present day central Rwanda became part of the kingdom. A ruler Ruganzu Nadoli invaded the independent communities of the Hutu's and formed a unitary state. Later in the 19th century, a group of independent Tutsi states existed, the most stable and powerful was the Gisaka in the eastern part of the country was forced into the National boundaries of Rwanda. The conquest of many Tutu states in the north and east occurred around the 17th century and continued into the 19th century. The Tutu control over the northern region (former territories of Ruhengiri and Biumba) was completed in 1920, under Mwami Rwabugiri's rule. He also had incorporated the eastern region into his monarchy, Bugoyi, Bwishazo and Kingogo.

Some historians state that the earlier Rwanda kings consolidated their power to suppress authority of local hereditary Lords and replaced them with their loyal supporter who were Tutsi. The political system resembled Japanese and European feudalisms.

When the Germans arrived in Rwanda, they strengthened the authority of the Tutsi hierarchy to continue to dominate the indigenous Hutus of the north and to suppress their resistance. Under the Belgium rule, there was a policy to establish a uniform and viable system of indirect rule. The majority of the local Hutus were removed from office and their authority was transferred to the Tutsi chiefs. The story of Rwanda continues on and the historical past is present today in some ways.

The independence of most African sates has occurred within the past 43 years. There are some countries still trying to form a stable government and viable economy. Independence was not easy nor will there be the calm and peace in an independent society.

Past Colonial Method of Control, Indirect Rule

The colonial powers prior to independence needed a method to adequately control the masses of their colonial subjects. The British used native administrators to assist in their rule and as an assurance of maintaining law and order, administration of justice, collection of taxes, daily operation of branches of local government and the supply line for forced labor.

This ingenuous idea was proposed by an Englishman named Lord Frederick Lugard, who was Britain's representative in the Mandate Commission of the League of Nations. The method was called "indirect rule".

Lugard has suggested to British authorities that the government should venture into East West Africa because there would be economic gains. As early as 1890, Uganda and Northern Nigeria were introduced to Indirect Rule. The Muslim population had a feudal society.

In 1900, Lugard wearing a military colonel's uniform was dispatched by the British Foreign office to go into the Hinterlands and take control of selected areas for the British and also prevent the Germans and French from annexing northern parts of Nigeria. Colonel Lugard was successful in organizing a native army which he recruited from the indigenous Hausa who had no true love for their Fulani rulers from North Africa. Lugard used white officers and noncommissioned officers (NCO) to command the native army. He was able to conqueror the Mohammedan Sultanates of Kano and Sokoto, Nigeria. Lugard decided to use some Sultans and chiefs who had surrendered and gave them some responsible positions in order to respect their religious customs. The British believed that this method was necessary to implement in Nigeria for governing large territories populated by what they referred to as primitive people.

It is believed that Indirect Rule or native administration was first used when Northern Nigeria was opened up to British trade and commerce. later Lugard became Britain's first Governor General.

Lugard had established an indigenous bureaucracy, utilizing feudal and rival political systems. Some chiefs had obtained their authority directly from the people through the elders and counselors. The British changed this and the chiefs were no longer subject to their democratic control of their citizens. Because under Indirect rule a native chief received its power directly from the colonial government and his power was limited by the government. The chief were responsible to the central government and they could be dismissed by the government. The British would justify indirect rule by saying "it educates the African in self government."

Dates Countries Became Independent

The following African countries were formerly under European protectorates or the League of Nations Mandates in the 1960's and after these countries were given their independence by the great colonial and imperial powers, Great Britain, France, Portugal, and Belgium. In 1997, the newspapers, magazines, and television will discuss the numerous problems that some Africa nations are experiencing in their efforts to establish democratic governments, eliminating poverty, forced labor and dictatorial rule. There is no excuse to blame others, however, one must address the historical implications that can be endemic to some of the problems today in African countries. An examination of the year they received their independence should in a most logical sense tell people that they can not correct all the ills that have been created today and some in those yesteryears of colored rule, especially when some countries have been abandoned by their exploiters.

Country	Colonial Power	Date of Independence
1. Angola	Portugal	November 11, 1975

2.	Antigua and Barbuda	Britain	November 1, 1981
3.	Bahamas	Britain	July 10, 1973
4.	Barbados	Britain	November 30, 1966
5.	Belize	Britain	September 21, 1981
6.	Benin	France	August 1, 1960
7.	Botswana	Britain	September 30, 1966
8.	Brazil	Portugal	September 7, 1822
9.	Burkina Faso	France	August 5, 1960
10.	Burundi	Belgium	July 1, 1962
11.	Cameroon	France	January 1, 1960
12.	Cape Verde	Portugal	July 5, 1975
13.	Central African Republic	France	August 3, 1960
14.	Chad	France	August 11, 1960
15.	Congo	France	August 15, 1960
16.	Djibouti	France	June 27, 1977
17.	Dominica	Britain	November 3, 1978
18.	Dominican Republic	Haiti	February 24, 1844
19.	Equatorial Guinea	France	October 12, 1968
20.	Eritrea	Ethiopia	May 24, 1993
21.	Gabon	France	August 17, 1960
22.	Gambia	Britain	February 18, 1965
23.	Ghana	Britain	March 6, 1957
24.	Grenada	Britain	February 7, 1974
25.	Guinea	France	October 2, 1958
26.	Guinea Bissau	Portugal	September 24, 1973
27.	Guyana	Britain	May 26, 1966
28.	Haiti	France	January 1, 1804
29.	Ivory Coast	France	August 7, 1960
30.	Jamaica		August 6, 1962
31.	Kenya	Britain	December 12, 1963
32.	Lesotho	Britain	October 4, 1966
33.	Madagascar	France	June 26, 1960
35.	Malawi	Britain	June 6, 1964
36.	Maldives	Britain	June 4, 1964
37.	Mali	France	September 22, 1960

38.	Mauritania	France	November 28, 1960
39.	Mozambique	Portugal	June 25, 1975
40.	Nambia	South Africa	March 21, 1990
41.	Niger	Britain	October 1, 1960
42.	Rwanda	Belgium	July 1, 1962
43.	Saint Kitts and Nevis	Britain	September 19, 1983
44.	Saint Lucia	Britain	February 22, 1979
45.	Saint Vincent and Grenadines	Britain	October 27, 1979
46.	Saint Lucia	Britain	February 22, 1979
47.	Sao Tome and Principe	Portugal	July 12, 1975
48.	Senegal	France	April 4, 1960
49.	Seychelles	Britain	June 29, 1976
50.	Sierra Leone	Britain	April 27, 1961
51.	Somalia	Italy	June 26, 1960
52.	South Africa	Britain	May 31, 1910
53.	Sudan	Egypt & Britain	January 1, 1956
54.	Surinam	Netherlands	November 25, 1975
55.	Swaziland	Britain	September 6, 1966
56.	Tanzania	Britain	December 19, 1962
57.	Togo	France	April 1960
58.	Trinidad and Toga		August 31, 1962
59.	Uganda	Britain	October 9, 1962
60.	Zaire	Belgium	June 30, 1960
61.	Zambia	Britain	October 24, 1964
62.	Zimbabwe		August 18, 1980

Zaire and Belgium A Reflection, 1997

When I read the newspapers and magazines in 1997 about civil wars and unrest in some African nations who are still under dictatorial rule, I must reflect back to my knowledge of the country's pre independence posture. I also must consider the pros and cons of the current political situation. A recent newspaper article stated that the President of Zaire, Mobutu Sese Seko was returning home after a convalescent stay in Switzerland and France. The author of the article did highlight some of Mobutu's dictatorial career. The article said that in 1965, five years after

Independence from Belgium, Lt. General Desire Mobutu seized power from Moise Tshombe, former leader of the Katnaga province (Sheba) a rich mining area. I infer that Tshombe was possibly the Belgium government's choice for president after independence, and not the rebellious or activist freedom hero Patrice Lumumba. One can not support the non democratic rule of Mobutu and his continual efforts to remain in political power while his country was experiencing serious problems internal and also the border conflicts with Rwanda. However, Mobutu did initiate some actions in 1966 to unify the nation which had previously been called the Belgian Congo. President Mobutu ordered colonial place names changed. Leopoldville to Kinshasa, Stanleyville to Kisangani and individuals were required to use African names. I often raise the question in world history classes, where is Belgium today in offering some healing techniques to her former cherished colonial empire that she relinquished in 1960 with open wounds of disunity, strife, tribal conflicts, economic problems and high rates of illiteracy. Yes, I ask where is the master of the Congo, Belgium. In 1973, while visiting Brussels, I also was asking what has she actually provided in political advice, financial assistance to assure that Zaire could move forward toward a democratic nation. I presume her major interests was enjoying financially her status as host to the North Atlantic Treaty Organization (NATO) headquarters which is located in Brussels. Belgium had other economic interests now not that of a former colonial state where she enjoyed the fruit of its labor and the minerals of its mining region for many years.

THE VIETNAM WAR, 1959-1973

Black Americans played an important role in the Revolutionary War, the War of 1812, the Mexican War, the Civil War, the Indian Campaigns, in World Wars I and II, and in the Korean War. From 1962 onwards, a new black soldier has been emerging not a laborer or body servant, a part time soldiers, or a rare hero, but an ordinary soldier, fighting and working on equal terms with whites in the military service of his country. The black soldiers who fought on the battlefields of southeast Asia are a monument to the fallen black heroes of history, who fought under the handicaps of unequal conditions, and emerged sometimes as heroes, and sometimes

Black Presence

as slaves. The Vietnam War portrayed to the world that there was no longer a need for blacks to prove their combat capability as black Americans, only to prove their fitness as American men and women. The heroic exploits and sacrifices of life by some African Americans were recognized with the awarding of the Congressional medal of Honor to 18 enlisted men and noncommissioned officers and commissioned officer. Some of those brave and courageous men of color were: Private First Class (PFC) James C. Anderson, U.S. Marine Corps, Sergeant First Class (SFC) Anderson, U.S. Army, SFC Eugene Ashley Jr., U.S. Army, PFC Oscar P. Austin, U.S. Marine Corps, SFC William Maud Bryant, U.S. Army Sergeant (Sgt.) Rodney M. Davis, U.S. Marine Corps, PFC Robert H. Jenkins Jr., U.S. Marine Corps, Specialist Six Laurence Joel, U.S. Army, Specialist Five Dwight Hal Johnson, U.S. Army PFC Ralph H. Johnson, U.S. Marine Corps, PFC Garfield M. Langhorn, U.S. Army, Platoon Sergeant Matthew Leonard, U.S. Army, Sgt. Donald Russel Long, U.S. Army, PFC Milton L. Oliver III, U.S. Army, Captain Riley Leroy Pitts, U.S. Army Major General Charles Calvin Rogers, U.S. Army First Lieutenant Ruppert Leon Sargent, U.S. Army, Specialist Five Clarence E. Sasser, U.S. Army, Sgt. Clifford Chester Sims, U.S. Army and Lieutenant John E. Warren Jr., U.S. Army.

During the Vietnam War era the African American women performed in an outstanding manner in the roles of nurses and other significant positions. In August 1868, Annie L. Grimes of Arlington, Tennessee attained the rank of chief warrant officer. Gloria A.Smith, Rockville, Maryland was one of the first black women marine officers. Cynthia Jean Walker was a black WAC who was the army's first WAC certified alcoholism counselor. Colonel Clotilde Dent Bowen was the first woman of color to attain the rank of full colonel in the United States military. She was a member of the U.S. Army Medical Corps. Colonel Margaret E. Bailey of Selma, Alabama became the first black nurse in the United States Army Nurse Corps to attain the rank of lieutenant colonel and full colonel. Musician Third Class (Petty officer) Evangeline Geraldine Bailey of Portsmouth, Virginia became the U.S. Navy's first female vocalist and also its first black female musician. Se.was a member of the U.S. Navy band.

The Vietnam War era provided an opportunity for the promotion of some black air force and army colonels to general rank and the eventual assignment to selected positions of responsibility and military prestige. Some of these officers were: Henry W. Brooks Jr., promoted to brigadier general in 1972 after 24 years of military service, later major general. Roscoe E. Cartwright promoted to brigadier general in 1971. Oliver William Dilliard was promoted to brigadier general in 1972. Frederic Ellis Davison was promoted to brigadier general in 1970's and later to major general rank. Edward Greer was promoted to brigadier general in 1972 after the completion of more than 26 years of military service. Arthur James Gregg was promoted to brigadier general in 1972 after the completion of over twenty-six years of military service. Later he obtained the rank of lieutenant general. James F. Hamlet was promoted to the rank of brigadier general on 1971 after the completion of over twenty-seven years of military service. Later he was promoted to the rank of major general. Julius Wesley Becton Jr. after the completion of over twenty-six years of military service was promoted to brigadier general in 1972. Later he was promoted to lieutenant general rank.

It was during the Vietnam War era that America and the world witness the promotions of two qualified officers of color to four star general rank. They were the late General Daniel Chappie James, U.S. Air Force and General Roscoe Robinson Jr., U.S. Army.

While serving as the Director of the U.S. Army Race Relations School, Germany, I would say it loud and clear to the students that possibly the most integrated segment of the American society is the United States Military Services, although some were still trying to get the message integrate now and provide equal opportunities to all personnel, namely two services who have made some creditable progress in recent years, the United States Marine Corps and U.S. Navy, the army and air force were definitely the pace setters and accomplished their goals without outside debate, political intrusions and civilian concern about recent new vocabulary of political correct, race cards, affirmative action, quotas, race preference and color blind society. Yes, it was during the Vietnam era that some courageous Americans of all color decided to integrate a previous segregated institution without long debates and judicial mitigation and litigations on issues of affirmative action legality. Therefore, when I see today successful enlisted, noncommissioned, and officer personnel who classify themselves as minorities, I know by passing this way of life how they really obtained their prestigious positions today based on their qualification and performance without people establishing quotas, restrictions and segregated policies for upward mobility strides. They should know that those who came before them are actually in most instances forgotten in name and thought. But somehow with God's blessed assistance and guidance of my hand with pen I will continue to write to my America the Beautiful and the world about those heroines and heroes of yesteryear.

Additional detailed information about the black presence in the Vietnam War can be found in **Black Defenders of America 1775-1973.**

PERSIAN GULF WAR - DESERT SHIELD DESERT STORM

Many questions were posed during and after the Persian Gulf War about the real black presence in the war. In 1991, the mass media presented a small and less factual presentation of the black participation in the Persian Gulf War. Their cameras and typewriters and microphones did not portray, write, and announce the most glorious moments of African Americans present in the war. At the conclusion of the war, they where still reporting the black community's controversy were too many blacks were being represented in the military services in relation to their numerical ratio and proportion to a census population of 44 percent. Around this reporting the headlines were still showing the recurring crime and degrading things that were occurring in the black communities by some few blacks and not the majority. African Americans were asking these questions: How many black pilots actually flew sorties over Iraq, if any? Were blacks flying the Apache helicopters? Did any blacks receive recognition for combat bravery or medals, such as the prestigious silver star? Why did we learn about the black POW weeks later after the white young lady was reported as a POW? Why was the picture and reporting of a man who actually directed the final tactical operation of the Persian Gulf War omitted? When a National Parade was held and a well prepared pamphlet was sold, where was the picture of this man? Who was the Deputy Commanding General of Desert Shield Desert Storm, the late Lieutenant General Waller? Where was the positive reporting of the black national Guard and Reserve units and not some of their possible shortcomings? Many of these questions did remain unanswered and are still insignificant to the controlling magnates of the media industry. In view of these omissions, I believe that is necessary to state some answers to the questions above by including the following researched information about the actual black presence in a war outside of the United States and its outcomes have become known to the world, yes pages in world history.

There were some black people who were wounded and casualties during the war.

Army private First Class Anthony Dress, adopted son of Vivian Dress of Grand Forks, North Dakota was injured during the said attack on the Dhahran, Saudi Arabia American Barracks. Dress had been present in Saudi Arabia for only one month when injured in the thigh area. The 23 year old soldier even though injured tried to assist one of the seriously injured soldiers.

Sergeant Christopher Stephens, former 27 year old member of the 3rd Armored Division was killed on February 26, 1991, in the Persian Gulf area when the "Bradley Fighting" vehicle he commanded was hit by Iraqi fire." On March 9, 1991, burial services were held for him at the Great Jerusalem Baptist Church, Houston, Texas. He is the son of Emma Stephans Bell. Mrs. Bell had four sons serving in the Gulf war Desert Shield-Desert Storm. They are Edmund, Willard, Timothy and her deceased son, Christopher. Christopher was married to Jennie Paden Stephens and they are the parents of five children.

Private First Class (PFC) Ronda J. Marshall, member of the 115th Mobile Army Surgical Hospital was presented at the site of a warehouse building converted into a military barrack that was struck by an Iraqi scud missile in Dhahra, Saudi Arabia. Two other guard members were also present. They were Specialist Michael W. Wilson and Specialist Anthony M. Tiggs.

Black Presence 327

The three soldiers had been cross trained at Fort Lee, Virginia as water purification specialists. Upon their arrival in Saudi Arabia they were attached to the 14th Quartermaster Detachment, a water purification unit from Greensburg, Pennsylvania (Reserve Unit). Members of the 14th quartermaster Detachment suffered some losses and injuries during the missile scud attack: PFC Ronda Marshall assisted in the rescue of wounded people from the burning military barracks. Minutes after the scud attack she stated in an interview "I am not a hero or anything, I was just doing my job."

Army Specialist Jonathan Alston, 27 years old, a native of Chapel Hill, North Carolina received the Silver Star medal for heroism in combat. Alston along with his friend Private Stephen Schaefer, 21 years old, of Claymont, Delaware were pinned down by the sniper fire. Alston and Schaefer had "approached an Iraqi sniper in his bunker who started firing immediately. Alston threw a grenade in the bunker and when it exploded, stored ammunition in the bunker caused a very gigantic explosion." Alston then sprayed the area with gunfire and threw in another grenade and was able to secure the bunker area.

Major Carlton P. Hairston, a native of Omar, West Virginia was born July 9, 1951. He is the son of Frank and Eunice Hairston. His father worked for many years as a coal miner in West Virginia. Carlton Hairston enlisted in the Air Force in 1969. He received his basic training at Lackland Air Force Base, Texas. Hairston decided to take a test for eligibility to attend the U.S. Air Force Academy in Colorado. He passed the test and received the highest score of those prospective candidates from West Virginia and being number one on the list, he was appointed to the Air Force Academy by West Virginia's Senator Robert Byrd. Hairston was the first Afro-American to be appointed to the Air Force Academy from West Virginia and the first to graduate. He graduated from the Academy in 1974 with a B.S. degree in Electrical Engineering and was commissioned a lieutenant, regular Air Force. Hairston completed successful training courses in pilot training in aircrafts T-37 and T-38, July 1975. He also completed pilot training at the Advanced Pilot Training school in the aircraft, C141A in November 1975. Houston flew the C-144A aircraft during the period 1975-1980. He was assigned as an aircraft commander on the C141A and was responsible for aircraft and crew on worldwide missions for the military Airlift Command. Hairston resigned his regular Air Force commission as a captain in September 1980. He then became an airline flight engineer during the period September 1980 to June 1987. He was second officer on B727 aircraft with Eastern Airlines. Carlton Hairston became a civilian airline pilot in June 1987 and was first officer on B-727 and DC-9 aircraft with Eastern Airlines. Hairston was a National Guard pilot on the C-130 B aircraft from March 1982 - January 1985.

He became an Air Force Reserve pilot in January 1985 and flew the C-120A aircraft until May 1986. Hairston continued as an Air Force Reserve Pilot and began flying the C-141B Aircraft in 1986. He was selected for major U.S. Air Force Reserve in 1986. He flew the C-141B Aircraft in "Operation Just Cause," Panama. On August 24, 1990, the U.S. Air Force called Hairston who was flying as First Officer, United Parcel Service to active duty.

This outstanding graduate of the Air Force Academy, superb civilian aircraft pilot and an accomplished Air Force Reserve Aviator flew C-141B Aircraft in Operation Desert Shield-Desert Storm in Saudi Arabia. He was also flying missions from the United States to Saudi Arabia after the war had ceased. He was scheduled to return to civilian status by August 23, 1991. The outstanding accomplishments of Major Carlton P. Hairston as a civilian pilot and U.S. Air Force Reserve and active duty pilot definitely can be a role model for young people of all skin colors to emulate. This versatile aviator of color who served so proudly in the Persian Gulf War must also be applauded for the following achievements in his rich and laudable civilian and military careers. Hairston was cited in Who's Who in West Virginia, 1983; qualified for the U.S. Air Force Academy Dean's List, High School Top 10%, Graduate and member of the Intercollegiate Karate team.

During the Persian Gulf War, the casualties by race were: 303 white to include 10 females, 64 African Americans to include 3 females. "Lest We Forget", some blacks who were killed in action or died of their wounds. Private First Class (PFC) Marty R. Davis, U.S. Army 19 years old from Salina, Kansas.

Black Presence

Lance Corporal Troy L. Gregory U.S. Marine Corps, 21 years old from Richmond, Virginia

PFC Jerry L. King, U.S. Army, 20 years old from Winston-Salem. North Carolina

Specialist Anthony Madison, U.S. Army, 27 years old from Monessen, Pennsylvania

Private Adrienne L. Mitchell, U.S. Army, 20 years old from Moreno Valley, California

Lance Corporal Christian J. Porter, U.S. Marine Corps, 20 years old from Woodale, Illinois

PFC Timothy A. Shaw, U.S. Army, 21 years old from Suitland, Maryland

Staff Sergeant Christopher H. Stephens, U.S. Army, 27 years old from Houston, Texas

Private Robert D. Talley, U.S. Army, 18 years old from Newark, New Jersey

Private First Class Robert C. Wade, U.S. Marine Corps, 31 years old from Hackensack, New Jersey

Corporal Jonathan M. Williams, U.S. Army 23 years old from Portsmouth, Virginia

Specialist James E. Worthy, U.S. Army, 22 years old from Albany, Georgia

There was an army specialist who was awarded a medal for bravery.

The Military Miracle

The United States military services have utilized the services of African-Americans through the years and in most cases as enlisted and non-commissioned officer personnel. During its support and enforcing of the Plessy vs. Ferguson doctrine of so called equal but separate, the military services had no intention to confront the social issues of personal racism and institutional racism. The black officers did not emerge until the late 1870's as a recognized segment of the officer corps even though they were on a segregated status. The military academies were instructed to enforce their desired exclusion of black candidates. It was in 1949 that the U.S. Navy decided to change its perspective of blacks as messman and stewards and realize that they could read a compass.

The United States Army experimented with two of its black West Point graduates. The second graduate, Lieutenant John Alexander, and its third graduate, Colonel Charles Young, to command all black Cavalry units. The racism was resplendent in 1917 when the senior black officers on active regular army duty became a behind the scenes controversy among President Woodrow Wilson, Secretary of War Baker and Senate Sharpe Williams of Mississippi. An incident concerning a white lieutenant named Albert Dockery who refused to serve and take orders from a black officer would lead to the eventual forced retirement of Charles Young with stated reasons as an alleged medical problem of high blood pressure. Ironically, Albert Dockery lived to be 100 years old. But, unfortunately he did not live long enough to witness the "Military Miracle."

In 1915, an officer named Beverly Perea had one dying wish and that was to be buried with military honors in Arlington National Cemetery. He became the first known black to be buried in the National Cemetery will full honors. This only became possible after the intervention of Mayor Curley of Boston and the favorable response of Secretary of War Garrison.

During World War I, it was necessary for the racist military society to assign its black officers to all black units as long as they would be fighting along side the French soldiers. An unfortunate staff study agreed to and referred to for many years after its conception in 1920 that blacks should not fight in combat and the black units should be commanded by white officers only.

The year was 1941, only 56 years ago and the regular U.S. Army had on its active role 2 line officers and 3 chaplains, a total of 5 black officers. The Navy and Marine Corps did not even give it a thought. Later, the army chief of staff would say, "There is no such thing as black aviation or in simple terms, black pilots, forget it." Yes there, are known factual imperfections of our U.S. military services, but it reflects the parallels of our American society and its civilian leadership that dictated to the Armed Forces its desire to perpetuate segregation in its military services.

What is a miracle? It is a "wonderful event, an extraordinary event, extremely outstanding." The trials and tribulations and the denials and ostracism of many black officers over the years who paid their dues so greatly and were rewarded with pass overs, force outs, retirements, remained in current grade until retirement and knew a lieutenant colonel was the highest and a colonel's promotion would be a rarity. Those brave black defenders were not to be forgotten because in an indirect way they brought us thus far to the miracle of our military in 1991. It is beyond any doubt and in a logical, historical perspective that the greatest advancement in our times in the glorious image of our military establishment is their decision to become color blind in their selection of a Chairman of the Joint Chiefs of Staff. Their laudatory action will not eradicate the present institutional racism that is in our military today in a covert manner, and it will not repay those moments, hours, days, months, and years of black officers of yesteryears attention to duty with little recognition. However, in a positive way it tells the entire Global population that judge not a people by their wealth and sometimes unfortunate members of their race, but examine their achievers and heroes and heroines and not their criminals. In 1991, America witnessed a miracle when a momentous decision was made to select and appoint an Afro-American as Chairman of the Joint Chiefs of Staff, U.S. Military, General Colin Powell.

UNITED NATION'S PEACE MAKER, RALPH BUNCHE

I can recall settling in a classroom many years ago in Banneker Junior High school, Washington, D.C. and one of my classmates was Joan Bunche, I only knew that her father was a professor at Howard University. A few years ago, when I arrived at my prsent college position. I shared an office with a colleague who had a large picture of Ralph Bunche on the wall and at that time, I asked a question, how many people today really know who Ralph Bunche was and his many outstandings contributions to World peace, independence for African nations and his peace making efforts in the Israel - Arab conflict in the late 1940's. I then proceeded to answer the question myself, because, very few if any of the media would ever recall the efforts of Bunche in the United Nations peace making involvement in its early years. Therefore, I have accumulated these missing pages of some true facts about the life and times of Dr. Ralph Bunche, the first African American to be awarded the prestigious Nobel Peace Prize.

Dr. Ralph Bunche was born in Detroit, Michigan. His parents died when he was thirteen years old and he was raised by an affectionate maternal grandmother, Mrs. Lucy Taylor who provided Ralph with great wisdom. Bunche learned about prejudice and racism in his early years. When he graduated from high school in Los Angeles, California. The Honor Society of Jefferson High School refused to elect him to membership even though he was the class valedictorian. In later years, the West side Tennis Club in Forest Hills would apologize for barring him and his son. Ralph Bunche had a goal to pursue excellence in education and his projected endeavors. He was a Phi Beta Kappa scholar, and Rosenwald scholar when he went to Europe and East African on a social science research council fellowship. Dr. Bunche earned his Doctor of Philosophy degree in the discipline of government from Harvard.

While studying at the University of California at Los Angeles (UCLA), Ralph Bunche was a member of its championship basketball team for three years and its football team. He suffered an injury that caused him to stop playing the game and his years as a basketball star caused a damage to the vascular system in his legs which he would suffer from in later years.

While serving as a professor in government at Howard University, Bunche used his talents of research in American government and International Relations and was instrumental in establishing a department of government and politcal science at Howard University. He also authored some interesting papers. He wrote on the *"Disfranchisement of the Negro"* and a *Comparative Study of Togo*. Ralph Bunche made a significant contribution to the manuscript written by Mydral Gunnar in 1944. *An American Dilemma*, author Gunnar acknowledged Bunche in the book when he wrote "the Chapter on *Political Practices*. *Today the data on southern politics in the chapter are for the most part taken from Ralph Bunche's seven volume study "The Political Status of the Negro" an unpublished manuscript. His investigation carried on with the help of several field workers are rich in material on the south."*

Ralph Bunche worked briefly as an acting chief of the United States Department's Division of Dependent Areas Affairs. During World War II, Bunche worked for the Office of Strategic Services, in the areas of Africa and North Africa. In 1945, Bunche participated in the Dunbarton Oaks Conference and the United Nation San Francisco Conferences. He also assisted in devising the trusteeship provisions of the United Nation's Charter and later he was appointed the head of the United Nations Division of Trusteeship and Non Governing Territories. He was promoted to the Undersecretary of the United Nations for Special Political Affairs. He headed the UN's team responsible for the decolonization of all the colonial protectorates except Portugual, Rhodesia and the Republic of South Africa.

In 1948, the United Nation's Secretary, General Trygve Lie appointed Bunche as the chief assistant to Count Folks Bernadotte of Sweden who was selected to be the UN meditator in Palestine. A seventy year old man secretariat was present in Palestine. On September 17, 1948, Bernadotte was assassinated in Jerusalem by an Israel's assassin. Bunche was selected to serve as acting mediator. The UN had ordered an immediate cease fire between the Arabs and Israels forces.

Dr. Ralph Bunche invited the Israel and Arab representatives to meet in Rhodes in the Dodecanese Islands for negotiation. Bunche was required to establish dates, time, and hours of the cease fire and he informed the Egyptian and Israels governments to make arrangements for the Armistice meetings. It was necessary for him to meet with both sides separately and requested the cooperation from both governments. Dr. Bunche was responsible for submitting proposals that would be acceptable for Israel and Syria. At one time, there was a deadlock for awhile and talks were suspended. Later Syria and Israel accepted a proposal and resumed the Armistice discussion. An Armistic agreement between Israel and Syria was concluded on July 20, 1949. Dr. Bunche was most successful in his mission as a United Nations mediator and above all an American statesman of color. Bunche was recognized by President Harry S. Truman, Foreign Minister of Israel, Moshe Shertor, and Egypt's Seyed Din, for his diplomatic achievements in the Middle East.

In the 1950's, he assisted Lybia and other black African nations in gaining independence. Bunche was responsible for having the countries who were involved in the League of Nations Mandate System to have their mandate transferred to the United Nations and trust territories. South Africa refused.

Ralph Bunche was responsible for a peace keeping force in 1956 to mediate disputes when the British, French and Israels attempted an invasion of the Seuz Canal area and Egypt. President Eisenhower had suggested United Nations intervention. The matter escalated when the Egyptian President Nasser demanded the foreign withdrawal and then the Israel attacked Egypt and of course, there has been no firm peace in that area in recent years.

When we read and hear about the civil strifes in the Congo and Rwanda-Burundi areas or the popular named country of Zaire, I still challenge the competent news media experts to reeducate the people about how some of the problems of today do have a relationship to what occurred 37 years ago in the formal colonial protectorate of a country named Belgium. Ralph Bunche was diplomatically involved in the early independence matters in Zaire in 1960. Bunche was asked to visit the Congo and assist in having the Belgium government give the new government an opportunity to establish a democratic government and have their people return to Belgium. He also was interested in preventing any interferences by Russia and give the United States an opportunity to assist the new government. While he was in the Congo he was arrested and almost shot because some black congolese soldiers mistook him for an un-tanned Belgian. In 1963, the UN troops left the country of Zaire or the Congo. It is quite possible that Bunche and the UN actions prevented Russian interferences and averted a possible war between Russia and the United States in the Congo region. The Russians did not pay their share of the Congo expense. France disagreed with the UN's actions and believed they were interferring in the internal affairs of Belgium. The British believed that the UN went too far in the Belgium Congo's situation. France refused to pay her costs of the UN's role in the Congo.

UN General Secretary U Thant sent Ralph Bunche to Cyprus and he was chief of the peace keeping operation on the island with 6,000 UN troops. The operations was assisting in the mediation process between the Turks and the Greeks.

Dr. Ralph Bunche died on December 9, 1971. He believed that the battle for peace can best be waged with patience and persistance. Today, the United Nations has its first African General Secretary. However, we must be reminded that an African American, Ralph Bunche is an image model for those of all colors to emulate his diplomacy of peace making in the years to come.

WEST INDIES

Geographical Facts

The areas extending from Florida south to the northern coast of South America and eastward is called the West Indies. They began in the north nearest Florida with Cuba and the Bahamas Islands and end with Trinidad off the coast of South America. The countries of Cuba, Jamaica, Haiti, and San Domingo (not Dominican Republic) and Puerto Rico are called the Greater Artilles. The lesser Antilles include the small islands, divided into the windward and Leeward Islands. The entire archipelago extends from Florida and the Yucatan to Venezuela and thus forms by enclosure the body of water known as the Caribbean Sea. Columbus called the islands the West Indies. Because thought that he was still in the Eastern hemisphere and had discovered a western route to islands similar to those which were known as the East Indies. Some have called the islands articles because Columbus was supposed to have reached the land of Antilia.

The Spanish settled in Santo Domingo and established the first European Colony in America and first introduced the dehumanizing system of slavery. They first tried to reduce the Carib Indian to a slave. They were not successful after exterminating some one million Indians in 1492, 60,000, 107, and 14,000 in 1514. Later they would commence the importation of the Africans for their future slave labor. The other European countries such as Britain, France, Netherlands, Denmark would become interested in the potential economic wealth of the West Indies. The prelude years toward colonization were the 1600's. In 1625, the British settled in St. Christopher, St. Kitts, Barbados and Tobago. Antiqua and Montserrat were settled in 1635 and St. Croix and Nevis in 1628. The Peace of Utrecht, 1713 recognized Great Britain's possessions of the Bahamas, Jamaica, Caymans, Caicos and Turks Islands. A French company settled some workers in St. Christopher in 1625 where the English had established a small colony, but the Spanish arrived in 1630 and drove them out.

The French established colonies in St. Eustatius and Grenada in 1625, Dominica, 1632, Martinique, 1635, and Guadeloupe, St. Bartholomew, and St. Martin in 1648. The Peace of Utrecht also recognized France's possessions of the western half of Haiti, St. Lucia, St. Croix and a part of St. Martin's along with the Dutch as co partners. The Dutch occupied St. Eustatius, Saba Aruba, Curacao and Bonaire. The Danish were in possession of St. Thomas, St. John and St. Croix. The Spanish were in possession of Cuba, Puerto Rico and the eastern half of Haiti or Hispaniola.

The Peace of Paris in 1763 was instrumental in the confirmation of Britain's new colored empire because Barbados, Antiqua, Barbuda, St. Kitts, Nevis, Anguilla, Montserrat, Virgin Islands, Jamaica and the Caymans were now under British control. All of these were acquired by settlement with the exception of Jamaica which had been taken from Spain and the Virgin Islands taken from the Dutch. In 1763, Dominica, St. Vincent, Tobago, Grenada and the Grenadines, were made part of Great Britain's Colonial Empire.

The Zambo

The genetic mixture of an African with an Indian was called in Latin America a "Zambo." The children of this union were classified as slaves. Spanish laws discouraged the cohabitation of Indians, blacks and mulattos. The Zambos were placed on a very low level of the Spanish social or "caste" system.

Early Fear of African Muslims

On May 11, 1526, Emperor Charles V issued an order that strong consideration be given when permitting the entrance of African slaves from Islamic communities such as the Wolofs into the colonies. The colonial masteres, feared the aggressive, literate and self-confident characteristics of those Africans who had been introduced to Islam. Some of the these Africans could read and write in Arabic.

Color Did Make a Difference in Colonial Spanish Colonies

The importation of African slaves into the Spanish colonies created a "color" problem when the African slave was altered genetically by exposure to his master and other ethnic peoples. During the seventeenth century, a classification was established to tell people who they were and were not from a visual physical and descriptive criteria void of actual biological reality and classification systen. A person's skin color, hair texture (wooly or straight), beard, thickness and thinness of lips, eye color, width of face, nose size, and body structure determined the classification. Another classification method was to classify according to skin color or (amount of melanin deposits or melanocytes in the skin tissues). Blacks were divided into several groups, one short hair, crisp, and crisp longer hair; and black, white, light, and dark mulattoes. Some slave owners would "brand" the blond hair and blue eye mulattoes on the forehead to prevent them from passing.

There was also a color problem with those persons who were genetically mixed with African, Indian, and European genes. They were referred to as Afro and Indo mestizos. This racial or ethnic group had increased greatly by the eighteenth century and many of them would cross racial lines back and forth for social survival within their communities. This situation caused Mexico to pass an ordinance that stated, "Those persons who are not Indians, nor chocolate colored (achocolatados) are called and considered Spaniards. The church parish records normally would have the category or classification written when the births were recorded. Sometimes there would appear "erasures" in the birth records.

Ironically, in the twentieth century as late as 1978, this author was able to see erasures changing a person's race from "colored to white in church records in the Fauquier County Court House, Warrenton, Virginia.

EARLY AFRICAN PRESENCE IN MEXICO

During the early sixteenth century, Africans were brought to Mexico as slaves. Many Africans lost the identity of their respective tribal or group name. Their conquerors devised many methods to designate them in accordance with geographical areas of origination and deportation. Some of the social groups that entered Mexico at one time as African slaves were:

Mali region: Mande Fu descended from the Soso.

Sudan area: Banda, called Canene when they entered Mexico.

Guinea (Cape Verde region) entered Mexico and were called Cape-Verde-Guinea

Wolof, entered in the 16th century.

French Senegal area: Serer - (mixture of Sereres and Wolof), entered Mexico under the name Berbesi.

Sierre Leone region: Mende, entered Mexico and were called the Cumba and another group was the Zape.

In later years, the social groups were called Ganga Negroes. The African population in Mexico in the 1550's according to records of taxation lists, official registers, and military reports, stated there were approximately 25,000 blacks, mestizos, and mulattoes in Mexico."

The West Indies Obsession of Color

The term "West Indies" refers to countries and their peoples. These group of islands extend from Florida south to the northern coast of South America and eastward. They began in the north nearest Florida with Cuba and the Bahamas Islands and conclude with Trinidad-Tobago off the coast of South America, Cuba, Jamaica, Haiti Santo Domingo and Puerto Rico. These islands are called the Greater Antilles. Smaller islands are referred to as the Lesser Antilles. The British called their former possessions Honduras and Guiana, the British West Indies. Other British controlled islands in the seventeenth century were Antigua, Anguilla, Barbados, Barbuda, Caymans, Jamaica, Grenada, Grenadines, St. Vincent Dominica, Nevis, and St. Kitts.

The population of the West Indies during the period of slavery and the slave trade was subjected to labeling or being named and called according to biological genetic structure.

The former colonial powers in the West Indies created a distinction and class system among Africans and persons of known descent. The classifications were:

Mulattoes - person born of a white and black parent.

Quadroon - person born of a white parent and mulatto parent.

Musties - person born of a white parent and quadroon parent.

Mustifinos - person born of musties parents."

There were numerous instances where these hybrid, or offsprings of these mixtures would assimilate and pass into the white community and would be referred to as English.

West Indian Musicians and Composers

Ignatius Sancho was born in 1729 of slave parents aboard a slave ship off the coast of Guinea enroute to the Spanish West Indies. His father committed suicide rather than remain a slave and his mother died at an early age. Sancho at the age of two years was bounded to two sisters. Later, he was befriended by the Duke of Montague who gave him an education. He was baptized at Carthagena and given the surname Sancho after Don Quiote Sancho. When the Duke of Montague died, Sancho lived in the home of the Duke's widow, Duchess of Montague and served as her butler. At her death, he received an annuity. He was given some assistance by the Duke's son-in-law. Later Sancho married a lady from the West Indies and they were the parents of a son, William. In 1803, his son published some of his father's letters. Some of his distinguished words were the Theory of Music and he was acclaimed as a writer, composer of music and a man of letters. Sancho died on December 14, 1780 and was buried in Westminster, Broadway, England.

Jose Silvesre Lafitte White was born in Mantanzs Cuba on January 7, 1833 the son of an amateur musician. White studied music under a black musician and was assisted by his father. At the age of four years, he could play the violin, at eight years White could interpret music and he was a composer at 15 years. He composed a mass for the orchestra of the Catholic Church at Matanzas. He organized a band on March 21, 1855. When White was 19 years old he gave his first concert in Matawzar and accompanied at the piano the noted Gottschalk. He played the Grand Phantasy of Osborn and Beriot on the themes of William Tell also the piece of the Cardinal of Venice with its 16 variations.

He arrived in Paris, France in 1856 and after performing before 60 professors, he was admitted to the Paris Conservatory of Music. In July 1856, he won first prize in a competition with 39 opponents and was honored with the title of Director interim of the conservatory due to the absence of a Professor Alard. He returned to Cuba after 18 years because of his father's health. While in Cuba, he gave concerts in Havana and Matanzas. Jose White returned to France in 1864 after playing before the king and queen in Madrid. The king presented him the decoration of Chevalier of the Order of Isabella, the Catholic. White played before Count Newekerker and Rossini at the Hotel de Ville in Paris, France. His musical pieces were Mendelssohn Concerto and the Phantasy of Paganini and his own composition Bolero for violin and orchestra. He also gave a performance for Napoleon The Third and his Empress Eugenie at the Tuilleries. While teaching at the Paris Conservatory of Music. White was admitted as a member of the Societe de Concerte. His former music professor, Alard presented him with a gold ornamented violin bow. White visited the United States in 1876 and appeared with the Theodore Thomas orchestra in at Philharmonic concert. On March 26, 1876, Jose White appeared in a concert at the Boston Theatre and he was accompanied by a concertist named Levy.

White went to Caracas for a concert and was decorated by the President. He received the order of the Bust of Bolivar. Later he went to Brazil where he served as Director of the Conservatory of Brazil. It has been stated that he was the tutor of the Emperor's children. He was the recipient of Paganini's famous violin, the double swan presented to him by Don Pedro. An outstanding man of color demonstrated a hundred years ago that there is diversity in the taste of the musical abilities of peoples of African descent. In a simple sense they can also play, composed and present their compositions in a most outstanding way as Europeans have done also through the years. Jose White a Cuban of color died in Paris, France in 1920.

Claudio de Salas Brindis was born in Havana, Cuba in October, 1800. He studied under Maestro Calvo and won a prize while playing with the Professor Ulpiano's orchestra. He performed before the Cuban military aristocrats and was praised for his superb performances. He presented concerts for Marshal Bertrant, General Tacon who gave him the title, Maestro Composer and Director of Orchestra, and General O'Donnell who would later imprisoned him until he was released by an admirer, General Concha.

In 1844, the Cuban Aristocrats imprisoned many Cubans of color and the incident was called the Escalera. The Negro poet Placido was killed in 1844. After Claudio Brindis' release from prison, he never regained his health and when he died on December 12, 1872, he was blind and poor. However during his successful music career he produced the Operetta, *"Matrimonial Yoke"* and later it was printed in Havana and dedicated to his friend, Captain General Concha. Two of his sons followed in his footsteps as musicians. One of his sons, Claudio Jose Domingo Brindis was born in Havana, Cuba on August 4, 1852, the son of Claudio de Salas Brindis and a wet nurse of color, who worked for the family of Count Don Jose Maria Chacon. He displayed a talent for music at a young age and was offered patronage by the Marquis of Somervelos. He studied under this father and at 10 years of age made his debut at the Havana Lyceum. He studied with Vandergutt and later was sent to Paris, France by his father and studied under the guidance of Charles Dancla, David Leipxick, Leonard and Sivoni de Salas. He won first prize while studying at the Paris Conservatory of Music. He was praised highly by the periodicals Le Siecle and L'Art musical.

He also studied at the Conservatory and Scala of Milan, Italy and in the Royal Teatro of Turnin, Italy and Florence, Italy and Prussia. He was praised for his performances in Berlin, St. Petersberg and London. His admirers called him the Negro Paganini, and king of the Octaves. de Sala visited North America in 1875 and organized the Conservatory of Haiti and assumed the title of Director of the Music Conservatory.

The outstanding talents and creative musical abilities of de Sala were so eloquently expressed in the European press reviews: *The "Courriere de*

Florence," Italy, says, "Chevalier Brindis de Sala is a young Negro, perfectly black, a son of Cuba of extraordinary talent, of a handsome and sympathetic appearance, it is said he speaks seven languages: he played last night, during the intermission of the Opera, two pieces on the violin. The young Negro was a revelation and filled with enthusiasm the audience. He is a violinist of admirable activity, his bowing is very quick and at the same time full of energy that carries the impression, the impetus characteristic of his race, he feels and feels with a passion that is shown in his eyes which have an electric expression." The "Gazette dei Teatro de Milan" says "Two nights ago in the Teatro of Manzoni during the intermission of the Opera the celebrated violin concertiest Chevalier Brindis de Sala delighted us with the magnificent sound of his instrument. Brindis de Sala is a sympathetic Negro of a vivid look and intelligence. As a concertist he merits the fame that precedes him, he pulls from the violin the sweetest sounds and passionate feelings, though, in the most difficult variations, he preserves a security, a good taste and purity of intonation most enviable." de Sala's brother, Jose de Rosario Sala was a noted violinist who lived in London, England.

Jose Mercedes Betancourt was born in Puerto Principle, Cuba. He was an violinist and a professor of music and director of an orchestra in the city of Santa Babel. In 1861, he published a book of his own composition under the name, Echoes of Tinima and he dedicated it to the Countess of San Antonio, wife of Governor Serraro who was then governor of the island. He died February 23, 1866.

Juan de Dios Alfonso was director of a Cuban orchestra and a composer. He died in Guanabacoa, June 1877.

Luis Jimenez was a pianist of talent who studied and graduated from a Germany conservatory of music.

Anita Otero lived in Humacao, Puerto Rico and was a talented musician of color. She was able to raise funds to enter the Paris Conservatory of Music. Otero became the first female of color from Puerto Rico to graduate from the Conservatory with honors.

Raimundo Valenzuela was a musician of color who was an educator in Havana, Cuba. He operated a music school and was choir director or master for some churches. He arranged sacred music for fifteen churches.

Some other West Indian musicians of note were Jose Maria Pacheco, Julian Rojas, Francisco Rendon and Evariste Quiros who was the Dean of the Maestro of Musica. Some of his clientele were white and black citizens. The musical abilities of African descent have been demonstrated throughout the world and definitely deserve a place of recognition in 1997 in the black presence in world history.

WORLD ARTISTS AND MUSICIANS OF COLOR

Contemporary literature in the 1990's will include the names of many talents in the music and arts areas, but sometimes we never hear of some greats of yesteryears. Ira Aldridge was a native of Baltimore, Maryland. He was an international actor who performed in Russia, Germany, England, Ireland, and Poland. He was regarded as an outstanding Shakespearian actor. He played roles in Othello, King Lear, Macbeth, Shylock, and Richard III. Aldridge died in Europe at the age of 59 years.

Samuel Coleridge Taylor was born in England in 1875, son of a black Sierra Leone physician and white mother. He studied piano, harmony, and composition at the Royal College of Music. He was a composer and teacher of the violin. He served as the conductor of the Royal Rochester Choral Society and also conductor of the Handel Society. When he first heard the Fisk University Jubilee singers, he became very interested in Negro spiritual music. He visited the United States and presented concerts in Philadelphia and Chicago. In 1905, Taylor published twenty-four Negro melodies transcribed for the piano. The themes were based on African West Indian and American Negro. A club was formed in Washington, D.C. in honor of Taylor and it was called "The Coleridge Taylor Society of Washington, D.C.

Black Presence

Through the years, I have read in some books and heard people talk about the genetic background of Beethoven. I have never believed the allegation of his being of African descent were true or had a sound basis of proof. However, I decided to include the following which I read some years ago in the one of my collectors items-book. In 1936, a distinguished pianist, lecturer and writer who had studied at the New England Conservatory of Music in Boston wrote a detailed and scholarly manuscript on the Negro musician. I was suprised to read the following quote: *"Coleridge Taylor, favorite authors, his biographies, Berwick Sayers speaking of the musicians' sympathetic appreciation of Browning, the English poet, says, without being aware of his history, he felt curious racial affinities with the former and held a theory that the expressed sympathy of the poet with the darker races was the outcome of actual blood relationship with them. Not only did the racial heritage of Browning intrigue Taylor, but the theory that Beethoven had colored blood in his veins interested him and he felt that the features and other physical characteristics of the great master confirmed the rumor."* Ms. Hare included a footnote that read an interesting description in a rare manuscript in the Royal Library of Berlin, *"short and massive, broad shoulders, short neck, large head, round nose, and dark brown complexion."* There is an uncommon portrait of the composer. The above account was quite interesting to me, because in 1973, I invited to speak to my class a German lady who was the curator of a small museum and a lecturer at the University of Munich at times. She stated very clearly to my class that Ludwig Van Beethoven was of African descent because one should see the picture of his grandfather. Author Cuney-Hare wrote, *"whatever blood Beethoven had, Samuel Coleridge Taylor was very fond of his genuis".*

A gifted poet of France in the mid 1800's was Auguste Lacaussade. He was honored by the French Academy and received the Prix Borden award. He was also honored and elected to membership in the legion d'honneur. He died in 1897.

Juan Latino (Juan de Sessa) was in Guinea around 1516. He came to Spain at the age of 12 years and later graduated from the University of Granada. He served as a professor of rhetoric, Latin and Greek. During the Spanish Renaissance, Latino wrote the *"Austridad"*, about Don Juan's victory over the Turk. (Juan was the son of Charles V of Spain). As a child, Latino had been a slave of a noble Cordoban family.

I have always been very fond of art and especially my most artistic sister, Ruth Greene Richardson. I have included in the following discussion some views about African art which people today are recognizing the creative works and abilities of the African artist through the centuries. An art critic, Roger E. Fry stated in his book, published in 1920 that, *"we have the habit of thinking that the power to create expressive plastic form* (plastic form is considered using the three dimensional interpretation of space as the basis) *is one of the greatest of human achievements and the names of great sculptors are handed down from generation to generation, so that it seems unfair to be forced to admit that certain nameless savages have possessed this power not only in a higher degree than we at this moment, but than we as a nation have ever possessed it. And yet, that is where I find myself. I have to admit that some of these things are great sculpture, greater than I think anything we produced ever in the Middle Ages. Certainly, things have the special qualities of sculpture in a higher degree. They have indeed complete plastic freedom, that is to say these African artists really can see form in their dimensions. Now this is rare sculpture."* Some art historians have said African art has influenced Pablo Piscasso, Matisse, Modigliani, Soutine, Elaine, Stern, Lembruch and Epstein. African art has a cultural significance, influential, exotic and has an aesthetic meaning.

The black presence in world history has been expressed centuries ago in the famous work of the Dutch masters. Black images were represented in architecture, decorations and religious themes. Flemish painters, Peter Paul Reubens used black figures, Albright Durer's portrait of a Moorish woman is called *"Katharina."* Rembrandt painted a work called the baptism of the *"Ethiopian Eunuch."* Jacob Jordaens' art piece is called *"Moses and Zippora".* Erasmus Quellinus painted the *Queen of Sheba* offering gold and precious stones to King Solomon. Some of the art works of Anthony Van Dyck depict scenes of stereotypes and the inferior status of blacks.

Black Presence

The European museums today have an enormous collection of African art and paintings that reflect the black presence in their countries at one time. Art is an expression of what the artists feels, creates and observes. I am sure that over the centuries, artists have observed the black presence at one time within their chosen scenario and surroundings to use their brushes of the trade.

George Polgren Bridgetower was the son of an Ethiopian Prince and German or Polish woman. John Frederick Bridgetower and his wife, Mary Ann were the parents of two sons who became talented musicians. George played the violin and his brother played the cello. George was born in Biala or Viala, Poland in 1799. Bridgetower's passport or travel permit described him as middle height, smooth brown face, dark brown hair, thick nose and a mulatto. George was a pupil of Haydn and Giorn or Jarnowic. He demonstrated his unusual talent at the age of 10 years. He once served as a musician for the prince of Wales or George IV. His first concert was in Paris on April 13, 1789. He once performed in London at the Drury Lane Theater where he played a solo between parts of Handel's Messiah. He published some compositions for the violin, mandolin, German flute and harps' chord. It has been stated that he was a friend of Ludwig Beethoven. On one occasion Bridgetower asked the assistance of Beethoven to prepare a concert. Beethoven had written a celebrated A Major Sonata, opera 47 for him. However, Beethoven decided to dedicate the composition to Rudolph Kreutzer of Paris. Some of Bridgetowers works were books of the Minuet for violin, and other notable manuscripts. Bridgetower died in London on February 29, 1860.

Chevalier de Saint Georges

He was born at Basse-Terre, Guadeloupe, December 25, 1745, the son of a Negro mother, Nanon and French father. His father was M. de Boulogne, a comptroller general. He was named after a famous ship, and his Christian name was given to him when his father took him to France. He received an education in France and studied lessons from Laboessierre, and Jean Marie Clair. His composition teacher was Mile la Chevaliered d'Eonde Beaumont of Carlton House, London, England. The Prince of Wales, George IV attended his concerts. During the winter of 1772-1773, St. George performed at the concert des Amateurs as a violin soloist in two original concertos written for violin with orchestral accompaniment. This performance acclaimed him as one of the first French composers of string quartet. St. George performed with the musician Jarnovitz. He served as a director of the concert des Amateurs. He was also interested in the theatre. He produced a comedy in three acts at the Comedie Italienne. He was a friend of the Duke of New Orleans and was given the title of lieutenant of the Hunt of Pinci. He wrote a composition *"The Anonymous Lover"*, and presented a two piece, The Girl Boy in 1787.

St. George served as one of the gendarmes of the royal guard and captain in the National guard in 1790. He gave concerts with Louise Fusil and Lamotte, a horn player at Lille, France and Belgium. He also published *La Chasse and Le March and de Marrons.*

St. George was trained in fencing at the age of 15 years and became quite proficient at 21 years. He was a master swordsman and excelled in horse back riding and skating. He was a very good swimmer and could swim the Siene River with one arm.

During the French Revolution, St. George went to Lille, France and became a captain and later promoted to colonel. He became the commander of the Black Legion, composed of West Indians who came to France to fight in the French revolution. He was also a recruiting officer.

Chevalier De Saint Georges was a brilliant French virtuosi, and composer who some of his works were present in the British museum and the Paris Conservatory. In 1912, a street was named in his honor in Basse-Terre, Guadeloupe. The life and times of St. George is another example of those missing pages of history about an outstanding musician of color who was present in historyin the 1700's. The research about this artist has revealed that there were black West Indians who did fight for the Frenchmen's liberty and equality. I believe that a person of St. George's notoriety can be a image model for young African Americans to emulate. He was a man who was able to become talented in another form of music, that is called classical. Black people have accomplished expert creativity in classical music over the years.

SOUTH AFRICA

An Early Zulu Musician

The year is 1996 and as we approach the new year, 1997, there will be many positive stories in magazines, newspapers and even cinema about South Africa today and its progress. While researching one of my books in 1990, I read several interesting articles written by writers of color prior to the 1940's. The authors were giving their views and observations about South Africa in the early years. One writer discussed a successful Zulu musician who was achieving some of his goals in 1937. Rubin Tholakele Caluza was born in Edendale, South Africa. He received his secondary education at Ohlange and Mariannhill. As a young man, he was able to learn basic principles of music from his grandfather who was the first conductor of the Edendale Mission Station Choir.

Aluza graduated from Hampton Institute (University) with a bachelor of music degree. While studying at Hampton, he organized a West African Quartet and they went on a tour of thirteen states. Their musical arrangements were African folk songs. Caluza studied in London after receiving a masters of music degree from Columbia University. He returned to South Africa and established music courses in many schools in his Zulu community. He was the first known African native to graduate as a Doctor of Music.

The South African Colored

An educator with creditable references and abilities wrote on South Africa's color obsession that was quite prevalent among the people of South Africa. He first discussed the historical background of the country in the 1500's and 1600's. Prince Henry the Navigator Diago Cao, Bartholomew Diaz and Vasco de Gama made their imprint on South Africa. When the East India Company and the Dutch East Indian Company arrived in South Africa, they met the Hottentots and Bushmen. The Dutch and English were pleased to converse with the Hottentots and eventually that first association would add some biological perspectives to the gradual disappearance of the original Hottentot people, who were genetically replaced by a visible mixed group who would become known as colored. Who were the coloreds of South Africa in 1937?

They were people living in the Cape Province. The 1936 Census included 767,984 colored. The Hottentots or colored were genetically mixed with the Dutch. The mixed colored were associated with the whites and spoke the Dutch or Afrikaan language. They had a social status legally above the Bantus. Some colored were able to purchase real estate in the white areas. The South African school system consisted of separate schools for whites, coloreds, Indians and Bantus. The Colored could vote whereas the Bantus in the Cape could vote only for special white persons to represent them in Parliament. The pay scale for colored was lower that the whites and the Bantu or natives the lowest.

The University of Cape Town admitted colored on equal terms with whites but not the Bantu, who attended Fort Hare Native College, a missionary college assisted by the government. The colored could ride in the same coaches with white. They could buy liquor but natives were required to have a fourth grade education before they could purchase liquor. The Natives could not compete in certain trades with whites or colored. They were required to carry passes after nine o'clock at night and information indicating their employment. The Natives were also required to pay poll tax. The colored did not have the above requirements imposed. There were separate churches for the colored and natives.

In the 1930's there were no enforced laws against intermarriage in the Cape Province. There were marriages between white and colored, white and Bantu, and colored and Bantu. There were certain terms used to describe colored who wanted to pass for white, there were called Negropeans. Some people would say privately that many prominent men, officials and clergymen were colored. In view of genetic diverse, there were many colored people with European or white relatives and possible with "royal genes."

It is interesting to learn that in 1937, the color obsession was very evident in South Africa and in 1997, the United States, confronts the problem in identifying people of different genetic structure with new terms such as biracial, and multiracial, because with increasing miscegenation among races in America, one can no longer say black or white, because the hybrid individuals are demanding to say who they really are genetically. The South Africans in the 1930's were experiencing a genetic diversity of among racial groups. These were mixtures between the Indians, Malays and Bantu and Colored, as sometimes a West Indian mixture or genetic strain. It has been stated that the founder of the Gow family in Capetown was a West Indian.

There was a great amount of illegitimacy among the colored, at one time 51 percent of the colored children were born illegitimate.

There were some distinctive colored who were able to obtain a higher education and prominent positions in their immediate community. A Dr. Abdurahaman was a member of the Capetown City Council for thirty years and also served as chairman of the Streets and Drainage Committee. His daughter, Mrs. Z. Gool also served on the city council. There were a few colored physicians.

The African Methodist Episcopal Church (AME) was instrumental in training some colored ministers. In 1997, South Africa is enjoying a long awaited independence. I was able to talk to a colored South African in 1973, who I thought was a black American at first. I was informed that they were a colored South African. I pose the question, how many Americans of all ethnic groups really know who the colored South Africans are and were yesterday. Yes, some nutritional reasoning or food for thought.

SOUTH PACIFIC ISLANDS

The Genetic Black Presence

I have used the term genetic black presence because I am sure that some historians anthropologists, scientists and laypersons will not in many instances acknowledge the black skin presence and other African physical features in some of these peoples especially when we classify people in America immediately by visible outside descriptions and not real genetic content of mixed genes especially in the hybrid, black, Negro or African Americans.

The following ethnic groups of people who inhabit these areas could very possible have strong contents of African genes that could vary from dominant and recessive, but somehow ignored by the Asian or straight black hair.

Micronesians	Melanesians	Polynesians
Marianas	New Guinea	New Zealand
Carolines	Bismarck Archipelago	Hawaii
Marshalls	Admiralty Islands	Somoa
Gilberts	Solomons	Tonga (small Islands)
Oceania	New Caledonia	
Palaus	Loyalties	
	New Hebrides	
	Fiju	

When the Portuguese and Dutch observed the Australian Aborigines, the Twi in 1769-7 they recorded in their journals that the physical description of the people were: "dark skinned wide nose, low brows, wavy hair and clearly distinct from African Negroes, primitive ancestors from Asia. None without the sophisticated knowledge of present day molecular biology. These early observers had already reached a conclusion that these people were in no way related to black Africans. Unfortunately, this early observation has been justified and evidence presented today to justify their thesis. I have often head the phrase a picture is worth a thousand words. Well, when I see pictures and read stories about some inhabitants of the Pacific areas, I pose the question. How can these pictures that portray people with distinct so called Negro or black descriptive features that are used by the United States to categorize or place people in a racial group and call them black, and culture view mainly posed on observation. However, these Islanders are classified as no way black or related to African peoples of black skin. I recently observed some pictures of black youngsters in a 1996 newspaper and a medical anthropologist was studying some children from Gorke New Guinea. The anthropologist was conducting research on the T-cells and possible relations to the leukemia virus. The physical descriptions of the children as I observed looking at the picture were wooly hair, Negroid nasal area and brown skin color. Now if those children were dressed in American clothes, latest styles and fashion, and they did not utter a word. In America, the beautiful they would be black. Negro or African American beyond a doubt.

In a 1995 newspaper article about Pope John Paul II's visit to Papua, New Guinea in the South Pacific, there were also pictures showing the people dancing in a welcome ceremony for the Pope. The people's physical description was definitely so called Negroid and dressed in American attire they would be mistaken for black people.

The realistic view is that over the years the cultural anthropologists and other have called the New Guinea populations as an ethnic composition of Negroid, micronesians, and polynesians. They clearly state that these peoples speak some 715 indigenous languages to include pidgin, English and Notu.

In September 1996 a popular magazine showed some New Guinea inhabitants along the coasts and the article was discussing how traffic jams were pushing more than one thousand aboriginal (first of its kind present in a region) farther into the interior. The article said their ancient rituals survive and the highland clan engages in mock battle practices for the real thing. Their weapons have been used since the domestication of plants and animals some 6,000 years ago. Their tribal wars were fought over pigs, land and women. The pictures clearly show peoples of district Negroid characteristics resplendent of physical descriptions used by America the Beautiful to call people African Americans, black or Negroes regardless of their genetic diversity.

A recent article that I read in a newspaper was about an aboriginal tribe that inhabit the Uluru National Park. The article said the people consider the caves of Ayers Rock which contain carvings and paintings to be sacred. The Uluru is a sacred site for the nomads. The cervices and caves in the rock can be regarded by the Aborigines like verses of a scripture. The people believe in a dreamtime as the beginning of all life, a time they feel is still with them The park was created in 1950. The people believe in a God Kuniya.

Previously the government deeded the land to the local aborigines and as agreed they leased it back as the Uluru National Park Ironically the picture in the magazine showed some people with visible physical descriptive Negroid features brown to dark skin and hair from curly straight to mild woolliness.

Nutritional Reasoning or Food For Thought

I decided to refer to my Webster's New Collegiate Dictionary for some definitions. The word Negro is defined as "a member of the black race distinguished from members of other races by usual inherited physical and physiological characteristics (inherited reception of genetic "qualities by transmission from parent to offspring, physiological - function and activities of life or living matter such as organs and tissues). Without regard to language or culture especially members of the black race belonging to the African branch." Negroid - a person of Negro descent. Negrito - "a group of Negroid peoples of small stature that live in Oceania the southeastern part of Asia." Papuan - "members of any of the Negroid native peoples of New Guinea and adjacent areas of Melanesia." Fijian - "a member of the Melanesian people of the Fiji Islands and their language is the Austronesian language, (language spoken from the Malay peninsula, Madagascar area. However, Easter Island and most all native languages of the Pacific Islands with the exception of the Australian, Papuan and Negrito languages).

"Australoid - "relating to an ethnic group including the Australian Aborigines and other peoples of southern Asia and Pacific islands sometimes including the Ainu (a member of an indigenous Caucasoid people of Japan)."

Filipino - "a native of the Philippine islands". There was no mention in the dictionary's definition of the Filipino's early ancestors. However, I decided to refer to an Almanac and World Atlas. The Almanac stated that the ethnic groups were "91.5 Christian Malay and the Philippines were anciently settled by various Malayan peoples in several waves of migration from Southeast Asia. The Spanish conquered the island in 1521." The World Atlas stated that most Filipinos are of Malay-Polynesian origin and there are some people of Pygmy (definition from Webster dictionary - "any of a small people of equatorial Africa ranging under five feet in height)," European and mixed descent".

Malay - "a member of a people of the Malay peninsula, eastern sumatra, parts of Borneo and some ancient islands". One historian wrote in a book many years ago that the Melanesians physical descriptive features were Negroid type, dark to black skin color, crisp curly hair flat nose and thick lips.

Now in consideration of the above discussion and realizing that people in 1996 could possibly care less what color or race were ancestral or aboriginal peoples were years ago and the fact is that they are who they are called today and in no way will identify with any genetic trace of black genes in their ancestral line, especially in the United States. I do not present any argument on this accepted reasoning, but just simple logic.

Therefore, where one considers the definitions of words discussed above and consider how they could actually define a person's ancestral heritage over thousand of years to Africa and peoples of black skin and wooly hair texture. Then the question could arise what is a black person out of Africa who has mixed genetically over many years with various populations and especially their conquers? One of course must understand that when their mixture was diminished through cellular groups of people living together and actual incest occurred within the groups the distinctive original dominant African genes could have become recessive and new mixture over the years dominant. But somehow as I often tell my college students, exposure to the sun did not sustain the amount of melanin in their bodies to portray to an observer black skin color. I also pose the question that if the controversial arguments on the origin of man and the many thesis using the complex route of reasoning. Why not consider the simple route and ask how has that black skin that possibly came out of Africa is still present today in many South Pacific populations. I also ask the question, why are those countries today researching the sickle cell gene and how did it arrive within their immediate environment?

A year ago, I learned some interesting facts from a female native of the Philippines who happens to be married to a retired army veteran of color and they are the parents of mixed children. She over heard me talking to someone about genetic diversity of people. She told me that when she attended school in the Philippines some years ago that they had to study about an ancestral tribal group of people who lived on the Philippine islands years ago possibly prior to the arrival of the Malays and Spanish conquers. She said those tribal ancestors were the first inhabitants of the area and that their descendants still live on the island and some can be seen visiting the main land of the Philippines. She described them as Negroid people, with dark skins somewhat flat nose, pygmy like people with wooly hair. This Filipino lady said they were called Negritos. Now I have never read any of this information about the Negritos in an American textbook or reference book. She was very sincere about the validity of her story. I did ask my Filipino barber about the Negritos and he did acknowledge that they had Negroid characteristics. I am in no way saying anything about black descent of the Filipino people in 1996. But I am presenting some food for thought about the early black presence on the Philippine Islands hundreds of years ago and the fact that some of the original Negritos descendants are present today and some authors have chosen to use the simple term pygmies as part of the ethnic composition of the Philippines today. I am sure that many of those original Negritos did not look at their conquer over the years namely Malays and Spanish and were never involved in the miscegenation process with invading strangers.

Therefore, when I write about the Black presence in the South Pacific Islands and the Philippines, the reader can use simple logic and realize why people do have a color obsession and consciousness in the World today. Recently, a popular American weekly magazine featured an article on an outstanding young professional, golfer of color. The article's author had to indicate its color awareness or obsession to state that the golf pro is "one eighth African American, one quarter white, one quarter Chinese and one-quarter Thai. (Remember some Almanac states that the Thai people are descendants of people who migrated from China after 1,000 A.D. and later came under the influences of people from the Indian civilization from adjacent states of Burma and the Khmer empire). Now if that professional golfer wants to declare his valid ancestral genetic blood line, what is the problem. The problem is quite similar, America still has a color problem. A few weeks ago, I attended the funeral of a graceful lady who physical description was white without any visible Negroid features. She lived 99 years and two months as a "colored person" and would tell you without any hesitation that she was black. Her ancestral lineage was Irish, African and Indian. She was probably the illegitimate grand daughter of General Robert E. Lee or some southern white gentleman. But she never desired to be a descendant of Robert E. Lee. Just as she desired to cherish her blackness, there are many people in America who represent the same genetic structure. But today they are characterized with so called political designed terms by the majority population as biracial, mixed race and multiracial. Also what about African Americans in general, where are the pure genes of African descent that would make them half African as the name African American denotes so clearly to those who accept it without any challenge.

I presume the statement by one of my instructors in history in 1971. "Who is a Negro, anybody who calls themselves a Negro and also one must consider some of the words of noted historian and author W.E.B. DuBois in 1928 when he wrote: *"names are only conventional signs for identifying things. Things are the reality that counts if a thing is despised either because of ignorance or because it is despicable, you will not alter nature by changing its name. If men despise Negroes, they will not despise them less if Negroes are called colored or Afro Americans. Moreover, you cannot change the name of a thing at will. Names are not merely matters of thought and reasons, they are growths and habits. As long as the majority of men mean black or brown folks when they say Negro, so long will Negro be the name of folks brown and black. And neither anger, nor wailing, nor tears will change the name until the name habit changes.*

But why seek to change the name? Negro is a fine word. Etymologically and phonetically is much better and more logical than "African or colored" or any of the various hyphenated circumlocutions of course it is not historically accurate. No name ever was historically accurate: neither English, French, German, white, Jew, Nordic nor Anglo Saxon." They were all at first nicknames, misnomers, accidents, grown eventually to conventional habits and achieving accuracy because, and simply because, wide and continued usage rendered them accurate. In this sense, Negro is quite as accurate, quite as old and quite as definite as any name of any great group of people.

Suppose now we could change the name. Suppose we arose tomorrow morning and lo, instead of being Negroes all the world called us "cheiropolide". Do you really think this would make a vast and momentous difference to you and to me? Would the Negro problem be suddenly and eternally settled? Would you be any less ashamed of being descended from a black man, or would your schoolmates feel any less superior to you? The inferiority is in you, not in any name. The name merely evokes what is already there.

Or on the other hand, suppose that we slip out of the whole thing by calling ourselves American. But in that case, what word shall we use when we want to talk about those descendants of dark slaves who are largely excluded still from full American citizenship and from complete social privilege with white folk?

Historically, of course, your dislike of the word Negro is easily explained: Negroes among your grandfathers meant black folks, colored people were mulattoes. The mulattoes hated and despised the blacks and were insulted if called Negroes. But we are not insulted not you and I. We are quite proud of our black ancestors as of our white. And perhaps a little prouder. What hurts us is the mere memory that any man of Negro descent was ever so cowardly as to despise any part of his own blood.

Your real work, my dear young man, does not lie with names. It is not a matter of changing them, losing them, or forgetting them. Names are nothing but little guide posts along the way. The way would be there and just as hard as just long if there was not guide posts, but quite as easily followed. Your real work as a Negro lies in two directions: First, to let the world know that there is much that is fine and genuine about the Negro race and secondly to see that there is nothing about that race that is worth contempt, you contempt, my contempt or the contempt of the wide, wide world."

W.E.B. DuBois wrote the above in a 1928 letter. I would like to know whether or not a popular minister and African American National leader read this letter or gave it some concern and thought when he probably on the spare of a moment suggested to the black and white community a new name for American blacks "African American." I ask this question in conclusion what will be the new name for the most distinct diverse genetic race of people anywhere, American blacks, in the 21st century? Yes, what is really in a name?

EMPLOYMENT OF BLACK CANNON FODDER

I can remember a former history professor stating in 1972 how over the years and throughout the world the black man has been used as a military asset to conquering armies. The distinguished professor and scholar would say it so distinctly, the soldiers were actually *"Black Cannon Fodder"*.

Blacks have served as soldiers since the early days of Islam, employed by the French in 1870's and used extensively by the Belgium government in the Congo to suppress the Arab slave trade and the eventual conquest of the Congo present day Zaire. History must remind people in 1997, that African soldiers from nine countries gave valuable military assistance to Belgium in the late 1890's in order that she would complete her desired conquest of the Congo Basin.

I ask the question where is Belgium today to present a reciprocal visit to quell the chaos and spoils of war in Zaire, Burundi and Rwanda?

Black Cannon Fodder

In the early days of Islam there was a practice to utilize Africans as soliders or "Black Cannon Fodder". The early presence of African soliders in Arab armies is another example of how people of color have been used to fight for their master's own gain and conquests.

Africans were used as soldiers by the Arabs to fight in combat, serve as security forces and bodyguards, and as a labor force. They were used by the Islamic or Muslim movements in the countries of India, Morocco, Egypt, Tunisa, and Bengal.

When King Leopold of Belgium sent Henry Stanley back to the Congo River basin to continue the Belgium conquest of the Congo, it was necessary to recruit a military force of Africans from nine countries. During the period 1883-1901, soldiers arrived from Accra, 591, Dahomey, 198, Egypt, 223, Ethiopia, 412, Lagos, 5,585, Somaliland, 2,315 and Zanzibar, 1,175.

The Congolese soldiers were part of the regular army and they were recruited from all areas of the country: Central Congo, 8,490, Kasai, 4,175, Kwango, 1,100, Lower Congo, 3,960, Stanley Falls, 5,175, Ubangi 2,880 and Ucle, 5,860. These regular soldiers were employed in 1890 against Mohammedan slave traders who continued the slave trade after an agreement by European and Americans to discontinue the raid. They had met in Brussels at the International Conference on Slavery.

On November 23, 1890, Sergeant Albert Frees from Monrovia, Liberia, led an expedition of soldiers to Chege and confronted Tippo Tip's son, Serfu's men upon crossing the Lomami river. Frees was successful in defeating Sefu and his troops. Sergeant Frees displayed unusual gallantry when an Arab army of 10,000 men crossed the Congo border on Lake Tanganyika in November 1893. Sefu was defeated and killed in the battle of Lulindi Maniema.

A native of Bangola displayed gallantry near the Stanley Falls station in a military action. His name was Bajoko. He was an intelligence agent for the state, and was nearly captured by the Arbas when he swam on the night of May 14, 1893 and carried essential information concerning the enemy. Later Bajoko was received by Kings Leopold and Albert in Belgium. Although the African soldiers were being used by the colonial power, Belgium too satisfied her personal gains, in many cases fought against their fellow countrymen. Those African soldiers did demonstrate that they had the abilities to fight under combat conditions and win victorious battles over the Arabs.

FRENCH EMPLOYMENT OF AFRICAN SOLDIERS

In the 1700's, soldiers of African descent were being used in battles of conquest and domination by the European countries. A distinguished French Marshal, Maurice de Saye, organized a regiment of volunteers composed of "Negroes, Turks, Tartars, Romanians. He also had one brigade composed of Negroes or blacks from the Congo, Arabia, Guinea, Senegal, and Santo Domingo. The troops of color were mounted on white horses and were under the immediate command of a Jean Hitton, a 'Sous brigadier', who stated that he was the son of an African King." These brigades fought in the war of the, Austrian Succession and other campaigns directed by Marshal de Saxe.

Blacks served in Dutch units as drummers, buglers and there was a Free Negro Corps of blacks and mulattoes in 1770. The Black Raiders assisted in an uprising in 1772. The Dutch East Indian army had black troops from Elmira. The Kumasi Ashante King provided recruits, the Donkos slaves captured in war. Blacks engaged in combat around 1844 and were present at the battle of Djagaraga on Bali in 1849 and some were decorated for bravery.

ROBERT AMBROSE THORNTON AND THE EINSTEIN YEARS

Robert A. Thornton was a master teacher, scholar and physicist and humanist. Thornton accomplished his goals with less resources, academic freedom and financial assistance than are available today. However, he was able to overcome many obstacles that could have denied him his outstanding achievements.

Thornton's sixty years of teaching experiences were endowed with unusual opportunities and exposures. He studied under seven Nobel Prize winners and had discussions with the renowned physicist, Albert Einstein at his Princeton Laboratory.

Who was Robert Ambrose Thornton?

When someone ask me who was Robert Ambrose Thornton? I will always say the following:

Robert Ambrose Thornton was a distinguished and great master teacher, physicist, humanist and scholar. He portrayed the true meaning of one performing his duties in a color blind and rainbow society. When he was asked to accept a teaching position at the University of Puerto Rico in 1944, he was ten years prior to the 1954 school decision "Brown versus The Board of Education" He was twenty years prior to his time when he was accepted for teaching positions in physics at the University of Chicago and Brandeis University in 1948 and 1953 respectively. He was twenty years prior to his time when offered a teaching position in physics at San Francisco State University in 1956. Robert Thornton was accepted by these institution because of his outstanding academic record and teaching qualifications. Thornton had obtained a very unique and rich teaching background prior to his acceptance of teaching positions at Brandeis, and the University of Chicago. Thornton served as a teacher, administrative assistant to the president of several universities, dean, department chairperson, associate professor, professor and emeritus professor.

Thornton taught at Kittrell College, North Carolina, Shaw University, North Carolina, Johnson C. Smith University, North Carolina, Talladega College, Talladega, Alabama, Dillard University, New Orleans, Louisiana, Fisk University, Nashville, Tennessee, Howard University, Washington, D.C., Praire View State University, Texas, and Tennessee State University, Nashville, Tennessee. The experiences at these nine predominantly black colleges/universities served as an early exposure and future background of his personal black awareness of the importance, significance and promising results of the Afro American institutions of higher learning. Although Thornton would spend a considerable number of years teaching in predominantly white institutions, he had served his early teaching years in the classrooms of black segregated institutions. He knew and was aware of the black students' problems and successes in predominantly black colleges and universities. Yes, Robert Thornton knew who he was, where he came from, but above all he knew that he was competent, qualified and could perform the duties of professor in physics and math, chairperson of a science department, administrative assistant to the university president, and dean of colleges/universities.

Who was Robert Ambrose Thornton? He was a scholar who was recognized because of his love for teaching and his personal and attentive approach toward assisting all students to learn and use their creative qualities. The academic and civic community recognized Thornton's laudatory achievements as a "Master Teacher". He was the recipient of two Rockefeller Fellow grants, served on the National Education Association's National Conference on Higher Education, appointed representative of the California State Colleges' Television Advisory Committee, recipient of the California State Colleges' Distinguished Teaching Award, and was honored by the San Francisco State University and the University of the District of Columbia with an honorary degree in science.

Robert Thornton was a philosopher who received many invitations to speak on various subjects relating to his philosophical and ideological beliefs. He performed these tasks quite admirably. Some of his major philosophical "topics were: The Task of Physics, The Role of the Democratic and Christian Ideals in Social Action, The Pursuit of Excellence and Commitment in the Educational Effort, Crises in Values, Science, Humanities and Human Values, The Exploration of Science and Morals, and The Value Crisis and the Inseparability of Black and White Education."

Thornton possessed an outstanding talent in music. He not only understood the physics of music, but he also understood how to perform as a successful bass baritone. He did not accept a musical career, but he never forgot his talent and love for voice. The Tennessean newspaper as early as August 24, 1928 reported about his well trained voice and also the voice of his colleague, R. Clyde Minor, a successful professor of Sociology, who later taught at Lincoln University of Missouri, Jefferson City, Missouri. The newspaper article read:

"Soloist show great talent in presentation of Oriental Cantata. Both of the male singers took part in the concert at Fisk University and it was a pleasure to hear them. R. Clyde Minor has a very agreeable tenor voice and his 'Ah Moon of my Delight' was much applauded. Robert Thornton has a powerful voice, very dramatic and well trained. 'Myself When Young', and 'As Then The Tulips' were admirably sung". Thornton would often sing one of his favorites "O God, Have Mercy St. Paul Mendelssohn". He was also a member of the Loring Club of San Francisco in the 1970's. Thornton participated in their annual concerts.

Robert Ambrose Thornton proved not only to himself and his colleagues but also to his students, friends and persons who would meet him later in life that he was a truly master teacher, scholar, humanist and physicist. His memorable moments with Albert Einstein also served as testimony to the facts that Robert Thornton talked, walked and thought with the scholars in the disciplines of physics and mathematics.

Robert Ambrose Thornton retired from the classrooms and also from our earthly presence on March 7, 1982, however his legacy of academic achievement and excellence will live on in the minds of those he helped to nourish academically and in the hearts he touched with his personable and humanistic love for all humanity. Yes, I can sincerely say that Robert Ambrose Thornton was indeed a master teacher, scholar, physicist and humanist.

Robert Thornton and The Einstein Years

A young college junior stood patiently and attentive as he attempted to hear the words of a world renowned scientist, and physicist. The speaker's address was delivered in the German language at the Belasco Theatre, Washington, D.C. in 1921. Even though he did not hear the full context of the distinguished speaker's lecture, Robert Thornton never forgot the exciting and impressive moments of seeing at the age of 24 years, Doctor Professor Albert Einstein. Whether it was fate or destiny, twenty-three years later, Thornton would write a personal letter to Einstein at his Princeton laboratory.

When Thornton had arrived at the University of Puerto Rico to establish a liberal arts curriculum in the engineering school at Mayaquez, he was interested in synthesizing a broad philosophic humanistic and human valued centered program within the school. Many of the students and faculty were skeptical of this possible approach. Therefore he believed that if he could obtain some support from a magnetic scientist and respected individual, that it would help him to present his philosophical, and humanistic program. Thornton realized that the circumstances that led him to write the letter were a combination of his imminent goals and also his intellectual, social, educational and economic factors.

A letter dated November 28, 1944 was written to Albert Einstein. The letter read:

"My work for the doctor's degree under the direction of Dr. Herbert Feigl of the University of Minnesota has just been completed. My chief work for the past fifteen years has been the teaching of various branches of college physics and mathematics in several continental colleges of the United States. Upon the recommendation of several professors of both the University of Chicago and the University of Minnesota, I was appointed visiting professor of physics at this branch of the University of Puerto Rico. There is a real attempt here to have a faculty of all races hence I come as the first American Negro to be placed on the faculty. I am to offer a course in modern physics next semester. Aside from the regular selected topics to be discussed, I plan to introduce as much of the philosophy of science as possible. Because of the lack of interest and knowledge of the wider implications of science in this part of the world, and because of my belief that a stimulated interest in certain philosophical aspects of science, particularly physics, I am trying to show the importance of present day trends in the philosophy of science. It is hoped by so doing that the prevalent practice of mere mechanical substitutions in formulas and the

consequent lack of perspective would be lessened. Then too, there is the hope that certain aspects of reflective thinking will be carried over into other areas.

I am wondering if you would be so kind as to write a short statement for me of your belief in having students develop an interest in the methodology and Philosophy of Science even within their undergraduate years. I have talked so much of your work in physics and also of your great active awareness in social areas that just a simple sentence or two on these matters would be a great inspiration for my students here. They are so isolated from many of the current lectures and contacts along these lines. Should this request prove to be inconvenient in any manner whatever please ignore the entire matter.

The master teacher would receive a reply to his letter from Einstein. The name Albert Einstein and his famous equation for the "Theory of Relativity" might be known to many persons. However, without assuming, in consideration of the young students, laypersons and individuals who have heard the name Einstein, but never gave it any indepth thought or consideration, the following brief biography of the humble and distinguished physicist who answered Thornton's letter is in order:

Albert Einstein was a physicist, educator and humanist. There are numerous books written on Einstein. Some are biographies, analyses of his works, and introductory books on Einstein's Physics. There are also some manuscripts written by Einstein. Who was Albert Einstein? Albert Einstein was the son of Herman and Pauline Koch Einstein, born March 14, 1879 in Ulm, Germany. Later his family moved to Munich, Germany, where his sister Maja was born in 1881. His first scientific curiosity was aroused when his father gave him a magnetic compass, At the age of twelve, he became interested in geometry. Einstein attended German Catholic schools in his early years. At the age of fifteen he became displeased with the strict discipline in the German schools and dropped out of school. This was in 1894. However, he entered the Polytechnic Institute of Zurich, Switzerland in 1896 and graduated in 1900. He had renounced his German citizenship in 1896, and in 1901 acquired Swiss citizenship. During this year, he completed his first scientific paper "Consequences of Capillary Phenomena".

Einstein served as a tutor in a private school in 1901. He received an appointment in the Patent Office in Bern Switzerland in 1902. The renowned scientist married a former student friend, Mileva Marie in 1902. They had two daughters and their marriage ended in divorce in 1919.

While working at the Patent Office, Einstein introduced his special "Theory of Relativity". After leaving the Patent Office in 1909, he made significant advances in his scientific professional career. He had received his doctor of philosophy degree from the University of Bern and was on the faculty of the University of Zurich and later a Professor of Physics in Prague in 1911.

In 1914, Einstein moved to Berlin, Germany as a professor in the Prussian Academy of Sciences and also Director of Physics. His General Theory of Relativity" was published in 1916. A paper on the "Cosmological Implication of General Relativity was published in 1917. Immediate fame came to Einstein in 1919 when a prediction of his theory was verified. In 1921, he was awarded the 1921 Nobel Prize in Physics for his research on the "Theory of the Photoelectric Effect."

Einstein visited the United States for the first time in 1921. Between the years of 1930-1932 he made three more visits. He lived in Belgium for several years after his return from the United States. In October of 1933 Einstein moved to America and accepted a faculty position at the New Institute for Advanced Study, Princeton, New Jersey. The noted physicist wrote the late President Franklin Delano Roosevelt and proposed plans for "atomic bomb research". Einstein served as chairman of the Emergency Committee of Atomic Scientists in 1946.

This outstanding scientist was offered the presidency of Israel in 1952. Albert Einstein remained at the Institute for Advanced Study, Princeton, New Jersey until his death, April 18, 1955.

The renewed, distinguished and outstanding physicist wrote Robert Thornton a hand written letter, dated December 7, 1944. The letter read:

"Dear Professor Thornton:

I fully agree with you about the significance and educational value of methodology as well as history and philosophy of science. So many people today-and even professional scientists-seem to me like somebody who has seen thousands of trees but has never seen a forest. A knowledge of the historic and philosophical background gives that kind of independence from prejudices of his generation from which most scientists are suffering. This independence created by philosophical insight is-in my opinion-the mark of distinction between a mere artisan or specialist and a real seeker after truth.

The Einstein Years

Thornton was surprised and very happy to receive the letter from Einstein with positive remarks of agreement. He posted a copy of the letter on a bulletin board and students and faculty were receptive to the comments by a distinguished scientist. The reciprocal communication between Thornton and Einstein was the beginning of a cordial and academic friendship that would last for ten years.

To show his appreciation and three years of friendship with Einstein, Thornton sent him a gift from Puerto Rico. Einstein wrote Thornton a letter in 1947, thanking him for the gift. The letter read:

"I was really moved by your kind gift and I hope that you find satisfaction in your work. With my best regards and thanks.

The gift was some hand-made handkerchiefs with his initials. Thornton wrote Einstein in 1949 to ask his opinion on a project. The project was "A Plan for the Improvement of the Teaching of the First Course In College Physics" The master teacher was an associate professor of physical sciences at the University of Chicago.

He addressed the letter to Einstein's secretary. Miss Helen Dukas. Thornton wrote:

"I am enclosing a paper which is part of the exhibit of the project which I mentioned. This is the material which I wish to have you give to Dr. Einstein.

The project is, "A Plan For the Improvement of the Teaching of the First Course in College Physics. " I feel that physics can be taught in such a way as to generate a wider cultural prospective. In order to do the teachers themselves must have this prospective, and enough competence in the relevant areas in order to teach for it. This means that the teacher himself must be a sort of generalists. "

It seems to many of us that the present mind-set against the necessity of explicit and scholarly interest in such pertinent areas as the history and methodology of science, and even the psychology of learning, can only be reduced by a joint effort *of those teachers who are interested in such matters. I know of many whom I have met through the American Association of Physics Teacher, the Seminar on Science Education, conducted by Mr. Conant at Harvard this past summer, and the Colloquium held at the University of Iowa, under the direction of Dr. G. W. Stewart who are now waiting for such an effort to be formulated.*

My project states that research must be done in three areas. First: the area of actual subject matter of physics with the following points in mind as the basis of the selection of the research. (a) Those parts of physics for which no explanatory basis, in terms of fundamental theory, has yet been achieved. An illustration of this type of research is found in the paper enclosed. My interest in this particular problem grew out of questions raised by students about the relation of Maxwell's field equations to the fundamental nature of matter. I have not answered these questions in the paper, but I do think that the paper points significantly to the desired answers. (b) The supreme values towards which the practicing scientist works is control and prediction. Communication with him about the cultural aspects of his endeavor has to start, at least, in terms of the values which he reveres. He must be shown that in order to talk about control and prediction, even in his subject matter area, he must know more than just the gadgetry of physics.

The two points above will have a practical effect upon the minds of the opponents who usually say that the rank and file of us who talk about methodology, history, and psychology know no physics. This is contended, not withstanding, the fact that eminent scientists like, Herman Weyl, Max Planck, Albert Einstein, James Frank, Philip Frank, Enrico Fermi, Neils Bohr, and many others have by their productions shown intense interest in the relevance of these scorned areas and their relations to their specific contributions. While the rank and file of physic teachers can not be held to the standards and achievements of these men, they should develop, to some degree, the more general prospective of these men.

Next: the logical framework of physics must be identified in order to point out those general conceptual devices which transfer from one physical situation to another. This research would include relevant historical considerations. (I am now preparing a critical analysis of the concept of operationalism in physics, this will be my exhibit of some of the types of analyses necessary. (This particular effort was suggested by questions raised in my class as to the nature and type of definitions used in science.)

Finally: small, laboratory and theoretical projects must be formulated as a basis for training the students for the application of their knowledge of physics in new situations. For example, physics as a prerequisite for entrance to medical schools presupposes its use in connection with certain biological phenomena. There must be some way to give to the student at least one or two experiments in a creative effort of dealing with biological and physical principles together. It is hoped that in this way he will catch the spirit of the "generalists." In this connection, I am getting the cooperation and advice from several authorities in three or four medical schools. They are helping me to prepare a small experiment of this type of laboratory exercises. The present laboratory exercises are sterile and require no imagination on the part of the students. We are suggesting the above types of exercises to replace, in part, the ones normally given.

I would go so far as to say that this would be an excellent example to the protagonist of the general education movement now current in the United States. I firmly believe that much of the confusion arises from the lack of genuine intellectual interest in all pertinent areas of knowledge such as methodology, history and psychology. I maintain that even though they claim intellectual interest, it does not manifest itself in a clear and communicable way to the consumers of this type of education. I include among the consumers, practicing scientists, not in general education, their children, and others who are subjected to this type of education. Specifically, I would like to have Dr. Einstein's reaction to the enclosed paper in its relation to what I have said in the letter.

After reading Thornton's letter and paper, Einstein wrote him a letter. Dr. Einstein told him:

"It seems to me that you have a reasonable idea in your mind, more cohesion and methodical understanding for the leading ideas and methods against a more or less incoherent bulk of facts. Not knowing the psychological attitude and mentality of the teachers, I doubt, however, that they will get from your pamphlet the essence of your intentions. I do not believe that your task can be achieved by any organized procedure where a number of people participate. The effective way would be, in my opinion, that one able person writes a good textbook. It is true, however, that success may depend from "political" factors for the judgement of which I lack the experience.

Thornton had the unique opportunity to visit Einstein seven times at his Princeton laboratory and home. However, he always cherished the memories of his first meeting with Einstein.

Upon his return to the mainland from Puerto Rico, Thornton visited Einstein at his home, 10 Mercer Street, Princeton, New Jersey. The first meeting was historical and an occasion that was memorable for Thornton in later years. Thornton said that when Einstein greeted him, he had anticipated to meet a pompous individual. However, Einstein quickly dispelled that notion, because in his characteristic sweater and "socks", he appeared very calm, down to earth and made one feel at ease. During his first visit, Thornton showed Einstein a mathematical formula he wanted to discuss. He was quickly writing the problem on the board and also trying to show Einstein how much mathematics he knew. Suddenly Einstein said:

"Professor Thornton, please go slowly, because I have had trouble with mathematics before. "

Thornton later stated that he believed those remarks were made by Einstein in order to let him know that he could make a mistake and that he should not be concerned about it, because Einstein also had made mistakes. Dr. Einstein was so ordinary that I had no feelings of inferiority when I was with him. I could exhibit my every weakness and he would help me declared Thornton. Einstein told Thornton that he was not a "Genius" as people called him. In his humble way, Einstein said: paid attention to what people were saying, worked hard on problems, criticized my own works, lived with ubiquity, if I did not succeed I would try again and get more ideas.

These qualities of Einstein impressed Thornton and gave him a motivated impulse for accomplishing his goals because the master teacher wrote:

"Einstein convinced me that intellectual excellence as a goal supported by books was something that no one could keep from having. In addition it would be a good weapon against tyranny and bestiality. "

During the seven private meetings with Einstein, Thornton was able to listen to and discuss some of Einstein's philosophies on science, education and excellence.

Thornton remarked that they discussed aspects of the theoretical foundations of several of the great theories of physics. They were classical mechanisms, electro-magnetic theory, quantum theory, and the elativity theory. Closely related to these discussions were items of philosophic and methodological character. That is, such items as simplicity the role of Operationalism, and the decline of mechanistic perception.

During such discussions the reasons for changes in or elimination of scientific theories were identified, said Thornton.

The master teacher declared that Einstein placed considerable stress on mental uneasiness about some already accepted scientific interpretations. In every case of our contacts written or oral, I would initiate the discussion by questions about the technicalities of a theory or the current interpretation, wrote Thornton!

Thornton said that he had been calling theories true or false. Einstein corrected that and told him that any theory is tentative. A theory can't be wrong, it is just like grammatical nonsense, the grammar itself is not wrong, the person makes it wrong.

Einstein and Thornton shared a mutual agreement on the belief that in order to achieve education, the pursuit of excellence and a commitment of responsibility to society, one must accomplish five things, they are:

1. *Give a person the proficiency and competencies which will enable one to make a living.*

2. *Set high standards of excellence*

3. *Share your knowledge*

4. *Be dedicated to the habit of truth*

5. *Experience the compassion of love.*

Thornton often told his audiences during a lecture that Einstein was total exemplification of these five values. Einstein also believed that one could not understand physics without knowing other things, such as philosophy, music, history and anything that would contribute to the fluency of ideas or would increase the volume of metaphoric usage (ability to make an analogy). These views were in agreement with Thornton's thesis on the "Transfer Analyses of Learning."

The master teacher wanted to complete some post graduate studies at the Institute For Advanced Study, Dublin, Eire Ireland in 1953. Thornton was to study "How To Relate the Quantum Theory and Einstein's Theory to Daily Affairs". Dr. Einstein wanted to provide the money for Thornton. However, Thornton had made arrangements to obtain the money from other sources. Einstein wrote a recommendation for Thornton to Professor Dr. Erwin Schrodinger of the Institute for Advanced Study in Dublin, Eire Ireland. Dr. Schrodinger was a distinguished Austrian physicist who along with Paul A.M. Dirac of England received the 1933 Nobel Prize in Physics for the "discovery of new fertile forms of the Atomic Theory." Thornton had expressed during a personal interview that "the greatest compliment I ever have had in my life was when Einstein wrote to Schrodinger."

The original letter to Schrodinger was written in German and a copy was given to Thornton. The original letter written in German and signed by Einstein read:

"Lieber Schrodinger.-
Ich hatte wiederholt Gelegenheit, mit Dr. Robert A. Thornton mich uber prinzipiel lefragen zu unterhalten. Einer einung nach hat er sinn fur das Wesentliche und sine allege meine Einstellung, die der unsrigen nahesteht. kh begreife und billige daher seinen Wunsch, an Eurem Institut ein Jahr tang zu arbeiten und wurde mich freuen, wenn sich dies realisieren liesse.

Mit herzlichen Grussen
Dein

A. Eitrstein´ "Albert Einstein

Several English translations of the letter that were obtained by Thornton read:

"Dear Schrodinger.-

I have repeatedly had occasion to discuss questions of principle with Dr. Robert A. Thornton. In my opinion, he has a sense of understanding and a general conceptual disposition that is very close to ours. I, therefore, comprehend and approve his wish to work at your institute for a one year term. I would be glad if his wish could be realized.
   With cordial greetings
         Yours

(Signed A. Einstein)
Albert Einstein

The letter was dated September 9, 1952. Unfortunately Thornton's wish was not fulfilled because Professor Dr. Erwin Schrodinger died before he could leave for Ireland. This personal and concerned interest that Einstein had for the master teacher was a very strong impetus in the future accomplishments demonstrated by Thornton in the remaining years of his teaching and administrative duties. He knew and was proud that he could tell the world without an air of egotism, that he, talked and walked with the *"Master Physicist", Albert Einstein. The letter* written by Einstein to Schrodinger in 1952, just three years prior to his death, contributed to the veracity and eliminates any dubiety as to how Einstein thought about the master teacher. This letter also illustrates the sincere and humanistic concern of one minority who had experienced the negatives of racism for another minority who also experienced the same. The mutual sharing of their intellectual thoughts and individual personalities was a true revelation of what the term "color blind" is about. This recommendation by Einstein refuted without any doubt the early statement by an Ohio State University Mathematics Professor to Thornton, that ... Negroes do not understand mathematics and physics." This letter and the personal photograph signed by Einstein and presented to Thornton were two memorabilia that were always prize possessions of the Master Teacher.

Thornton recalled a visit to Einstein's house in Princeton where he observed only one honor hanging on the wall, He learned that Einstein kept all of his diplomas, citations and awards in a box. Einstein explained to Thornton about the only honor displayed. He told Thornton that he had received a letter from the Zurick Institute in Switzerland inviting him to Zurick to receive an honorary degree. Einstein did not answer the letter. (Thornton stated that Einstein was known to answer every letter received). Einstein said that when his relativity theories were made public, the Zurick Institute "laughed at him" and did not believe him. He also had failed an entrance examination for acceptance at the institute. However, when the theory was accepted as valid, he received an invitation to accept an honorary degree. When he continued to ignore the invitation, the Zurick Institute sent his friend to convince him that he should accept the invitation and travel to Switzerland. He finally decided to go to Zurick, and he appeared in a straw hat and ordinary street clothes. Through some persuasion, he donned the ceremonial robe. Einstein had his personal thoughts about assuming administrative positions. When Thornton told him that he had been a "Dean" Einstein replied, "What a pity!" As an administrator, you must take your work home. To be a good scholar, you do not take your work home' Thornton explained that Einstein who worked at the Patent Office, used his time after work to study physics and accomplish his research.

Thornton commented on a discussion with Einstein about race. His views toward Blacks were humility and belief in the quality of excellence for upward mobility. I told him about some of the hardships I had suffered as a Negro and his responses were always directed toward making me feel that in some sense these hardships were stimuli for doing creative things said Thornton. The master teacher believed that his being Black and Einstein Jewish helped their relationship tremendously.

While discussing a physic problem during their meeting, Einstein misunderstood a phrase that Thornton used and the response by Einstein was quite humorously. Thornton often enjoyed telling this humorous story:

"During a visit to Einstein's laboratory, I told him that I had been working on a 'black body' problem in Physics. When referring to the 'black body' and its emission of wave lengths in a spectrum. Scientists describe the numbers and their relationship in three different basic ways: tables, graphs and equations. You have two numbers associated therefore you can represent them in three different ways.

One way is to just draw a graph and use two sides. If one of the values is called X, and one is Y, what is the equation that relates to the two. This was the problem I had. (reference the equation).

When I arrived at the laboratory I stated to Einstein that I was having trouble with my black body problem. Einstein evidently misunderstood me and replied: I certainly have sympathy for all of your people on this problem. We had quite a laugh about this misunderstanding."

While serving as a Visiting Professor at the University of the District of Columbia in 1981, Thornton was initiating plans and developing a proposal to complete an indepth study of Albert Einstein's views on education and especially in terms of its functions, aims, human qualities and its obligations to society and the individual. Thornton believed Einstein's views on education were little known, and had been overshadowed by his great achievements as a scientist. A major goal of the proposal was to develop means for disseminating his study and encourage others to carry on further explorations into Einstein's thoughts and to investigate the possibilities of appropriate implementations.

Thornton envisioned that there was sufficient material available on the views of Einstein about education not only for extended study but also enough to initiate a whole new series of investigations about his contributions over and beyond the technicalities of the scientific revolutions of the 20th century.

The study would also show that, in Einstein's view all good education is an endeavor to show the essential unity of man's search for the truth in the very variety of its method and contents. Such a broad view of education does not contradict the importance of specialization. Specialization is a supplement to the broad view, reference to a broader context gives special training a greater meaning and interest. Only through specialization and application is the common heritage of culture and knowledge vitalized and extended, wrote Thornton.

Thornton had written some personal recollections and thoughts about Einstein in his proposed project "Einstein-Education-Human Values". He wrote:

"In my repeated conversations with Professor Einstein the issues of education were often discussed. He, at all times, emphasized the importance of the role of education in understanding and realizing the conditions for a healthy and productive society. He would point out the importance of work, reason, excellence and the great sentiment of love with its qualities of sharing and compassion. He firmly believed that a human education is one which helps its receivers use their superior training as a stimulus for courageous and creative thinking and doing. This use often having to be done even at the expense of suffering unpopularity.

Throughout my entire contact with him, in letters and conversations, there was always present his great dedication to the development of man's humanistic qualities. He viewed conceptual understanding as central to the whole problem of humanistic education. Einstein considered any study humanistic if it went beyond the mechanistic and utilitarian aspects of the subject. Going beyond, to him, meant placing due emphasis on the human content, the philosophical ingredient, and the historical setting, He would in no way endorse fragmentation, narrow specialization or provincialism. If treated in this manner, he said, all studies are of humanistic value. Einstein insisted that the natural sciences and particularly physics were legitimate members of the liberal arts spectrum if understood in terms of their conceptual, philosophical and historical content.

At present, when many are beginning to see that a return to liberal arts is essential, it would indeed be significant to have the dominant scientist of the 20th century add his voice in its favor. In Einstein's life and works we find a new conception of humanistic- education, one which is highly relevant to the world of modern technology and industrial society.

Professor Einstein views are remarkably similar to earlier advocates of a liberal education. One is reminded of the ideas of such men as Erasmus of Rotterdam, Montaigne, and Wilhelm von Humbolt. They held that the best medium for the formation of a harmonious rich and imaginative personality was the liberal arts, but this tradition was always to be interwoven with the concrete interests of the professions. Einstein insisted that there be no false dichotomies between professional and humanistic educations. He wanted to avoid esoteric aloofness.

In my conversations with Einstein he seemed anxious to make it very clear that he was speaking not as a recognized creative man of science but rather as a well-informed citizen who had experience in the educational world.

The master teacher declared that the public image of Einstein is centered around his scientific contributions.

Thornton's personal feelings were that for too long people have been preoccupied with the technicalities of Einstein's contributions to sciences

Thornton earnestly pointed out that Einstein must be seen in the broadened context of his immense humanity. He further stated that his proposed project would give a full well documented description of Professor Einstein's views and concerns about education and human values. "The unity and cohesion in the findings would be assured by adhering to his views about education's function, aims, and humanistic qualities, and its obligations to society and the individual, said Thornton.

The demise of Thornton in March, 1982, precluded the master teacher from completing the project on "Einstein-Education-Human Values". However, it is fortunate that he was able to write some of his proposed outlines and thoughts about the project. In 1981, the "master teacher" was suggesting a study that would be beneficial today, in 1988, in assisting many educators and researchers in understanding that many problems in our schools today are incidental to the absence and recognition of humanistic values in education. There is a serious need today to prepare the student to be versatile in his interdiscipline curriculum and be academically prepared to confront his future years of increasing advances in science and technology. The years of experience and study by a great American scientist and educator, Albert Einstein could cause a very significant input to the many themes, and theories in the hundreds of proposals and studies being tested in classrooms today to correct current problems and deficiencies.

The ideas and philosophies of Einstein and Thornton on Transfer Analysis and Humanistic Education could contribute to solving some of the classroom problems of learning and comprehension.

The seven meetings with Einstein presented some opportunities for Thornton to observe his character and humanistic finess. Thornton described Einstein as

"a thorough going humanist, a very compassionate person who taught me more than mathematical techniques. He always appeared relaxed and listened intently to what I said. He always portrayed a great sense of dignity. Einstein's hearing and conversation were never trivial and it was always serene. I had heard the stories about Einstein appearing a little absent minded but I had no way of knowing that, because he remembered everything I ever told him. He was an older man when I knew him. However, I did not come with the expectation that the older you get, the less creative you become. I think the shift of creativity in him was toward broader generalizations.

Einstein was not particularly interested in minutiae. When you are young, that is when you are more apt to be measuring the diameter of an atom. He was philosophical and my beam was on his. We discussed the nature of simplicity and what the ingredients are that make up a theory. During our discussions, Einstein would always say 'Do you have anything else to ask Professor?' I maintained contact with him until 1953, two years prior to his death. I wish I had spent more time with him. I could have but I did not.

Thornton remembered Einstein by many things: his outstanding accomplishments in physics, the first letter he received from him, other letters, a personal autographed picture of Einstein, and the inspiring and informative meetings he had with him. However, the master eacher would often read a quotation from Einstein, because these following words not only depict the intimate character of a genius of physics but also a genius in understanding his fellow man. The following words would always be a definitive memory for Thornton of Albert Einstein, the man who did exert himself to answer Thornton's letter, and the man who tried to give in some measure his assistance as he believed that he would receive in turn from others:

We exist for our fellow man, In the first place those upon whose smiles and welfare all our happiness depends, and next for all those unknown to us personally but to whose destiny we are bound by the tie of sympathy. A hundred times every day I remind myself that my inner and outer life depend on the labor of other men, living and dead, and that I must exert myself in order to give in the same measure as I have received and am still receiving.

A. Einstein

Further reading see *Robert A. Thornton, Master Teacher Scholar, Physicist, Humanist*

The Einstein Years

In 1932 at the request of the *Crisis Magazine*, Dr. Albert Einstein sent a message to American Negroes. Einstein wrote:

It seems to be a universal fact that minorities, especially when their individuals are recognizable because physical differences are treated by the majorities among whom they live as an inferior class. The tragic part of such a fate, however, lies not only in the automatically realized disadvantages suffered by these minorities in economic and social relations, but also in the fact, that those who meet such treatment themselves for the most part acquiesce in this prejudiced estimate because of the suggestive influences of the majority, and come to regard people like themselves as inferior. This second and more important aspect of the evil can be met through closer union and conscious educational enlightenment among the minority, and so an emancipation of the soul of the minority can be attained. The determined effort of the Negroes in this direction deserves every recognition and assistance.

A CANADIAN AMERICAN PHYSICIAN

ANDERSON RUFFIN ABBOTT was born in Toronto, Canada, on April 7, 1837, the son of Wilson R. and Ellen Toyer Abbott. His parents had emigrated as free people from Mobile, Alabama to Toronto in 1835. Abbott received his education at Toronto Academy where he was an honor student, and Oberlin College, Ohio, Preparatory Department, 1856-1858. He graduated in Medicine from Trinity College, University of Toronto, Canada. He was a licentiate of the medical board of Upper Canada in 1862. Dr. Alexander T. Augusta was his mentor.

Dr. Abbott was determined to join the U.S. Army during the Civil War. He was somewhat influenced by Dr. Augusta who received a commission in the U.S. Army. Abbott wrote the Secretary of War E.M. Stanton several times stating that he wanted to be an assistant surgeon in the Army in one of the Colored regiments. He was appointed an acting assistant surgeon with rank of captain on September 2, 1863. Abbott was one of the eight black physicians to be appointed to the Army Medical Corps and a founder of Freedmen's Hospital. He served as chief executive officer of Freedmen's Hospital for several months. The memoirs of Dr. Abbott revealed some interesting historical experiences. Dr. Abbott stated that when he was traveling to Washington, D.C. from New York in July 1863 with Mrs. A.T. Augusta, they were abused by two thugs at the New York train depot. They were able to elude the men and find safety until the train departed for Washington, D.C. Abbott wrote that they were probably some of the early victims of the New York draft riots. The riots were responsible for the deaths of many innocent black people.

Dr. Abbott gave an account of how he and Dr. Augusta were warmly received by President and Ms. Lincoln at a White House "levee" in the winter of 1863-1864. Abbott wrote:

> "We appeared in full uniform and were met by Mr. B.B. French, a commissioner of the Treasury Department, who conducted them to the president. It was probably the first time in the history of the U.S. that a colored man had appeared at one of these levees. What made us more conspicuous of course was our uniforms.

Colored men in the uniforms of U.S. military officers of high rank had never been seen before."

Youth and adults that quote might not have any historical significance to you, but to me it has. You see President Lincoln was recognizing two ranking officers of color not field soldiers but two men who had mastered the discipline of medicine. They were welcomed by the president of the United States prior to the official ending of slavery for some 4,000,000 black people. Today in 1996, some 153 years later, many people take it for granted or could care less when they read about the eventual appointment of high ranking black military officers. Probably because I have studied and written about the black military experiences for some 25 years, I have several inferences about recent events. You see youth and adults, the glamour of sports, humorous movies and television specials and the recurring articles on black crime and poverty, do become the first and last impressions and perspectives of black by some Americans and foreigners. I believe they must be reinformed and reeducated about people of color who have overcome many obstacles without the so called affirmative action and equal opportunity measures. Therefore when I review the historical trails of black people over the years, I believe we as a people have in many instances done the impossible and white, black and all colors of people need to know that. They must understand that the positive history of African-Americans will not be found in the curriculum of white educational institutions especially on the collegiate level. Many of the institution's students will be aware of the popular athletic and musical abilities of black Americans. This is a fact and a reality. The accomplishments of Dr. Abbott have prepared the way for the present attainments of some people of color today.

Dr. Anderson Abbott was on duty in the contraband camp Washington, D.C. from June 26, 1863 to June 25, 1864 to August 21, 1865'. He was the director of Abbott Hospital in Freedmen's Village, Virginia. He resigned to his position in 1866 and returned to Canada where he passed the primary examination for the degree of medicine at Toronto University in 1867 and 1869 and became a member of the College of Physicians and Surgeons, Ontario, Canada.

In 1871, Abbott married Mary Ann Casey, Toronto. They were the parents of five children. Abbott practiced in Chatham, Ontario, Canada and was appointed coroner of Kent County as probably the first black appointed to that position in Canada. He was elected president of the Kent County Medical Society. Dr. Abbott was an acting resident physician of Toronto General Hospital. He also served as president of the Wilberforce Educational Institute from 1873 to 1885 and on the board of Chatham Collegiate Institute. Abbott served as an associate editor of the Messenger, a publication of the British Methodist Episcopal Church. He was also responsible for the integration of schools in Chatham.

In 1881, Dr. Abbott moved to Dundas and was appointed director, vice treasurer and president of the Dundas Mechanical Institute, 1883. His civic interest was noted when he was appointed high school trustee and chairman of the Internal Management Committee 1885-1889. He also served as a warden of St. James (Anglican or Episcopal) Church and the registrar of the St. James guild. In April 1890, he was elected a member of James S. Knowlton Post No. 532, Grand Army of the Republic and Surgeon of the post in 1892. Dr. Abbott was appointed an aide de camp to the commanding officer of the Department of New York GAR. In this capacity at that time, Abbott had achieved the highest rank and prestige ever awarded a black in Canada or the United States.

Dr. Abbott returned to the United States in 1894 and was appointed surgeon in chief of Provident Hospital in Chicago, Illinois. He was licensed to practice in Illinois and Michigan. Abbott had other talents besides medicine. He was a writer, lecturer and journalist. He gave lectures on the subjects of history, poetry, Darwinism and medicine. He wrote articles for the *Planet, Banner, New York Age* and *Colored American*. He also had an interest in the Niagara Movement and W.E.B. Dubosis' projects. The distinguished military surgeon, Dr. Anderson Ruffin Abbot died on December 29, 1913 in Toronto, Canada.

A DIPLOMATIC HISTORIAN OF COLOR, MERZE TATE

In 1972, while a graduate student at Howard University, Washington, D.C., I had a unique opportunity as a student in Dr. Merze Tate's diplomatic history class to listen to her outstanding and most informative lectures. I believe this late scholar should not be forgotten and should be made known to others today and also in future years.

Dr. Merze Tate was born on a farm in Michigan in 1905. She graduated with honors in 1927 from Western Michigan University. She received a masters degree in history from Columbia University and a doctorate in political science from Harvard University's Radcliffe College. Dr. Tate received an economics degree from Oxford University and she studied at the Geneva School of International Studies.

Dr. Tate's illustrious teaching career included: 1927-1932, high school history and civics teacher in Indianapolis, Indiana, 1935, history instructor and dean of women at Barber-Scotia Junior College in North Carolina, 1936, she became the history and social science department chairperson at Bennett College for Women, North Carolina. Dr. Tate taught at Morgan State University, political science and served as dean of women. She served on the faculty of Howard University form 1942 to 1977.

Dr. Merze Tate's impressive professional career included the writing of books and scholarly papers. She was the author of manuscripts on European diplomacy, history of Hawaii, great power rivalries in the Pacific, disarmament and nuclear weapons, United States and the Hawaiian Kingdom, and Hawaii Reciprocity or Annexation.

Dr. Tate lectured and taught abroad. She was a Fulbright lecturer in India in 1950 and 1951 and lectured under the auspices of the U.S. Information Agency in the Indian Subcontinent, Thailand, Singapore, Hong Kong, Japan and the Philippines.

Dr. Tate was a member of Phi Beta Kappa and the recipient of four honorary degrees. She was a philanthropist who made endowments and funded scholarships at universities where she had studied and taught. Dr. Tate will always be remembered as one of my outstanding and motivating professors.

COLOR OBSESSION

I have included this discussion on color obsession in this book because I believe that some of the articles and research that I have completed over the years will enable the reader to think about other views on this volatile subject in our present ever increasing polarized society in 1997. I first realized this in the early years of my research in American, African and European history that I have noticed that many of the so-called people of color were miscegenated and racially mixed and often referred to as of African descent, mulattoes, mixed, slave mother "African father, quadroon, mustie, zambo, creole, but never did I see "multiracial", biracial, half white, half black and other popular terms today. I must state very clearly that I am sure that many of the personalities that I discuss in this book lived and died as white people mentally even though they were aware of the presence of their black genes.

Color obsession is quite obvious when several American National magazines in 1993-1995 and 1996 publish articles on a multiracial society. A magazine in 1993 discussed how immigrants came to America many years ago, and talked about the slaves who came from Africa. Yes, the subject of slavery is the starting point to address designated and assigned culture to Americans of African descent. They were also introduced to a naming system that would continue through the 1990's, assigning names such as slave, darkey, nigger, coon, colored, colored American, Negroes, Afro Americans, blacks and African Americans. We must remember that there was no intention or considerations to assess the apparent biological changes in physical description of the original African slave who arrived in America in the early years. Biological diversity that occurred genetically during slavery with the European, Indian, and in some cases the Asian was insignificant to the census takers in 1860. Why do I say 1860 because when I was researching my book, *Thomas Sewell Inborden An Early Educator of Color*, the Virginia census for Loudoun county, 1869, listed the family of Levi and Hannah Proctor as mulattoes. His wife was formerly Hannah Rector who was related to one of the distinguished first families of the local area. Thomas S. Inborden's mother was Harriet Proctor Smith, daughter of Hannah and Levi. I was able to locate several letters where T.S. Inborden did mention about his genetic inheritance. In a letter he wrote to his daughter, Dorothy, T.S. stated:

"I am Indian for a large part. I have at least half white aristocracy which has given me the spirit of independence and an attitude of the equality of any man who walks the face of the earth. I have some French and Dutch extraction. These inherent qualities have given me tenacity and personality that has made one more than anything else except perhaps my environment. In all my life, I have never cared for the cheap and rashy element of people. I have had to mix with a great many of them. I have always tried to put myself with those who were looking upward and onward, especially those who wanted to be somebody. When I come into a bad environment and can not remake it, get out of it. The one thing to consider is whether one course will lead us to wealth or woe".

"I have never said nothing about my father. He died not an old man with Brights disease. (Kidney disease) I have seen him on several occasions when he came to my mother's house. He was one of the cleanest and finest dressed man I ever saw. He was a typical southern gentleman. He was well educated and has the finest cultural bearing. He has one son who clerked in the Conrad's store in Upperville where we all traded. I was too young to understand it but all of this was the tragedy of the old days for which none of us seemed responsible".

I researched the papers and self biographies of Thomas Sewell Inborden for eight years. At first, I did not understand his views on race and how he felt since he could pass as a white man day or night because of his obvious Caucasian physical features. However, as I studied his papers, I realize that Thomas S. Inborden lived and died as a proud man who was sensitive to his blackness, aware of it and proud and also respected his other genetic racial characters as stated above. He once wrote *"It is fine to speak to people who have a sympathetic spirit especially when you have a feeling that you have an unpopular subject. My racial identity was not clear in the mind of a gentleman who introduced me. He said something like this: Professor Steiner of the University of California said somewhere that if he had to be born again, he would like to be born a colored man, so that he might be able to study the colored problem from the inside. We have with us today a gentleman who understands the colored problem, and who was not born colored either"* These may not be the exact words, but it is the thought. *The first thing that I had to do was to dispel the audience of the fact or statement just made, that I did not have to be born a colored man, and that I wanted them to know that the traditions of our country and the laws in many, if not all the states, had said that any man is colored who has one iota of Negro blood in his veins. I am glad to have the honor to address you as a colored man."* If this occurred in 1920 and I read in a newspaper an article written by a very popular news correspondent or columnist about the young outstanding golfer who prides on his genetic diversity, then can we really say we are color blind today. Because just as Inborden had distinctive white features in 1920 and chose to live as a man of color and be aware of his white genes, can the young golfer and other people of color who have mixed genes voice their own self awareness without people expressing their rightful, personal opinions sometimes expressed without the historical awareness that this color obsession is a continual American custom, just revised and televised in 1997.

The following discussions will address the facts bearing on problems of color obsession, and a speech that was delivered on the Diversity of African Americans.

Facts bearing on Color Obsessed Problems

1. Race is a social construct involving prejudice, myth and superstitions.

2. Binary approach of race, white or black

3. Skin color is the dividing line of binary or two races.

4. Some Spanish or Hispanic Americans and native born Americans prefer not to use the binary rule.

5. Desire to change census category and lose minority solidarity.

6. Science of race - reality; people in 1997 simply see race as descriptive physical features, namely skin color, nose shape, eyebrows, hair.

7. Differences in academic opinions on race by scholars such as cultural and physical anthropologists. Some of them believed race is not a biological concept.

8. Population biologists have developed an approach to explain race by analyzing genetic marks in selected populations. They have learned that there are more genetic differences within one race than there is between that race and another. Some of these genetic differences are difficult to explain. An example would be, if one would select at random any two black Americans and an analysis is conducted on their 23 pairs of chromosomes, the results could show that their genes have less in common than do the genes of one of them with that of a random white person. This research adds some support to my simple statement that African Americans not Africans are probably the most diverse individuals on this planet biologically as a group. Now when one considers traits, people are sorted by traits and different groupings are produced and they are called non concordant. You are not obtaining equal traits.

9. One drop of blood theory - historically this theory has had many variations or exceptions. In the 1800's, the state of Virginia would tolerate a person with less that one-fourth black genes as white and later defined white as having less than one sixteenth black genes. Many states, especially in the south began to enact laws to prohibit whites from marrying any black person. The legal significance was present in American society in 1986 when the U.S. Supreme Court ruled that a lower court could force a Louisiana woman with negligible African ancestry to be legally defined as black.

10. Evaluation and biology of race. Some scientists will argue that if original man and woman evolved from the African continent, then the blacks should be categorized in one race because their ancestors did

not migrate out of Africa, but stayed on the continent. Whereas the Asians, traveled north and east toward the Pacific Ocean and the whites toward the European continent. Because of the biodiversity of the genes possibly through years of mutation (changes) and environmental factors, the Asians and whites produced different physical features when they migrated out of Africa. These differences relate to the theories on the origin of man. Some scientists have proposed reasons for shared traits among so called different racial groups. An anthropologist wrote in 1995 that the dark skin of the black African social groups could be due to evolutionary changes for survival, because they evolved with selected genes to produce melanin to protect them from the equatorial climate. The scientist also said the long nose structure of North Africans and northern Europeans show that they evolved in a cold climate and their nose from a physiological or functional provides the moistening of the air prior to it reaching the lungs. It was also stated by the scientist that the thin, tall burly structures of the African group such as the Masai from Kenya evolved to release the body heat and the short squat bodies of the Eskimos evolved to retain the heat. These views were discussed in an article published in 1995.

11. One can not ignore the possible effects that early racist writers of the Early Explorers of Africa has had on the social, cultural, scientific, and academic literature through the years that are still meaningful to some people today in assessing the African Americans' intelligence and cultural values. The books are in the libraries and the so-called scholars and experts still use all forms of media to express their opinion that sometimes in an indirect way will parallel the thoughts of the early racist views of explorers like Stanley and others, especially in the equatorial areas of Africa (Congo). I read the following views of an early explorer who told the history of his travels and exploration in Africa in the 1800's. The book was printed in 1889. Some of the observations of the Congo in equatorial areas of Africa and its people were:

"There are valid differences between the tribes in constant intercourse with each other. The seasons are dry and rainy and could affect the people. In equatorial Africa, sheep become black and cows in some districts do not give milk after the calf is weaned. In the malarial districts, no cattle can be found. Wild animals are of a degenerate and degraded type. The foreign plants and vegetables when brought to equatorial Africa lose many of their distinctive features. If one traverses the intervening countries between Egypt and Senegambia, they will observe the physical qualities of the people and have no difficulties in recognizing almost every degree or state of deviation displayed showing a gradual transition from the characteristics of the Egyptian to those of the Negro without any broadly marked line. The native of the highlands are more reddish in color and their hair less wooly. The features are more prominent and less prognathous (jaws somewhat projecting beyond the upper face), higher forehead and greater intelligence than the native of the coast swamps, the true Negro. On the west coast, the natives are also of a darker hue than the interior. There is a constant movement toward the west that the more intelligent light colored and physically fine formed interior tribes on reaching the coast swamps soon degenerate to the true Negro type. The native of Sierra Leone are tall and really handsome and the Liberian Krumes and Senegal Wollofs are of great stature and wonderful strength. It is considered that the great branches of the African race are developed Negro types and the Negro represents a degree rather than a distinct race and nearly all the degenerate types known as Negroes are found on the border of their ancestral tribes. Thus the east coast of African shows us the Abyssinian more resembling Arabs than Negroes. The north African gives us the Kabyles and Berbers. South Africa gives us the Kaffir families and the Hottentot and Bushmen. The Sennaar tribe of Niger and Lake Tchad more approach the Arab. But, when these families verge upon low and intertropical region they at once develop Negroid branches. The brown, reddish or olive colored races are more numerous than blacks, and for some hill tribes who chose to live far from the hot swampy districts, thin lips and prominent noses are the rule. Precisely the same peculiarly is noticeable in the South Pacific Sea Islands."

The writer also said, "*Those people of the higher latitudes are of a light brown or olive tint near approaching white. While those of the low and moist island are directly of the Negro type. Therefore, the Negro is simply an intertropical African in a humid locality.*"

DIVERSITY OF AFRICAN AMERICANS

I delivered a speech to a high level government agency in 1995. This speech will provide some information about the differences of black Americans.

I sincerely believe that the residuals effects of Americas dehumanizing system of slavery and its many years of covert and overt forms of racism and especially institutional racism have taken their toll in the education and miseducation of many Americans of all ethnic groups. Today, 1995, people of all ethnic and racial groups have the stereotype visions of African Americans. Vision portrayed through the news media, television and the mind tranquilizer of humor and laughter that actually omit the serious and scholarly representation of a diverse or different people.

Today, I would like to address some very significant true facts and thoughts for you to consider about the Diversity of African Americans. A diversity that is quite profound in biological, social, economic and political perspectives. These diversities should reflect that African Americans, blacks, Negroes, Afro Americans, colored, Afric, Ethiopians, slaves, free people and the infamous words nigger and darkey all have been used to describe black people. Biological diversity represents the miscegenation or race mixing of the African slave during slavery with European, Indian, and in some cases Asian genes. This occurred over a period of at least 250 years. Of course, as long as the original slaves and mixed slaves reproduced among themselves, yes, we have many blacks representative of their dominant African genetic heritage. However, in 1995 the African American today whether they agree, reject, or care less, are still representative of genes of other races. There was one group of blacks during slavery that were given different names because of their visible resemblance of a half mixture other than African with European.

Black Presence

They were assigned the names of octoroons, quadroons, mustie, mulattoes, high yellows and chestnuts. Unfortunately, the biological genetic diversity and genetic offsprings of an African or half African and a white person created a problem for the slave and master. This was the beginning of a division among African peoples of their beautiful ebony skin color who in some instances had already been divided by social groups or tribal groups. Many of the mulattoes were born free or later freed by their biological white father or purchased their own freedom as some other slaves did. They created their own community when freed and this was the beginning of a mulatto class within the divided black community. This was also the start of disunity among African peoples in America based on the degree of lightness of the skin and certain physical descriptions. Some mulattos developed a self concept, individual pride and superiority that they were different from other blacks. They developed the life styles and a new culture based on the majority white culture. In later years, the U.S. Census in 1860 and 1870 would identify the family as mulatto. There were also some blacks prior to the 1860's who owned slaves. Yes, skin color is an obsession in America today, possibly a residual effect of yesterday. This early social division among blacks did have an effect on the unity of blacks. This social division was portrayed in community activities to include burial societies, churches and clubs among blacks and later some colleges would reflect the color problem. In South Carolina, in the 1870's there was a Brown Men's Society for lighter skin blacks. Episcopal churches in Charleston for blacks would reflect a difference. This was a beginning of segregation within a segregated society perpetuated by blacks. The point is simply black people over the years in culture, values, folkways, morals, speech and religious beliefs have been quite different from other ethnic groups in America. I am saying historically and realistically that blacks do not think the same or act the same as unfortunately, the 10 o'clock news would give a first impression to those who do not know the way it really was.

There are many majority members and even some black representatives of all classes of society which include managers, government leaders, military leaders who honestly believe that the so called unfortunate street element of blacks and a few blacks who act out the antics of weekly stereotype humor shows to include popular talk shows are actually how most African Americans really are. Occasionally, upper level managers are concerned about hearing some employees of color use in their office or hallway jargons of slang and fad terms dis, yo, mo, and pressing, but I sincerely believe that these speech patterns and even dress styles are not accepted by most people of color.

Economically and politically blacks are diverse and the residual effects of segregation and exclusion over the years justify some of these conditions of poverty, ignorance, illiteracy and low performance in pursuits of some goals. But these are not based on a desire in most cases and definitely not on any physical or mental differences because this overall population of a mixed hybrid of African and others today could be demonstrating his weak genes rather than his African genes, then the Bell Curve would have another meaning. Diversity political, one must realize that blacks have been denied the right to vote in the majority of cases for many years prior to the thrust of Civil Rights drive in many areas of our country. Yes, some did vote and many in the south were led to the polls by their masters or former masters. Case of point, when a former confederate body servant filed for a confederate pension in 1921 a statement in his support read "Leroy Jones lived with my grandfather and my father", wrote a white man. He also wrote, "he was what was known as a white man's Negro and voted with us in every election and causing ill feelings among other blacks. Old Leroy told us he was going to stick to his white folks". If there was one there were more. Yes, some blacks did vote under those conditions. There were many blacks after the Civil War with no where to go who remained with some former masters or other majority member or share croppers. Yes, there were white sharecroppers but they were eventually able to move toward upward mobility without another burden, an inferior segregated life style. One must realize that the truth is that prior to 1954, there was only one major minority in America as far as race and enforced separation, the black woman and black man, - Black people. The Civil Rights Movement of 1960 gave long overdue considerations to the American blacks. Prior to 1954 and especially World War II. There were two categories of race in the U.S. Army, Navy, Mararines, and Air Force, Negro and white, everyone else who were not Negro or black were considered white. Since the dehumanizing slavery system blacks have been considered by non

Black Presence

There are so many variables to the problems of African Americans today and also those who do not really understand the diversity of blacks and their long historical road toward equality. Again, the youth, black and others do not understand black nationalism, multicultural and Afro Centric and affirmative action and quotas in daily discussions today.

I do not have the solutions to any problems. However, as a concerned American of color. I have some inferences, suggestions and logical thoughts and crucial facts we must consider. First, that the intent of Brown vs Board of Education 1954 has not been met. We do have a polarized society. Yes, still based on living patterns, cultures, churches and most aspects of life to include schools. How can people communicate and erase the fears of others and stereotypes. The educational system does not assist the problem. Why? Because the standard curriculum of public textbooks are oriented toward a 98% of the majority's history in America. When one pursues an education whether in a black or majority school system they must satisfy those requirements. Then how will others to include blacks really understand blacks when persistent negative impressions are shown on radio, television and other news media. There is definitely a need for white youth and others to be reeducated about the positive achievements of African Americans in America's society. There is a strong necessity for all Americans and foreigners, especially, to be reeducated about the truth of African Americans and their past and present conditions, some sustaining pains that linger. They cannot be compared with other Americans including people of color from the West Indies and Africa. This is a distinct and different American of color. Many of these things are not known to some black youths who appear to act out of ignorance and negative characteristics in our society. All blacks do not support their actions. African Americans over the years were confronted with these problems, situations and legal accepted conditions in America and I repeat 35 years cannot correct those past injustices and denials. The trials and frustrations and state of low self esteem and thoughts of inferiority were accepted by many blacks when they could not overcome these experiences. Many survived, some did not. There were separated families and recurring illegitimacy during slavery and also denial of an education and the right to enjoy the better things of life.

families and recurring illegitimacy during slavery and also denial of an education and the right to enjoy the better things of life.

Let us not forget that other Americans will and have constructed monuments, museums and elaborate structures to remind not just Americans but the world of their past inhumane treatment and injustices. People of all races study and discuss the negatives and humor of blacks. African American and other groups must be reeducated. Many black youth today are not aware that a baby born years ago at home or in the separate wings of segregated hospitals in the north and south began their first month of growth and development in a restricted neighborhood across the railroad tracks. Of course, his physician was white because there were no black doctors in the town.

On Sunday, church worship was separate. Some Catholic churches reserved a section in the rear. When school age was reached, youngsters started school in an inferior classroom setting to include buildings, textbooks and sometimes state approved low quality of teachers. When children would go to the grocery stores on the corner, friendly Jewish merchants had a writing pad to give them credit before the emergence of the credit card. They did not take the flight to the suburbs when they closed shop. They went upstairs to their their living quarters. They did not need plastics and bullet proof glass to fear some belligerent black. Their securely force was their black customers who shared a sense of mutual respect, communication, trust and loyalty and not fear. That was the way things were.

When the young black child reached maturity, they were aware that the laws of the land sanctioned the segregation in ice cream parlors, restaurants, skating rinks, bowling alleys, theaters, Griffith Stadium, home of the Red Skins' barber shops, and hair dresser. (But in the 1950's a fair skinned black lady who lived in the black community would prefer to pass as white to have her hair done at a white salon on Connecticut Avenue). Some blacks would pass as their physical descriptions dictated as Spanish, Indian and others to go to white theaters in Washington, D.C. Young black children would enhance their inferior and denial status in America when they would always see white faces in the performances of their duties as policemen, bus drivers, firemen, state troopers. In 1976, the state of Virginia had 1,000 officers all were white except 3 who were blacks. Can 35 years correct that without some boost and acceptance of qualified blacks. One would see white municipal judges, firemen, store clerks, insurance agents (economic most white insurance companies only wrote term insurance for blacks, not ordinary, especially Metropolitan. There were no black parole officers, prison guards, milkmen, or secretaries. The black youth must wake up and smell the real coffee because he or she is living in a new time period and opportunities are available some facilities are open and people of all races are willing to assist them think positive and strive for excellence in the pursuit of education. Even though covert institutional racism is still present in the community, private business and government, one can overcome them with education, faith, strong self concept, high self respect and morals for one's self and above all strong family support not the peer pressure or fads. Now, I am not naive, they cannot do this alone because residual effects of the past still have clouds on black progress. Some people still believe that blacks are outstanding in entertainment, sports, and music because they all have rhythm, song and dance skills, are religious and emotional and loud. I believe the most diverse and different race of people in the world is the distinct African American in the U.S. who collectively does not think or act the same if you really know them. Why do I stress this because the nonblack youth especially white needs to be reeducated about why and how some black people think the way they do. They continue to see injustices in America and the legal actions of some lawyers who try to convince judge and jury that blacks have completed the goals of integration and affirmed assistance. White people and others need to know through their own dominated educational system that these stories of truth occurred and the knowledge of these facts could alter predetermined opinions. There are many whites and even blacks that will say the past is fine but remember that other people have the same problems. I tell them nicely. Yes, but if I drive a Volkswagen and you a Mercedes and we leave our starting points at different times. You leave one hour ahead of me, there is no way for me to catch up with you unless someone does something miraculously to cause that to occur. I call these positive accomplishments of blacks under all the conditions of yesteryears and even today miraculous when they first realized the truth devoid of rhetoric and faced the situation and accomplished these wonders against many odds and with the concerned assistance of many white Americans and others without quotas because they were quotas for exclusion without affirmative action plans because the affirmative action plans were to affirm segregation then and forever until of course America the Beautiful was threatened by a surprise when their poor and wealthy blacks came out of wilderness in the 1960's and demanded in a nonviolent way for America to change. Dr. Martin Luther King had a dream and the fact that the dream has not been fulfilled today even though there is not a closed door, not a whip, not a chain, but because the legal reinterpretations of congressional and Supreme Court decisions that have brought us thus far are now being altered or changed based on a belief of reverse discrimination. Yes, there are discussions today about affirmative action and quotas. I must say that our government along with the business world has a history in resisting equal employment for blacks. Case of point in 1969, our largest civil service employer the Department of Defense had only 6 blacks on the GS-15 grade level. In the past 30 years, many blacks have moved from the status of messenger and custodians to clerks, laborers, technicians, computer specialists, analyst, typist and a few higher positions. Many blacks today still appear on a curve between GS-5 and GS-12.

There are many leather chairs still not filled in the upper level positions with people of color. But let us examine the situation. With the tables turned, and it's not racism, if there was a black dominated government in the work place and blacks were in charge, they would hire many blacks in all positions just as whites have done over the years. But there is one difference, the blacks would not have had a four hundred year history of being dominated by legal means by the white population, there is a difference. Therefore, people must not point the finger and accuse a race of people as being responsible for past injustices prior to their birth. But all must be reeducated of what happened and the residual effects that exist today that have caused the problems we are experiencing in 1997.

In view of all these complexities of racial polarization in America. I must state emphatically. There is a need for managers and employees to listen to each other, learn something about each other's differences. Stop stereotyping each others. Use tact. The minority employee must maintain their self esteem, be prepared, qualified and ten times better and then stand at the door and trust that concerned managers will open it without any reservations on one's capability. If agencies throughout government would take actions immediately and avoid the standing practices and long mitigations and extenuations and give qualified loyal employees an opportunity based on their performance void of the employers personal view then we can move toward a color blind society, to include the work place. After 300 years of toils and struggle, I believe America still has the faith and desire to survive and achieve. But the majority view of superiority, power and control must stop. When they are qualified include them in your inner circle of favorite friends. Let us be frank and realize that in today's civil service system, fully qualified and satisfactory is not the means toward rapid upward mobility for promotion, most outstanding is the mark of the day and someone who will accept you if you are qualified. The employee must possess the qualification and the employer must be considerate. The military has been somewhat successfully in using these approaches.

Ladies and gentlemen, sometimes I realize that the future in the African American advances appear bleak and doomed. However, I am not a pessimist but optimist and I sincerely believe like Dr. Martin Luther King that there are some white people and others who really would like to see an equitable American society. The day is coming when there will be a black president. When I have recollected about our beautiful past and proud race, I deeply believe that the continual closed door toward progress, bell curve, Rutger's president statement and a political party plans to eradicate affirmative actions, will not prevail forever. Because I ask, what race of people have accomplished so much in a span of 130 years since removed from slavery? This is a proud and sustaining thought that gives me the optimism that there will be better tomorrows for people of color even if barriers are present in our time. I also believe that maybe not yours nor my tomorrows, but one tomorrow some day, America will really portray, for all peoples devoid of hate and ostracisms, a feeling of love and welcome. It is in the future and it must come if we all expect to survive together here in America the Beautiful.

BIBLIOGRAPHY

Primary Sources

Manuscript Collection

Thomas Sewell Inborden Papers

Manuscript Division, Library of Congress, Washington, D.C.
  Newton D. Baker Papers
  NAACP Collection
  Carter G. Woodson Papers

Moorland Spingarn Research Center, Howard University, Washington, D.C.

Anna J. Cooper papers
Mary Anna Shadd papers
Lucy Slowe Collection
Mary O.H. Williams, Collection

National Archives, Washington, D.C.

Camp McGrath, Bantgas, Philippines, Island Post Returns RG 98, 1909-1915

Liberian Dispatches, WDC. GS RG 165, 1912-1915
Military Intelligence Division Papers (Colonel Charles Young), RG. 165

Military Pension Files, RG 15, Adjutant's office

Miscellaneous Letters from Legation of Haiti, Records of the Department of State, RG 59, National Archives, 1906-1907

State Archives

Alabama State Archives and History, Montgomery Alabama
Miscellaneous Manuscript Papers

Hall of Records, Maryland Archives, Annapolis Maryland
Miscellaneous Manuscript Papers

Newspapers

Afro American (Baltimore) and (Washington D.C.)
Atlanta Journal and Constitution
Chicago Tribune
New York Times
Washington Post

Periodicals and Magazines

Journals

Blood
Journal of American Medial Association
Journal of the American Pharmaceutical Association
Journal of Hematology
Journal of Medicine
Journal of Pharmaceutical Sciences
Lancet
National Medical Association
Negro History Bulletin
Negro History Journal
Pediatrics
Science

Magazines

Crisis
Ebony
Jet
National Geographic
Opportunity
Southern Workman

Interviews

Allen Harriet, conversation with Harriet Allen, Interviewed, 1988, 1989, 1991-2, Washington, D.C.

Miller, Inborden Dorothy, conversations with Dorothy Inborden Miller, 1976-1979 and 1992, Washington, D.C.

Personal Notes

Class lectures, unpublished and published articles, notes and manuscripts, of the Library of Robert Ewell Greene.

Secondary Sources

Books

Alford, Terry, *Prince Among Slaves*. New York: Harcourt Brace, Dovanovich. 1977.

American Colonization Society *Liberia*. February, 1893 Bulletin No. 2.

Batuta, Ibn. *Travels of Ibn Batuta.* London, 1927.
Blakley, Allison, *Russia and the Negro.* Washington, D.C. Howard University Press. 1986
Borch, Samuel. *Egypt From the Earliest Times*. London, 1875.
Budge, E.A. Wallis. *A History of Ethiopa*. 2 Vol. London: Methuen 1922.

Castro, Fidel. *In Defense of Socialism.* New York: Pathfinder Press, 1969.
Cox, Oliver C. *Caste Color and Race*. New York: Modern Readers, 1970.
Cullen, Contee. *Color*. New York: Harpers and Brothers Publishers, 1925.

Diop, Cheikh. *The Origin of Civilization Myth or Reality.* Westport: Laurence Hill and Co., 1974.
DuBois, W.E.B. *The World and Africa.* New York: International Publishers, 1946.

Edwards, Paul ed. *Equiano Travels*. London, 1967.
Enan, Muhammad Abdullah. *Decisive Moments in the History of Islam*. Pakistan: S.H. Muhammad Ashrof, 1940.
Erman, Adolph. *Life in Ancient Egypt*. London: MacMillan and Co. 1894.
Esler, Antony. *The Herman Venture.* New Jersey: Prentice Hall, 1996.

Finch, Charles S. *The African Background To Medical Science*, 1990.
Foy, Felician, ed. 1992 *Catholic Almanac.* Huntington, Indiana: Our Sunday Visitor, Publishing Division Inc., 1992.

Gann, L.H. and Peter Duigan. *Burden of Empire.* New York: Frederick Praeger Publisher, 1967.
Graham, Richard ed. *The Idea of Race In Latin America, 1870 - 1940*. Austin: University of Texas Press, 1990.

Greaves, Richard L. etal. *Civilizations of the World V. 1 and V. 2*. New York: Harpers Collins College Publishers, 1993.

Greenberg, Joseph H. *Languages of Africa.* Bloomington: Indiana University, 1966.

Greene, Robert E. *Black Defenders Of America 1775-1973*. Chicago: Johnson Publishing Co., 1974.

Greene, Robert E. *The Planter, A Brief Sketch Of the Civil War Steamer And Its Pilot Robert Smalls*. Washington, D.C., R.E. Greene Publisher, 1980.

Greene, Robert E. *They Rest Among The Known*. Washington, D.C.: Yancey Graphics, 1981.

Greene, Robert Ewell. *Delta Memories A Historical Summary*. Washington, D.C. Yancey Graphics, 1981.

Greene, Robert E. *Black Courage 1775-1783, Documentation Of Black Participation In The American Revolution.* Washington, D.C.: National Society Of The Daughters Of The American Revolution, 1984.

Greene, Robert E. *Colonel Charles Young, Soldier and Diplomat*. Washington, D.C.: R.E. Greene Publisher, 1985.

Greene, Robert E. *The Saga Of Sydney A. Moore*. Washington, D.C.: R.E. Greene Publisher, 1985.

Greene, Robert E. *Teach Me To Learn Biology Simple To Complex* Washington, D.C.: R.E.Greene Publisher, 1987.

Greene, Robert E. *True Tales, For Children, Young Adults And Adults*: Washington, D.C.: R.E.Greene Publisher, 1987.

Greene, Robert Ewell. *Robert A. Thornton, Master Teacher, Scholar, Physicist And Humanist*. R.E.Greene Publisher, 1988.

Greene, Robert E. *The Conway - McAfee, People Of Color*. Fort Washington, Maryland, R.E. Greene, Publisher, 1989.

Greene, Robert E. *Leary - Evans, Ohio's Free People Of Color*, 1989.

Greene, Robert E. *Swamp Angels, A. Biographical Study Of The 54th Massachusetts Regiment*, Fort Washington, Maryland: Bo Mark/Greene Publishing Group, 1990.

Greene, Robert E. *Black Defenders of The Persian Gulf War Desert Shield - Desert Storm A Reference And Pictorial History*. Fort Washington, Maryland: R.E.Greene Publisher, 1991.

Greene, Robert E. *They Did Not Tell Me True Facts About The African American's African Past and American Experience,* Fort Washington, Maryland: R.E.Greene Publisher, 1992.

Greene, Robert E. *Who Were The Real Bufflo Soldiers? Black Defenders of America*, Fort Washington, Maryland: R.E.Greene Publisher, 1994

Greene, Robert E. *Physicians and Surgeons, Real Image Models for Youth and Adults*, Fort Washington, Maryland: R.E.Greene Publisher, 1996.

Greene, Robert E. *A Biography - Thomas Sewell Inborden, Early Educator of Color*, Fort Washington, Md: R.E.Greene Publisher, 1997.

Hallett, Robert *Africa To 1875.* Ann Arbor: The University of Michigan Press, 1970.

Hare-Cuney, Maude. *Negro Musicians And Their Music*: Washington, D.C. Associated Publishers Inc., 1936.

Herodotus, *The Histories*. New York: Penguin Books, 1965.

Howard, C. ed. *West African Explorers*. London: Oxford University Press, 1951.

July, Robert W. *A History of the African People*. New York. Charles Scribners and Sons, 1974.

Johnston, Henry Sr. *Liberia V. 1*. London. Hutchinson and Co., 1906.

Lee, Ulysees. *The Employment of Negro Troops.* Washington, D.C. U.S. Government, 1966.

Lewis, Bernard. *Race and Color In Islam*. New York: Harpers and Row Publishers, 1970.

Lewis, Bernard. *Race and Slavery in the Middle East*. New York: Oxford University Press, 1990.

McKay, John P. and others, *A History of World Society V. II Since 1500*. Boston: Houghton Mifflin Co., 1996.

Micheli, Mario De. *Picasso*. London: Thames and Hudson. 1967.

Morner, Magnus. *Race Mixture In the History of Latin America*. Boston: Little Brown and Co., 1967.

Myrdal, Gunnar. *An American Dilemma*. New York: Harpers and Brothers, 1944. V. 1 and V. 2.

Nascimento Do Abdias. *Brazil Mixture Or A Massacre? Essays In The Genocide Of A Black People.* Dover, Massachusetts: The Majority Press, 2nd ed. 1989.

Payne, Elizabeth. *The Pharoahs of Ancient Egypt.* New York: Random House, 1964.
Pipkin, J.J. *The Negro in Revelation in History and in Citizenship.* St. Louis, Missouri: A.D. Thompson Publishing Co., 1902.
Powell, Raphael P., *The Invisible Image Uprooted.* New York: Philemon Co., 1979.

Ramos, Frank U. *O Negro Brasileiro* 2nd ed. Rio de Janeiro, 1940.
Rawlison, George. *History of Ancient Egypt V. 2.* New York: A.L. Burt Publishers, 1880.
Richardson, Clement. *The National Encyclopedia of the Colored Race.* Montgomery of Alabama: National Publishing Co., 1919.
Rogers, Joel A. *100 Amazing Facts About The Negro.* New York: J.A. Rogers, Publishers, 1934.
Roland, Joan G. *Africa: The Heritage and The Challenge.* Greenwich, Conn. Faucett Publications Inc., 1974.
Rotberg, Robert I. ed. *Africa and Its Explorers. Motives Methods and Impact.* Massachusetts: Harvard University Press, 1973.

Shapera I. Livingstone's *Private Journals 1851-1853.* Los Angeles. University of California Press, 1960.
Scobie, Edward Black Britannia. *A History of Blacks In Britain.* Chicago: Johnson Publishing Co., 1972
Sertima, Ivan Van ed. *Blacks In Science, Ancient and Modern.* New Brunswick, N.J., Transaction Books, 1985.
Sinnette, Elinor D. *Arthur Alfonso Schomburg.* Detroit: The New York Public Library and Wayne State University Press, 1989.
Skinner, Elliott P. *Peoples and Cultures of Africans.* Garden City, New York, Doubleday Co., 1973
Snowden, Frank M. *Blacks in Antiquity.* Cambridge, Mass., Harvard University Press, 1970.
Stanley Henry M. *Stanley In Africa.* Chicago: Standard Publishing Co., 1889.

Stems, Peter N., et al. *World Civilizations The Global Experience*. New York: Harper Collins College Publishers, 1996.

Stoddard, Lothrop. *Clashing Tides of Colour*. New York: Charles Scribners and Sons, 1935.

Trimingham, Spencer J. *A History of Islam in West Africa*. New York: Oxford University Press, 1970

Upshur, Jiu-Hwa L., et al. *World History V. 1* New York: West Publishing Co., 1991.

U.S. Government, DA Pamphlet 550-43. *Area Handbook for the United Arab Republic* (Egypt), October 1972.

Vansina, Jan. *Kingdoms of the Savana*. Wisconsin: The University of Wisconsin: The University of Wisconsin Press, 1970.

Vlahos, Olivia. *African Beginnings*. Greenwich, Conn: Fawcett Publications Inc., 1967.

Wesley, Charles H. *The Changing African Historical Tradition*, Washington, D.C.: Associated Publishers, 1925.

Williams, Chancellor. *The Destruction of Black Civilization*. Iowa: Kendall Hunt Publishing Co., 1971.

Woodson, Carter G. *African Heroes and Heroines.* Washington, D.C. The Association Publishers Inc., 1939.

Woodson, Carter G. *The Negro In Our History*, Washington, D.C. The Associated Publishers, Inc., 1939.

Young, Charles. *Little Handbook of French Creole as spoken in Haiti*. 1905.

INDEX

A

Abbott, Anderson, 381,384
Abu Tig, 41
Aesop, 32
Afars, 65
African Brazilian, 60
African Brazilian Return
  to Roots, 175
African Cardinals, 35
African Kingdoms, 62
African Kingdoms, Past
  and Present, 51
African Kingdoms and
  Societies, 50
African Nationalism and
Independence 310-322
African presence, Mexico, 338-335
Africanus, Scipio, 31
African Sculptures, 63
Afro Cubans, 168-169
Agass, Kizlas, 41
Ahmed, Mohammed (Madhi), 41,48
Ainus, 38
Anu, 11, 14
Allen, Harriet, 12,13
Alessandro de Medici, 37,38
Alexevna, Maria, 161
Alfonso, Juan, 343
Aldridge, Ira, 344
Almargo, Diego, 97
Alvarado, Pedro, 97
Amazing Grace, 127
Amazons, 104
Ambedicar, B.R., 28,29

Amen, 14
American Colonization Society, 216-218
American Revolution
Amir ibn al-as, 45
Angola, 69
Angostura, 178
Antarah, 48
Anu, 11
Atlanta, 314
Ashanti King, 63
Azikiwe, N., 311

B

Babylonians, Bohia, 61
Bailey, Margaret, 323
Bakr, Mohammed, 45
Baker, Vernon, 296-299
Balboa, 97
Bamboula, 168
Baptista, Pedro, 92
Battle of Uhud, 43
Becton, Julius W. Jr., 324
Beethoven, Ludwig, 344-345, 347
Beihari, Abid, 44
Beja, 33, 65
Belgium Congo, 96
Belkin, Ivan, 163
Berbers, 59, 60
Betancourt, Jose, 343
Black Cannon Fodder, 359-361
Black Military in Islam, 42,43
Black Presence with Spanish Explorers, 97

Black Resistance, Brazilian
Slavery 173
Black tankers, WW II, 283
Blanco, Teodora, 169
Blemmyes, 33
Bonaparte, Napoleon I, 153, 155,156,
Bond, Horace, 312
Bolivar, 178-179
Bonaparte, Pauline, 158
Bonaparte, Napoleon III, 163,164
Boxer Rebellion, 275
Brazilian African Vocabulary, 174
Braziian Slavery, 128
Bridgetower, George 347
Brindis de Salas Claudio, 341-342
Brooks, Henry W., Jr., 323
Brotherhood of Negroes, 179-180
Brown, Wesley, 290
Brues, Alice, 23
Brunet, General, 159
Bueno Aires, 178
Bumba, 58
Bunche, Ralph 314,332,335
Busiris, King, 33
Byrd, Robert, 327
Byron, 163
Byzantine, Empire, 36

C

Caluza, Rubin, 349
Carter, Arthur, 292
Carter Jr., Edward, 299
Carthage, 30
Cartwright, Marguerite, 312
Cartwright, Roscoe, 324
Casado-Cespedes, Miquel, 169
Catholic Saints and

Cardinals, 34
Caturla, Garua, 168
Chacabuco, 178
Cheops, 15
Chinese Boxer Rebellion, 208-209
Chosnoes, King 49
Christophe, General, 158,159
Chuma, James, 96
Churchill, Winston, 289
Cibola, 168
Cinthio, Giraldi, 36
Clapperton, Hugh, 99
Clement VIII, 37
Cleopatra, 33
Colonial Indirect Rule, 318
Colonial Treaties, 166
Color Obsession 385-391
Columbia' slaves, 64
Cook, James Captain, 95
Congo River, 68
Constantine, 32
Contradanzo Criollo, 165
Conway, Ewell, 12,13
Corry, Joseph, 99
Cortes, Herman, 97
Cortez, Herman, 170
Cortez, John, 168
Count of Baghdad, 41
Crowther, Adjai, 96
Cuban Music, 168-169
Cuban Personalities, 169-171

D

Dalits, 29
Danakil, 64
David, al adlam, 45
Darwin, Charles, 1

Davis, Benjamin O. Sr., 290
Davis, John 95
Delgado Manuel, 169
Delgado, Martin, 169
Deccans, 46
DeGaule, President, 306
Dessalines, General, 158,159
d'Anthes, 162
Decisive Moments in Islam, 49
de Olano, Nuflode, 97
Diagne, Bloise, 276
Digna, Osman, 49
Dillard University, 94
Dionysus, 33
Diop, Cheikh, 10,24
Discovery of the Antartic, 94-95
Diversity of African Americans 391-399
Dhul-Nun al-Misri, 39
Djibouti, 65
Don Juan of Austria, 38
Dravidians, 25-30
Dubois, W.E.B., 10,65, 311-312, 358-359
Dulama, Abu, 45
Duke of Florence, 38
Duke of Urbino, 37
Dumas, Alexandre Davy, 153-156
Dumas, Alexander II, 154, 159-160
Dumas, Alexandre, III, 160-161

E

Early Bantus, 63
Early Egyptians, 10
Early Interest in Haiti, 215-216
Early Observation of
Early Explorers, 97
Early Explorers, 92
Einstein, Albert 361-381
Eisenhower, Dwight, 296
Emperor Charles V, 37
Enhla, 57
Ermann, Adolph, 15
Estenoz, Evaristo, 168
Ethiopia, 72
Ethiopia, a Profile, 90
Etienne, Eugene, 276
Etruscans, 32
Euripedes, 32
Evans, James C., 297
Eve Theory, 1
Estevan, 97

F

Fauset, Jessie, 311-316
Fife and Drum Corps, 143-144
Flavian Period, 33
Fox, John, 301-302
French Revolution, 152
Fulani, 64

G

Garamantes, 33
Garirdo, Juan, 168
Georges de Saint Chevalier, 347-348
Ghana, geography, 53
Ghana, a Profile, 54

Gines, Micaeha, 170
Gines, Theodora, 170
Githakas, 58
Giulio de Medici, 37
Goncharova, Ekaterina, 162
Goncharova, Natalya, 162
Gordon, General, 49
Gomez, Sebastian, 17
Gouled, Hassan, 65
Grajales, Mariana, 169
Graeco-Roman Experience, 31-34
Great Rift Valley, 69
Guatemala, 133
Guilo, 37

Heracluis, Emperor, 49
Hipolita, 179
Hittites, 9
Holland, Milton, 198
Holland, William, 198
Hollis, Levy, 310
Homefront War Efforts WW-II, 288
Homer, 32
Huguley, John W. III, 304
Hunt, Gibbs Ida, 316
Hurston, Zora, 103

I

Ife, 63
Iliad, 32
Impressions of slavery, 107
Inborden, Thomas, 200
Ippolito, 37
Iras, 33
Isis, 14, 32
Islam and Muhammed, 40
Ismali, Mawluy, 43
Issas, 65
Italian Renaissance, 36-38

H

Habshu slaves, 46
Haiti, 157, 215
Haitian Ruler, 209-210
Hamiclar, 31
Hammurabi Code, 10
Hannibal, 30
Hannibal, Abram, 133-137
Hare-Cuney, Maude, 345
Harrith, Zayd, 44
Harvey, Peter 95
Habanera, 168
Hairston, Carlton P., 327
Hall, Jacques, 19-25
Haley, Alexander, 291
Hassan ibn Ali, 45
Hastie, William, 68
Hausa, 64
Hayes, Roland, 316
Hellenistic Period, 33
Henson, Matthew 92-94

J

Jacobins, 157
Jacobins and Reign of terror, 152
James, Daniel C., 324
James Jr., Willy, 300-301
Japan, 38
Jernagin, W.H., 316

Jimenz, Ghirardo, 170
Jimenez, Juan, 343-344
Jobson, Richard, 98
Johiz, al, 45
Johnson, Charles S., 314
Jose, Amaro, 92

K

Kalanga, 57
Kalawant, Waubat Khlan, 47
Kasongo, 96
Kawammu, Emperor, 38
Kenyatta, Jimo, 62,311
Khofre, 15
Kruschev, Nikta, 312
Khufah, Ibn Nadba, 45
Kikuyu, 58-159
Kopcsak, Peter, 286
Korean War, 307-310

L

Labouret, Mary, 154
Laboy, Marie, 161
Langston, John, 198
Lacaussade, Auguste, 345
Latin America, 168
Latin America Dance, 177
Latino, Juan, 345
League of Nations and Mandate, 276-281
Leakey, Louis, 6
Leakey, Mary, 6
Leclerc, Charles, 158-159
Lee, William, 197-198
Leopard, 180

Lee, Ulysses, 292
LeFall, LaSalle, 37
Lewis, Cadjo, 103-106
Liberia, 216-234
Liberia, Dangerous Mission, 218-225
Livingstone, David, 100-101
L'Ouverture, Isaac, 153
L'Ouverture, Placido, 153
L'Ouverture, Toussaint, 153,156-159
Logan, Rayford, 316
Lorenzino, 38
Lorenzo, Guiliano, 37
Lorenzo the magnificent
Louis, Joe, 290
Lugard, Frederick, 318-319
Lumumba, Patrice, 312
Lwo, 51

M

Mboya, Tom, 312
McCalla, Eric, 11
MacCalla, Johnetta, 11
Marceo, Antonio, 170-171
Madhi, al Ibrahim, 47
Makatubu, 96
Malcom X, 10, 40
Mahouts, 31
Malinke, 64
Malawi, 67
Mande, 58
Margaret of Parima, 37
Marghi, 58
Mariaho, Ainaro, 61
Maro, Sakanouye, 38-39
Martin, San, 177

Matabele, 57
Matthews, Mark, 293-294
McManus, Luther, 310
Medici of color, 37
Medina, Ramirez, Maria, 169
Mena, Gonzalo, 179
Mendez, Lorenzo, 170
Mesopotamia, 8
Mexican War, 184-186
Miller, Dorothy I., 200-201, 269-270
Miller, Walker, 267-270
Minoans, 30
Minoan Kilts, 34
Misjah, 45
Moncada, Guillermo, 179
Monnerville, Gaston, 305-306
Montejo Francisco, 97
Moody, Harold, 312
Moreno Slaves, 178
Morgan, Henry, 292
Mortenol, Helidore, 275
Mt. St. Bernard, 154
Mt. Cenes, 154
Muhammed, Elijah, 40
Mustanir, 46
Muezzin, 47
Mzilkazi, 57

N

Napata, 32
Narmer, 14
Nascimento Abdias, 131
Ndebele, 57
Nedjeh, 45
Nefertari, 15
Nero, 32

Neronian Period, 33
Neur, 62
Newton, John 126
Nguni, 57
Nicholas I, 162
Niger River, 68
Nkrumah, Kwame, 312
Nile River, 66
Ninth Cavalry and Biogenetic Diversity, Philippines, 258-264
Niza, Marcos, 97
Nkrumah, Kwame, 54
North Pole, 94
Nosseyeb, 46
Nyerere, Julius, 68

O

Odyssey, 320
Ootah, 94
Organization of Africa Unity, 313
Osiris, 14
Otero, Anita, 340
Othello, 36
Ouhab, Mabed Ibn, 47

P

Pacheco, Jose, 344
Padmore, George, 311
Palmer, Nathaniel, 95
Park, Mungo, 68, 98
Partition and Domination of Africa, 164-167
Pasha, Ali, 41,43
Pasha, Hicks, 48
Passerini, Cardinal, 37

Patton, Georges Jr., 286-287
Perry, Admiral, 93-94
Persian Gulf War, 325-332
Peter The Great, 133-136
Phelps-Stokes Fund, 314
Phillips, Elizabeth, 292
Philippine Insurrection, 207
Piscasso, 346
Pizarro, Francisco, 97
Plutarch, 32
Pope Gregory XVI, 35
Pope Pius VIII, 35
Powell, Colin, 65
Praire View State University, 198
Prelude to Partition
 of Africa, 95-96
Punitive Expedition
  Mexico, 255-257
Pushkin, Alexander, 161-163
Pushkin, Nadezhda, 136-161
Pushkin, Sasha, 161
Pushkin, Sergey, 161

Q

Quiros, Evariste, 344

R

Rabah, ibn Bilal, 46
Rendon, Francisco, 344
Rivers, Reuben, 302-304
Robespierre, 154
Robinson, Roscoe, Jr., 324
Rochambeau, General, 159
Rodionovna, Arina, 161
Rodriquez, Socorro, 170

Rogers, Joel, 133
Romantiscism, 159-163
Rojas, Julian, 344
Roosevelt, Franklin D., 289
Ross, Lucy, 94
Rwanda, 317-318

S

Sadat, Anwar, 15, 44
Saint Benedict The Moor, 35
Salm, David ibn, 45
San Lorenzo, 38
Saint George, Chevalier, 153
Sala Rosario, Jose, 343
Sancho, Ignatius, 340
Schomburg, Arthur, 37
Second Punic War, 31
Selassie, Haile, 78, 79, 80, 84, 90,
 91, 312-313
Serapis, 32
Seven Hundred and Sixty First
 Tank Batallion 285-287
Seven Image Models of Bravery, 295
Shaka, 57
Shaw, Thomas, 304
Shumari, 96
Sickle Cell Disease, 4
Sierra Leone, 69
Sixty-Second U.S. Infantry, 195-197
Smith, Proctor, Harriet, 199-200
Smith, Professor, 98-99
Smithsonian, 19
Soliman, Angelo, 37
Sophocles, 32
Source of Slaves, 132
South African Colored, 349-351

South Pacific Islands, 351
Sotho, 57
Spanish American War, 202-206
Stanley, Henry, 96
St. Avold, France, 303
St. Martin de Porres, 34
Stewart, Ollie, 289
Stowers, Freddie, 272
Sufism, 39-40
Suhaym, 45
Sumerians, 8, 10
Survival of African Religion, 174-175
Swazi, 57

T

Tanzania, 68
Tate, Merze, 385
Taylor, Samuel Coleridge, 344
Thalassemia, 4,5
Thebes, 33
Thomas, Charles L., 299-300
Thomas, James, 298
Thomson, Joseph, 96
Thornton, Robert and the
 Einstein Years 28, 361-381
Three Musketeers, 160
Tib, Tippu, 96
Tobias, Channing, 314
Toure, Sekou, 312
Troy, 32
Tsonga, 57
Tswana, 58
Tulan, Ahmed Ibn, 43
Turkish Units, 44
Tutsi, 58, 66
Ty, Queen, 33

U

Uganda, 69
Uledi, 96
Umar, Caliph, 45
United Nations, 332-335
U.S. Civil War 186-201
Uruguay, 177
Untouchables, 26, 27, 28, 30

V

Valenzuela, Raimundo, 343
Velasquez, 97
Velasquez, Ann, 34
Velasquez, Manuel, 170
Vieira, Antonio, 92
Venice, 36
Vietnam War, 332
Virgin Islands, 67

W

Washshi, 43
Wa-Ndorobo, 58
War of 1812, 180-183
Watson, George, 301
Wesley, Charles, 3
West Indies, 335-344
West William 194-195
Wheeler, Charles, 100-102
White, Jose, 340-341
White, Walter, 311
Williams, Eric, 312
Woodson, Carter G., 92
World War I African American
 Presence, 266-275

World War II, African
 Presence, 305-306
Wright, Richard, 316

X

Xeres, 32

Y

Yoruba slaves, 61
Young, Charter, 225-254
Young, Bar Ida, 316
Yeargan, Max, 31

Z

Zahir, 46
Zambo, 337
Zani, 42
Zansi, 57
Zanibar, 69, 70
Zeus, 33